Flyboy 2

FLYBOY 2

The Greg Tate Reader

GREG TATE

Duke University Press *Durham and London* 2016

Printed in the United States of America
on acid-free paper ∞
Designed by Amy Ruth Buchanan
Typeset in Chaparral Pro by Westchester
Publishing Services

Library of Congress Cataloging-in-Publication Data
Names: Tate, Greg, author.
Title: Flyboy 2 : the Greg Tate reader / Greg Tate.
Description: Durham : Duke University Press, 2016. |
Includes bibliographical references and index.
Identifiers: LCCN 2015049621
ISBN 9780822361800 (hardcover : alk. paper)
ISBN 9780822361961 (pbk. : alk. paper)
ISBN 9780822373995 (e-book)
Subjects: LCSH: African Americans—Music—History and
criticism. | Popular music—United States—History
and criticism.
Classification: LCC ML3479.T35 2016 | DDC 781.64089/96073—dc23
LC record available at http://lccn.loc.gov/2015049621

Cover art: Robert A. Pruitt, *Stunning Like My Daddy*, 2011.
Courtesy of the artist.

For Mama Tate—still the First Reader who matters the most . . .

For Dr. Chinara Tate—Rock On Starchile in the wilds of Cognition and Nutritional Justice

For the Grand Sun Nile Steven Woods—dreamer, bon vivant, best-dressed man in Gotham, and the inventor of three-dimensional dragon sculptures

Contents

2. She Laughing Mean and Impressive Too

3. Hello Darknuss My Old Meme

4. Screenings

5. Race, Sex, Politricks, and Belles Lettres

Introduction
Lust, of All Things (Black)

"There are only two subjects—race and sex—and we alternate between the two." We recall the filmmaker Sandye Wilson dropping this maxim on Lisa Jones around 1986. Most likely after Lisa had made some self-deprecating comment about the content, or supposed lack thereof, of one of her own smart, racy, surreal plays about the politics of Black desire for her company Rodeo Caldonia High Performance Theatre. Wilson's quip stuck with me (and to me) because like every other growing American boy I had long been equally obsessed with both of those vast, irreducible, and inexhaustible subjects. Race, generally equated with politics, is really in the American context a branch of metaphysics, aesthetics, and anthropology representing a far broader body of concerns where you can readily leapfrog between sex, death, religion, criminality, linguistics, music, genetics, athletics, fashion, medicine, you name it, in the name of African liberation and self-determination. For a Black American artist at this stage of history race is the gift that keeps on giving, an encyclopedic way of framing, examining, and mirroring the world in ways that can aspire to be as poetic, prophetic, polemical, and poignant as that metamorphic, metaphoric machine we know by that crafty and elusive catchall "Black Culture."

Of course, what I myself have really been intrigued by all along is something less quantifiable than Black Culture and even Black Identity and Black Consciousness, and that something is what my friend Arthur Jafa has termed Black Cognition—the way Black people "think," mentally, emotionally, physically, cryptically how those ways of thinking and being inform our artistic choices.

Stanley Crouch once told me he thought my real subject was Myth, and to a certain extent that's true, inasmuch as I think that the most fabulous things about any people are the legends they produce. But as true as that is, I'm interested in the play and whimsy, the process as it were, which preceded the formal production of the myth. Black Rock guitarist Ronny Drayton relates how when he was learning to play, older cats told him when he studied someone's solo to try and imagine that player's intentions—what had he been feeling to make him play a certain way, what story was he trying to tell. James Baldwin was once asked if he thought Black people were better than white people. Baldwin replied in the negative but went on to say he did think Black people had a greater capacity for *experience*, which I always took to mean we had the best stories and storytellers. (This is how we know Jesus was Black—he talked a new religion into existence and it stuck.)

The arenas where Black people have had the most visible, visceral, and profound impact on the modern world have been those in which we can freely repurpose our experiences, our wagging tongues, our fun. Black Cultures and Black Cognition tend to privilege the structuring and stylizing of the bloody improvisational moment. What's proven remarkable about the way Black people play with such self-invented forms is how we inevitably devise these call-and-response languages that other folk, worldwide, feel compelled to emulate.

As in physics, where the most esthetic equations are generally proven to be the correct ones, the most beautiful and approximate abstractions of the forces of nature, Black improvisational languages in music, dance, poetry, art, and athletics owe their charisma to their elegance, their risk taking, and to their invitational, democratic, come-one, come-all viral, virile, vulnerable, vernacular engineering.

Because I had been intensely reading listening thinking arguing about jazz, blues, and funk in this high-handed way since I was, oh, the age of twelve, by the time I was twenty-three and began writing for the *Village Voice* I was a sure case of precocious cogitation and preparation meeting opportunity and maybe even destiny. I also knew like Crouch, Baraka, and Ellison before me that Black music was a unique, insightful mechanism for comprehending how people of African descent had survived, transcended, transmuted, and transmogrified their horrible American experience. What I knew that my critical elders didn't by sheer dint of generational accident, access, and affinity was that hip-hop mattered from the get-go. That once again, the African American working class, best described by my old landlord and mentor A. B. Spellman as "the most despised and feared group of people on this earth," had created another vernacular, improvisational form for addressing their condition and the condition of the world. Of course I also knew hip-hop mattered because it replicated, revoiced, and extended rhythmic, sonic, and collage effects Miles Davis, Ornette Coleman, Sun Ra, Jimi Hendrix, and George Clinton had renovated in their very Afrocentrically Expressionist musics of the sixties and seventies. More to the point, I recognized that if I wanted more of where that marvelously head-chargey kind of funk came from, it was only going to come from hip-hop.

Though born in 1957, I am not a child of the sixties but, like most who define the hip-hop generation, a child of the seventies. What being a child of the seventies meant for any young Black man trying to become a writer middecade was coming to terms with Black feminism in literature, visual art, and politics and the innate, emergent, and self-authorizing power of Black women in general. This leg of the journey began at Howard University in the midseventies, where several annual writers' conferences made clear that the most provocative, innovative, and insistent voices in African American novels, poetry, drama, and criticism in the moment were named Audre Lorde, Adrienne Kennedy, Toni Morrison, Jayne Cortez, Ai, Thulani Davis, Ntozake Shange, Gayl Jones, Michelle Wallace, Barbara Smith, Alice Walker.

Being at Howard at the time also meant becoming aware—via filmmaker and professor Haile Gerima's courses—of "3rd world cinema," which included an independent Black cinema movement led by Gerima's UCLA classmates Charles Barnett, Larry Clarke, and Julie Dash, the work of Ousmane Sembène, and the revolutionary cinema emerging from Cuba, like *Lucia*, and Argentina's *The Hour of the Furnace*.

Being at Howard then also meant encountering the Africentric expressionism of the Africobra school of painters, many of whom were then teaching or lecturing at the school—Al Smith, Frank Smith, James Phillips, Nelson Stevens, and the late department chair, Jeff Donaldson (not to mention the phenomenal Ethiopian Skunder Boghossian).

Being the child of lifetime Pan-Afrikanist Florence Tate meant the same woman who introduced me to the recordings of Aretha Franklin, Malcolm X, and Nina Simone via heavy rotation in our home would also "break" the music of Jimmy Cliff and Fela for us. Being the brother of Brian Tate, one of Washington, DC's first Black punks, meant the Clash, Bad Brains, Talking Heads, the Sex Pistols, James White and the Blacks, and Siouxsie and the Banshees became enveloped in my conception of the funk. Becoming friends with Vernon Reid in 1979, three years before I moved to New York, meant I actually knew someone who was inventing a life for himself at the intersection of free jazz, punk rock, hip-hop, and harmolodic funk. A combustive mixture of elements downtown Gotham loudly proclaimed was going to be late twentieth-century art's new lingua franca. Becoming a friend of Linda Bryant—Tribeca's only African American gallerist and conceptual art curator—meant meeting David Hammons, Senga Nengudi, Bill T. Jones, Adrian Piper, Houston Conwill, Lorna Simpson, and Fred Wilson, moments after becoming aware of their existence and sensibilities. What befriending Thulani Davis in the midseventies meant was that when she told me to send Robert Christgau some work I did, and when Christgau said, "The more writing like this I get in the paper the better I'll like it," I knew I was being given a license to ill on paper. Coming into the game my influences were the usual suspects—Baraka, Ishmael Reed, Pynchon, Marquez, Lester Bangs, and Hunter S. Thompson. Coming into it at the once all-seeing all-thinking all-knowing *Voice* meant I could be me, be free and not what somebody's style manual said I had to be—a monumental gift to a young writer. Being at the *Voice* throughout the eighties and early nineties also meant jumping into a hotbed slash clusterfuck of radical-critical Black American thought—straight gay feminist and supermacho—thanks to my writer and editor colleagues Thulani, Carol Cooper, Stanley Crouch, Playthell Benjamin, Nelson George, Barry Michael Cooper, Harry Allen, Lisa Jones, Lisa Kennedy, Hilton Als, James Hannaham, Jill Nelson, Angela Ards, Yvette Porter, Ben Mapp, Donald Suggs, Peter Noel, Paul Miller, Joan Morgan, Rob Marriott, dream hampton, Karen Good. Nice work y'all. We about rocked that joint. For a good hot minute. C'est le muhfukn vie. Quoth the ravens forevermore.

But so there I was, in the right place at the right time with the right rhymes and other progressive right Negroid and Caucasoid rhymemakers. It was also the crack time and Reagan time too, have no doubt. And living on Sugar Hill in Harlem's Washington Heights, where one night all the Jamaican weed dealers got ushered out and all the Dominicano dealers went to work with seemingly no legal impediments the next day, you got to see and hear—pop pop pop 'til the breakadawn—what the drug war was really about. This was also a time when police brutality and other forms of hate crimes were up and Minister Farrakhan played the Garden more often than Run DMC and Jesse Jackson was running and running and by the time Public Enemy released *It Takes a Nation of Millions to Hold Us Back* it did seem like Amiri Baraka's Nation Time all over again—that Black people were coalescing into some kind of movement for justice and freedom and Afrocentric/ghettocentric expression everywhere, in local politics, in film thanks to Spike Lee and the Hudlin Brothers and John Singleton, in theater thanks to August Wilson, and thanks to the crew coming through the *Voice* at that time in weekly journalism as well. When future scholars want to know what it felt like to be Black, think Black, marinate Black in Gotham City in those decades it is to the *Voice* archives they will go. Believe that.

Of course a lot of us back then also all believed hip-hop was the unstoppable revolution come. Not hard to understand since like jazz in the sixties it seemed to present a breathtakingly novel reformulation of its avant-garde baadass attitude every other week. Ergo a lot of *Voice* people wound up at the *Source* and *Vibe* too, thereby creating the journalistic culture and profession that now allows Nelson George, Barry Michael Cooper, and myself to sit back and laugh at the fact that "hip-hop journalist," a label once considered oxymoronic, is now something you can proudly scribble as occupation on your tax return.

I feel like I was somewhat removed from much caring about the state and fate of hip-hop by the time Tupac and Biggie began publicly feuding, certainly by the time they were murdered, but this isn't true—I still care very deeply and know that's just a wounded protectiveness talking. Like a lot of folk, I also knew the party, the hip-hop movement, was truly over when Puffy, a major talent scout but no talent, got the nerve to get on the mic—and went platinum! This became the handwriting on the wall if only because it signified that Black Mediocrity was now as commercially viable in hip-hop as Black Genius, the same fate that had already befallen jazz and soul in the eighties.

But hip-hop, like Black music always has been and always will be, is the most accurate arbiter of the zeitgeist, of the consciousness of the people and of the age. And insofar as this moment is defined by sex, shopping, terror, and virtual life and death, hip-hop remains our most prophetic cultural pulse taker, raker, and shaker. Bush, bin Laden, Fifty Cent, Paris Hilton, Fox News, ringer tones, and the iPod shuffle—these are actually what constitute our real world, people—a world of loops, break beats, random bombings, bootleg videos, faked realness, and manipulated fears; it's all of a piece, it all runs together nicely, don't you think, quite wickedly in fact, welcome to the twenty-first century, "not what you hoped for is it?," love it or leave it, sing along with me.

Premillennium tension and my hip-hop divorce aside, however, by the midnineties I was trying to make a little music of my own. Threw myself wholeheartedly, really, into Black rock improv bands with oblique feminist names like Women in Love, Mack Diva, Strange but Beautiful, Medusa Oblongata, and, since 1999, Burnt Sugar, the Arkestra Chamber. The latter of which more than anything is about me trying to make the genre-bending Black music I'd like to hear but cannot find. I got so much joy out of it that I found myself thinking in moments of ecstasy and delirium that I'd rather be a mediocre musician than a great writer. It's not true, but I relate to the sentiment simply because like anyone with a heart, I love the social part of music far more than the social part of writing, which is, need it be said, nil. The real drawback, though, for a critic composing and performing music as a coprofession is that your edge and killer instinct go kaput. Another occupational hazard of a profession as narcissistic as playing live music is that you can become less concerned with what everybody else is doing. So though I continued to write about music I allotted more time in the nineties to writing fiction, plays, and lyrics, as well as literary, film, theater, and visual arts criticism and op-ed pieces. I also felt emboldened enough to get a little raw and personal in the sharing of certain sexual obsessions at the behest of Rebecca Walker, who for her book *To Be Real* commissioned what became published in the *Voice* as "The Black Lesbian Inside Me"—a rare occasion of my Black male-feminist fantasies run amok.

Now comes the sound of a man patting his own back, if not ducking his own *sic*.

What I've come to realize upon reviewing this quarter century's worth of work is that I have come to occupy a somewhat unique position in the constellation of African American writing by keeping one ear to the street, one ear to the academy, and a phantom third hearing organ to my own little artsy-fartsy corner of Gotham and Brooklyn's Black bohemia. By addressing myself to sifting through the crossfire messages all three were beaming into my brain, I have managed to carve out something of a sui generis, signature, and quite eclectic legacy in African American criticism. That I was able to do so and maintain the ability to constantly laugh at myself while thinking out loud and growing up in public is what I think makes these pieces somewhat still readable years and decades after the fact. It also, I'd like to believe, gives them some kind of useful purpose as a rude and proper model for my literary inheritors. A little something of a tool kit for the next intrepid scribe who wants to take on all of Black Culture, Sexuality, Consciousness and Cognition, high and low, 'hood and hermeneutical. A field guide for an array of rhetorical operations she can deploy whenever she's ready to toss her vernacular riffs and metafoolishness (per George Clinton) into the high-critical tabloid mix of her generation's "changing same" moment (per Amiri Baraka), and at an uncautious, self-indulgent, talking-out-that-ass tempo roughly equivalent to the child's own brazen temperament, unbridled curiosity, bloody improvisational nerve, and beautiful, dutiful, devotional lust for all things Black. Our Black lives, creative acts, political plots, and trans-African legacies *been* mattering HERE for a good long while.

The
Black Male
Show

Amiri Baraka

1934–2014

> I think about a time when I will be relaxed. When flames and
> non-specific passions wear themselves away. And my eyes
> and hands and mind can turn and soften and my songs will be
> softer and lightly weight the air.—AMIRI BARAKA

Nabokov told us that all a writer has to leave behind is his or her style. Amiri Baraka made the reading populace deal with a rowdy, robust gang of style. Miles Davis (whose powers of concentration, condensation, and cool Baraka emulated in his poetics) once said he only had use for musicians who could play a style—stone-cold-bold originals. Originality, like style, is generally what's left after artists eliminate all excess from their repertoire—all the corny stuff that seems better suited for somebody else.

Born October 7, 1934, in Newark, New Jersey, Everett Leroi Jones shed hosts of styles, skins, friends, foes, and belief systems on the way to becoming Amiri Baraka, the iconic legend of literary and political lore. Like Miles, he got beaten bloody upside the head by upsouth redneck cops for being a model of uppity nigra defiance. Like Miles, Baraka walked away with brains, cojones, and swagger intact . . . intensified, even.

I'm Everett LeRoi Jones thirty years old. A Black nigger in the universe. A longer breath singer, would-be dancer, strong from years of fantasy and study.

LeRoi Jones is the byline the world first came to know him by (simultaneously) as a poet, jazz critic, playwright, essayist, and fiction writer. As Langston Hughes biographer Arnold Rampersad notes, Baraka and Hughes are the only writers in the Black American canon to distinguish themselves in four genres of writing: poetry, fiction, drama, and the essay. (Ntozake Shange belongs on that list too in our humble—more fodder for diatribes to come.)

Every writer can tell you about the one book that changed their life, changed their mind, made becoming a writer a fait accompli. For this writer here, that book was Baraka's *Black Music*. His *Blues People* is standard reading for anyone wanting to know the history and socio-cultural-political significance of The Music to The Struggle, but *Black*

Music is The One by freedom-swing musicologist Baraka that turned your boyee out. Made him leap overnight from being a fourteen-year-old Marvel Comics / sci-fi nerd to a precocious warrior nerd for the cause of freakishly-rad jazz improv.

Black Music introduced superheroic otherworldly entities calling themselves Sun Ra, Ornette Coleman, John Coltrane, Cecil Taylor, and Pharoah Sanders. And did so deploying a style that was as incandescent, indelible, and whiplash smarting as the music itself. Laid down like grammatical law in *Black Music* is the mandate that music journalism seem as possessed by furies as The Music. Count this reporter among those writers who owe their adult vocation to being swept up by Baraka's elegant prose juju at a tender, volatile age.

The fledgling career of LeRoi Jones became noteworthy in 1959 with publication of his chapbook, *Preface to a Twenty Volume Suicide Note*, which contains the poem of the same name now known as a much-anthologized classic. In a scant eighteen lines, a gothic young Jones parses dissonant melody from his sorrows and hallucinations, confesses alienated harmony with everyday chaos, then achieves spiritual renewal observing the mysteries of infant curiosity.

At that moment, Euro-American poetry and fiction was being resuscitated by the bebop-inspired artistic offspring of the so-called Black Mountain and Beat Generations; Jones, then ensconced in Gotham's East Village, swiftly bonded with the inner circle (Charles Olson, William Carlos Williams, Robert Duncan, Robert Creeley, Allen Ginsburg, William Burroughs, Frank O'Hara, Willem de Kooning, Larry Rivers, et al.) via books or bars. Jumped onboard their drunken boat like 'twas lifesaver, barnacled onto their methods and milieu until they became his own.

Jones arrived in the East Village as a refugee of the U.S. Air Force and of Howard University—where he served time with homecoming queen Toni Morrison, studied the blues with Sterling Brown, sociology with E. Franklin Frazier, and Dante's *Inferno* with the great Afro-Classicist Nathan Scott. (Bombardier training was his metier in the Air Force, or the "Error Farce" in Jonesology.) Soon after arriving on the Lower East Side he became betrothed to the former Hettie Cohen, also a poet, and within scant years also became the father of two darling daughters, Kellie and Lisa—who rolling stonishly gained stepsister Dominique DiPrima in this period.

By the time *Preface* was published, Jones had become a promising fixture of the Village's modern art–damaged bohemia. Hardly content simply hobnobbing with the Beats' pale male star chamber, the energetic and ambitious Jones read, wrote, and edited like a fiend, thought very deeply upon all things poetical, personal, and darkly sonorous, and while sipping cocktails, dashed off his own jazz and come-what-may-tales accordingly.

This proto-fly-brother in the ointment also devoted as much time as humanly possible going out to hear music of the great Black modernists who further ignited his literary passions—John Coltrane, Thelonious Monk, Ornette Coleman, Cecil Taylor. These giants, among others, would provoke him to conjure his two aforementioned seminal classics of Black musicology, *Blues People* and *Black Music*.

By 1965, a barely thirty-years-old Jones had published the five now-canonical works that would forevermore ensure his presence on Africana syllabi across the land and guarantee his dramatic works would become mainstays of off-Broadway and regional theater well into the twenty-first century: *Blues People* (once again, church sez Amen); *The System of Dante's Hell* (a broken-beat fictive odyssey through his childhood, adolescence, and young manhood); *The Dead Lecturer*, his rapturously mordant second volume of death-obsessed née death-defying poems; *Home*, a book of cultural essays and belles lettres; and that first bevy of earth-scorching plays—*Dutchman*, *The Toilet*, and *The Slave*.

In 1959, the year twenty-five-year-old Jones published his *Suicide Note*, a thirty-three-year-old Fidel Castro and a thirty-one-year-old Che Guevara took over Havana with a rebel army that overturned the U.S.-supported and Mafia-friendly Batista regime. In 1961, Jones accepts an invitation to join a delegation of upstart American artists for a visit to postrevolutionary Cuba. In Havana he gets to rap with Castro and Guevara. The Cuba voyage, essayed on in *Home*, documents Jones's slow turn away from poetic disengagement with tings politique. This gradual 180 will later be propelled into *r/evolutionary* overdrive by the assassination of Malcolm X in 1965.

That catastrophic event will provoke Jones's 1966 exodus from the East Village (and his young family) up to Harlem for race-man/race-manic repurposing and action. Treating the denouement of Ellison's *Invisible Man* like personal prologue, Jones, having made the Village his underground asylum, tunnels his way out of existentialism, emerges more upright than a *Pithecanthropus erectus* atop the manholes of Lenox Ave, declares himself learned in the ways of Western men and his own 'groidal Self, and thereupon screams his right to be Blacker Than Thou like a postgraduate King Kong.

MLK and the civil rights movement had never moved Jones the way Malcolm X had. But that movement, or at least a young firebrand faction led by Stokely Carmichael, also began moving X-ward around

'66—demanding civil rights now get down with some Black Power. In the years between 1965 and 1972, Jones will come under the sway of Kwanzaa creator Maulana Karenga, who'll compel an epochal name change: Imamu Amiri Baraka (rough translation: the Wise Beloved Prince).

He shall also wed the woman who'll become his forty-five-year life partner, Amina Baraka, with whom he'll embark on parenting six additions to the Baraka line—Ras, Shani (Rest In Power), Obalaji, Amiri Jr., Ahi, and Jones. He shall also transmogrify from heady Beat ingénue to the Father of the Black Arts Movement. Other milestone works of poetry, drama, fiction, and music criticism quickly follow—*Black Magic Poetry, Black Fire, Tales of the Out and the Gone, Black Music, A Black Mass, Slave Ship*. He'll take to the stage and read poems or direct plays with the same jazz vanguard peers he'd written so exquisitely about earlier: Sun Ra, Albert Ayler, Don Cherry, Sunny Murray, Milford Graves.

In 1966 Harlem, he'll obtain government funding (made available to stave off an eastward migration of L.A.'s 1965 Watts uprising) to produce street concerts featuring Ayler, Graves, and Sun Ra's Cosmo-Drama Intergalactic Myth-Science Arkestra. Returning to Newark in 1967, he'll form a performance group commune, Spirit House Movers; during Newark's riotous uprising of that year, he'll be held captive by a giddy gaggle of cops intent on killing him under the jail before Jean-Paul Sartre intervenes from Paris. (Another French, Marxist cultural icon, filmmaker Jean-Luc Godard, will later show up at Spirit House more in pursuit of irony than comradery.) Later in court, a Newark judge and DA will attempt to convict Baraka of inciting a riot with a poem.

By 1968, Baraka had become a resolute Kawaida-principles-following, Black cultural nationalist. The demands of all this newness meant rallying, conferencing, speechifying, etc. became as central to Baraka's existence as the more lyrical aspects of his production. His writing didn't go cold unattended (quite the opposite), but his writing career, as such, became enmeshed if not subordinate to his political fervor.

Since some of the fervor was expended in verbally assaulting pink-skinned people in general, and occasionally Jews in particular, those in the commercial American publishing industry who fit those descriptions, or were empathetic to same, saw fit not to publish any new books by Baraka for another three decades. (Trust that Baraka's literary executors will soon discover piles of manuscripts, as the man never stopped writing as prolifically as you or I exhale.)

The Black Arts Movement that Baraka godfathered (in ways alleged by some former da cap enforcers to be as Corleonean, and even Caligulan, as Conceptual) transformed the relationship between Black American society and its poets, painters, dancers, novelists, and serious musicians. It challenged Black artists to be more accessible and engaged with grassroots folk; it raised esthetic, political, and historical consciousness within Black America, bourgeoisie and working class alike.

The Movement also fostered radioactive waves of self-love, ethnic pride, tribal bonds, and identity. Some commentators (like this reporter) believe Baraka's rhetorically excessive brand of hypernationalism, while not faultless re charges of Jew baiting and whitey-hating, was a necessary countersupremacist corrective: the centuries of self-loathing that legal forms of American racism had imposed on folk of African descent required extreme countermeasures.

Say this for Baraka—he gave back to redneck racism as good and as bad as he got. Mama Tate, who maintained a friendship with the Barakas for decades, always liked to say, "Ooh, that man has a wicked tongue. Glad he never put that tongue on me!" A now dearly departed DC coworker, Harlee Little, described Baraka as a "word magician" capable of casting linguistic spells on his enemies liable to hurt them bad. To Baraka, once a rabid fan of Mandrake the Magician, Black Arts had a meaning and purpose beyond the obvious—that of deposing pale-skinned demonic forces with poetic conjuration.

Some Baraka admirers, colleagues, cronies, and debunkers (like the Black Panthers) found the cultural aspects of his nationalism a tad too cultish and indulgent in pseudo-African pageantry for their taste. The Movement's near-blind idolatry of all things Black as more beautiful than anything produced by the pink man got parodied by genius Black comic minds like Richard Pryor and George Clinton as soon as they felt safe.

Yet without the precedent and rage of the Black Arts Movement, it's doubtful that various Ivy League schools, and even many HBCU's, would've gotten pressured by students to either create African American studies programs or die. Many currently employed Black professors/celebrity-intellectuals at upper-echelon schools wouldn't have jobs today, nor would such cultural touchstones as *Soul Train*, BET, *Essence*, the National Endowment for the Arts Jazz Masters Program, or the Alvin Ailey Company have found the funding or the audience to exist.

Black Arts branded blackness in ways market-savvy, capitalist America could understand. Baraka's own poetic dynamism also gave rise to the generation of Black Arts poets who would ultimately lend hip-hop its tongue-lashing voice—David Henderson, Nikki Giovanni, Sonia Sanchez, Amus Mor, Jayne Cortez, the Last Poets, Carolyn Rodgers, Mari Evans, Gil Scott-Heron. The equation is simple: no Black Arts Movement, no lyrical precedents for Public Enemy, Boogie Down Productions, Nas, Wu-Tang Clan, Mos Def, Kanye, or Jay Z. Without Baraka's Black Arts Movement there'd have been no radicalizing or modernizing lyrical precedents for hip-hop's streetwise poesy to build upon.

As the sixties became the seventies, those on the front lines of that ongoing Power Move we euphemistically call the Struggle (notably Baraka's Congress for African People, the Black Panthers, Young Lords, etc.) raised the stakes by guiding their radical vision and agenda more concertedly toward seizing electoral power in urban America—rallying hard to see that Black faces got voted into high urban mayoral places. The former goal led to the first National Black Political Convention in Gary, Indiana, circa 1972, which Baraka was instrumental in organizing and rousing with a speech (one Mama Tate, who was there, still remembers with passion).

Within two years, the grassroots folk of Newark, Gary, Oakland, Detroit, and DC had their first Black mayors and congresspeople. That moment's political vanguard also aligned themselves with national liberation movements in Cuba, Vietnam, Algeria, Palestine, Guinea-Bissau, Mozambique, Angola, and South Africa. The turn toward identifying with the revolutions being waged by other peoples of color around the globe resurrected the inclinations of Malcolm X and Martin Luther King Jr. in this regard.

In 1974, though, Baraka made a swift left turn away from being Mr. Super Pro-Black to becoming an avowed Communist. (Under Baraka's fast-moving, ideology-switching hand, the Congress of African People eventually became the Revolutionary Communist League [Marxist-Leninist-Mao Tse-tung Thought], which later merged with some Pan-Asian, Chicano-Latino socialists to become the League of Revolutionary Struggle.)

The suddenness of Baraka's move struck some devotees like an ambush in the night; other less invested Black radicals considered these exotic switcheroos hilariously routine for the mercurial Baraka. Many position papers and sloganeering poems soon followed, as did epiphanic apologies for early acts of anti-Semitism by Baraka's younger, class-struggle-clueless self. Our man also declared himself to be an anti-Zionist. In 2003 this distinction didn't dissuade New Jersey governor Jim Greever from attempting to snatch back Baraka's Poet Laureate of New Jersey title after he dropped his incendiary take on 9/11, "Somebody Blew Up America." This bromide insinuates that various and sundry forces—George Bush, Condoleezza Rice, Ariel Sharon, the CIA, state of Israel—all knew the attack on the Towers was imminent, and took pains to ensure that all of Israel's WTC-employed folk avoided the workplace that horrific day. From the meshuggenah, our takeaway was that anyone who thought Amiri Baraka couldn't still Set It Off didn't know who they were dealing with.

By 1980, Baraka had merged forces with the multicultural League of Revolutionary Struggle, while back in the post–civil rights money jungle, the radical wing of Black American intellects had begun to come in from the cold at spots like Yale, Harvard, Princeton, Brown, and Columbia. Other old cells, like surviving members of the Black Liberation Army and Weather Underground who'd held tight to paramilitary dreams of plotting the Fall of America, got either killed or captured and sentenced to supermax federal prisons for forever and a day. For his part, Baraka would spend the next twenty-five years teaching literature at SUNY Stony Brook, with short stints at SUNY Buffalo, Rutgers, and his alma mater, Columbia University, along the way.

Baraka's changes in political philosophy never took him far from The People or The Music he loved or from prolific writing. He returned to music writing, a vital gumbo published as *Digging* a few years back contains definitive, up close and personal writing on the only two figures, musical or otherwise, who Baraka ever insinuated intimidated him in print: Nina Simone and Abbey Lincoln.

The Barakas' family home in Newark became legendary in the eighties and nineties among younger artists and intellectuals of the funk and hip-hop generations for the generous, open verbal jam sessions convened there. At these, one might walk in (as my drummer friend J. T. Lewis did) and find yourself irrevocably immersed in hours-long conversations with "Nikki Giovanni, Ishmael Reed, Sundiata (RIP), and Harry Belafonte all under one roof."

In that same era, if one was engaged in social-justice movements against apartheid or gang-related violence in urban America or rallying for Run Jesse Run (and later Obama) or even conscious rap conferences at Howard University—all the forums in other words which defined The Struggle in the eighties to the aughts—well, there you'd inevitably find a still physically vital, politically vigorous, and satirically unsparing Amiri Baraka.

Furthermore, if you were in New York on the jazz club and concert sets, you'd see him still giving up the dap by his presence (worth way more than Jay Z's to those in attendance) to the most advanced veteran musicians and young turks of our time. Baraka never stopped spitting lyrics with the world's greatest players either—check YouTube for the vintage clips of him holding down the bandstand with champs like David Murray, Henry Threadgill, and William Parker. Check as well for his appearances with the Roots, Boots Riley of the Coup, and on HBO series *Russell Simmons Presents Def Poetry*.

At seventy-nine, our man Amiri refused all prognostications of him being anybody's fossil. His out-the-blue jettisoning from the scene creates a power vacuum in our brainwaves. One of the many immeasurable losses of his absence is going to be those must-read memoriams Baraka wrote in bloodfire for our Struggle's most vaunted fallen soldiers, like James Baldwin.

So many once-hot causes, personages, and organizations dissolved around Baraka seemingly ages ago—as many of his most beloved younger comrades (notably filmmaker St. Clair Bourne and Sékou Sundiata) shocked him by transpiring long before he did. In their honor, one suspects bruh's twinned passions for art and social justice sustained and gained in incendiary intensity. The poet and publisher Jessica Care Moore recently broke how any event, poetical or political, "always got more gangsta" whenever Baraka shuffle-bopped into the room.

To this, we can testify recalling a gathering of Black Arts veterans convened by the producers of the *Eyes On the Prize* PBS series to discuss a continuation on the Black Arts and Black Power movements. Speaking last, Baraka rose and let the producers know that if they couldn't come correct in narrating those coterminous histories, "We will come find you." Since that *Eyes on More Flammable Prizes* series never happened, assume some figured they couldn't get it right—or Left—enough, and didn't need Baraka on the prowl for their heads.

Let none assume Baraka's too far gone now not to suddenly jump up and roundhouse they petit-bourgeois comprador asses from beyond the grave *with the quickness*.

– 2014 –

Wayne Shorter

INTERVIEW CONDUCTED WITH CRAIG STREET

Wayne Shorter has had an abiding impact on the evolution of modern music since his emergence as a primo saxophonist and composer in the late fifties. First with Art Blakey's Jazz Messengers from 1958 to 1963, next with Miles Davis from 1964 to 1969, then again with Weather Report, his cooperative band with Joe Zawinul from 1970 to 1982. The past decade has garnered high-water marks for his stellar quartet.

Shorter's influence as a writer of indelible works for the modern jazz idiom is matched only by Charlie Parker, Thelonious Monk, and Ornette Coleman. His compositions for Miles Davis, and for his own Blue Note albums in the sixties, set a high bar for melodic, harmonic, and emotional sophistication. His tenor saxophone playing brought more introspective nuance and intellectual complexity to the horn than anyone since Lester Young. With Weather Report, Shorter's soprano statements evolved into pristine miracles of tonal brevity. He could wring as much soul out of one note as others would out of entire careers. *Native Dancer*, Shorter's collaboration with Brazilian singer-songwriter Milton Nascimento, was deemed an instant classic upon its 1974 release. The kind of once-in-a-lifetime production like Coltrane's *A Love Supreme* that redefined the breadth and cosmopolitan scope of African American music.

Interviewing Shorter is like trading wits with a hybrid of precocious teen and wizened sage. There's a pure delight in each novel thought and sensation that borders on cognitive ecstasy—not only for Shorter but for his interlocutors too! Always coupled, a la Sun Ra and Ornette Coleman, with a profoundly philosophical take on his art and times, humanity, generally, and the very fabric of the cosmos.

. . . . .

Wayne: Every Saturday my mother used to come home from work (she had two jobs) and she'd bring clay, watercolor, and X-Acto knives. My brother Alan and I, we'd sit in the kitchen at a round table making Captain Marvel and Captain Marvel Jr., the Frankenstein monster, the Wolfman. One time we tried to make the whole world. He made a hundred people and I made about 150. We also made the Second World War. Remember the Red and Blue Armies in Russia?

There was a guy named Jimmy Tyler from Jersey City, New Jersey. He played almost exactly like Charlie Parker. And that almost made a wide void for me. The trying makes the void. And he was trying, but he got caught by the wayside. He got distracted by the so-called other elements of nature, not so organic. Along with others that age. I was sixteen, seventeen, didn't know nothing about how to intercept, how to save somebody's life.

When I was growing up, what I was doing was making everything abstract. I'd go to a party and they'd be playing all this Bullmoose Jackson stuff. All these fine ladies around and I'd be saying, "Hey, don't yawl know Billy Eckstine?" I'd go to the record bin while they were slow dragging and throw on some Bird, and they'd say, "Get him out of here, he's crazy. Don't invite his ass to no more parties." Me and my brother Alan, they tagged us. "Don't invite them two to no more parties. They too weird. Abstract and all that."

I'd go out to the couch where the girls would be sitting and all the bad guys—the good-looking guys—would grab a girl by the hand, wouldn't even ask her and say, C'mon, let's dance. Once I saw a guy slow dragging with *two* girls. I'd go over to a nice-looking little girl, she'd kind of lean forward like I was going to ask her to dance, and I'd say, "Let's talk about Saturn. How many them rings around there? How many you think there are?" So the word went around that they want to talk about science fiction, fantasy, all that, and they *out*. And we stayed there. We held on to it.

When I heard Dizzy, Monk, those people back then, I identified with the contrast between what people were doing and what they were not doing. What Dizzy and them were playing, their style, was not about what everybody else was about. And people were not aware of that contrast, they were missing it. And I found they were missing every other thing that was like what bebop represented. They were missing it all in their areas of specialization. They were missing it at the movies. They were going to see the funny movies and I was going to see the odd movies. I was going to see *Rocketship X-M*. And they used to say, "You like that odd shit." I'd say, "You ever get inside that odd shit?" I'm crazy, man. It feels good to be crazy. It's healthy.

All through high school that stuff was happening to me.

Cat used to walk the hall and never be with a girl. Always walked the wall. No books. You say, "Where your books man?" He says, "In the locker. Lost the key, forgot the combination."

We had a guy who was leading a band we used to call The Group. We told him, "We want you to front the band." Because he walked around with this suitcase full of all these arrangements and couldn't read a note of music. But he would do like Dizzy and wear a beret and glasses and everything. His name was Jackie Bland. He said, "My name is Bland. It should be Jackie Bland's band." We said, "No, we calling it The Group. You just frontin'." And we used to go to the bandstand and put a blank piece of paper on it like we were reading.

My brother Alan, he played alto sax, wore gloves and glasses when the sun was out. People would ask him, "What you gonna do?" He'd say, "We going to pray." They couldn't tell whether he said to play or to pray.

There is a monster amongst us.

I like to have fun, man, because The Door is coming closer. My brother called me and he said, "Wayne, The Door is getting closer." I said, "What you mean The Door?" but I knew what he meant. Miles knows about The Door, that's why he's having a lot of fun now [laughs].

Greg Tate: After reading your other interviews it's a surprise to find that you're so gregarious.

I'm just as gregarious as these eggs. Do you mind if I partake? I'm going to do like when I was in school—listen to the radio, do homework, watch TV, talk on the telephone, and get an A [laughs]. I'm jumping around. I'm the kind of person who jumps around when he talks because everything is connected.

The word "jazz" to me means "No Category." It's an intangible word. Some of those other words are tangible because they become something people can use to block, run interference, corner the market on something. More than the money, it's like telling somebody what to feel. Like when they shout, "Rock and Roll!" and all that stuff like that.

Rock and roll to me is like a knife. That knife in the hands of a murderer and that knife in the hands of a surgeon.

Craig Street: Same knife, different ends.

Hitler tried to make the ends more important than the means. And some others who think they're in charge of South Africa. Weather Report was asked to go down there, you know? They asked us two and three times. I said, No. Got to where they asked through some intermediary people. I said, "You all don't have to be all incognito—I ain't being incognito about the answer."

I asked my grandmother one day, "Where did we come from?" Because she was talking about her aunt who was in slavery and sold to a Spanish guy in New Orleans and he got her declared free and he married her. I wanted to find out some more about that, and I said, "Grandma, What's going on?" And she went into her room and she came out and brought me this book called *Race and Sex* by J. A. Rogers.

I've given two sets of J. A. Rogers books away. One to Bobby Thomas, the drummer who used to be with Weather Report, and one to a girl who was taking Eldridge Cleaver's class out in Berkeley. She asked me, "What is 'code'"? She wanted to know where did slavery code and slang come from. So I sent her J. A. Rogers's books and then I wrote a whole thing down about code and she got an A.

I read a lot of books. Got a ton of books in my house.

I'm reading this baaad book by Lord Dunsany. It's about marriage. This guy marries this elf girl. The first night they have dinner, he wants her to say grace and she refuses. That's the story. There's another book he did called *The Charwoman's Shadow*. She stands in the garden and the line is like this: *Dusk was falling but it was already midnight in Carlotta's hair.*

GT: There's an attention to detail in your writing that could almost be called sculptural. Where do you think that derives from?

I guess I see that the littlest thing equals the big thing. The little thing has got to be in there, all the details got to be in there.

I like this phrase: A million dollars does not exist without one penny, but one penny can exist without a million dollars. I like that, brother! [laughs] And there's a third something in there too. When you can see that something is existing without the premise, you know it's jive. It's just acting like it's existing. It's saying, "Here I Am," and you're saying, "You jive"—the penny ain't in there.

Before we went to work, Miles would call me up and say, Wayne, come on down and watch some television with me. We'd watch *Days of Our Lives*, that kind of stuff. We used to have fun. Like, he'd call the Hilton hotel and say, "Give me the cook." And he'd tell the cook how to season something. He'd say, "Light on the pepper, that's right, and give the carrots three minutes, you got it." That's the kind of stuff that brings out whatever's happening in the music for me. That simplicity, you know?

One time we were sitting at the Plugged Nickel and Miles said, "What do you do with your hands when you ain't doing nothing?"

I said, "Well a lot of people do this [makes a shrug, palms up]." Miles said, "That's right—but what do you do with *yours*?"

When we did that album *Miles in Berlin* he asked me, "Do you feel like you can play anything you want to play?" So I said, "Yeah."

And dig this: After I said, "Yeah," he said, "I know what you mean." Like he was talking to himself and I became him.

I think that Plugged Nickel album represents the highlight of something. Wynton Marsalis came to my house and he asked me to play it. (I can't do his voice because I haven't seen Wynton in a long time. I like to talk in the voice of the person who's talking rather than talk for them in my voice.) Wynton found the record and he said, 'Stella by Starlight,' dig it." And I said, "You want some chicken or some juice or something." And he said, "No I want *that*."

Once Miles asked me, "You ever play like you don't know how to play?" I thought about that—because you don't just let your hands go anywhere because that means you know how to play. But to play a horn like you're with a girl you want to talk with and you act like you've never been on a date before. To make out like she's the only one you ever talked with. That's what Miles was getting at when he asked about playing like you never knew how to play. I've heard directors say, "Do it like you've never had an acting lesson," to try and get them past the clinical thing. But then the next level is to do it like you've never ever had a lesson. And I heard that in the Plugged Nickel stuff. Wynton told me that was something he wanted to get to because all of a sudden all of the training and everything didn't mean nothing. Like Bird said, "I practiced everything I could and when I got on the bandstand I forgot all of that stuff."

Miles's place was jumping at one time. I'd be there and Miles would say, "Play me something." And he'd be in the kitchen cooking pigs' feet and collard greens. Cannonball Adderley would be walking around talking about, "That's gonna be something to reckon with."

One time I was at Miles's house and he got a telegram from Frank Sinatra asking, "Why don't we do something together?" Miles showed me the telegram and said, "Dig this Wayne, dig this shit." So he wrote on a piece of paper for the messenger to take back: "I don't want to get in your way so stay out of mine." [laughs] The bad people should just be together. To eat ice cream and talk, not just to play music together.

I got a letter from a doctor who'd heard *Native Dancer* and he said, "This makes me want to be a better surgeon." I think the importance of playing could be nailed down to something like this. Well, not nailed down. Think of it as a nail you're hammering eternally because the nail is soooooo long.

My mother told me that one time when she was in school the teacher asked, "How many want to be lawyers?" or this or that. Then she went down to the lower echelon and asks, "How many want to be garbage men?" One guy raised his hand. And she asked him why and he said, "Somebody's gotta do it." Now I see guys collecting garbage around my house and I wonder which one of them wants to be a better garbage man.

Art Blakey used to say, "I don't want them to see me—I want them to see a great big drum." When he's playing now Art looks like he's attached to the drums. Other people can be so disconnected. We had a cab driver who was disconnected from the steering wheel. He was putting the brakes on at imaginary stops. We were almost late one night because he missed the street eight times. Up in the air sometimes you can feel some pilots are not connected, not a part of the plane. I've gotten so I can feel the smoothness of the teamwork between the mechanics on the ground and the pilot, especially in heavy turbulence. The pilot will be making his little light jokes and I'll be wondering, "Is he attached to the computer?"

Life is really a ball man. Don't you feel that?

Are either one of you married? I've been divorced two times and I had a ball in both marriages. The next one is going to be the complete ball. They say when you get married more than once it's like being with the same person. The first one and the second one are the same person because my karma is the same. Now the next time I get in that rocket ship, my karma will have been broken and I'll be able to recognize the one person I always made a commitment to be with eternally. People are very fortunate when they can recognize the one person they always made a promise to be with. When you say "I do," that's deep man. That commitment is a part of karma building. You can live together and make believe you're doing what married people do but marriage is not the ceremony or the paper. Marriage is, "What are you going to do when you get married? What you gonna do when you get your own band?"

Living together is only about a degree of commitment. In Zen Buddhism they talk about a Greater Vehicle and a Lesser Vehicle. Lesser meaning when you become monkish and you're practicing this enlightenment process for yourself, as a priest, not going out into secular life. The Greater Vehicle means spreading out into the world. It means commitment. Commitment exemplifies what I believe about the law of cause and effect or the difference between inductive thinking, which the Western world has a lot to do with, and deductive thinking. In the Orient that living together thing ain't even in it. The marriage is like a whole, and the parts take care of themselves. But living together is like being a part of something and you try to make it a whole. And the whole is always kept separate because the whole of the commitment has not been committed yet.

Another word I don't like is "direction." If something is a style and it stays there, then people ask, [adopting a pompous British accent] "What *direction* are you going in aesthetically?" If you put on a style of clothes is that the direction?

I rather like instead the term "value-creation." Direction to me is blinders. But value-creation is taking off the blinders and making value out of every moment. In Buddhism we talk about how there are a thousand lifetimes in a momentary existence. Actually saying that the working of karma is like that. Even the simple act of eating is building karma.

My karma makes other things react to it. Makes a woman either attracted or repulsed. Or in a total inference—total inference, dig that!—either I chase fortune or fortune chases me.

[Wayne turns to an actor doing a crying scene on TV] She's building karma now with that onion. There's a life condition for what she's doing. She's in the world of absorption. And in the world of absorption you can't really make a drastic effect on something. That's why Buddhism considers that Christianity cannot, in a certain world-way, make a drastic effect until people's karma is not harmful. Because Christianity is harmless, not harmful. It's altruistic in its actual conception.

People mess with Christianity, Christianity doesn't mess with people.

Affecting change can really happen if it happens individually, on a one-to-one basis. Enlightenment is going on all the time. If you're concerned about anything, it's happening already. Think of the individual as the same as when you talk about a million dollars not being able to exist without one penny. Enlightenment among the masses isn't going to have nothing to do with no organized nothing. Enlightenment is awakening.

I also don't like that word "concept." Like, let's make a *conceptual* album. With our album *Atlantis* we didn't try to make no big thing out of it. I was sitting there doodling and came up with that crest that's on the back of the album. I said, "What is this? Looks like some kind of family crest or something like that." And something started to happen. Wasn't no words, but it was like something pushing up to be heard. And I wrote down A, T, L, and finally wrote down Atlantis. I said, "Let me check this out tomorrow."

Went home, went to sleep, and the next day it got stronger. It wouldn't let go. I'm not trying to make anything mystical or magical out of making an album, but whenever you do something, something comes along, hitches a ride on along. It's like that episode of *Twilight Zone* where the gremlin hitches a ride on the wing and made the flight much more than what it was. That's what I'm talking about.

You see the movie *The Crusades*? So Saladin says to King Richard, "Hmm looks like a nice blade you have there." Richard takes a big two-by-four, cuts it in half. Saladin says, "You show me the strength of your arm, not the sharpness of your blade." So Saladin took out his nice Saracen blade, got a piece of silk, threw it in the air, and it went *swish. Well.*

You know who Pop Warner was? Used to be backstage at the old Apollo? They used to ask him, "Pop, how you feel?" He'd say, "One motherfucking tooth in my mouth and *it* got the nerve to ache."

After we wrap the interview and step into the hallway to leave, Wayne peeks his head out the door and yells at us, "Get married!!!"

– 1985 –

Jimi Hendrix

The history of Black Americans and rock music is a long, strange, twisted, and exhilarating affair. The Jimi Hendrix story screams right from the heart of it. Since the 1860s, Blacks have been inventing forms of popular entertainment that have transformed the country's mass-entertainment marketplace. Our folk have also unceremoniously discarded those forms from cultural relevance at the drop of a hat—especially whenever the latest thing starts to look like it's in need of preservation as a remnant of those "never were" good old days. When it comes to music, Black America generally tends not to be impressed by the good old days. This is why in our music, as the trumpeter Lester Bowie once noted, the tradition is innovation, not nostalgia.

That observation applies equally to our mid-nineteenth-century marching band and church hymnal composers and those who came later to establish minstrelsy, ragtime, New Orleans jazz, swing jazz, bebop, blues, rock 'n' roll, soul and funk, house music, and hip-hop. The upside of this is that Black American music remains fluid, dynamic, transformational, and vital to each new generation, rather than static and reactionary. The downside is that, from one generation to the next, African Americans know less about our tradition of innovative musical geniuses and their contributions to world culture than plenty folk do elsewhere.

Jimi Hendrix looms large among those lapses in our collective consciousness. His absence from a general celebration of African American heroes is both absurd and symptomatic of a more widespread problem: cultural and political amnesia.

Some of that can be attributed to the fact that until recently, Black Americans have been largely a people running from a horrible past toward a more promising future. In the twentieth century our nomadic musicians always led the way on these fugitive pilgrimages, opening up spaces, internal and external, where Blacks could feel a little bit freer to be themselves (and really, to just *be*) in public.

Jimi Hendrix, over his too-brief twenty-seven-year life span, proved to be one of our most agile and adept freedom fighters. Decades after his rumor-shrouded demise Hendrix is still one of the most misunderstood and misapprehended of the group. We're here to rectify the situation.

James Marshall Hendrix was born on November 27, 1942, to Al and Lucille Hendrix in Seattle, Washington. His parents had met on the dance floor at a local jitterbug contest. They soon became a prizewinning dance couple in the area. In March 1942 Al joined the Navy, leaving his pregnant wife in Seattle.

She delivered their firstborn while Al was stationed at Fort Benning, Georgia. At that moment Al Hendrix sat in an Alabama stockade for allegedly *thinking* about going AWOL to see his spanking new son.

When Al returned home he found that his young son had been shuttled between various family members and neighbors. Lucille was a hard-drinking, party-hardy woman who would die of liver disease when young James was sixteen. She was too impoverished and too enthralled by the local nightlife to care for the child herself. James had been named Johnny at birth, after, in all probability, an area hustler with whom Lucille ran. This was a sore point for Al and helped drive a wedge between the troubled couple that eventually ended their marriage.

Al began his life as a single father after the birth of Leon, his second son with Lucille. Although he was a highly skilled factory laborer (machinist and electrician) and jack-of-all-trades, the senior Hendrix was not always able to care for both of his sons. Segregation and racism kept many men of color out of union trades for which they were well qualified. Al was forced to give Leon up to foster care when the boy was eight years old.

Young James loved his mother dearly but saw her only intermittently, at first because Al forbade it; later mostly because Lucille was just not trying to be around. One can't help but be struck by how much young James took after his parents—Al's work ethic and extraordinary mechanical aptitude, Lucille's impulsive spirit and romantic wanderlust, her concomitant love for adventure and stimulation. That he and his mother would both die from liquor-related complications sadly caps off the narrative of Jimi's familial family legacy—a tale beyond ironic and tragic.

Al and young James lived in virtual poverty until James's teens. About then is when his father's work as a landscaper became more lucrative. Friends and relatives remember the boy who would become Jimi Hendrix as a shy, dreamy-eyed stutterer—albeit a quite proud and dignified one. He might come to school wearing shoes with holes in them, but, by all accounts, he still carried himself with a self-possession that bordered on aristocratic.

Young James grew up listening to his father's favorite music—the modern, electric guitar–driven blues of Big Bill Broonzy, Jimmy Reed, Elmore James, and Muddy Waters. Around age twelve he started emulating the plucking of those idiomatic giants on the household broom. When his father asked him why so many bristles from the broom were turning up on the floor, James offered up a shamefaced explanation. Al was so moved that he went to a local pawnshop and bought himself a saxophone and a real guitar for his son so they could learn to play together. As Al put it in Joe Boyd's *A Film about Jimi Hendrix*, "I let the sax go after a while because I figured he was going to do more with the guitar than I was going to do with the sax."

According to the multimedia artist Xenobia Bailey, a Seattle-born friend of the Hendrix family, the community in which she and the Hendrix clan grew up was one where music held a cherished place in many a Black household. Some homes even had basement areas that were set up as clubs, with bars and miniature bandstands where visiting musicians like Ray Charles and Ike Turner would routinely drop in for after-hours jam sessions. There was also a unique multigenre and multigenerational aspect to the music Seattle's Black folk made back then. Bailey says she hasn't heard the hybrid anywhere else since—a freewheeling blend of jazz, blues, church music, and rock 'n' roll that made for a heady and seamless hallucinatory hybrid. Contrary to popular belief, the fabled esoteric eclecticism of Jimi Hendrix probably has more roots in what he heard in Seattle than in the swinging London scene he got airlifted into near the end of 1966. Bailey also has a perspective on Hendrix himself—she shockingly doesn't believe that he was such a great guitar player—least not when compared with others in their community who she unwaveringly claims were far more accomplished. Bailey says those better guitarists ended up in jail or dead by the mid-1960s. Meaning her argument is beyond dispute by anyone not from that time and place. When Bailey describes those players' gifts, however, their attributes are not far removed from those valorized by Hendrix devotees: the ability to make the instrument "talk" (or emulate conversational speech and full control of the instrument at a high volume). Bailey also recalls that Hendrix and these other embryonic guitar masters often got together after school to loudly jam for hours in a house she'd pass by on her way home.

Hendrix's brilliant flowering was many road-dog years and cross-country R&B shows in the making, but Bailey's anecdotes make one realize how much nurturing Hendrix was given by the musical proclivities of Seattle's postwar Black community.

One reason Hendrix didn't wind up in prison, or worse, is that right after graduating from high school he got arrested for "joyriding." That one brush with jail pushed him to join the U.S. Army and train as a paratrooper. While stationed at Fort Campbell in Kentucky, Hendrix successfully completed twenty-seven jumps and earned a Screaming Eagle patch—a goal that had been on his mind even before he enlisted. He saw a homeboy with one emblazoned on his Army jacket. Jimi Hendrix entering the Army to pursue a Screaming Eagle is prophetic, comical. But Hendrix also later remarked that some of the inspiration for his trademark booming and whooshing guitar noises came from the sounds he heard the wind and jet engines make when he jumped out of planes. Proof once again, that there's no experience, as the saying goes, that's ever lost on a true artist.

While performing in bands with other soldiers, Hendrix met an affable bassist named Billy Cox, who would later rejoin him after the Jimi Hendrix Experience disbanded and the Band of Gypsys trio project arose with drummer Buddy Miles—another R&B road dog Hendrix had also met earlier.

Hendrix was honorably discharged from the Army in 1961 and wasted no time in finding work on the legendary chitlin circuit, the nationwide network of nightclubs and theaters throughout segregated Jim Crow America. Top R&B entertainers were often bundled together on package tours that might feature as many as ten different acts a night. The circuit got its name from the fact that the only place in many cities for a Black person to eat and sleep in those days was someone's home or a boarding house, places where the fare was universally soul food—pork chops, mac and cheese, cabbage, collard greens, and that staple of the antebellum plantation diet, chitterlings, or more popularly chitlins: hog intestines, the offal of the pig. Not even the most fervent connoisseur of chitlins would deny how much they stink while cooking, and that foul odor may have led some sure wit among the performers to liken their working environment to the stench of fried pig guts.

It was on this circuit that Hendrix would really learn and perfect his craft while observing a host of legends—Sam Cooke, Jackie Wilson, Hank Ballard, Ike and Tina Turner, Sam and Dave, Little Richard, and the Isley Brothers.

Little Richard, born Richard Penniman in Macon, Georgia, described himself at the 1987 Grammys as "the architect of rock 'n' roll"—after declaring himself the winner of The Best Rock Artist award. His piano-pounding, highly dramatic flair, and pancake-makeup transvestism left an indelible mark on later performers such as James Brown, Jackie Wilson, Mick Jagger, David Bowie, KISS, and Hendrix. Richard once remembered Hendrix as someone who "didn't mind looking freaky, just like I don't mind." Richard also proclaimed that when "Hendrix got to whanging and wailing on that guitar, making it go woo woo, it made my big toe stand up in my boot."[1]

Hendrix's own reflections on his time with Richard emphasized less about Richard's bigfoot love and admiration for him than about the memory of being fired in New York for insubordination. It was at that point, in 1964, that he decided to settle in Gotham for a bit to try jump-starting a career and finally play the music he heard in his head. To hustle some coin he'd still go back out on the circuit as needed. By this time he'd developed a reputation as one of the best guitar players on the soul music scene.

Hendrix's personal tastes remained partial to the 1950s blues favored by his dad and to the even older acoustic-blues musicians of the 1920s and 1930s such as Robert Johnson, Lightnin' Hopkins, Son House, and Bukka White. Black popular music was undergoing a seismic shift by 1964. Partially caused by the advent of Motown Records out of Detroit, partially by the British Invasion wherein highly and unabashedly derivative Black-influenced rock from the UK hit the U.S. charts hard: primarily thanks to the Beatles, the Kinks, the Who, the Hollies, and the Rolling Stones.

Hendrix's greatest influence came not from across the Atlantic pond but from the Minnesota-born singer-songwriter born Robert Zimmerman then known to the world as Bob Dylan. Coming out of the protest tradition of folk music pioneered by figures such as Lead Belly and Woody Guthrie, Dylan transformed everyone's idea of how poetic and polemical a pop song's lyrics could be with every successive album he made for Columbia Records. Dylan had been signed to the label by the legendary A&R man and producer John Hammond—a man also instrumental in bringing Count Basie and Billie Holiday to Columbia. (Hammond might have brought Robert Johnson there too if the musician hadn't died before Hammond could track him down. A dozen years later, in 1972, Hammond signed a skinny young Dylan-inspired singer-songwriter guy out of Ashcroft, New Jersey, by the name of Bruce Springsteen. A decade on he closed out his prescient career by bringing into the label's fold a very Hendrix-inspired Texas guitarist named Stevie Ray Vaughan.)

Hammond's son John Jr. is a guitarist and singer who, like Hendrix, was a faithful student of older blues songs. In 1965 Hammond Jr. invited Hendrix to play with him at Cafe Wha? in New York's West Village, right down the street from Folk City, where Jimi's idol, Dylan, often performed. In late 1965 Hendrix shuttled between Harlem and the Village, slowly weaning himself off the circuit. He was then surfing from rooming house to rooming house with his girlfriend Fayne Pridgon, a former flame of Sam Cooke's. He sustained himself as best he could on meager earnings from downtown club dates and the occasional tour with Ike Turner or the Isley Brothers. Hendrix also did many low-budget recording sessions with various little-known and now forgotten R&B and pop hopefuls. He even did a session with the buxom blonde actress Jayne Mansfield.

Hendrix put together his own band, Jimmy James and the Blue Flames, finally giving himself the space to do things that were frowned upon during his circuit sideman gigs—wearing loud clothes, playing an even louder guitar, and doing old-school blues guitar showman tricks like playing the guitar with his teeth and behind his back while suggestively humping it like a hyperfrenetic sex machine.

Hendrix was not enamored of his own voice, but he did sing blues of his own invention as well as a few cherished Bob Dylan songs—most notably "Like a Rolling Stone." On the Village club strip, Hendrix was occasionally seen by various record company folk hoping to discover the next Dylan, but he went pretty much unnoticed during his Jimmy James days—even though he had already developed much of the look, performing style, and sound that would make him a rock god just two years later.

His luck finally turned in 1966, when a young English fashion model, Linda Keith, then involved with Rolling Stone Keith Richards, wandered into the club and was floored by Hendrix's dynamism. Keith brought a well-known record executive down to hear Jimi, but the man, Keith recalls, spent most of the night waiting to be impressed. The Stones also dropped by to give Hendrix the once-over. Possibly because of how alluring Linda Keith found him, they too sat through his set less than dazzled. Keith then had the inspiration to approach the man who would become Hendrix's first manager and producer, rock bassist Chas Chandler, who'd recently exited the moderately successful British Invasion group Eric Burdon and the Animals. Chandler saw immediately why Keith had been raving about Hendrix; after much discussion and hand-holding, he convinced a suspicious and nearly penniless Hendrix to accompany him to England, where they would begin the strategic process of propelling him to stardom. It's said that what clinched the deal for Hendrix wasn't the promise of fame and fortune but Chandler's agreement to introduce him to Eric Clapton.

The checkered history of African American artists exiling themselves to Europe to escape racism and secure respect for their gifts stretches back to the nineteenth century and continued into the twentieth via Josephine Baker and a host of bebop-era musicians including Kenny Clark, Dexter Gordon, and Johnny Griffin. Hendrix, however, was the first Black American artist to be taken to Europe by an Englishman who fulfilled his express purpose in making his managerial client as big as any of his own countrymen.

Speculation has always run rampant among Hendrix fans as to whether Jimi would have ever gotten a break in the United States like the one Chandler gave him in the United Kingdom. Count this reporter among those who'd vote a definite No. The reason for this is simple: Hendrix did not possess a Black church–approved singing voice to impress the major R&B producers of the day such as Berry Gordy or Jerry Wexler. Among the movers and shakers in that world, the standard for Black male vocal prowess leaned toward Ray Charles, Sam Cooke, Jackie Wilson, Otis Redding, and David Ruffin.

No one in America was likely to sign or market a flashy Black blues and soul guitarist whose own lyric-writing and vocal inspiration was Bob Dylan. And certainly not one who wanted to create his own genre of music out of everything he'd assimilated to date.

By contrast, the UK's pop-music culture was more open-minded, having observed the massive global impact of its own artists tinkering with blues, rock, and soul verities.

In Lennon-McCartney, Pete Townsend, Jagger, and Clapton, Hendrix found simpatico creatives who well knew the recorded roots of American music. Like Hendrix, they too were intent on wringing something novel, clever, and brutally modernist out of their madcap distortions and maniacal appropriations of that tradition—not far in effect from the derangement of European painting that the Cubists had been driven to attempt after seeing African masks and sculpture. (The market value that got attached to the Brits' productions after esthetically embracing Mama Africa also runs parallel with visual modernism.)

Hendrix instantly benefited from the UK music scene being smaller and more centralized than the vast fifty-state-wide sea-to-shining-sea expanse of America's music consumption base. Even if Hendrix had landed a major deal in the States, he would have had to concoct three-minute songs for the Top 20 in the hope they might one day get him on AM radio or network television and raise his profile on the soul circuit. In London, Hendrix was able to sidestep the circumscribed tried-and-true African American way to showbiz success. Hendrix skipped over Motown's civil rights–era integrationist dreams to join the emergent hippie counterculture and become a movement bellwether before the hippies even knew their own brand name.

The UK provided Hendrix with a lower bar for duty-free entry and overnight overseas success—one that required no big-name managers or labels and little in the way of artistic compromise. For the first time in his professional life he could play music he'd composed in whatever way he chose, all without worrying about alienating the U.S. music industry's gatekeepers—label heads, pop radio programmers, the savvy and merciless patrons of the Afrocentric chitlin circuit.

The UK was not free of racism, but it didn't share the United States' history of racially motivated lynching for miscegenation. So London was also a place where Hendrix, who'd attended an ethnically mixed high school in Seattle, suffered no violent repercussions for being seen nightly in the company of pink-skinned women. (After mega-success in America, Hendrix's open dalliances with white women would be overlooked by even the ordinarily racist white youths who flocked to his concerts. The jazz trumpeter Lewis "Flip" Barnes, who grew up in integration-resistant Virginia Beach, Virginia, recalls seeing Hendrix there in 1968 and being amazed that "white boys who called me nigger every day at school were drooling over Hendrix and acting like they'd have freely given Jimi their girlfriends if he'd wanted them.")

Because Chas Chandler had already been attached to a successful British group, he was able to bring his American client to the attention of swinging London's most prominent tastemakers—the musicians, models, fashion designers, gallery artists, record producers, filmmakers, and ad agency creatives—who told everybody else what was hot, hip, and happening on the metamorphic scene. Much of what Chandler devised to promote Hendrix could be viewed as mere publicity stunts, but they were all extremely ingenious, well calculated, and, in a couple of instances, even diabolically effective. One of the more outstanding schemes unfolded on a night soon after Hendrix's arrival, when Chandler took him to a club featuring Eric Clapton's then-new band, Cream. At the time, Clapton was considered by musical London to be the greatest guitarist in the world. Members of Clapton's fervent fan base became infamous for scrawling "Clapton Is God" on public walls and bathroom stalls all over the city.

That Chandler brought Hendrix to see Clapton, whom Jimi much admired for his work with Cream and two previous groups, the Yardbirds and John Mayall's Bluesbreakers, was one thing. That he asked Clapton if his young and colorful Black guitar-slinging friend could sit in on Clapton's gig was practically unheard of. Who would be cheeky enough to suggest such a thing? The setup was well played and the fix was in. Having heard and seen Hendrix in New York, Chandler knew that while Clapton and Jimi were both monster guitarists, Hendrix was the more eye-popping and extravagant showman and wouldn't be shy about deploying every circuit trick in the book—especially if it meant daring to wrest away devotion from a local deity. Years later, Clapton would recount how Hendrix not only proceeded to pull out the stops but also played "Killing Floor" by Chicago blues avatar Howlin' Wolf—a song which Clapton confessed he lacked the technique to even to attempt at the time. When Clapton tells the story he seems recovered enough to give himself a chuckle while still a bit transfixed in Hendrix's fast-approaching high beams.

When the time came for Hendrix to put another band together, Chandler and Hendrix decided on a young jazz-mad drummer named Mitch Mitchell (who worshiped drummer Tony Williams and Elvin Jones) and Noel Redding, a rock guitarist whom Hendrix liked for his frizzy orange Afro and who reluctantly became the bold new band's bassist. With only three songs in their repertoire, Chandler debuted the Jimi Hendrix Experience, on January 24, 1967, at the prestigious Marquee club and packed the joint with the UK rock scene's elite. Within weeks the group had an album deal and was booked in London's most advanced new studio, where a heady and accomplished young engineer, Eddie Kramer, worked. Kramer was a recent departee from the Beatles' famous studio haunt, Abbey Road. There he'd apprenticed with the Fab Four's eminent producer George Martin. Hendrix also soon made the acquaintance of an electronics genius, Roger Mayer, who gave Jimi first dibs on various gizmos he'd recently invented to alter the guitar's stage sound with the tap of a boot. The sounds of these devices remain the stock "stomp box" arsenal of rock guitarists everywhere for dialing in distortion, wavy watery tones, and pitch-shifting, bass-boosting presence (the Octave Divider). The wah-wah pedal would come later from another inventor. Hendrix also got access to some of the first larger-than-life-size amplifiers that had just rolled off the assembly line, right as the volume level of rock music begin to edge skyward.

Are You Experienced?, the 1967 debut album Hendrix and his newborn band made with these supersonic devices, dazzles and bewilders many accomplished guitarists today, even those who know every riff, lick, and chord progression by heart. The virtuosity, creativity, vision, and brash brinksmanship Hendrix unleashes on the album's ten cuts still blasts forth from the speakers with earth-shattering intent. On one song Hendrix even intones a proclamation announcing the martial plan behind his weaponized sound. "To your world I must put an end / May you never hear surf music again." Six of the most frequently covered Hendrix songs ever written come off the original UK version of the album—"Purple Haze," "Foxy Lady," "The Wind Cries Mary," "Manic Depression," "Third Stone from the Sun," and the slow blues "Red House" (which was dropped from the American release) and Billy Roberts's "Hey Joe."

Thirty-three years later, *Are You Experienced?* still sounds like something an avant-garde troupe of extraterrestrial soul men left behind before heading back to Alpha Centauri. The passage of time has not made it a period piece because nothing else in the period even vaguely resembles it in design or feeling—not even the Beatles' alien, experimental, and epochal *Sgt. Pepper's Lonely Hearts Club Band.*

In the history of the electric guitar, Hendrix is the Before and After picture. Partly, this derives from his peerless knowledge of every major guitarist and guitar style in blues, jazz, folk, pop, and rock 'n' roll that had preceded him as well as his working familiarity with classical and flamenco guitar, South Asian sitar, and Arabic music. Hendrix freely references all of that information on the album and in ways that show he's already figured out how to make them sound like personal inventions. Ones that matter most because he's using them in his own inimitable fashion. Hendrix and Kramer took advantage of a then newfangled recording process called multitracking, which had been developed in the BBC's sound engineering labs in the 1950s for use in radio theater. This technology gave musicians and producers more flexibility in the recording and postproduction process, allowing someone as fecund as Hendrix to lace the same song with different freaky-deke guitar parts.

By 1968, studio technology had evolved so rapidly that four-tracks had become yesterday's news. Hendrix's next album, *Axis: Bold as Love,* was made a year later with an eight-track machine. *Electric Ladyland,* his third (and for many, his masterpiece), produced in between tours throughout 1968, used sixteen-track boards. Some of Jimi's songs have as many as fourteen layered guitar parts on the same cut. (Check out his 1968 studio version of "The Star-Spangled Banner," where the guitars are made to sound like a one hundred-piece symphonic string section.) *Are You Experienced?* still mystifies and amazes today because it remains difficult to fathom how a trio made that convulsive and roaring a sound with such limited technology. The term "psychedelic" had not been in use long when the album came out, but the record's mind-altering powers were quickly recognized to be the equal of any drug.

The association of Hendrix with drug use rivals his musical reputation in some sectors of mainstream society. To this day he is widely thought to have died of a heroin overdose, like his compadres Janis Joplin and Jim Morrison. His autopsy found no evidence he'd ever used heroin, however. Hendrix, in fact, died from asphyxiating on his own vomit after taking an accidental overdose of sleeping pills in combination with a suspiciously high volume of red wine. (A second inquest in 1990 into the puzzling circumstances of his death led some to conclude he may even have been murdered. Various parties around Jimi at the time suspected his business manager, Michael Jeffery, of being the culprit and believe an accomplice may have been Jimi's last known girlfriend, the Swedish painter and professional figure skater Monika Dannemann. Neither is alive today: Jeffery died in a mysterious plane crash off the coast of Majorca in 1973; Dannemann committed suicide the day after revelations from the second inquest made front-page news in London.)

When Hendrix died, his bank account contained only a few hundred thousand dollars. The lone payout Jeffery gave Jimi's father amounted to $250,000. After Jeffery's demise, the Hendrix family, led by Al Hendrix and friend/executor Alan Douglas, hired famed civil rights attorney Leo Branton to investigate the money trail and determine exactly how much loot Jimi's four-year superstar career had actually garnered. Branton discovered that Jeffery and his associates had tax-sheltered millions of dollars in an offshore Bahamian island firm to which neither U.S. nor British tax agencies—nor Hendrix himself—could gain access. Hendrix had often been paid in cash for his expenses; when larger expenditures came up, like studio costs or housing, Jeffery's office took care of payments. Hendrix had become more focused on the business end of things as he got older, wiser, and more successful, but the frenzied pace of his professional life distracted him.

Hendrix discovered that LSD was a common cocktail chaser in swinging London, and all the literature one can find on its effects suggests that it produced spectacular hallucinations and extended the range of sensory perceptions to an extremely acute degree. Some people claimed to have visions of God while tripping on acid; the guitarist Carlos Santana, of the famed San Francisco–based band that bears his name, believes that the LSD trips experienced by musicians such as Hendrix, John Coltrane and Miles Davis, and others played no small part in provoking the wide-screen dream quality of the period's best music. Over the course of the three studio albums released during his lifetime, Hendrix would provide more than a few fans with the sound track for their own trips; for the rest of us the music stands as our closest sonic replica of an LSD excursion.

The close-knit, collaborative relationship Hendrix had with his chief engineer, Eddie Kramer, accounts for some of this. Hendrix heard exotic and esoteric sonorities in his mind; he and Kramer found ways to re-create them in the studio: the torrential winds he'd experienced when making parachute jumps; the tidal rush and lulling murmur of oceans, above and beneath the water; all those other transdimensional aural manifestations Hendrix created which we have no reference for other than his music. With only guitar, heart, and hands, Hendrix was capable of producing noises that evoked all manner of things—global catastrophes, human trauma and animal anguish, lust, howling winds, raging infernos, cracking lightning storms, peals of thunder, supernovas, black holes, dark matter, superstring brain waves. When you see clips of Hendrix pulling off all these effects live and in real time, you realize just how in command of his instrument, amps, and stomp boxes he was, even while pushing them to extremes their builders could scarcely have imagined. Hendrix was musically aware enough to know about the experiments with tape manipulation that European composers such as Stockhausen, Xenakis, and Ferrari had been doing since the 1950s to generate strange tones and resonances. From his time in Greenwich Village he knew about the high-pitched bestial growls and psychotic screams that jazz saxophonists like John Gilmore and Marshall Allen in Sun Ra's Arkestra, Albert Ayler, Pharoah Sanders, and John Coltrane were bursting forth with in the 1960s as well. It had always been Jimi's ambition to have his guitar lines flow with the smooth sustain and controlled vibrato he heard in the work of saxophonists and violinists. His fleet fingerwork and penchant for high volume accomplished some of this; the new technologies he found in London for extending the guitar's tonal palette and dynamic rage accelerated the process.

On top of all this, Hendrix was also one of the most charismatic, visceral, and physically graceful showmen who ever graced the twentieth-century stage—as choreographically spellbinding and well coordinated in his way as James Brown and Michael Jackson were in theirs—the main difference being that his guitar became like a third leg or even a hyperkinetic dance partner. Hendrix and his guitar are so scarily aligned that every note is perfectly in sync with a facial or bodily expression that matches the rhythm and emotion of what he's dropping on his ax. Was his sound the embodiment of his spirit, or was his body the source of his sound? Like his disciples in George Clinton's Parliament Funkadelic, Hendrix wanted to free your mind but expected your ass to groove and follow along too.

Jimi's voice was not the infinite resource that his guitar was, but in the studio he created a sensuous half-sung-half-spoken persona for himself that was capable of great subtlety, supple phrasing, seductive humor, and dramatic sensuality. He was in the tradition of all the other great bluesmen who preceded him in being a natural, fanciful, and witty storyteller.

Hendrix loved the English language as much as any other adroit lyricist of the tongue. He was a fan of science-fiction literature and film—in particular stories about apocalyptic alien invasions. At least three major songs in his canon—"Third Stone from the Sun," "Up from the Skies," and "1983 . . . (a Merman I Should Turn to Be)"—tell of the human population's obliteration by space invaders or disasters.

The oblique title of his second album, *Axis: Bold as Love*, metaphorically conjoins Armageddon and a romance gone awry. Mystical references and allusions turn up in his songs from southern Black American hoodoo folklore—a source common to blues poetry since before Robert Johnson went down to the crossroads. Both versions of "Voodoo Chile" on *Electric Ladyland* draw on this lineage. Other lyrics freely cross-reference the Bible, astronomy, medieval literature, and Native American myths—the last likely derived from the Cherokee roots of his maternal family. Death and mortality make frequent appearances, as do startling premonitions of his own death. Hendrix accepted death as a side pocket of life and may not have expected a long life for himself. He openly mourned his mother throughout his adult years, dedicating two of his most beautiful ballads to her, "The Wind Cries Mary" and "Angel," which was composed after Lucille visited him in a dream.

The Experience became a ridiculously busy and much-exploited touring machine during 1968, not least because the group was among the first in rock to pull down as much as $50,000 to $75,000 for one-hour gigs. For three men to do this with only a couple of roadies in tow made for quite a box-office haul. By comparison, James Brown was, by 1967, making as much but doing three times as many gigs, and paying much of it out to a twenty-two-person band and personal attendant entourage.

Chandler broke Hendrix in the UK and Europe shortly after *Are You Experienced?* by putting the group on the road, opening for acts whose audiences were unprepared for Jimi's flamboyance, volume, and highly sexual suggestive stage antics—most notably the teen-friendly, studio TV–manufactured band the Monkees. Chandler engineered those appearances just for the scandal he knew would ensue; he also knew it would get the group thrown off the tour. (It took only one gig.) Breaking the Experience in the United States represented a whole other challenge. Opportunity arrived with news of the 1967 Monterey Pop Festival in California—the Summer of Love, as it became known—the year that Americans became aware that there were drug-taking, unmarried, and unwashed long-haired hippies in their midst—ones given to public cohabitation in the Bay Area's notorious Haight-Ashbury district. The Monterey festival took place right in this countercultural epicenter.

The event had been concocted by John Phillips of the Mamas and the Papas and other West Coast music insiders to present a showcase for what the promoter saw as the best and most serious rock music of the day. On its titular board of governors was Beatle Paul McCartney, who told them no festival with those aspirations could possibly be legit if the Jimi Hendrix Experience wasn't on the lineup.

The roster for the festival eventually included the Who, Big Brother and the Holding Company featuring Janis Joplin, Jefferson Airplane, the Grateful Dead, Sam and Dave, Booker T. and the MGs, Lou Rawls, and Otis Redding, who was to make a career-expansive appearance (one that Redding barely enjoyed, as he perished when his plane went down in a Nevada lake only a few months later). Hendrix went on second to last, at which point he and the band blazed through a set of originals and covers that included B. B. King's "Rock Me Baby," Bob Dylan's "Like a Rolling Stone," and the Troggs' "Wild Thing," which morphed into a frenzied feedback soundclash that saw Hendrix grind his guitar up against his man-size Marshall amp so vehemently a roadie had to bodily bolster it from behind. Jimi performed somersaults while soloing; for his finale he set a hand-painted Stratocaster guitar aflame with a lighter, then pounded it on the stage floor until it shattered to bits, howling in its destruction like an animal tortured, gutted, and slaughtered by a madman. The documentary director D. A. Pennebaker's handheld film of the performance captures every spectacular nuance in graphic, close-up detail. After Monterey, the Jimi Hendrix Experience would hardly ever be off the road in America or Europe for much of the next two years. In 1967 alone the group played 255 shows.

The making-it-up-as-they-went-along aspect of the fledgling rock business led to a transatlantic helter-skelter schedule of one-nighters; the group might play Cleveland one evening, Belgium the next, then Los Angeles the night after that. The schedule induced permanent jet lag, which inevitably took a toll on Hendrix, Redding, and Mitchell's cama-raderie and creativity. The group that had stunned London with its ad hoc but ready-made synergy in 1967 sounded more than a little ragged around the edges, sometimes even dispirited, by late 1968. That Hendrix managed to complete the double album *Electric Ladyland* despite touring and band strife is a testament to his ambition, will, and skill at deliver-ing magical results. The studio was a refuge for him. It was where he felt most liberated and focused as an artist. Eddie Kramer recalls Hendrix spending hours recording a single riff over and over until its tracking met his exacting standards. The Allen twins, Arthur and Allen (later known as the Aleems, Tunde and Taharqa), became Hendrix's studio background singers and were already among his best friends in New York—they'd known Hendrix since his days scuffling for R&B gigs in Harlem bars, and recall how his work ethic preceded his celebrity. They also tell of seeing him hunched over a small record player in their shared apartment, working well into the night practicing songs by John Lee Hooker, Lightnin' Hopkins, and Muddy Waters until the chords, fingering, and timing became second nature.

As Hendrix's ambitions as a songwriter, composer, and player grew, so too did his dissatisfaction with his bandmates, Redding especially. A fair amount of *Axis: Bold as Love* and *Electric Ladyland* features Hendrix on bass. The story goes that while he played, Redding was allegedly across the road downing pints in a pub and sulking over the interminable studio time and over being told what to play. Hendrix also began to disdain his wild-man stage image and the expectation that he'd have to bump and grind or burn his ax at every show. He longed to be taken seriously as a musician and to play outside the box of the heavy-rock trio. He told an interviewer, "We did those things mostly because it was fun. They just came out of us, but the music was still the main thing. Then what happened was the crowd started to want those things more than the music."

By midsummer 1969 the Experience was a wrap. Hendrix retreated to a house in Woodstock, New York, to jam with compadres old and new. Finding a replacement for Redding proved incredibly simple: A call went out to Jimi's Army and chitlin circuit pal Billy Cox, who was then off the road for a spell and living in Kentucky. Over the next year, with many drastic changes and events to come, Cox would become Hendrix's most stalwart musical companion and pal.

Hendrix explained his new agenda to the press: "I plan to use different people at my sessions from now on. Their names aren't important. You wouldn't know them anyway. It really bugs me that there are so many starving musicians who are twice as good as the big names. I want to try and do something about that. Really I am just an actor—the only difference between me and those cats in Hollywood is that I write my own scripts. I consider myself first and foremost a musician. A couple of years ago all I wanted was to be heard. Now I'm trying to figure out the wisest way to be heard."

Besides Cox, he brought two percussionists to the upstate house, veteran Juma Sultan and young buck Jerry Velez, as well as a second guitarist, Larry Lee, who in the early 1970s would become Al Green's lead guitarist and music director. It was with this core unit that Hendrix spent most of the summer of 1969. Mitch Mitchell was initially invited to drum but is said to have felt alienated by all the Black brotherly love surrounding Jimi at that point. Whether Mitchell realized that Hendrix may have spent the previous three years overcoming his own alienation in the very white-dominated rock world, the historical record does not say. When Mitchell did come around, it was during the two weeks before the now legendary Woodstock Music and Art Fair scheduled for three days in August.

The Woodstock band Hendrix dubbed "Gypsy Sun and Rainbows" was scheduled to perform during the closing sunrise event of the festival; by that time much of the near-million-strong audience from the previous two days and nights had scattered out of sheer exhaustion. For the faithful, though, Hendrix and the band played for almost two hours straight. They performed songs old and new, then unleashed an a cappella interpretation of "The Star-Spangled Banner" that has since become the default sound-track anthem for every PBS and History Channel documentary about Vietnam and 1960s-era political upheaval.

Surprisingly, Hendrix was not always against the war in Vietnam. Like many working-class and middle-class African Americans of the time who weren't members of the Black Panthers or the Black Arts Movement (that is, like most of us), he was pro-American and even jingoistic when the subject was communism. One friend, Eric Burdon, recalls Jimi as having a "right-wing attitude" when he first got to England. In 1967 Hendrix told a Dutch paper, "The Americans are fighting in Vietnam for a completely free world. As soon as they move out, they [the Vietnamese] will be at the mercy of the communists. The yellow danger [China] should not be underestimated."

After Woodstock, Hendrix found himself at the mercy of the multimillion-dollar business that owned a fair piece of him. His manager, Michael Jeffery, once showed up at the upstate house with some Mafia-connected guy who put a bull's-eye on a tree and shot point-blank rounds into it while Jeffery pressed Hendrix to do a gig at a Mafia-owned club. What Jeffery's nudging and cajoling could not accomplish, the mob guy's marksmanship did, and Jimi unhappily acquiesced.

Hendrix wanted to fire Jeffery but was too intimidated to do it on his own. He sought out alternatives, notably Alan Douglas, a producer who'd made records in the 1950s and 1960s with such jazz luminaries as Duke Ellington, Charles Mingus, Eric Dolphy, and Betty Carter. Douglas would later produce the Last Poets' first recordings. Douglas tried to set Hendrix up for a session with Miles Davis and Tony Williams, but the word is that Miles balked, demanding $50,000 beforehand, and the session was canceled. Douglas was also unable to pull Jimi away from

Jeffery; what might have happened when Jeffery's contract was up at the end of 1970 remains a matter of speculation.

In December, Hendrix began work on the very lyrical, driving, and opulent music that would appear on the posthumously released albums *The Cry of Love* and *Rainbow Bridge*—originally intended by Hendrix to be a double album titled *Gypsy, Sun & Rainbows*. He also formed his one and only all-Black group, Band of Gypsys, with Billy Cox and Buddy Miles. Even forty years after Hendrix's death, the sight of a completely African American trio of hard-rock musicians can be startling. Except for a brief window in the 1990s when the all-Black rock bands Living Colour, Fishbone, and Bad Brains each had contracts with Columbia Records and maximum MTV exposure, such a sight has been rare since Hendrix's death. For Hendrix, though, the idea did not come about because of any long-suppressed cultural-nationalist tendencies. In the years of poverty in New York that had preceded his sojourn to England, he had signed album contracts with various low-level producers, hoping to jump-start a solo career. One of these deals resurfaced in 1969 and obliged Hendrix to give the contract owner, one Ed Chalpin, the right to profit from his next full-length album. Jeffery decided they would give Chalpin a live album of new material instead. Out of this end-run strategy the Band of Gypsys was born.

The concert album was culled from the four sets Band of Gypsys performed on New Year's Eve 1969 at the Fillmore East in New York. It quickly became, upon release in June 1970, the first Hendrix album to viscerally connect with young Black people. The solid, muscular grooves laid down by Cox on bass and Miles on drums were the funkiest Hendrix had built on his post–chitlin circuit career. White rock critics tend to slag it off as a jam-happy throwaway. Yet for those Hendrix fans who also like funk in their rock 'n' roll stew, the album remains a milestone. Although Mitchell would rejoin Hendrix soon after the Band of Gypsys fell apart—due as much to Jeffery's interdiction as to, some say, that Buddy's scat singing annoyed Jimi—the foundation Cox and Miles provided allowed Hendrix to lock into his band's rhythmic powerhouse in ways Mitchell's messier, jazzier style precluded. The result, heard on the original well-edited album and on later full concert CDs, shows how highly evolved Hendrix had become as an improvising guitarist. One whose extemporaneous mastery and blending of genres was as deeply exploratory and relentlessly magical as the best jazz saxophonists of the day.

Before Hendrix, the guitar had stunning but circumscribed roles in blues and R&B as a mostly accompanying instrument whose solo space was limited to a few bars here and there. Early 1950s rock 'n' roll guitar pioneers Bo Diddley, Sister Rosetta Tharpe, Chuck Berry, Ike Turner, and Elvis's man Scotty Moore firmly established the guitar as a defining ingredient in the emergent genre. Yet until Hendrix came along, no one had shown how versatile and explosive and imaginative a single guitar player could be on one album or in one show. Pete Townsend of the Who credits Hendrix with making him take the guitar seriously. But what Hendrix really did was make the guitar and guitar players as prominent, necessary, and fashion-forward as lead singing in late twentieth-century popular music. Along with Sly Stone and James Brown, he also became a pacesetter for the younger Black (and some non-Black) musicians who redefined R&B and electric jazz in the 1970s—Santana; Earth, Wind & Fire; Rufus featuring Chaka Khan; the Isley Brothers; War; Mandrill—and Miles Davis, Herbie Hancock, Chick Corea's Return to Forever, and Weather Report too. One of Hendrix's last concerts, the Isle of Wight Festival, also included a post–*Bitches Brew* Miles Davis band featuring two electric keyboards, electric bass, and an electrified horn of Davis's—all the result of Miles's decision to propel jazz into the high-voltage big-tent concert world of late sixties arena rock.

In September 1970 Hendrix spent his last time onstage jamming with members of War, just hours before he was found dead in his London apartment. The transplanted West Coast musicians were then backing up his old friend Eric Burdon, whose former bassist Chas Chandler had been Jimi's UK-born savior from poverty and obscurity in America. The poignant torch-passing symmetry of those connections between the doomed Hendrix and his heir-apparent brothers in War now seems taken from some Aquarian-age variation on a Greek tragedy.

– 2010 –

Note

1 *Jimi Hendrix*, dir. Joe Boyd (Warner Bros., 1973).

John Coltrane

In an art form more celebrated for its sinners, John Coltrane held the honor of being the music's first saint. There have been three figures in jazz history who have changed not only the artistic rules of the game but the social field on which it has been played too—Armstrong, Parker, and Coltrane. The status of each icon is also in dialogue with the others.

Armstrong's entertainment value stands in marked contrast to Parker's aloof and self-destructive serious artist profile, Coltrane's search for God redemption, goodness a gentle rebuke to them both. By the time I began listening to jazz in the early seventies you felt Coltrane was everywhere and nowhere in African American culture—politics, religion, literature, visual art, and even music. Well, especially music—because unless your name was Ornette Coleman or Sun Ra you labored under the shadow of Coltrane. To such a degree that not until recently have I been able to hear Coltrane's music as a stand-alone sui generis thing. When an artist is so surrounded by admirers, flatterers, and copycats the originality of what he or she proposes can be lost and even trivialized in what we come to understand as their style. If artists live long enough, rest on their laurels often enough, that style can become a trap and a parody of itself. With Coltrane though we have the rare fortune to witness in retrospect how an artist of prodigious Promethean will, talent, and force creates a means of expression bent toward not perfecting a style but the man himself. Coltrane brought ethics into jazz, front and center, and in a way that couldn't stomach the man being less than his art. He once said he wanted to be a force for real good in the world and that the pursuit of art required what he described as a constant "polishing of the mirror."

Coltrane's recording career spans 1955–1967. In that time he made several pivotal studio recordings with Miles Davis, three posthumously released live recordings with Thelonious Monk, and forty-five studio albums under his own leadership. What you get to hear across the span of all those tracks is a man chasing perfection, or at least his mien chasing his own perfectibility and capacity for profundity. If we all live long enough, the artists we love get more intriguing to us in different ways— some by merely surviving, some by becoming more visibly, audibly vulnerable and even broken like the Billie Holiday of *Lady in Satin*, others by sustaining their great generosity of spirit into their golden years like Ellington and Armstrong. What makes Coltrane unique is that his artistic pursuit was ultimately of things that art can at best only poetically suggest, a unity between humanity and cosmological creation itself. He's also rare in this most improvisational of musics in being an artist whose career has the anathema of a destination point—a single work that looms as a centerpiece, his quartet's *A Love Supreme*, quite possibly the most cherished jazz recording of all time. Miles Davis's *Kind of Blue* (upon which Coltrane and Cannonball Adderley performed saxophone miracles) is likely the most often played in homes and restaurants worldwide. But *A Love Supreme* is the fixed point by which we have come to assess Trane's progression from student to master—everything before is seen as prologue; all that followed as extended coda and epilogue. (Perversely, though, *A Love Supreme* is not my own notion of Coltrane holy grail. That ranking is occupied by the little-recognized and posthumously released *Sunship*, one of the last studio recordings of the same quartet that erected *A Love Supreme*, and certainly the freest of their freedom jazz forays.) *A Love Supreme* is also, as Ashley Kahn has pointed out, a genuine singularity—a completely secular work about things spiritual that is anything but preachy or academic and has been known to move even atheists to genuflection if not tears. In truth, *A Love Supreme* is as flesh and blood, as animal, as a piece of music can get and as philosophical, conceptual, and mysterious too, in the bargain. By the time the Coltrane quartet released *A Love Supreme*, Coltrane was already the artist to watch in jazz for a host of reasons—his own mercurial development had garnered the respect of hard-core jazz devotees during his time with Miles and Monk; his first recordings with Atlantic, especially "Giant Steps," had made those impressed with technical legerdemain in jazz sit up and take notice. Trane had also had a bona fide jazz radio hit with "My Favorite Things." Yet he used his popularity to form a bridge between the young turks and the old guard by openly endorsing and supporting avant-garde musicians like Ornette, Archie Shepp, and Cecil Taylor—this at a time when members of Trane's generation like Miles and Mingus openly criticized them and, oddly enough (given who was talking), even questioned their mental health.

Coltrane was the kind of artist whose jug could contain worlds and multitudes and still not compromise or corrupt his own principles or plans. The paradox of the avant-garde jazz movement, the thing which made it so prey to charges of charlatanism, was that it both simplified and complicated the jazz listening experience at the same time. For better or worse the avant-garde made jazz a more self-consciously and self-avowedly intellectual, experimental, mystical, and political music, more science fictional in keeping with the space-age space-race times, and more Afrocentric. It was a movement that demanded the audience get with the program or get out and, Sun Ra excepted, early on made few concessions to good old-time entertainment. This made for real starving artists among the avant camp (Coltrane compatriot Pharoah Sanders once said he survived eating only wheat germ and peanut butter during his lean mean freshman days in the movement). The numerous kindnesses the already quite financially secure Trane showed his hungry cubs, from actual cash loans to buying cats groceries to obtaining record deals for them, are now part of jazz legend and further shore up the claims made for Trane's sainthood.

What surprised me in coming back to Coltrane's oeuvre in recent years is how time has made his music sound even more original and exciting. Some of this is because where he was once the dominant voice of a radical Black jazz culture, jazz today is anything but Black and radical in its rhetoric and expression and there are no dominant figures or dominant ideas. The upshot of this where Coltrane is concerned is that where once you had to work hard not to reference him, today there's little around that sounds even remotely reminiscent of the music he made with McCoy Tyner, Elvin Jones, and Jimmy Garrett—especially in terms of galvanic gut-wrenching emotional intensity. What the Coltrane Quartet's music had was two of music's more elusive qualities in combination—melody and gravitas in equal measure. You can hear those qualities in certain Black voices that came to the fore in the sixties, Otis Redding, Nina Simone, Martin Luther King, Malcolm X, and in certain rappers today, Chuck D, Rakim, Nas, GZA, Scarface—but the Coltrane Quartet, like MLK, also gave voice to a sorrowful empathy for the human condition—one which daily demanded everything be laid on the line. You can't buy that level of commitment, you damn sure can't fake it, you can only deliver it from the viscera and maybe even bleed for it. McCoy Tyner has said he knew it was time for him to leave the band when he saw Trane bleeding from the mouth while blowing and not even seeming to care.

That degree of indefatigable discipline and unbridled passion can still render so many fans of the Coltrane quartet speechless, enchanted, focused, uplifted. An avowed atheist and libertine late friend used to say that when he wanted to hear God he listened to Coltrane. We always figured our friend was hedging his bets—hoping that the devotional ardor Trane's music evoked in him would provide deliverance enough for his sins.

– 2006 –

Gone Fishing: Remembering Lester Bowie
October 11, 1941–December 8, 1999

The jazz realm we refer to as the Avant-Garde isn't generally recognized for having produced a plethora of great wits. The form's sonics already exceed most folks' notion of radical extremes, so the idea that the abyss could be winking back is likely too terrifying to ponder. Art Ensemble of Chicago trumpeter Lester Bowie was the jazz avant-garde's trickster god. His sudden passing in 1999 provoked us to gather testimonials about his boldly theatrical and sagacious derring-do from his equally game-changing generational peer group.

Oliver Lake

Lester and I met in high school in St. Louis and from that point on we were always hangin' out. He was a leader then—on his soapbox preaching, calling the shots as he always did. If you were ever around Lester, you were definitely following. He was a prodigy on the trumpet—started around the age of ten or eleven and was playing gigs by the time he was fifteen. He had a hard bop band back then that was one of the most exciting bands I'd heard up to that point. He was always trying to get as much experience as he could. The first band I toured with was with him backing up people like Solomon Burke and Rufus Thomas. I remember we left St. Louis for the West Coast with two trumpets and by the tenth gig this other cat was ready to quit because Lester was playing so much stuff. He played with carnival bands, circuses, funk bands, marching bands, anything that called for trumpet, he wanted to do it. All of that came into play when he got with the Art Ensemble. But when he heard them, that was it for him. No more hard bop.

Henry Threadgill

Lester was like a colonel, a go-getter. He had that leadership quality. He had an energizing spirit that could amass people and move things forward. He was about the breaking down of all boundaries. In the sixties he pushed the idea of everybody in the ACCM (Association for the Advancement of Creative Music) getting out and taking the music beyond Chicago—which meant not just the United States, but everywhere. Musicians who don't go anywhere don't gather any information. The music we were creating wasn't coming from one stylistic concept, so we needed as much information as we could get from all kinds of places and all kinds of music. It was really good to have somebody like Lester around pushing everybody out. That had a major impact. He was on the go constantly, tirelessly. He didn't have time for no jive stuff. It had to be authentic, real, happening. You ever hear him do "Hello Dolly"? People tried to say that was a joke like they tried to say Rahsaan Roland Kirk was a joke, but humor doesn't lessen the seriousness of what you're doing. It actually broadens it. What would life be without comedy? It would be a drag, wouldn't it? Lester had a vocabulary that was about bringing all of these so-called light things to the forefront. When he became the second president of the AACM the first thing he initiated was a four-day twenty-four-hour concert. We were sleeping in the theater and getting up to play in shifts. That was the kind of thinking he had. He was a salesman, one of the chiefs. He could throw up a dream and take cats on a journey.

Craig Harris

Lester and all the cats in the Art Ensemble of Chicago had incredible vision, almost unheard of in the so-called jazz scene and especially in the edgy area of music they were playing. Their business organization and infrastructure really gave me something to aspire to. In the late seventies and eighties the Art Ensemble used to move around like the big rock acts, with two vans, four or five roadies, and a drum tech. They had a bus twenty years ago. It was a lemon, but they had a bus called The Sludge or something. Funny thing is when they rode into town, Lester would be in front riding shotgun on his motorcycle wearing a black leather jacket, smoking his cigar, looking like the scout and the general.

Steve Turre

We became good friends after I joined Brass Fantasy, and we used to go fishing all the time. Go out to Sheepshead Bay and catch bluefish, blackfish, and fluke. We'd also talk about our dreams. Lester had visions, and a lot of the things we talked about while we were fishing came to fruition.

There used to be a joint over in Newark called "L.C.," an old-time jazz-soul joint with the organ trio kind of thing. I used to gig over there with different guests like Cassandra Wilson, Arthur Blythe. Lester did one with me. This is in the hood where people just want to tap their foot, and we were just playing straight ahead, playing the blues. Man, Lester played the shit out of this stuff—he was swinging, playing the changes, and it was popping. He sounded a lot to me like Blue Mitchell in that straight-ahead style. The innovators of the AACM, Muhal Richard Abrams, Lester, and whatnot, were rooted in the tradition, and could play Charlie Parker if they wanted to and then go on and do what they did. It's quite notable that of all the elders that are still with us, Max Roach was at Lester's funeral. Max, being an innovator himself, recognized that Lester was contributing something of lasting value to this art form.

Max Roach

He was an original. That was my take on him and Anthony Braxton and that whole school that came from Chicago. Originality—that's the thing that marks us in our music. I'll tell you a wonderful story: Kenny Dorham was working with Bird, writing charts for Billy Eckstine's Big Band,

and had his bachelor's degree from Texas University. He was also going to Manhattan School of Music to get a degree in music education so he could teach. One day he told me, "Man, they flunked me on trumpet. I'm going to the NAACP about this." He didn't understand that when you take trumpet you have to sound like every other trumpet player, or else you can't play with the orchestra. That's the mark of classical music, but with us the mark is you've got to have your own personality. Lester and all the guys who came out of the Chicago school understood that. That what's happening is not how much you play but what you play. At Lester's funeral, it was just fabulous when all the trumpet players played and marched around the church at the end. There wasn't a dry eye in Saint Peter's. It exemplified what that whole school is about in being very spirited and collective. They understood that the essence of this music is not about imitating but being yourself.

Thulani Davis (from her eulogy for Bowie)
Lester was sartorial splendor. He strode in classic two-tones in spring, classic boater in summer, and the perfect leather for riding a 750 or a Harley. He gave notes on the new shops in Soho, and how to flash just the right glint of watch and silk at the mortgage desk. He reminded me of home, especially when he came back from Maryland with a whole crate of crabs. He was never stingy or shy when it came to good living. He was the man in the corner booth in a hotel in Tokyo with the best cognac and the Cuban cigar. The man who knew the chef at the best restaurant in Sicily, the one to see on where to buy clothes in Milan, or Paris, or anywhere. After knowing him twenty-six years when I ran into him I still always felt like I should have on better clothes, but he helped me get easy with the gray hair. Lester was the kind of guy who would never be old, always tough, always proud, who always made you want to have his respect. Getting it was like you finally got yourself a handmade suit.

Craig Street
I was fortunate in having seen people like Miles and Hendrix, Sly Stone enough times to recognize that nothing they did was ever random or by accident, that it was always with intent. Lester was in that vein. Lester was a masterpiece.

Butch Morris
Lester and I did a duet tour of Holland in the late seventies and I don't think I've ever learned so much just sitting next to somebody. At the risk

of sounding corny, he had a knack for the vernacular of the horn. Sitting next to Lester you could, for example, see what the Cootie Williams stuff was about at close hand. He encompassed and synthesized the whole trumpet vocabulary. He brought the whole continuum of the trumpet lineage into the avant-garde, brought the whole trumpet baggage with him in a way that was obvious—pointing back without quoting.

One of the most impressive things Lester did when we first met was describe Rasul Siddik's playing to such a tee that years later when I walked into a club and heard this trumpet player I knew it was Rasul, because Lester had described his technique so well.

Craig Harris

Lester was part of that great continuum of St. Louis trumpet players that includes Shorty Baker, Clark Terry, and Miles Davis. He used parts of the trumpet that most people don't deal with: the low tones, the pedal tones, the growls and smears. Always doing it his way, never mimicking, and always honest. He taught me how to use the horn when you're tired. He used whispers in his playing and he taught me how to play soft. Told me that'll put years on your career.

Deborah Bowie

It's kind of ironic now, but right before he got sick he was thinking, "I'm not going to be able to play this way much longer. What am I going to do?" I was always reassuring him that he could do whatever he wanted to do musically, but he said he just wanted to go to Maryland, fix up the house, be a regular guy, and fish. I don't know if it was a true feeling, but I think he wanted to stop and do something totally different that had nothing to do with music. I think he always played so hard and was such a die-hard stage musician that he didn't want to look at the possibility of doing something else.

He would always dive into stuff—like when he came off an Art Ensemble tour, went to Nigeria, and ended up staying in Fela's camp. Before that trip he had this whole thing about how he was going to be an African and have several wives. Staying around Fela for about six months changed his mind about having more than one wife. When he came back, that's when we got married. After Fela, one was enough. I don't think he was worried about his legacy, but because Art Blakey was also born on October 11, he said, "I guess I won't be played when I'm gone, because that's Blakey's birthday too." During the six months that he was sick he got an award from the mayor of Chicago, who declared it

Lester Bowie Day. He said Dizzy had told him that when you get one foot in the grave, that's when they start giving you all these awards.

I told him, "You can't leave me. I'm going to jump in there with you," and he said, "No you're not." I asked him what would you do if it was the other way around. He said, "Well I'd be sad for a little while, then I'd sell the house in Brooklyn, and move to Maryland and go fishing." He was a realist. He handled everything in life that way, and that gives me strength.

Famadou Don Moye

Ain't nobody ever did shit for us, and we never made it an issue of getting into the politics of the mainstream. We were never part of that, never have been, and never will be. That's why they can all really kiss our asses now. They labeled what we did "hate music"—"weird," "avant-garde"— and Lester never got his proper credit as an innovator of the trumpet tradition, but we're happy with how things turned out. We're not bitter or complaining. We realized early on that there was some kind of game going on. Understanding that to be a given, we kicked ourselves in the ass every morning to do what had to be done: taxes, office work, orientation for roadies, maintenance of our vehicles, blah blah blah. We have our own publishing company and we've paid for all of our shit. Fifty percent of the income the Art Ensemble makes goes into production, 50 or more, minimum. What does this shit mean? It means I'm sitting up in my goddamn fifteen-room house winterizing.

We got all kind of shit going on that's got nothing to do with music. Music is not enough, you've got to have life. People think we're about some kind of mystique, but we're just some regular motherfuckers trying to raise our kids and have regular lives. This thing is about thirty-five years of cooperative economics. More than music it's about sustaining our lives as opposed to the tragicomedy of the starving artist bullshit.

We never considered ourselves to be expatriates. We just went to Europe to work, not to say fuck America. Lester was always instrumental in establishing a base of operations for us, a headquarters. He also brought the element of family into the thing, because when they all went to Paris in 1969 he brought his wife, Fontella Bass, and their two kids, and they had two more kids while we were over there. Lester's whole thing was always tempered by the reality of having two kids.

The music was the focal point. It qualified what we were doing. Otherwise, ain't no reason for no grown man to uproot his family out of the kind of successful career Lester was having as Fontella's musical director, and go to Europe on some bullshit. You can believe that the structure of the whole thing was definitely calculated. When we got the house in Paris, Lester put five $1,000 bills down on the table, said, "We'd like a house," and the next day we had a house. Before that, we'd been staying in an insane asylum just outside of Paris. The doctors were jazz fans, and gave us rooms and rehearsal spaces in this nuthouse.

When I joined the Art Ensemble, we would rehearse eight hours a day every day, and afterward sit down and have a home-cooked meal in a home environment with the kids and the dog running around, just normal shit. Lester was more a diplomat than any of us—he'd been a Harvard fellow, a Yale fellow, and down at Dartmouth, and had a capacity to communicate with the intellectual and cultural elite. But he was also a regular motherfucker, with six kids and nine grandkids.

All the kids came out alright. None of the kids are in jail or dope fiends or were teen pregnancies, none of that shit. Two of Lester's sons work for us and his daughter is now a PhD candidate at the University of Chicago. She came out on the road and took care of her daddy at the end.

I did the Lester Bowie forum. That's how I got two homes, and everybody in the band has homes too. Lester turned a lot of people on to the whole schematics of that—Craig Harris, Oliver Lake, Steve Turre, Cecil Taylor, Betty Carter—turned 'em on to quality of life for your ass. Cats used to come around and talk to Lester about getting a home, and he'd customize a program for 'em. He was like, "Do you want a house, or are you just a renegade motherfucker?" A significant point for me is that, at the time of Lester's demise, his house was paid for and he had health insurance. It wasn't a situation where he was sick and we were running around doing benefits trying to collect money for Lester because he was in the paupers' wing unable to get proper treatment. We always had quality of life wherever we were, and Lester was the king of that.

– 1999 –

The Black Artists' Group

Before there was Barack Obama, there was freedom jazz, Malcolm X, Freedom Riders, Martin Luther King, Minister Farrakhan, and gangsta rap. Which is to say the sound of a people yelling to be free and un-fucked-with by any rhetorical and sonic means necessary. The question of what jazz signifies today besides great chops has been at issue since the 1990s. Devoid of any palpable connection to grassroots Black Liberation politics, what—besides history, nostalgia and professionalism—does all of today's virtuosity even mean a lick? The larger question of what other kinds of Black American music are doing to disturb the peace in the Obama moment is less fraught with anxiety. Being Black and ghetto-born in modern America remains a de facto down-pressed political condition for millions of slavery's descendants; the American music industry like the American sports industry still depends on the ghetto's vast talent pool to feed its multibillion-dollar plantations. But alas, poor jazz, what cultural resistance movements can it claim even spiritual allegiance with now? The progenitors of hip-hop, techno, and house not only reclaimed luminous chunks of soul and funk for themselves in the eighties and nineties but also rifled and sampled those parts of freedom jazz and electric jazz that their parents transported from the funky-free radical sixties to the seventies. Public Enemy's Bomb Squad, De La Soul, and A Tribe Called Quest can testify. The spirits of Ellington and Sun Ra are arguably more alive in any hip-hop record than in any jazz released over the last quarter century. Those paradigm-shoving DJs Grandmaster Flash and Afrika Bambaataa, Marley Marl, the Bomb Squad, the RZA, and the Dungeon Family all done made it so—carried forth the notion that Black experimental music can operate at artful extremes and still shock, jock, and mock that booty-rock.

Black American protest politics and Black American musical experimentation have been joined at the hip since before the spirituals. Reading Eileen Southern's monumental tome *The Music of Black Americans* will provide more evidence than we have space to recite here. When Chicago's AACM and Amiri Baraka's Harlem-then-Newark-based Black Arts Movement kicked off in the midsixties they followed in the footsteps of a century's worth of community organizers who placed Black performance at the center of their activism.

Ragged turns of radical Black history—from the Haitian revolution to the Watts riots—connect Buddy Bolden blowing modern jazz to life down by the Mississippi River in the nineteen-oughts to the formation of St. Louis, Missouri's Black Artists' Group near the mighty river's northernmost point in 1968.

By the late sixties jazz will have become beset by the same crisis of identity every other modernist art form was suffering from—a crisis brought on by the recognition that formal purity, linear progression, and the Great Man Theory of History have their creative limits. The best jazz musicians who found their voice after Coltrane's death tended to find it in accordance with politically conscious, community-minded collectives. After the departure of the Messiah (Trane), his fellow trailblazers—Miles Davis, Ornette Coleman, Sun Ra, Cecil Taylor—all proposed musical answers to the desire for playing with not just feeling but greater tribal meaning.

Miles led Bolden's descendants back to Congo Square with a polymorphous electrified twist; Ornette decided the blues should go after the head of Pierre Boulez. Sun Ra continued his carnivalesque marriage of Afro-futurism (and retro-futurism) swing and multiphonic starship navigation. Cecil Taylor wrought symphonic forms out of ninety-minute piano solos via an African Code Methodology.

The members of the AACM and BAG smashed together atoms that had split off from all of freedom jazz's maestros. Just about everything any literate lay listener would want to know about the AACM can be found in *A Power Stronger Than Itself*, author and member-trombonist George Lewis's masterful history of his fellow Chicago avant-groidd homegirls and homeboys. Benjamin Looker delineates the rise and fall of BAG in his essay "Point from Which Creation Begins." Looker is a less storied intellectual figure than Professor Lewis (who isn't?) but no less indispensable a wellspring on his subject.

In my own freedom jazz-radical circle in 1970s Washington, DC, the members of BAG who migrated to New York during the so-called Loft Jazz years quickly became crowd favorites—especially when they took the town with their own bands or those including California and Chicago-born fellow travelers. All were engaged in creatively rejuvenating the music's guerrilla front lines. We knew the St. Louis crew had emerged from a collective akin to the AACM but never much questioned how it might have been different. Thanks to Looker we know that BAG's idea of a Black artist included many nonmusicians who also possessed exceptional talents as choreographers, theatrical directors, poets, literary scholars, and painters. (Art historical recognition of BAG member Emilio Cruz's hallucinatory visual work is shamefully overdue.) We also discover through Looker that BAG's multidisciplinary folk often collaborated on massive intramural events and ceremonies equally informed by high-European modernism and the highly esthetic Afrocentrism Amiri Baraka's Black Arts Movement proposed. Musical homework in those days meant more than building your conservatory or bebop chops.

BAG's leading musical avatars, saxophonists Oliver Lake, Hamiett Bluiett, and Julius Hemphill, and trombonist Joseph Bowie, made enduring contributions to extending the freedom jazz vocabulary, vernacular, and lore in the seventies and eighties. The former trio formed the still-vibrant World Saxophone Quartet with David Murray in 1976; Bowie helped invent punk-funk with his Defunkt brigands—who recently celebrated their thirtieth anniversary with a triumphant Lower East Side return gig. Hemphill's desire to extend BAG's multimedia legacy to New York was seen in the various permutations and presentations of his freedom jazz opera *Long Tongues*, which took its inspiration from Ralph Ellison. (Confession and transparency time: this writer contributed some scraps of libretto to the 1990 Apollo Theater production of *Long Tongues* thanks to DC-based producer/presenter, painter, and longtime Hemphill supporter Bill Worrell.)

In 1972, BAG began dissolving due to internal conflamma and withdrawal of government funding—yes, after the inflammatory response of Black America to MLK's 1968 murder in over one hundred cities, the powers that be decided bankrolling Black Aesthetic–driven clubhouses as far away from the capital beltway as St. Louis might drain off energy for more property-damaging radical pursuits; once the feds realized the Fire Next Time was under control and fading in memory, a group like BAG was toast. (Unlike the enduring AACM, whose Maroon identity, infrastructure, and integrity was built on the kind of grassroots comradery and the ingenuity that only American urban impoverishment can produce.)

In the wake of BAG's dissolution, members Lake and Bowie, along with drummer Charles "Bobo" Shaw and trumpeters Floyd LeFlore and Baikida Carroll (future composer for playwright Ntozake Shange) struck out for Paris as a working ensemble. Apparently this group left behind only one live recording of an extensive French campaign. *In Paris, Aries 1973* has finally been rereleased after being a coveted cult item for nearly forty years—thanks to the very freedom jazz–savvy Thurston Moore. This group's freedom jazz making will not be a revelation to anyone who owns any Art Ensemble of Chicago sides. Yet because this edition of *In Paris* is only available as limited-edition vinyl (loss of original board tapes forced the manufacture of reproductions from the seventies vinyl version) I found myself—as frequently happens whenever seventies music is magically spun on the antique turntable—returned to a state of analogue innocence and freedom jazz paradise regained. My reviewer's copy of *In Paris* got dusty, skipped a couple of times, and may have been slightly warped in shipping. However, I treasure these technological imperfections as much as I do the audible intimacy of the setting and that incredible sense of emotional, cerebral, and political presence that only French freedom jazz–loving crowds provide in my humble experience as spectator and bandmate. Bobo Shaw also comments on the Parisians: "We were amazed by the French audience. People seem to concentrate and participate completely."

Freedom jazz is more often extolled (or reviled by certain Philistines) for its chaos, density, and noise quotients but the tradition's open embrace of silence, space, balladry, and ambience can also be heard in the earliest work of Sun Ra, Cecil Taylor, and Albert Ayler. AACM and BAG musicians deploy African, Asian, and "toy" instruments as composerly coequals. On *In Paris* the BAG-men deploy percussion, bells, congas, marimbas, et al., just as pianistically as their Art Ensemble brethren (albeit if your notion of "pianistics" includes Cage's prepared expeditions to Africa and Indonesia). This borrowed conceit, and other Midwestern tendencies, such as healthy solo horn and percussion expositions in the middle of ensemble concerts, were still fresh enough additions to freedom jazz's conceptual repertoire in 1972. All of these gambits and family jewels were approached with a game attitude by the Black Artists' Group on the gig.

The listening value of this recording as a recovered document is severalfold. There is first to recommend the spirited generosity and affability that can be heard going on between the members—they give each other plenty room to stretch and breathe; the opening pace is leisurely and introspective, fanfares, bird calls, animal gibberish, bikehorn farts, erudite strains of trumpet and flute slowly emerge as if from a deep slumber, members amble about the resulting soundscape as if they'd wandered onto a very liberal production of *Waiting for Godot* where they can interject their own pungent dialogues and discourses on To Swing or Not to Swing and whether To Be or Not Freeboot.

What freedom jazz–loving Midwesterners—from Sun Ra to Bowie, Threadgill, and Lewis—brought seventies freedom jazz Big Apple rodeo was brotherly love and roughhouse roustabouting. New York freedom jazz could never sound less than fit for urban expressionist combat, but the cats from the nation's interior and Western edge always made the enterprise seem less sermon-on-the-mount and more sharp barbershop banter when not outright vaudeville. Fans of Lake, Bowie, Shaw, and Carroll know them as virtuosos adept at creatively improvising in any idiom you'd care to name—from bop to funk to twelve-tone. What you can't know until you hear *In Paris, Aries 1973* (the zodiac reference is in memoriam to BAG bassist Kada Kyan, who fell ill and passed on to the beyond before the trip) is how conversational, elated, and relaxed the group sounds unleashing all that artillery—especially on the record's four elastic compositions: "Echos," "Something to Play On," "OLCSJBFLBC Bag," and "Re-cre-a-tion." *In Paris* is a welcome addition to a small and brilliant canon of mature, atmospheric album-length freedom jazz works which includes the Art Ensemble of Chicago's *People in Sorrow* and *Urban Bushmen*, Marion Brown's *Afternoon of a Georgia Faun*, and Bennie Maupin's *The Jewel in the Lotus*—all intimate gatherings of extrasensory improvisers who utilized the freedom jazz platform to fulfill a post-Coltrane ideal—the spontaneous creation of aleatoric symphonic works by a pan-idiomatic and boundary-free hive mind of spiritually connected virtuosi.

– 2011 –

Butch Morris

For those who follow jazz, the question of whether the music's exploration period is over is deadly serious. After Ellington, Monk, Miles, Ornette, Cecil Taylor, Sun Ra, and Coltrane, what epic journeys are left? Only a few intrepid souls have even attempted to answer the question. Count the Art Ensemble of Chicago, Henry Threadgill, and Lawrence "Butch" Morris, among the expedition leaders.

[The late] Morris (1947–2013), an L.A. native, was among the wave of Midwestern and Californian musicians who migrated to New York in the 1970s and reignited the jazz avant-garde. His contemporaries include folks such as David Murray, Oliver Lake, Arthur Blythe, and the late Julius Hemphill of the World Saxophone Quartet. His late brother was the esteemed bassist Wilber Morris. "Butch," as he was known to all and sundry, first came to our attention as a cornetist on some of Murray's earliest albums; he later came to impress as the conductor of the David Murray Big Band. It's as a conductor of improvisational ensembles that Morris came to stake his bid for jazz immortality.

In the late seventies, he began developing a method he would term "Conduction," a *patented* vocabulary of hand signs and baton gestures that would enable him to alter arrangements on the bandstand with the fluidity of a soloist. Some of the best early examples of conduction can be heard on David Murray's *Live at Sweet Basil*, volumes 1 and 2 (1984), and on Morris's own *Current Trends in Racism in Modern America* (1985). More up-to-date variations are to be found on Morris's ten-CD boxed set *Testament: A Conduction Collection* (New World Records, 1995), which includes sixteen conductions recorded over a ten-year period in Turkey, Japan, Italy, Germany, New York, and Florida.

What made the conduction process fascinating was knowing that nothing was written down and watching the graceful, balletic Morris literally pulling music out of the air. The instruments Morris favored tended toward the exotic for jazz. The last ensemble I saw him with comprised four acoustic basses, two cellos, three violins, piano, drums, oboe, trumpet, and trombone. On the conductions from Turkey and Japan, some players use traditional folk instruments like the *kemence* and the *koto*.

Morris's family turns out to have been very musical. Besides brother Wilber, his sister Marceline was an award-winning concert pianist in her youth, while his older brother, Joseph, was a citywide clarinet champion who went on to become a champion boxer in the military. Butch took up trumpet at the age of fourteen; he credits Miles and Gil Evans's collaborations with sparking his own music awakening.

After graduating from high school in 1966, Morris enlisted in the Army; on the same day, he was drafted. His first post after basic was Stuttgart, Germany, where he got to rile southern rednecks with his Nina Simone and John Coltrane records. "I wasn't listening to that music politically until those guys brought it to my attention," he says. "After that, I'd play it whenever they came in the barracks drunk. A lot of fights broke out from me playing Nina Simone."

Morris might have missed Vietnam had he not put in for a transfer. "I started taking pills for my nerves because a lot of crazy stuff started happening in the barracks, like homosexual rapes, drugs, killings, and a lot of racist stuff. The doctor told me he couldn't give me any more pills because I'd become dependent. I put in for a transfer and told them, don't tell me where you're sending me. They made me a medic when I got to Vietnam because they were short on medics. They'd bring a guy in and say, 'Morris, sew him up and ship him out.' That was my training.

"The thing that trips me out was that the day I almost lost my life was the day the colonel said he wanted some flowers on his desk. I went out to this field to pick flowers, and we got shot at. When I got back, it hit me that I could have been dead because this colonel wanted some motherfucking flowers."

Morris returned home intending to study prosthetics and, instead, discovered Arthur Blythe and Bobby Bradford, two pillars of the West Coast free jazz scene, rehearsing in his mother's garage with brother Wilber. "What they were playing was really the Black revolution," he says. "It was a very melodic free music. It was ruthless, but there was some romanticism attached to it. I heard it as all this black that they had sprinkled a little blue on. What they played would go so deep in your soul, man. It also made me think, "Now that's some bad shit, but where is *my* shit at?"

Morris found his answer in composition (he is an extraordinary melodist, a kaleidoscopic arranger) and later, in developing conduction.

"When I began seriously composing, I found I couldn't get notation to do what I wanted it to do. When I hear a lot of notated chamber music, it sounds like it's music that's still on the page—like music you see instead of music you hear. I was trying to figure out how to get notated music to rise up off the page."

Though Morris is as trained as they come, his approach to music making has more in common with hip-hop producers like The RZA than with his jazz contemporaries. Not only in its results, but in Morris's attitude toward his player-haters: "I've forged ahead fueled by resistance. A lot of times, the more resistance I met, the more courage I got in a strange sort of way. A lot of people say, 'Well, you can't do that—what gives you the right? Improvisation is supposed to be free.' Of course I can do it; you see me doing it. That's a very European notion, that improvisation means just play what you want. There is a system, a vocabulary. All I want to do is teach you the system so I can create a structure around what you have to contribute."

Are we talking chaos or democracy here? You needed to hear and see Morris do his thang before you decide. While you were making up your mind, Morris kept on waving his magic baton and conjuring up the most multiculturally inclusive sounds this side of a United Nations summit conference.

"What I'm interested in now is the symphonic orchestra," he says, "because it's stagnant, even the twentieth-century stuff. And it doesn't matter whether it's Penderecki, Xenakis, or Boulez. It's not my taste, and it doesn't get in my body. Whether my music is considered jazz or not, I still consider myself a jazz musician, and whether you think my music swings or not, it still contains the things that make swing happen, which are combustion, ignition, and propulsion. What I'm talking about is how you get from under there, how you heat an orchestra up, how you ignite that shit and set it on fire. That's what I'm talking about."

– 1997 –

Charles Edward Anderson Berry and the History of Our Future

The poet Amiri Baraka likes to asks this relevant rhetorical question: *If Elvis Presley is king, who is James Brown—God?*

In this same vein, Little Richard once held the Grammys hostage by declaring himself the Architect of Rock 'n' Roll.

Now while I do believe the Godfather of Soul to have been an African deity on loan to the world, the flesh, and the devil, I must confess to finding Brother Penniman's statement as arguably askew. Because while Brer King Richard is certainly the Great Emancipator of androgyny, abstract expressionism, and glam in postwar American music—as well as the man who begat the ecstasy of agony one hears in James Brown, Otis Redding, Gene Simmons, and Ziggy Stardust. Yet for all of that, the Real Architect of Rock and Roll, we would counter, the Master Builder, as it were, of this house we all currently inhabit could be none other than tonight's most honored guest, Mr. Charles Edward Anderson Berry.

Every form of music needs a daring and original framer of its constitution and its constituent parts—primarily so that all those who follow that intrepid strict constructionist soul might have a strong structural reference to aspire to. And a lyrical key to the gateway—a Rosetta Stone, as it were, to translate the mysteries of the Master's tongue into a language any fool could clearly understand and repeat to others.

Such a person generally provides a formal and symbolic transparency to his chosen music. Kind of like that of life science's double-helix, an iconic figure who binds together the thing's major figures and its minor grooves into an illustrative and spiraling totem. The kind of thing many people will come to admire from miles around. Come hear you play that guitar till the sun comes down.

Fletcher Henderson's big band was not truly swinging until Louis Armstrong spent a year and a half in the orchestral mix sonically seducing his fellows into the sweetbread of syncopated rhythm. Dizzy Gillespie tells us that while he, Thelonious Monk, and Mary Lou Williams had worked out the complex and highfalutin theory of bebop years before they met Charlie Parker, it wasn't until they heard Bird that they knew how the music called their music was supposed to sound—how all those higher intervals were supposed to flow together with love and affection, be kept moving strong and in the right direction.

Somebody asks Louis Armstrong how is it that he plays so beautifully. Pops told 'em, "I just imagine a big ol' fruit tree, and try to pick the ripest fruit."

Every spanking new musical twist needs an avatar to hang, plant, and pluck its ripest fruit upon, its own Johnny Appleseed. The music we call rock and roll was bequeathed Mr. Johnny B. Goode himself, Chuck Berry. Berry is the iconic template and the role model of every cocky, geeky, and charming guy with a radical guitar style we've seen since who roams the land reeling and rockin' to the beat of his own boogie while confessing to immense sexual frustration and extreme landspeed velocity.

The bell-ringing guitar intro to "Johnny B. Goode" is as heraldic, annunciatory, and emancipatory an invitation in American music as those new beginnings heard on Louis Armstrong's "Weather Bird," John Coltrane's *A Love Supreme*, the Rolling Stones' "Satisfaction," and Jimi Hendrix's "Voodoo Chile." All of which let all other musicians know that there was a new sheriff in town. All are musical exemplars of what us folk here in critical theory land like to call an epistemic break—hell, an epistemic breakdown, really. Some hella krunk nouveau knowledge that interrupts, disrupts, and transforms our sense of life's possibilities and the kind of folk we believe to be forces for apocalyptic change in the world too.

From this end of history's telescope it might seem inevitable that the cat known to the world as Chuck Berry would have become the true Crown Prince of All Rockers. Yet as we know from his joyride of an autobiography, one clearly written in his own quite literate hand, Chuck Berry could also have become a master carpenter and jack of all building trades like his hardworking dad, Henry William Berry Sr., *or* a car thief, reform school recidivist, professional women's hairdresser, photographer, stenographer, or boxer.

Mr. Berry is also the beloved son of a mother, Martha Banks Berry, a college-educated woman who taught high school English for decades. A mother from whom we surmise came Berry's lyrical command and romance of the language. Had the guitar not become a teenage obsession Mr. Chuck Berry might have spun his wordsmith skills into a literary career, perhaps one not unlike two other dark and compositionally talented sons of the Corn Belt addicted to writing and wanderlust—Joplin, Missouri's James Langston Hughes and Oklahoma City's Ralph Waldo Ellison.

Mr. Chuck Berry fell to earth on October 18, 1926. This astrologically marks him as a Libra, and an air sign, just like your current speaker, who was born ten days before the launch of Sputnik.

October 18 is a birthday day Mr. Berry shares with quite a diverse and motley crew: actor Joe Morton of *Brother from Another Planet* and *Scandal* fame, blues diva Jessie Mae Hemphill, anti–civil rights Dixiecrat Senator Jesse Helms, singer/songwriter Laura Nyro, playwright Ntozake Shange (of *For Colored Girls Who Have Considered Suicide* fame), alleged Kennedy assassin Lee Harvey Oswald, and more recently the young slasher—singer/songwriter/producer/actor—Ne-Yo.

Astrologers tell us that October 18 people are dynamic, spirited, energetic self-starter types who refuse to sugarcoat their opinions to please others and are ambitious to the point of seeming aggressive. October 18 people do not like playing in the background but tend to have great analytical intelligence and often do very well as engineers, architects, designers, city planners, teachers, and musicians. People born on this date we're also told are extremely budget minded and have the patience to save for big-ticket items. Like fleets of multicolored Cadillacs and their own theme parks. (Many of you have been to Graceland but who here has been to Berry Land?)

The year in which Mr. Berry joined the human race—the year of our lawd childe 1926—turns out to have been quite a generous one for providing a ripe and bountiful bevy of iconoclasts, innovators, prophets, and anarchists of many stripes. Musically 1926 delivered unto the world Miles Davis, Morton Feldman, Big Mama Thornton, Joan Sutherland, Ray Brown, John Coltrane, Iannis Xenakis, David Tudor, Tony Bennett, and Oscar Brown Jr. To other areas of human endeavor 1926 was kind enough to provide Fidel Castro, Jerry Lewis, Hugh Hefner, Marilyn Monroe, Steve Hercules Reeves, Neal Cassady, *To Kill a Mockingbird* author Harper Lee, the master of grindhouse cinema Roger Corman, Green Lantern illustrator Gil Kane, Beat-poet laureate Allen Ginsberg, *Young Frankenstein Blazing Saddles* director Mel Brooks, Robert Bly of *Iron John* fame, and France's own Michel Foucault. (Mr. Foucault, we feel compelled to add, was most notably the author of a three-volume set, *The History of Sexuality*. Each volume seems well applicable to a Chuck Berry discussion: *The Will to Knowledge, The Use of Pleasure, The Care of the Self*. A major dissertation beckons on the Foucault/Berry connection but for time's sake we'll save that discursive magic trick for some other Case Western fellow from another time and another galaxy far far away.)

Nineteen twenty-six was clearly a spectacular year for birthing folk hell bent on doing things My Way *and* The Highway. Obviously Berry fits that annus mirabilis of a mix like a mojo hand in a blacklaced love glove.

History also gave Berry's brinksmanship spirit a shove by dropping his essence down in the "Show-Me" state of Missouri. From a Black perspective Missouri historically matters for several reasons—not least because for 143 years, from 1702 to 1865, Missouri was a state where the institution of slavery was legal. In honor of Mr. Berry's well-known mathematical acumen I will further report that according to the 1820 census, ten thousand captive African persons lived in Missouri and constituted one-fifth of the state's population. According to a state audit of 1860 the estimated base commodity value of all the enslaved Africans then in Missouri would in today's terms amount to $1,142,838,790. This number of course merely reflects the value priced on their human stock and not the wealth their labor continues to produce through compound interest. A more developed Case Western conversation about the question of reparations in Missouri will also have to await a later day. But let's take a break here to watch a reverie by Mr. Berry himself on the history of slavery and his personal memories of segregation in the state.

Even though we're here tonight paying tribute to the debt rock and roll owes to Chuck Berry it would be irresponsible if we didn't pay some attention to the debt owed those African warrior-souls, enslaved and free, of an earlier America who helped make Chuck Berry and his music humanly possible.

According to exploreStLouis.com, "early census figures show blacks, both free and slave, lived in St. Louis from its earliest days under French and Spanish colonial rule. In fact, black settlers were listed among those killed defending St. Louis from the British in the Revolutionary War Battle of Fort San Carlos, which took place on what are now the Gateway Arch grounds."

Missouri is notably where in 1847 an enslaved man named Dred Scott and his wife Harriet first sued for their freedom in what eventually became infamously known as the Dred Scott Decision of 1857—wherein ten years later the U.S. Supreme Court determined that people of African descent brought into the States under slavery were not to be considered U.S. citizens and neither were their descendants. It is said that this decision helped to hasten the onset of the Civil War but Dred Scott himself died within a year of finally receiving his freedom.

Among Mr. Berry's regional ancestors are the first all-Black regiment of the Civil War, the Sixty-Second Regiment of United States Colored Troops, organized in Missouri in 1864. Members of this regiment were also the key founders of Lincoln University. One thousand and sixty-eight members of the Fifty-Sixth U.S. Colored Infantry are buried in Missouri. A prominent white abolitionist publisher, Elijah Parish Lovejoy, died defending his printing press from racist attackers. One of Lovejoy's young employees was an escapee from slavery named William Wells Brown, who became one of the first published African American novelists and playwrights. Brown's 1853 first novel is titled *Clotel; or, The President's Daughter: A Narrative of Slave Life in the United States*. It tells the story of a Black woman named Currer who is described as a mistress of Thomas Jefferson and whose daughter is the book's nominal protagonist.

Laws of the time forbade the education of Black children and made it a fineable and jailable offense. But in 1835 an ingenious minister, the Rev. John Berry Meachum, established his Freedom School aboard two steamboats he built himself and anchored in free U.S. government–owned territory in the middle of the Mississippi River. One of the Freedom School teachers, Elizabeth Keckley, purchased her freedom in 1854 and later became First Lady Mary Todd Lincoln's seamstress in Washington, DC. Ms. Keckley went on to write a book titled *Behind the Scenes, or, Thirty Years a Slave, and Four Years in the White House* about her experiences.

What the compelling, courageous, and ingenious sagas of Lovejoy, Meachum, Wells-Brown, and Keckley tell us is that long before Chuck Berry was a twinkle in his loving parents' eyes, his (and Miles Davis's) regional ancestors in the St. Louis, Missouri, and Alton, Illinois, areas, were courageously and creatively outwitting the slave system and defining the pursuit of American scrappiness on their own spirited, renegade, antiracist terms.

When we read about Chuck Berry's music we often encounter terms like "hybrid" and "crossover" and "border crossing." This too seems perfectly in sync with the state of Missouri itself—the only one in the union that borders a record eight of our nation's other states. The Gateway to the West is a territorial crossroads. It is one of the few places in the United States where the Northern Hemisphere's pre-Columbian Native heritage can be visibly seen from across the Mississippi River. The latter bit is thanks to places like Monks Mound—a cosmopolitan construction of earth built around 1100 BCE that has the same base size as the Great Pyramid of Giza—13.1 acres. Like the Great Pyramid, the mound has likewise been found to have been built with extreme mathematical attention given to various astronomy coordinates. A ritual game called Chunky, we are told, was once played on the mound's plaza. This game involved tossing spears with a "great deal of judgment and aim" at a chunky stone that was rolled across the field. (Perhaps Chunky had a baby and we can call him or her rock and roll too—Ba-dum!)

St. Louis history with regards to twentieth-century kulcha before and after the rise of Chuck Berry will not be undersung tonight either. The Texas-born Father of Ragtime, Scott Joplin, had great success during his time in the area, both forming an opera company and composing his opera *A Guest of Honor*. This work celebrated Booker T. Washington's 1901 White House dinner with Teddy Roosevelt. This event had inspired Black folk and scandalized segregationists everywhere. The self-anointed Father of the Blues, W. C. Handy, confessed that the sheet music he composed for his famous "St. Louis Blues" was based on melodies he had heard while walking the city's streets. Like some of Chuck Berry's compositions it freely combines elements from both the blues and from south-of-the-border musics of African descent. (In Handy's case that music was the Congo-Angolan-derived "Argentinian" tango and not the Afro-Cuban airs that would later compel the creation of Mr. Berry's crossbred Afro-Latin glory "Havana Moon.")

Josephine Baker, the woman who became variously known as the Bronze Goddess, the Black Pearl, and the Creole Goddess, was born bred and cornfed in the same town as Mr. Berry in 1906. Ms. Baker certainly set a great precedent for taking a world-class talent that had been honed on the St. Louis scene to international glory. Not to mention fighting in the French resistance and actively supporting the civil rights movement. The godmother of African and voodoo dance in America, Katherine Dunham, also spent much of her life in the area. About herself Dunham once said words that could readily be used to describe Mr. Berry's impact: "I certainly feel my career was a great career because it inspired so many many people, literally hundreds of people to follow a new kind of life and to realize that they could make out and advance their own professional and private and social lives." Dunham also said that while she once hoped the words on her tombstone would read "She Tried," she later realized they would have to read "She Did It." Ditto à la Mr. Chuck Berry again. As previously mentioned, jazz's own Prince of Darkness, Miles Davis, arrived in East St. Louis by stork circa 1926. As Miles's daddy was a quite-well-off dentist and hog farmer, young Davis made good his escape from the area a decade earlier than Chuck Berry. Unlike Miles, though, Mr. Berry has maintained a tight and close connection to his spawning grounds. In this way he may have also been an inspiration for a young and Princely keeper of the Berry flame from Minnesota also not known to venture away from home for long.

Richard Pryor once observed that we only hear about old wise men because a lot of young wise men are dead. As a young adult Chuck Berry pursued several career paths and passions. Most of these we'd consider honest labor; others we'd consider hobbies, a remainder just plain illegal, carpentry, construction work, auto assembly line, photography, women's beautician school, car thievery, reform school, boxing. Fortunately for us, the worst of these options ended in utter disaster and the best were superseded by the far more lucrative returns which early on derived from his music making.

Berry's apprenticeship as a club performer in St. Louis found him outdrawing Ike and Tina Turner on a regular basis and sharing stages with the great Albert King. All the real guitar fans here tonight will note that pushing the six-string strangulation envelope seems to have gone viral in 1940s and '50s St. Louis. True to his nature as a high-handed and sophisticated musical eclectic, Chuck Berry himself provides us with a list of key influences that could not be more diverse—Louis Jordan,

Harry Belafonte, Nat King Cole, T-Bone Walker, Muddy Waters, and what he generically refers to as "hillbilly music." No artist of any significance is reducible to a laundry list however. Jorge Luis Borges tells us that the greatest artists tend to reinvent their influences as much as the other way around, and Chuck Berry is no exception.

Folk are often given to wonder just what did Chuck Berry do to render his music so essential to the bloodstream of twentieth-century (and now twenty-first-century) popular music. It's no easy thing to give an answer in plain English nor to separate the many moving parts from the generous and loving whole. Sensibility tends to be an indivisible thing with the artists who endure—everything from shoes to work tools to Cadillacs seems to be of a piece. In the film *Hail! Hail! Rock 'n' Roll*, you get the sense that director Taylor Hackford, Keith Richards, and Eric Clapton all seem confused as to whether Berry knows how great his impact has been. And these are perfectly legitimate concerns for guys whose young repressed British lives Berry changed forever. This concern may be a tad off the mark though for the guy whose greatest creation was not his musical oeuvre but Chuck Berry a man in full—the dude himself. (Not to get all anthropomorphic and whatnot but like, dig: If you were the Sun how much time would you spend thinking about the light you cast on the Moon? Just sayin' . . .)

Befitting his architectonic mind-set, that of a man as comfortable in the world of blueprints and structural designs as on stage, Berry's most influential songs repeatedly do something that only James Brown's do in my humble estimation: They embed and encode the thermonuclear energy of rocking and rolling into highly detailed song forms. This is simply not true of a lot of music we all know and love. If you learn to "correctly" sing and play a Stevie Wonder song there is no guarantee that you too will sound Wonderful. Learning "Voodoo Chile" will not transform you into a Hoodoo Man or help you acquire a Foxy Lady. And unless you're Nina Simone, figuring out how to play and sing George Harrison's "Here Comes the Sun" is not necessarily guaranteed to brighten anyone else's day to a supernova level of luminosity.

If, on the other hand, you learn any James Brown or Chuck Berry song note for note, you will find yourself having become funky enough to funk up a room and your roommates may indeed find themselves rocking and rolling till the break of dawn. Learn to play the bass line to "Cold Sweat" and you will be grooving. Learn to play "Johnny B. Goode" as originally executed and you will thereafter and forevermore be a rocker.

Generous souls that they are, Brown and Berry already did all the heavy conceptual lifting for us. They already took everything away from the song that was not elegantly funky or just plain rocking those socks off. Michelangelo said, "Every block of stone has a statue inside it and it is the task of the sculptor to discover it." Mike also declared unto the heavens, "I saw the angel in the marble and carved until I set him free." Well, ditto babe: This is how Papa got a brand new bag and Beethoven got rolled in his sarcophagus.

Berry's greatest innovation was the entrepreneurially driven rhythmic logic that led him to blend the 4/4 of boogie woogie with the 2/4 of hoedown hillbilly music while elocuting his lyrics in a timbre designed to attract (and then confuse) the country and western crowds who showed up to his dances on the side of the tracks and the Mississippi River. That he did this during Jim Crow née American apartheid's brutally slow wane was equally rad. As Berry found out when he was booked by Country and Western promoters on the basis of "Maybellene" and then told there was no way in hell he'd be allowed to perform when they saw his face at the door. Heard him knocking but Oh No No No neither *he* nor nobody looking like him could come in.

We'd argue that the classic 2/4 beat we know as the quintessential engine of rock and roll became the genre's percussive signature because it rides so comfortably beneath Berry's indelible and immortal songs on the subject. Those songs remain among the most beautiful products ever conceived in the taboo-defying and transgression-embracing alchemist's lab known as American race mixing. Let's take a moment and acknowledge how diabolically clever it was of Berry to adapt his music to the one beat that already made truckloads of Midwestern and Southern-based white Americans feel at home in their own bodies. How brilliant and commercially correct Berry's instincts were to construct songs that grafted his licks, riffs, and sentiments on top of the rhythmically white familiar.

By the same token this meant some of Berry's best music would not find universal appeal among African Americans who preferred variations on 4/4 to move and groove to. As dance rhythms go, the Berry-beat can look not quite so natural a dance rhythm for even the most adept of us. You only have to watch the 1973 clip of Berry on *Soul Train* to see how much strain the then-best dancers in Black America endured before freely allowing that hillbilly beat to get up under their skins (http://www .youtube.com/watch?v=fT17IPu8amU).

What Berry only describes in his book as a "hillbilly" beat is also the backbone of many Black Pentecostal church services, a version of which we hear on the late sixties R&B/gospel instrumental anthem "Amen Brother" by the Winstons. The song's four-bar break beat section at 1:26

by that group's drummer, Gregory G. C. Sylvester Coleman, later became the basis of UK-bred "drum & bass" or "jungle" music—another eurhythmic genre many a Black American preternaturally obedient to the spooky chain-gang syncopations of the 2 and the 4 tends to find a tad constrictive on the floor (http://www.youtube.com/watch?v=GxZuq57_bYM).

There is no part of a classic James Brown song that is not funky from stem to stern. This is why hip-hop producers will sometimes only sample James shouting "One!" to make a beat meatier. In the same vein, if your intention is to become a rock-and-roll singer, songwriter, guitarist, or performer, the recorded legacy of Chuck Berry, audio and visual, requires only astute mimicry to transfer the feeling of the thing into your own body and transfer that feeling to others. This is why there are so many gosh-darn rock bands in the world and why once upon a time when young people of Negro origin still played instruments there were funk bands all across this great land. Because Chuck Berry, like Mr. James Brown, is in that rare category of artists I like to call the Body Snatchers. Artists with not only the power to possess your soul with their musicality but to dispossess one of all manner of zombie-stiff anxieties, neuroses, and inhibitions.

Now over in hip-hop, there's a thing we call "lyric lovers' rap." Meaning rap for those fans of the culture who love the wit of the word slinging as much as they love those phawnky beats. When you actually parse the lyrics of songs like "Maybellene" and "Too Much Monkey Business" you realize Chuck Berry is also one of the godfathers of rap music. You want to talk about florid sexual braggadocio and machine-driven rhetorical erotica? Classic Berry rivals any young buck in today's world of krunk:

> As I was motivatin' over the hill
> I saw Maybellene in a Coupe de Ville.
> A Cadillac a-rollin' on the open road,
> Nothin' will outrun my v8 ford.
> The Cadillac doin' 'bout ninety-five,
> She's bumper to bumper rollin' side by side.

Want to talk about antiauthoritarian militancy in rhyme? Well younger Chuck B. occasionally sounds like the prototype for Public Enemy's Chuck D, especially in these lines from "Too Much Monkey Business." Kick it Yo. (At this point in the lecture the writer attempts to recite Berry's "Monkey Business" in a Chuck D cadence over the vocal album version of Public Enemy's "Shut 'Em Down"):

Been to Yokohama—fightin' in the war
Army bunk—Army chow—Army clothes—Army car, Nah!
Too much monkey business—A—Too-too much

Bob Dylan has said that after he heard Chuck Berry he knew he'd never have a day job. Dylan paid his ultimate homages to the King of Rock with the cadence he used to deliver his classics "Highway 61 Revisited" and "Subterranean Homesick Blues." "You know poetry is my blood flow," Chuck Berry reminds us in *Hail! Hail! Rock 'n' Roll*.

What was also in Chuck Berry's blood flow was free love at a time when his fellow darker brethren were being rabidly hung, strung, drawn, and quartered under mere suspicion of being too free with their love anywhere near women of the Caucasian persuasion. As he relates in his memoir magnifique, Berry spent nearly four years of his life between trials and incarceration for the alleged crime of sex with white women. Berry is often described as one of the first major crossover artists in American popular music—but we should never forget that what he was crossing over from was a world where Black people and pink-skinned people had to be roped off into segregated sections to prevent physical contact during his concerts. Through no fault of his own other than being a Brown-Eyed Handsome Man, Berry was often the beneficiary of uninvited smooches by non-Black audience members. More than once, Mr. Berry had to be escorted to safety while pitchfork-and-torch-bearing Frankenstein-movie-style mobs were forming and frothing to exact a very high price for Mr. Berry's charismatic presence. In his autobiography, Berry recounts one such event occurring on a Meridian, Mississippi, campus where he heard one young southern cracker-gentleman tell another, "That nigger asked my sister for a date." Another fellow frat boy whipped out a switchblade to underscore his disgust at this fantasy. This vignette exemplifies what Berry describes as "Southern Hospitaboo," a conundrum Berry relates as having puzzled his own father for a lifetime: "Why is it so," pondered Mr. Berry Sr., "that black hands could knead the dough of the bread that white tongues savored yet blacks could not be favored to feast at white tables?" For his part, Chuck Berry describes in his memoir feasting and savoring from many white tables over the years—especially those set by various southern belles.

We need also add that the lifelong polyamorous Mr. Berry was, as he reveals in his self-penned book, also a pioneer in the realm of open marriage: His beloved and most devoted wife of six decades, Themetta "Toddy" Berry would rank for many an American man (and woman) as a head-of-the-line candidate for rock-and-roll sainthood.

Nobel Prize–winning author Toni Morrison points out that one of the truly amazing things about the Black experience in America is that bestial treatment did not produce a bestial people. The history, generosity, and charismatic capacity of African American music can be readily viewed as a triumph of the civilizing strains of our music over the savagery perpetually visited upon our communities. Tony Bennett reminds us that any civilization is judged by what it gives to the rest of the world. America, he says, can say it gave Louis Armstrong to the world, a statement to which I'd say Louis, yes Tony, but we need also be as proud that we gave 'em Chuck Berry too. Matter of fact, thanks to Carl Sagan embedding "Johnny B. Goode" in the cosmic archives of earthly civilization on *Voyager 1*, we can also say America gave Chuck Berry to the universe. Roll over my brother Beethoven, tell Lord Sun Ra the news.

– 2014 –

Lonnie Holley

Like many of old-school R&B's soul tenor voices, Lonnie Holley is really a preacher. Like any modern shaman worth his salt, he also has own gospel to spread. When we listen to his debut album we can hear echoes of other preaching tenors who know what to do with a bit of vibrato—Aaron Neville springs to mind, although Holley's celestial roadhouse keyboard work brings to mind Sun Ra in a whimsical mode. Holley's thematics have little to do with life among the stars though. In fact, his laments for his fellow earth creatures are very much about our contemporary seduction by the connectivity bars of our beloved digital devices.

Lest anyone mistake him for a Luddite without a clue, we should mention that Holley too maintains a Facebook page from his perches in Atlanta, Georgia, and Birmingham, Alabama, the Magic City where he, like Sun Ra, was born and bred. Unlike Ra, Holley left, came back, and stayed—returning to support a humungous extended family that included his own mother's twenty-six other children and his grandmother's sixty-six grandchildren. Holley has also, since his twenties, done something else beyond Sun Ra's imagining: established world recognition for the visionary visual art he continues to produce, against the odds, obstacles, and outright hostility he's confronted in the land of his birth. Ironically enough—or perhaps not so ironically, given the history of U.S. Blacks in the "dutty" American South; the city of Birmingham, in pursuit of airport expansion in the nineties, cruelly and callously bulldozed dozens of pieces Holley had constructed on land where his grandfather had built an ancestral sixteen-room home in the 1950s. After a protracted legal battle the city of Birmingham would eventually be made to award Holley $165,700 and relocate his family of fifteen children to nearby upscale Harpersville, Alabama—much to the chagrin of his ensconced neighbors there. Despite setbacks, Holley's work was exhibited at the White House during Bill Clinton's reign and was chosen to represent the United States during the 1996 Olympics in Atlanta. A major 2003 retrospective organized by the Birmingham Museum of Art also traveled to Birmingham, England, that same year.

The magnificent southern-based African American tradition of multimedia art making Holley belongs to has only recently begun to receive serious critical attention in the USA. A stellar 2011 Indianapolis museum exhibition of Thornton Dial, the tradition's still-productive eighty-nine-year-old grand master, had magazine critics frothing superlatives like "America's Picasso." A 2002 Whitney Museum showing of sui generis nonfigurative quilts by families of women from the isolated islet of Gee's Bend, Alabama, stunned and delighted New York art denizens. One prominent scholar of abstract expressionism claimed their artistry meant the history of his field would have to be rewritten.

Holley's own voluminous body of work, now housed and still harvesting fruit in a warehouse compound in Birmingham, is as formidable—formally, conceptually, cross-culturally. The twenty-page booklet enclosed in the album contains many sterling examples. Among this writer's favorites are "The Music Lives after the Instruments Is Destroyed" from 1984, which makes exquisite use of a ruined Gibson SG guitar, amputated saxophone parts, and plastic flowers, and "Keeping a Record of It (Harmful Music)"—an assemblage from 1986 that combines a discarded turntable and stylus with a bovine or canine animal skull—and a monstrous assemblage from 1994, "The Fifth Child Burning," a title which also appears on the album in song form.

All can be seen in the long section on Holley that appears in the massive two-volume *Souls Grown Deep: African American Vernacular Art of the South*. About the incident which inspired that sculpture Holley says, "A little girl in Birmingham had burned to death in her own house. . . . These things in the artwork had all come out of her own burned down house. Her parents was not home. They had given her luxuries but not their own time. Four little girls had died in the bombing at the Sixteenth Street Baptist Church in 1963. They was the victims of racism. The 'fifth' child had died of family neglect. We got to look past racism sometime and find the blame within ourself."

Holley's own art practice was birthed in 1979 by his response to another costly eruption of murderous flames—the masterful sandstone tombstones he made after two nieces perished in a house fire. Holley's virtuosity with this medium has earned him the nickname of "The Sand Man."

Holley's fairly late turn to publicly offering his music composition, performance, and now recordings yielded astonishment and early core support from two Atlanta-based American indie rock princes, Bradford Cox of Deerhunter, and Cole Alexander of Black Lips. Both have performed with Holley in Atlanta, as has the ATL's reigning Afro-folk diva, Doria Roberts. Holley's album, though, is a solo project foregrounding his vocal lamentations and keyboard work.

As a boy, Holley was given up by his mother to an alcoholic carnival performer who took him on the road at the age of one and a half. The artist feels trauma initiated his relationship to sound and experience. "I was too little to understand what was being engraved on my brain but I always sung and moaned about what I saw and what music those carnival people used to satisfy them. That carnival lady sold me to a whiskey house owner where I lived from ages four to twelve. Right after I got there, a drunk man attacked me with a poker iron, juked it right into my brain. In my music I'm singing about my brain lifting me when nothing else could help."

Holley dates his desire to perform and record his own music to a 2002 visit with the aforementioned quilters from Gee's Bend, Alabama. "They were doing a recording of their music for the Smithsonian and I sang with them. After that is when I first begun to lock down some of my own music for a record company." Holley cites Marvin Gaye, Stevie Wonder, Bob Marley, and Michael Jackson as his soul inspirations. His freestyle singing and home accompaniment on discarded keyboards has been going on for decades though. A recurring theme on the album is society's digital addictions or, as Holley calls it, "CTM," his hilarious translation of "computer technology management" as "cold titty mama." "If we're not managing our habits and using these technical things they'll kill us because we'll overload them and burn 'em out. You all have created your new mama. Half the people who had good jobs in America were fired by a computer, by cold titty mama."

Holley sees music as a healing force—even for the obesity which plagued folk in his own family. "Some people don't listen to the right music to burn away fat. I play music to make your body move but you don't have to dance to have music move your body. The right music can make your brain burn away this excess energy that has piled up within you while you're just sitting down. I make music to build the spirit and to burn the fat away."

– 2013 –

Marion Brown (1931–2010) and Djinji Brown

To be real, it was the late Marion Brown's son Djinji who embarrassed my ass when he asked, "Damn, Greg, isn't there room for an article on a Black genius before he dies?" Mr. Brown the elder is a saxophonist, educator, essayist, and painter, whose discography includes albums with John Coltrane, Archie Shepp, and Brian Eno, in addition to more than thirty titles under his own name. Djinji is a rhyme artist and hip-hop composer who's down with the Boom Poetic / Soup crew organized by those doyennes of flava, Sha-Key and 99. They were most recently seen wreckin' shop at Lollapalooza, but Djinji didn't make it. In June Mr. Brown suffered a series of strokes, and his son took to overseeing his treatment and care.

I knew of Djinji's existence long before he knew of mine because of "Djinji's Corner," an eighteen-minute composition on my favorite album by his pops, 1970's *Afternoon of a Georgia Faun* (ECM). This was back in the heyday of freedom jazz, or fire music, when musicians like Mr. Brown were throwing out the rule books, developing new methods of improvising, channeling their chakras and nervous systems into sound. These days, that era gets dogged by some reactionary critics who would have you believe that those cats couldn't play conventionally or had just plain gone nuts.

Djinji and I visited Mr. Brown in August at the Brooklyn hospital where he was recuperating from three operations. His movements were slow, but his grip was firm. Father and son show tremendous love and respect for each other's artistic endeavors, strengthening the spiritual link between the musics of their generations. What follows is a lyrical freestyle on Black musical philosophy in the words of the elder and then the younger Brown.

Afternoon with a Georgia Brown

I'm a Virgo. Virgos are loaded with music and art. And some common sense. Sonny Rollins, Wayne Shorter, and Charlie Parker are all Virgos. In the sixties, I wanted to develop an individual approach to sound, melody, emotions—the kind of sound to make a lady want to lay down in a minute. What makes the saxophone sexy is where the sound comes from—straight through your solar plexus, which is connected to the whole sexus. The music we did in the sixties came from a place that a lot of people aren't familiar with. Kind of bourgeois, bookish, heady, and individualistic. We did a lot of talking about what we were going to do, and instead of rehearsing we'd wind up having an eight-hour dialogue about all kinds of stuff. Ornette Coleman talks like he plays—convoluted. He can say things that only make sense when he starts it. By the time he gets to the end of it, you don't know what the subject is. We all do that. It's characteristic of Black talk, telling stories that go in and out of each other like Bach's counterpoint.

John Coltrane's music was awesome and frightening to the degree that you knew you wanted to even pretend like you could do it. And his music was very hip-and-pelvis too. Very gut. Trane's thing was mystery. He liked to talk about things that were shrouded in mystery, things for which there were no concrete answers. Just a lot of nice explorations. John was easy to talk to. You'd find yourself making sense to him when you couldn't make sense to nobody. He understood so much. One night after my solo at the East Village Other, I walked off into Trane's arms because I had pneumonia. He just held me so tight I felt like I would just melt back into his body. It was a transporting thing. I felt like I'd left the planet.

Playing free always gave our music a pickup, gave it a lift it might not have had otherwise. Even if I felt lost, I knew I had to play, so I just kept going. And you'd always have one person in there who could pull it all together, usually a drummer like Sunny Murray, Rashied Ali, Andrew Cyrille. What they'd do would put everybody in their right lane. Sunny Murray's sticking was fantastic. He played some passages that sounded like they were being played by a thousand bumblebees.

What we're hearing right now in jazz sounds like a bunch of guys who all studied with the same people. We're not hearing very many extensions of individual creativity. I hear a lot of pointillism in hip-hop. Little dots all over a certain area with scratches and splashes organized into rhythms and patterns.

My son Djinji's music has grown a lot over the years. He's learned how to develop things. The content was always there, but it lacked development. It's like learning to conjugate verbs.

Djinji's Corner (A Bronx Tale)

In hip-hop, we don't have a sense of sacredness about our music yet. Not like my father's generation did. They knew where they were going to, man. There's this feeling I get freestyling that's like in Carlos Castaneda's books where he talks about running through the Gates of Power and you can't see shit. When we're in the cipher and it's on, I know it's how those brothers felt to the tenth power. Like it's dark and it's clear. Sometimes when I'm rhyming on the mike, I feel like there's nothing inside of me but blackness—no veins, no organs, just a shell physically, but open and full of universes from my toes to my hair follicles. There are rhymes coming out of me, because there ain't no stomach, there ain't no heart, no intestines to get in the way of that shit.

Hip-hop is in the purest form of an African tradition, orally related, and we don't have no books that can tell you the shit you need to feel. There ain't no hip-hop Bible. Ever hear of Old DJ Mario from the Bronx? He couldn't read or write, but he built his own speakers. Give him a manual, he'd throw that away. Our education has come from outside of the classroom. From our dance to our murals. Fuck the Sistine Chapel— we've done the third rail, you see what I'm saying? Risking our lives for a ten-piece on the third rail. Michelangelo, We are with you—do you hear me? Picasso, We are with you—do you hear me?

– 1994 –

Dark Angels of Dust: David Hammons and the Art of Streetwise Transcendentalism

In the continuum of Black American interventions into spaces culturally marked "Whites Only," David Hammons's emergence and tactical maneuvering in the American and international realms of the modern art world seem as voluble as Nat Turner's and as inevitable as Miles Davis's. Educated in the sixties—in the Los Angeles of the Watts riots—Hammons follows in the footsteps of activists and artists such as Malcolm X, Amiri Baraka, James Brown, and the Black Panthers, who made manifest the degree to which being Black and Black forms of being, especially those found in the urban streets, could be erotically and politically poeticized and positioned as countersupremacist provocations to Black American self-renovation and agency. Martin Luther King Jr. and the civil rights movement mobilized the Black American desire to end legalized racism; more radical figures sought to awaken the community's perception of its innate beauty, genius, and power of vernacular disruption. Inspired by this sentiment as much as by the technocratic funk and erudition of jazz icons Thelonious Monk and John Coltrane, Hammons proceeded from the notion that Black American culture readily contained an inexhaustible wealth of gestural, metaphorical, and material resources. He then went about developing a practice that pursued street cred and modernist cred with equal authority (and intensity), and with sly, shamanistic wiles. The influence of the Black experience on modern art has been well documented—how African art acquired by intrepid anthropologists found its way to ravenous European artists, such as Picasso, in search of antibourgeois, antiauthoritarian inspiration from outside the institutional cosseting of museums, universities, and the church.

The midcentury pursuit of African formal expressivity as a counterforce to rationalist modernity became manifest in the impact that Thelonious Monk and Charlie Parker's virtuosic improvisations on the blues and Tin Pan Alley ballads had on the aesthetics of artists Jackson Pollock, John Cage, and Andy Warhol. The notion that an "America first" formalism and classicism could emerge from fetishization of the pop-familiar had long coursed through the post-African paramodernity of Black American music and dance. The increasing desire among American creatives for a visual modernity of their own gave rise to the dominant categories of postwar American visual art: abstract expressionism, pop, minimalism, conceptualism, performance art, video art. However, postwar American visual culture was equally influenced by the liberatory political actions of the African American body politic in this period. The mass mobilizations and theatrical staging of protest and self-determination politics by the civil rights and Black Power movements in the sixties and seventies, those movements' grassroots creation of personality cults proved as viral as the Hollywood machine. They produced the notion of an American public sphere that could be artfully and anarchically occupied and manipulated.

Black American political action provoked other repressed American constituencies to take dramatic street action for their constitutionally guaranteed due—Hispanic, female, gay, antiwar. The organized counterattack and overreach of the federal branch against all those contesting constituencies turned America's urban centers into battlegrounds, real and symbolic, where not only opposing political passions but opposing representations of American cultural style and identity were challenged or destroyed by fire. American notions of the spectacular and the prophetic shifted from the silver screen to the television, from the gallery wall to the street in the 1960s, because the dark gods in the street started doing more than just shouting back and made "Black" and "street" synonymous in the American psyche. The movement and school of American street painting we know as graffiti—but among hip-hop devotees more correctly understood as writing, tagging, and bombing—is thought to have begun in Philadelphia in the late sixties by an intrepid teenager named Cornbread (Darryl McCray), who not only tagged his name but a levitating crown (presaging Basquiat by a decade and visually predicting that artist's well-known encomium that his work was about "royalty, heroism and the streets"). After tagging up his reform school, McCray would go on to tag an elephant in the Philly zoo and the Jackson 5's private jet. A stylish bombing of the biggest and baddest targets, these acts also mark a self-authorized assault on private property rights and state control of public space. The proliferation of writing, tagging, and bombing on the world's biggest rolling canvas, the New York City subway system, continued the combative tradition of artfully Africanizing jihad by stylish, gladiatorial degrees. Bombing's mobilization of the repressed energies in the city's guerrilla creative core eventually produced several early masters of war—Crash, Futura 2000, and Rammellzee among them. Hammons is a generation older than these writers, and by the seventies, he was showing in L.A. galleries with a community of fellow travelers such as John Outterbridge, Betye Saar, and Noah Purifoy—a group as much influenced by Arte Povera as by the Watts Towers. What is evident in the most stellar work Hammons produced at this time, his legendary "Body Print" series, is his interest in representing both the materiality and the ephemerality of blues and jazz, and Black folk, especially Black street folk. The creation of this series required actual Black bodies and Vaseline—a skin product of particular cosmetic significance to Black Americans—and marked the last time that graphic figuration would be a dominant feature of the artist's work. It was also not the last time he would articulate an inherent tension between Black conceptual bodies and negative white space.

Despite the commercial success of the Body Prints, Hammons decided he'd exhausted that vein and stopped making them in the 1970s. In that refusal, Hammons established himself as the Duchamp of America's streetwise artists, an elusive illusionist whose practice became focused on creating a body of work the art world could not easily ignore, categorize, claim, or disclaim, either. Hammons spent the next twenty years making his relationship to the street the essence of his practice, which extended beyond the various and multifarious works he created. Joseph Beuys became another valued point of reference alongside Duchamp. For Hammons, whatever an artist did outside the white cube—or found and transformed out there—was art too, whether or not it was ever exhibited. Having already experienced success inside the art world when he was barely twenty, Hammons committed himself to proving how little validation an artist needed from that world to be significant, productive, prolific, and influential. In a 1986 interview in *Real Life* magazine, Hammons told art historian Kellie Jones why he preferred the streets to galleries for his work: "The worst thing in the world is to say, 'well I'm going to see this exhibition.' The work should instead be somewhere in between your house and where you're going to see it, it shouldn't be at the gallery. Because when you get there you're already prepared, your eyes are ready, your glands, your whole body is ready to receive this art. By that time, you've probably seen more art getting to the spot than you do when you get there. That's why I like better doing stuff on the street—because the art becomes just one of the objects that's in the path of your everyday existence. It's what you move through, and it doesn't have seniority over anything else."

Hammon's tactical evasion of art world fame and fortune reached its pinnacle in correspondence with that eighties moment in New York when many graffiti artists were hungry for gallery legitimacy, and the pursuit of celebrity beset the city's art world like a plague. While the meteoric and doomed Basquiat was being fêted in princely fashion by dealers from Berlin to Beverly Hills, Hammons was selling immaculately white and perfectly round snowballs in the company of squatters and junkies on the Lower East Side (*Bliz-aard Ball Sale*, 1983); bagging elephant dung from the Bronx Zoo; collecting greasy brown paper bags from Harlem BBQ joints; and catching lice from the hair he swept and saved for the wire-sculptural work that would eventually produce his dreadlock colossus (*Untitled*, 1992). During this period, Hammons built a shanty house in Battery Park City for a 1985 work called *Delta Spirit*. A shrine of sorts, in the tradition of self-constructed habitats in the Mississippi Delta, it was made from discarded lumber, evoking similar rickety shelters still visible there and in South Africa. That *Delta Spirit* was erected near Wall Street, where auction blocks selling enslaved Africans once thrived, only heightens the site specificity and poignancy of the work. Later would come his short film collaboration *Phat Free* (1995), a recording of a performance in which Hammons goes kicking a bucket around Harlem—one of Hammon's many oppositional asides about the mentality of hip-hop culture. If one had to name two Hammons works that epitomize and provocatively strike a balance between his love for Black American street folk and his critical intentions toward that community, they would be 1986's *Higher Goals*—a fifty-foot-high basketball pole and hoop encrusted with African-esque decorations composed of discarded soda bottle caps bent to resemble cowrie shells—and his 1989 circular assemblage *Night Train*, made from trashed bottles of Night Train and Thunderbird wine (legendary Harlem wino favorites).

Like the Alabama painter/sculptor/assemblage artist Thornton Dial, Hammons believes there is a magical and even dangerous aura specific to organic and industrial materials that have been touched by Blackfolk. Hammons told Jones, "I have information on Black people's hair that no one else in the world has. It's the most unbelievable fiber that I've ever run across. I was actually going insane working with that hair so I had to stop. That's just how potent it is. You've got tons of people's spirits in your hands when you work with that stuff. The same with the wine bottles. A Black person's lips have touched each one of those bottles so you have to be very, very careful."

In Basquiat's and Hammons's work, one recognizes a shared obsession with bringing visual recognition to the aspects of Black life that elegantly and eloquently teeter between functionality and dysfunction, form and chaos, vision and apocalypse. In light of Basquiat's fate, it's impossible not to read the apparitions in his work as possessing a marked-for-death aura. With Hammons, you also get fatalism and sly gallows humor, but because his works often take their complex feelings about race, death, and desire into the public square, they presume no transcendence or representation of folks' circumstances that cannot be critiqued by the folk themselves. This was never more apparent than in 1988, when his installation *How Ya Like Me Now* was attacked by Black men with sledgehammers. The work in question, shown in a vacant lot in Washington, DC, near the National Portrait Gallery (which had no representation of Black Americans on display at the time), depicted a billboard-sized drawing of Jesse Jackson that Hammons had given blue eyes, blond hair, and pink skin, along with the taunting inscription of the title (taken from a popular song by hip-hop lyricist Kool Moe Dee).

The piece's street critics, not in on the joke, interpreted Hammons as an alien interloper out to insult a Black hero rather than to expose an American electorate for whom Jackson's primary disqualification as a presidential candidate was his skin color. Hammons took the assault in his usual acerbic stride: When the work was moved inside, he placed several sledgehammers on the floor in front of it, sardonically attaching the defacers' toolkit (and brutal misreadings) into the work.

Having become an art historical figure and an unpretentious and unaffected art world star on his own savvy outlier terms in the nineties, Hammons has become more familiar to regular gallery-goers, curators, and collectors, but he remains an elusive trickster-figure. He exhibits more inside these days, albeit with his own arch twists on what coming in from the cold can mean for the adoring hordes who now show up to see his work.

In 2002, before the opening of his exhibition *Concerto in Black and Blue* at New York's Ace Gallery, idle chatter speculated on whether Hammons might use the Lascaux-scale rooms to install a major retrospective. Instead, gallery visitors were given slight plastic objects which emitted a faint blue light, and then entered a space of near-total darkness. Once there we were only able to make out the silhouettes of our fellow blue-glinting spectators. Hammons had evaded and avoided the obvious once again. In works such as 1989's *Highfalutin*—a recombinant construction that morphs a basketball hoop into a crystal chandelier— and *Hail Mary*, 2006—from a series of seventy-two dusty drawings that record the impressions of a dribbled basketball—the artist continues to mine, mock, and memorialize the streets.

In 2006, proving he's lost none of his desire to set the bourgeoisie aflame, Hammons and his wife, Chie, exhibited two floors of expensive fur coats that they'd torched to ruined perfection. The show occurred at an otherwise barren townhouse atelier on the Upper East Side. Clearly, Hammons's street ethos and 'hood-elevating aesthetics continue to repel the domestication that's expected to follow rebel artists into respectability. What Hammons's practice has bequeathed the modern scene more than anything is a nomadic sense of the street as not just a canvas but a carnival in constant tumult to which attention must be paid and for which argumentative translations will be made. Concomitant has been his commitment to taking the art world down to ground level every chance-operation he gets. In the realm of so-called street art, Hammons looms large as the field's philosopher-king and most agile demolitions expert.

– 2011 –

Bill T. Jones: Combative Moves

"So who's this Bill T. Jones?" asks Homeboy, wandering through the Brooklyn Academy of Music after the Bill T. Jones / Arnie Zane Dance Company's last of four appearances at the Next Wave Festival last December. Fortunately, Homes wasn't looking to me for an answer. Coming correct on Jones can take longer than a New York minute when you're swerving like a madman for that Senegalese diner up the ave. Artsy-fartsy New Yorkers have been following Jones's career since he and his late partner, Arnie Zane, began blowing up the spot with their movement experiments in the late seventies. Last year the MacArthur Foundation dropped one of their "genius" awards on Jones for being a modern dance innovator. Ironically, the choreographer probably reached his largest Black audience last October when he graced the cover of *Time* representing a "Black Renaissance" in the arts.

Still/Here, the work of Jones's company performed at BAM and which will be taken around the country through April, was inspired by the artist's own life experience. Jones, a gay man, was diagnosed as HIV positive a decade ago; Zane, who was also his lover, died of AIDS in 1988. In the piece, Jones uses movement to illuminate the human struggle with disease and dying. The impetus came from the survival workshops Jones has been leading since 1992 in hospitals throughout the country. In them, he conducts interviews and movement exercises with intimate groups of patients of all ages, races, genders, and classes. Incorporating video and audio segments taped at those workshops, *Still/Here* ranks among Jones's most complex and emotionally resonant works. Miraculously, it avoids becoming mired in morbidity or pity, allowing the audience to experience the combativeness of the "unwell," as Jones refers to those like himself.

Jones's troupes, a mad multicultural lot, are more diverse in body type and ethnicity than any other dance company around. For instance, Odile Reine-Adelaide, a bald, beautiful, statuesque sister from Paris, stands in sharp contrast to 250-pound Lawrence Goldhuber—not that he can't move like Tinker Bell when he wants to. When asked what he demands from his dancers, Jones drops a list that would impress a marine drill sergeant. "I'm a good choreographer," he says, "but I need people around me who give, give, give. I need people with well-developed feet, flexible legs, and strong backs because I do a lot of back work. I also want to know what your politics are. Stand behind your politics, whatever they are. They try to make me Mr. P.C., but I'm not. I don't treat women like shit because I don't want to see women treated like shit, and I try to learn from women how not to treat them like shit because I don't think anyone teaches us how." Balancing art and politics with aplomb, Jones has a knack for pushing his issues in your face without pushing you away.

Translating his vision of the ultimate abyss took Jones two years and required the meticulous choreographer to intensely scrutinize his four collaborators: composers Vernon Reid (of Living Colour fame) and Kenneth Frazelle, the legendary folksinger Odetta, and Jones's good friend videographer Gretchen Bender. He asked Reid to work on his next big commission when they were introduced several years ago by Jones's sister, performance artist Rhodessa Jones. "When the piece revealed itself," he recalls, "it give me pause. Vernon is a heterosexual young Black male, so why should he want to deal with my issues around mortality, fueled by my particular affliction? I'd been disaffected by the rock world when people like Mick Jagger and David Bowie denied their sexuality—like, 'We were just kidding, that's not really true.' But I looked deep into Vernon's eyes, and I saw a gentle, intelligent human being. One who still had the rebel spirit on all levels, which to me translates as 'Let people live.'

"I chose Ken Franzelle because I wanted one section to be informed by a Eurocentric classical sensibility. He's a very unassuming man whose father was a bluegrass musician. The man he lives with is a paraplegic, and they had just finished being buddies to someone who had died of AIDS. The project had a lot of meaning for him. I told him his section should use things people said in the survival workshops. He said, 'If you mean sung speech, I think it should be somebody like Odetta.' Oddly enough, Cicely Tyson had just introduced me to Odetta, and I was thinking of something with her separately. So this guy was already putting that together for me. I listen to those things. I feel those kinds of things are channeled to me, or sent to me—I don't want to sound too New Agey about it.

"Gretchen Bender, Arnie, and I used to get together back in the eighties and talk about the 'mediazation' of culture and television as a tool through which we manage our mortality. When I decided to videotape the survival workshops, Gretchen and I decided that was one way we could get a large world to come into this dance world. For that, I needed a person I knew and could trust. Understand that this woman was so close that when Arnie was sick, she would come sleep in the bed with him. We've been through the fire together. If I'm going into the world of the 'unwell,' there are very few 'well' people I would go there with."

Jones is very conscious of the ghettos he occupies as an HIV-positive gay Black artist. He also resists running from or being marginalized by those who are racially, politically, sexually, or metabolically different. "What I do expect for people is decency," he says. "Don't lie to me about who you are in context to the company. If you are straight, be straight. I know straight guys who come to the company and think they have to be gay. That's ridiculous. If you're a white middle-class person, be that. That's okay; there's room for you here."

– 1995 –

Gary Simmons: Conceptual Bomber

"I was definitely a crayons-and-Play-Doh kind of kid," recalls Gary Simmons. "I was always drawing my ass off. The problem was keeping my shit on the paper. I was one of those kids who was constantly drawing on the walls and the furniture. What I was really into was those Lego building blocks. I used to make these big, crazy things. They'd be like little cities. My mother would say, "What the hell is that?" I'd say, "This is the headquarters of Starbase, or something."

Simmons, thirty, still can't stay in one place when it comes to making art. Conceptual to the max, he'll work with any material to get his point across. And Simmons's points usually cut with the slicing wit of a switchblade. Check *Mr. Klanman*, a cast concrete effigy of a Ku Klux Klan member posed to resemble a lawn jockey (in place of Old Black Joe out on the grass, you have Cracker Jack dressed in his cross-burning Sunday best). Or *The Garden of Hate*, a onetime installation for New York City's Whitney Museum at Phillip Morris in 1992, which replicated a small-town square with an azalea arrangement at its center shaped like a Klan cross.

Outside of the Klan motif, there's *Lineup*—an installation that debuted at the 1993 Whitney Biennial—in which several pairs of gold-plated sneakers sizes ten and up are held for questioning in front of a police lineup wall. That same show featured *Wall of Eyes* from Simmons's series of "erasure drawings"—chalk illustrations of visual stereotypes that point up the smear job historically done on the Black image. Bringing a high degree of technical skill to his assaults on the racist imagination, Simmons feels as compelled to make beauty as he does social commentary.

Generally a jovial brother, this six-foot-plus visual terrorist from Laurelton Gardens in Queens brings the power-move mentality of hoop players and hip-hoppers to the art game. While growing up he hung out with local graffiteros, but he wasn't down with a particular crew. "I was more like a tagger," he says. "I wasn't really so much a piecer. I have mad respect for them because those kids have real serious skills, but I'd never say I was a graffiti artist. I just liked the excitement, but something told me that all the money and hype just weren't going to last. It just seemed like being a court jester to me, like, Let's get the Negroes in here to entertain us for a little bit."

A graduate of the School of Visual Arts and Cal Arts, these days Simmons is firmly ensconced in the mainstream art world. He has an installation at the Hirshhorn in Washington, DC, until February 12, and a major new work in the Whitney's *Black Male* show through March. His primary American dealer, Metro Pictures in downtown Manhattan, is planning to host his one-man show in March, with exhibitions slated to follow in Paris and Los Angeles in the fall.

Simmons's collectors tend to be white, wealthy, privileged—and, I would imagine, mad implicated in the antiracist discourse sublimely raging through his work. How he maintains his integrity, independence, and most important, his subtlety while working on the art world auction block involves some major trickknowlogy. When a collector buys one of the erasure drawings, for example, he's paying a lot of money for a piece that's on the verge of disappearing. "You're buying this thing where I'm going to come into your house, draw on your walls, and that's the piece," says Simmons. "The work is ephemeral and if it gets erased, sorry, that's it. So I get an empowered moment of drawing on an institution's walls, erasing it, and leaving this nonmark behind me."

Not surprisingly, Simmons's influences are "the infiltrators": Marcel Duchamp, Joseph Beuys, Cy Twombly, and David Hammons. "The ones who took that myth-of-the-crazy-artist thing and flipped it on you. Everybody that was trying to fuck with you. Those niggas were the best for that."

Likewise, in his own work, Simmons attempts to flip the script on his racially charged subject matter like a man intent on mediating a sucker to death. "My strategy," he says, "is about stripping emotions out so my work's not anchored to one person's experience. I think it's egocentric when people say, 'My life is my art.' My life is not my art, you know. I listen to CDs, I go the movies, I watch cable TV like everyone else. Where the art comes in is when you throw out a question visually that makes you rethink something that's in your everyday experience. I'm not into snapshots of life; I'm more into the blueprint.

"Film and music are big influences for me," Simmons continues, on a roll, "because the way a filmmaker approaches a scene is about some form of seduction. I love Quentin Tarantino. He's the king of seduction right now. The key to his work—which I like to think relates to mine—is that all that violence is muted by humor. If I could say I have a tool, seduction is it. In art, you can't scream at somebody; it won't work. But if you can visually seduce them, then they want to be there. If you use seduction as a hook and make it as lush as possible—which for me means sampling familiar things—then you got 'em in love. Once they're there, then you can kick that ass."

– 1995 –

The Persistence of Vision: Storyboard P

"Charlie Parker's father was a tapdancer," that inductive analyst, Miles Davis, once proclaimed. "That's why he played that way." Swing, funk, blues, and rhythm aren't just genres, they're things that happen to bodies in motion, driving the most rhythmically adept and coordinated of folk to fits of spontaneous creation, such as catching the Holy Ghost, speaking in tongues, blasting out bebop cages with freedom jazz dervishes.

This crucial relationship between African American musicality and physicality has always been rather sidelined in the music press. The performative conversation between African American musicians, composers, and dancers—street, social, and modern—has always been the more sophisticated, fluid, and ingenious one.

At twenty-two, Storyboard P is a state-of-the-art model of a twenty-first-century African American dance improviser and theorist. From the moment we first saw him work on YouTube we were dumbstruck by how his moves resembled Ray Harryhausen's stop-motion animations and CGI à la the Terminator or the *Matrix* trilogy. More than any dancer we'd ever seen, he made his wraith-like, mime-like, cyborg movements appear faster than twenty-four frames per second, and sometimes so freakishly slower you'd swear his spatial traversals had been artificially manipulated. Another revelation came upon seeing Story being interviewed online. That clip made clear he wasn't just a feral, fecund mover and shaker of modern street dance, but a deep thinker about practice and process.

Story's dance can resemble the jerky kineticism we associate with those genius spasmodic figures in early silent comedies—Charlie Chaplin, Buster Keaton, Keystone Cops. Footage of those cinematic pioneers was originally shot on hand-cranked cameras at irregular, uncontrolled frame rates. The illusion of more lifelike movement we expect in films today is due to everything being shot and projected at twenty-four frames per second. Between each one of those emulsified frames is a black one, invisible to the naked eye, that your eye uses to evoke the sense of natural ambulation.

In that aforementioned YouTube interview, Story shows out with movements that replicate the black frame of projected film and the persistence of vision—the cinematic-projection phenomenon where the eye recursively tricks itself. To such illusionistic mastery can be attributed the degree to which his choreography has both the fluid motion of movies and the hyper-artificiality of animatronics. Soon as we heard Story break all this down in minute detail, we knew bruh was on that proverbial Next Level with his shiznit.

Like any streetwise superhero, Story has an origin story. In his case, it also happens to be a Brooklyn story—one that unfolded first in the Brookdale section of the borough's fabled Bedford-Stuyvesant nabe. He recalls a perturbed grandmother making him dance at family functions so as to cure him of preteen shyness. It was his father, however, who saw in those fledgling first steps something that demanded he enroll his son in a nearby African dance class. Story remembers not wanting to go, for all the reasons toughie younguns generally don't want to take dance classes in the hetero-anxious 'hood. He recalls excelling at the African forms to such a degree that the lead drummers instructed he stand in front and demonstrate to others how venerable Motherland moves were meant to be done. (Specific dance forms are as fastidiously studied and revered in working-class African American culture as bebop melodies are by initiates and devotees of the saxophone.) When he got older, his dad put him in the prestigious Harlem School of the Arts, situated a long ways uptown in upper Manhattan's most famous 'hood. To a turf-conscious Brooklyn kid, Harlem can loom as more hostile and alien than the dark side of the moon.

Appropriately enough we met in Harlem at the generously donated library of the Romare Bearden Foundation, which itself was housed in the famous Theresa Hotel building where Castro stayed during his first UN visit after the revolution. Romare Bearden was the most renowned African American visual artist of the twentieth century and an innovative translator of blues, jazz, and African sculptural strategies to two-dimensional forms. Hearing Story unspool his thoughts on fracturing space and time surrounded by Bearden's eclectic book collection insinuated a continuum and a complementarity.

It was at the Harlem School of the Arts that Story began to discern the artistic merit of the dance he saw every day in his 'hood.

"When I started taking class there, I realized what we were doing in the 'hood was more advanced, in terms of movement, than what they were teaching in their hip-hop classes. When people say 'street dance,' they always think of a battle or something disorganized—but it's sophisticated really, what we do in the streets. It's high math, and real dancing, with combinations."

Story's Brooklyn story is also a Jamaican story—not only because more folk of Jamaican descent live in BK than on the island itself, but because the Brooklyn scene where he honed his craft in the early oughts was fueled and dominated by Jamaican DJs and B-boys. "We'd get a battle mixtape and we'd ponder on whatever dance was current. Then we'd put a little extra spin on it, start creating. I'd have a vision of a step, and then do that dance around the local park. 'Bogle-ing' was big in Brooklyn when I was coming up. Some of the drug dealers saw me doing my thing around the neighborhood and they started paying me to battle. So I'd go around the parks and battle to keep a little change in my pocket.

"My friend Nelson," Story continues, "knew about a show called Flex in Brooklyn that happened downtown in the Fulton Mall. When I saw that party, I was dumbfounded because I had already had a vision of some of the things I saw there—some of the glides and the floats. It caught me off guard the first time I saw someone glide, the illusion behind it. By Monday I was gliding at school: 'Hey, I'm in the hallways gliding now.' And they're like, 'Wow, P!' and 'Son, how you do that?' The earliest steps were just about seeing and imitating. I'd also conjure stories about how I was with a certain group of dancers, just to create a buzz around myself.

"I started learning some of the techniques of the dances, and made my way up through the Brooklyn reggae club circuit. I was in a group called Bad Company, and then, over time, I made it to a group called Main Event, who were the biggest dance crew in Brooklyn at the time. After they drafted me, my name blew up in Brooklyn."

Story can sometimes be randomly seen around Brooklyn dancing freestyle with young acolytes on the veranda of places like the Brooklyn Museum of Art. Yet though he strives to maintain those connections he mostly works as a soloist professionally—as in commercial vehicles like director Kahlil Joseph's bullet-time balletic film for Flying Lotus's "Until the Quiet Comes." Story's own prolific flow of self-produced clips on You-Tube often feature fellow travelers, but his evolutionary curve has become so radical and artfully sui generis few can keep up.

Like any boundary-crossing urbanite who clubbed hard in his early twenties, Story has watched the vibrant underground that spawned him turn to shite.

"The scene has changed now. The dancing used to be part of the dancehall reggae scene in Brooklyn, but over time they became separated—the clubs started shoving the dancers out. The dancers had delivered a cult following by then though. So we began producing these events we called Battle-Fest. The first Battle-Fest was in 2005. We promoted it through flyers in the neighborhood. The whole thing was like, 'Real dancing is back in Brooklyn.' So you could come freestyle and battle against another person, and if you won, you got a trophy.

"Battle-Fest got on the legendary Mr. Wiggles web page." (Wiggles, aka Steffan Clemite, is one of the most revered progenitors of the electric boogaloo and poplin' styles *Soul Train* addicts know from that show's seventies heyday. He still performs with the famed Rock Steady Crew.) "That's when these old-school poppers started coming and hating on our style. They'd say, 'Oh, that stuff—that's not dancing.' But that's where the first buzz came from: from big haters like Mr. Buddha Stretch. I have to mention the names of the big haters of what we were doing in Brooklyn. Over time I started traveling and battling, and I met an old-school dancer, Shock-a-Lock, who became a mentor. He taught me a lot about aesthetics, and evolved me. Made me want to get onstage and learn more about the psychology of performing."

Story is as much fueled by his loyal opposition as by the acceptance of wiser old heads.

"The haters were very helpful. I learned that was just part of the game when people would actually come up later and say, 'I was just hating to try and psych you out, get you to stop.' Because they could see where it was going. That turned into me really getting good at what we call the 'bruk-up' style. Flexing, we also called it. I battled everyone and beat everybody that was good in Brooklyn. To the point where people started saying what I was doing wasn't 'bruk-up' anymore."

Even in the freebooting world of street dance, there are reactionaries who like nothing better than to impede the inevitable flow of progressives like Story. What he says next about the conservatism of some of his fellows will sound familiar to any experimental musician. Whether in academia or on the pavement, there will always be those gatekeepers for whom the old rules matter more than Generation Next results.

"What's sometimes weird and limited about dance is that when you mix together different styles and do them all well, people want to try to box you in. Especially when you step out of highlighting one particular style, like popping. People couldn't fathom what I was trying to do. They got sick of me playing the eighties songs like ['Sussudio' by] Phil Collins—'Why you playing that?'—but I was creating."

At moments of revolution in artistic form, innovation frequently involves discarding flashy displays of technique. The reduction of ostentatious moves in favor of subtler ones is often read as laziness or limited ability. Remember how long Thelonious Monk languished under that now laughable misperception in jazz, and you'll dig immediately where Story is coming from.

"When I was sixteen I would hear a song and do six routines in thirty seconds—what we call burnouts, where you just hard-glitch-out. That's what I was known for: going hard like I was pulling out a machine gun, going wild on you, and the battle was done. But over time, as I wanted to work on the detail of certain things, I had to slow it down. That's where a mastering of sitting comes in. When you're sitting on a muscle and sitting on your core, you're finding those little in-between grooves, to get it more digital, more animated, more about the anatomy of the steps. This requires a little more strain and a little more patience but now I'm speeding that up more. The sitting is a hardening process. It's sort of like a Mack truck pushing through space: it's heavy, but the more momentum it gets, the faster it gets. That's how my technique is. I have a masked technique. I know how to mask what I'm doing. Because when you have the technique down, then you have to find ways to hide where it's coming from. So that people will only see the illusion you're trying to create, and not the technique. I've created this hybrid style, mixing in different things like ballet, because I've been chasing this vision. The roots of my vision are really from the golden age of professional jazz dancing—the 1940s golden age era of the Nicholas Brothers. The vision is to get there, with my technique animating it. I want people to know I'm not just dancing effortlessly, but formulating it so that it's knocking and pulsing."

Story studied filmmaking at an HBO satellite program in Brooklyn during his late teens. Given that background, and his proficiency with home production, Story wants to elevate his own profile and that of true-to-the-asphalt modern street dance simultaneously.

"Part of my vision is to start a film company. Take what we're doing now in Brooklyn and put it on film. Because our style is very theatrical and we put certain elements in that make our performances like Cirque du Soleil at times: magic tricks, different characters like Sinbad gone reggae, or *Clash of the Titans*–style monsters and creatures. The name Storyboard came from when I was in film school and somebody said, 'It looks like you sequence your moves, like you're writing them out for a film.' And that's actually what I'm doing in my mind when I hear a song: I'm taking notes in my head and actually trying to portray what's written there, which is like scribble-scrabble. You know when you write everywhere on a page, even upside down too? Well, I started interpreting that as: If I do a move, it should be awkward because of how I have it written out in my head."

All this dancing about architecture isn't to say Story isn't ambivalent about making the transition from street self-determination to more lucrative venues. He's well aware of the cheapening and disposability effect big money has had on past forms of street dance like breakdancing and vogueing. He also has boundaries where flat-out industry exploitation is concerned.

"I want to get into using things like masks and makeup more, but it's important to always acknowledge the foundation of what we do, which comes from the streets. I always want to have my street following. Because that's my base, and if other things fall apart, I want to always have that. If I lose my base it's over for me. Having that base is what allowed me to walk away from a Cirque du Soleil audition when I realized I didn't want to dance for them."

At the Cirque du Soleil audition in question, Story came ready to display his style and was told he'd have to do some company choreography as well. When he saw video cameras out, he backed away rather than provide an opportunity for his moves to be facilely assimilated into Cirque's.

"I went to an audition for their show *Michael Jackson: Immortal*. If you have a specialty, they ask you to come out. But when you get there they tell you that you must learn their choreography before you even do your specialty. And I think that's bullshit. Because there's people who are dancing for their tour who just do their specialty and don't do Cirque du Soleil's choreography. That makes a difference for me, when I can do my own thing—because I can animate Michael completely, and not do the cliché Michael Jackson that people know. I'm good enough to do Cirque's choreography, but I didn't want them to say I wasn't good enough and still be able to hold on to my material, pick out bits here and there. I'm smarter than that. So I didn't give them nothing. Basically, it was just lack of respect. Afterwards a lot of the other dancers there told me, 'Story, you taught me a lot about integrity by walking out.' When you tell them you're a street dancer they want to hold their nose up at you, treat you a certain way, and you really have to put your foot down."

Story's way of moving—the elegance, the whiplash control, and the muted aggression beneath it—will remind many of Michael Jackson. The truth is that he's even light-years beyond MJ as a dance artist, if not quite in his league as a total showman. What he appreciates most about MJ is more ephemeral and existential than terpsichorean—the intention behind the man's physicality more than the mesmerizing bravura.

"When I was growing up, I was scared of Michael," he admits. "When Michael came on, I used to cry—I don't know why . . . probably because of *Thriller*. When I was coming up, the top style in our circle was gliding—that illusion. Everyone who danced had to have some foot placement for sliding. What I learned was that foot placement in your sliding smoothens out your up top. So that if you pause and have some animation up top and smooth it out, then it becomes surreal. So that's what I learned from watching gliders—that I could do any type of dance up top; I could shimmy, anything, even if the stop-motion is in there too. That was a game changer for me. That's when I said, what if you could put that effect on four styles and make it look like one seamless flow? That's what I think Michael did. That's really what his vision was—to be unreal as a persona. A lot of people overlook that. That's why a lot of people never get Michael Jackson. They only see the movement, but not the concept behind it. Because the moonwalk is like a ghost walking—it's really a phantom he's portraying. People think it's like walking on the moon, but that's a space walk. A moonwalk is the energy from the moon being attended to—it's more eerie."

Animation is a word Story returns to often when describing his technique. "'Animation' means something that has life. Miming is emulating with your body. Film is just miming and emulating visually. You personify it with a face so it comes out like Freddy Krueger from *Nightmare on Elm Street*. When I had dreams and certain visions, they always looked cinematic to me. When we were creating in Brooklyn we'd take inspiration from movies like *The Matrix* and pull a concept from a leap we saw there. Other influences would be Jerome Robbins, Tim Burton, and Maya Angelou, because I'm also a poet. I got serious about dance early, but didn't fully embrace it, because I'm into literature and I wanted to be a writer. So on a strict formal level, I see myself writing things, but giving you a visual presentation, metaphorically. With the movement being like Tarot cards moving, you know? Not always being literal, but more multidimensional."

When Story spoke of street dance having a higher math dimension he wasn't just blowing smoke to the rafters. His description of how he fractures, splits, and sculpts time into ornate movement details and temporal counterpoint will be resonant for anyone who's spent deep listening time with Monk, Miles, and Wayne Shorter.

"I have different biorhythms I use when I dance—like a four-count. I'll break that into a sixteen so that, in a smaller count, more movements will happen, be superimposed. This makes it hyperrealistic. So that, say, with one move of your arm, if you pop it, you'll actually pop it in six places. When you move like that, it's like an armature coming to life and starting to grow. This is what makes the movement more like stop-motion; more so than regular pop-locking. You have accent marks, and the vibration of the movement itself which is smaller than a one-count. It's so meticulous and small that if you're practicing for a long time people will not even understand or see what you're doing. I've experienced that for a while. But you have to practice until it hardens and you're inside the music. Until, when people look at you, you seem to have become the music. First the instruments and then the really small accents. Sometimes there's even ambience in the studio that you pick up in your body. It becomes that meticulous."

Story even likes to use the body's propensity to malfunction during athletic events as inspiration.

"Your friend 'Charley Horse' is in your body, right? [Story refers here to the slang for that ambush of stiff-muscle cramps that can sideline gamers with excruciating pain.] When we tighten up, the air stops going in that area, that's why it becomes stiff—you get a charley horse because there's no oxygen. If you're pulsing, the air is coming in and it's hitting, so you start feeling that muscle more. It breathes and then it gets stiff—there's that balance. So it becomes like a pulse, like electricity flowing. Now, when you hear music your brain knows that muscle exists, so your brain starts controlling it and it'll become automatic after a while. When you're freestyling this means you can access that feeling right away."

Story's take on the relationship between music and motor activity evokes Yoruba and Hindu thinking on such matters. "I think we channel music through our brains and our endorphins lock into certain things and they command you to move in certain ways. You don't even have to work on it too much. When we're practicing and creating animation, we just practice pulses. Pulse, and then breathe."

Shades of Terry Riley, anyone?

Given the rigor of his ideas about movement and the extreme demands Story puts on himself to convert them into actionable technique, Story has become a bona fide outlier in the world of Brooklyn street dance. A stranger in a familiar land of a thousand dances and gifted movement technicians. Rather than surrender to frustration, Story, like any autodidact with a cause, transfers alienation into just getting better on his own highfalutin and high-posting terms. "Sometimes, having a conversation with my circle or my community can be very agonizing because I feel so underappreciated as someone who loves learning, and applying steps to different areas. I don't want it to turn into bitter ego because it's really more self-mastery I'm chasing. If I feel like people aren't listening, or they're comparing me to Chris Brown and I can't get a video on YouTube, then I'll say, 'Let me just keep mastering a little more now.' That's how I think, know what I mean? Because sometimes, when you're performing animation, there comes a point where the audience is completely quiet. And if you're not confident in what you're doing, you'll jump out of sitting in the surrealism. So I practice just staying there, forcing the audience to experience that—get them out of their attention-deficit disorder. This thing people have today from television, and whatnot, where they can't just go watch something and pay attention, or read a long book."

– 2013 –

Ice Cube

Reggie Hudlin, a man who knows his guilty pleasures and the markdown they tag on his soul, admires Ice Cube's *AmeriKKKa's Most Wanted* as a work of "evil genius." Less sardonically, an engineer and coproducer on the project told Vernon Reid that in the midst of recording "A Gangsta's Fairytale" he realized everyone involved would definitely be going to hell. That's the track where Cube has a moppet ask him, "Why you always kicking the shit about the bitches and the niggers? Why don't you kick some shit about the kids man, the fuckin' kids?"

For the uninitiated, Ice Cube—who appears at the Apollo this Saturday—is a former member of N.W.A, the Los Angeles-based group Niggaz with Attitude that shook the shit of East Coast rappers and fans alike with *Straight Outta Compton*. That record not only put listeners within point-blank range of L.A. gang mentality, but did so nonjudgmentally, without any sense of moral distance, going so far on some tracks as to use Black on Black violence as the metaphoric base for the group's boasting. In a music built on revenge fantasies and sensationalism, N.W.A brought reality closer to the foreground. As the gunshots echo from West to East, out here L.A. gang violence sounds like nothing but Black genocide turned in on itself. To hear a group endorse and uphold it with the relish of N.W.A not only seemed shocking but intolerable, if not inhuman. Yet what they also put to the test was the argument that rap was the voice of Black Americans who had no voice elsewhere. If the mentality N.W.A spoke out of prevailed in their area, and rap was reality music, why shouldn't their music bear a one-to-one relationship with their social context? Ice Cube was a major voice on that record, contributing some of the dopest, deadliest rhythms to the record's centerpieces, "Gangsta

Gangsta" and "F— Tha Police." The latter tune inspired the FBI to register a letter of protest with the group's record company.

Last year Cube left the group, charging disputes over royalties and other issues with the band's manager. He went on to make *AmeriKKKa's Most Wanted* with Public Enemy's production unit, the Bomb Squad. The album highlights Cube's remarkable abilities as a storytelling rapper. He identifies himself as a kind of crime reporter for the Black community. While he can be as lurid and grotesque as 2 Live Crew's Luther Campbell, he's redeemed somewhat by being a hell of a better artist, a true poet of the streets. You might be revolted by what he says, but his inclusion of violent detail rarely seems gratuitous and is always wickedly entertaining to boot. If you hear the Cube in the tradition of the griot, the outcast who records and recites the tribe's history no matter how unsettling the tale, you also have to see him in the tradition of hard-boiled crime writers like Mickey Spillane and Jim Thompson. The question becomes why can't a rapper be given the same artistic license as a novelist to concoct his stories as he sees fit, no matter how brutal? Why is it that when a rapper tells a violent story, he becomes incriminated in his tales in a way a filmmaker doesn't? Maybe because he can't hide behind the camera? I'm not closing the discussion, just asking a question.

The nicest thing you can say about AMW is that there truly is something to make everybody mad. Take white people for instance: "It's time to take a trip to the suburbs / Let 'em see a nigga invasion point blank on a caucasian / Cock the hammer, didn't crack no smile / Take me to your house, pal." On the other hand, you might as well pistol-whip a Pan-Africanist as have them endure a line like, "You want to free Africa? / I just stare at ya / Because we ain't got it too good in America." Cube might win a few brownie points with the nationals when he slags off Arsenio, who he claims to like "about as much as the bicentennial," but I've yet to meet anything roughly resembling a human being who can stomach the verse in "You Can't Fade Me" where he drools, "Nine months later . . . why did I bang her? Now I'm in the closet looking for the hanger."

On the other hand, though at last count the album contained fifty-seven utterances of the bitch-word, it also contains Yo-Yo, a female L.A. rapper who goes toe-to-toe with Cube on "It's a Man's World," KOing his sexist ass with some severe comeback lines: "To me you're not a thriller / You come in the room with your three inch killer / Think you can do damage to my backbone / Leave your child in the yard until it's full grown? / I'm gonna put it like this my man / without us your hand'll be your best friend. / So give us a credit like you know you should / If I don't look good, you don't look good." You might consider his extension of album space to Yo-Yo noblesse oblige, or just good business practice since he's producing her upcoming Atlantic album. I think it's just a reflection of the better part of his nature.

It's hard not to like Cube when you meet him since he comes off as a straight-shooting sonuvagun who saves all his bravado for his work. There's very little in his posturing that makes you think he feels a need to impress anybody with his manhood. At twenty-one, Cube's got a round boyish face dappled by sprouts of facial hair that may one day decide to become a full beard. He stands about five foot seven in a chunky body that gracefully mimics a boxing combination at one point and offhandedly manages a hip-hop pirouette the next. As Barthes said of photographs, every face has a punctum: a central point of interest that makes it hang together. With Cube it's his eyebrows, as furrowed and demonic as a djinn's. Considering how many folk I know, myself included, think he needs to make a date with the exorcist, the eyebrows seem more than appropriate. His laugh, always a telling thing about a man, is a hearty chortle, sounding deviously confessional and private at the same time.

The abandoned lumberyard warehouse in south central Los Angeles where we do our interview is also where Yo-Yo is shooting the first video for her LP, "Stompin' to tha 90's." Until you go to South Central, you don't know what an American bantustan is. Relative to Hollywood, South Central might as well be a Louisiana backwater. The way this city is laid out, you could live here and not even know there is a Black community.

When I step into the warehouse, Cube and his boys, the Lench Mob, are gathered in a semicircle shooting the shit: What I catch of the conversation has to do with some woman who claimed she lost T-Bone's gold chain. T-Bone told of how quickly the chain was returned when he went directly to the woman's mother with this distressing news. "Fifteen minutes after I got back home her mother called to tell me that I could come pick up my chain when her daughter came home from work." For all the implied malice in this story, the interaction between the Lench Mob and the thirty or so young sisters assembled for Yo-Yo's video seems very familial and playful. These L.A. brothers remind me more of easygoing southern Black men than their urban northern hip-hop counterparts. At one point T-Bone and another brother played patty cake with some of the sisters. Not exactly the sort of brotherly love you'd expect to see exhibited by America's most wanted. The women in Yo-Yo's video, by the way, were wearing T-shirts that read "Intelligent Black Women's Coalition." These words ran around a woodcut-like drawing of an African American Lady Liberty holding a flaming chalice in one hand and a book emblazoned with TRUTH in the other. For a rapper with a reputation as a mad dog sexist, Cube doesn't seem threatened by sharing his success with a sister who looks like she could stomp all over him in a minute.

Yo-Yo will be in full effect for a rematch when the Cube show rolls into the Apollo. When I asked the Cube how he thought New York would respond to his show, he replied, "I don't know man. Because the brothers in New York . . . last time l played there with N.W.A I was told the reason we got a mixed reaction is because, 'They didn't like the way y'all wear your hair.' What kind of shit is that? Fuck that. The hair don't make the man. The man makes the man." Cube promised that his show is going to be basic. No dancers, no smoke machines. Just beats and rhymes. "All a true MC needs is a mike and his tracks."

. . . . .

Greg Tate: What was your upbringing like?

Ice Cube: I had a moms and a pops. I was a cool youngster. I wasn't never into no trouble-trouble. I used to do what teenagers do. It wasn't nothing major. My father is a landscape artist and my moms work at UCLA. She, uh, shit man what she do over there? Something about the library. I never really got into it with her. A couple of times I went on the job with my father but not really because I was into my own thing. You know kids, last thing they want to do is work. After school I'd just come home and hang out with my homeys. We used to shoot hoop, play football in the street. Chase girls. The usual. Hang out talk about each other. That was when we were kids. Then when we got older folks started to do crazy shit like break in cars, break in houses, stupid shit like that.

Tate: So you never did any of that?

Ice Cube: Yeah [laughs]. But I didn't do it a lot because I figured one day I might get caught. And the biggest problem I had was not the police but my pops! Because yo, if I got caught out there, my ass was as good as gone. The people I hung out with, some of them had both parents, some of them just had a moms that was there. In my case having both parents worked out, but it's really on the kid, how the kid wants to be, you know what I mean. If he wants to fuck up he's gonna fuck up, one parent or two. It does make a difference what kind of home the kid comes from but it's still up to the kid. Just because the mother and father are an alcoholic doesn't mean you have to be one. The reason there's a lot of broken homes is because when we was brought here, look what they did. They separated the tribes, separated the families so you don't have that backbone structure, that do or die for the family kind of thing. So a brother can't handle it and he's outta there. Fucking Italian family, yo, the family got to stay together no matter what.

Tate: Many people feel the Black family was more together twenty-five or thirty years ago.

Ice Cube: Yeah because the struggle was clear. It was right in front of you. Now it's a hidden struggle—motherfuckers think they got it good.

Tate: What do you think the struggle is today?

Ice Cube: It's the same one. It's no different, that's the thing. They done found a new way to play us. They can't play us straight up so they gotta throw shit behind us and to the side of us. The struggle is still for Black people to get what the fuck we're owed by this system.

Tate: So where do you see hip-hop as fitting into that struggle?

Ice Cube: What we're doing is making Black people know themselves. Mentally the people in South Africa have it better than we have it over here because they know who they're fighting. Over here the brothers are so mixed up and turned around they don't know who is the enemy. Now I heard even in South Africa they're pulling the same old trap. They're making the Zulu tribes fight the people that's following Mandela. So once again, the Caucasian is conquering. Same shit happening here, bloods and crips. Long as you don't go to the white neighborhood with that shit, y'all can stay down there and kill each other, who cares?

Tate: The impression we have of the gangs on the East Coast is of a powerful criminal enterprise that doesn't give a kid a choice as to whether they can belong or not.

Ice Cube: You got a choice. If you want to hang out you got to be down. If you don't want to be down get the fuck outta our face. It ain't like Hollywood do it. Like you're walking the hall and they say, "Hey buddy, you better be in our gang or we'll kill you." Everything is done for material reasons. Like you say, Yo if I'm in a gang I got a little power, all the girls gonna look at me and say oooh—that type of thang. Most definitely fear of my father kept me from hanging out with the gangs. That's where I rested my head, that's where I ate, can't rock that boat, pops wasn't having it.

Tate: *Before you got into music what kind of things did you think about doing with your life?*

Ice Cube: Football, usual things like sports. I went to architectural drafting school, that was like a fallback for this rap if it didn't work. I did a year. Haven't needed it. Yet.

Tate: *You got a way with words. Were you good in English in school?*

Ice Cube: Nope. I was good at math. I wasn't good at English or vocabulary or none of that shit. I didn't think the shit was gonna help me earn no money. I didn't want to learn it straight up. Now with math, I knew when I made my money I wanted to know how to count it. Math will help you in life, but what the fuck I need biology for? They need to have a whole new list of classes. English, cool, you need to learn that. They need to have a course on how to raise babies, given the percentage of people who leave high school and have babies. See they'll make some shit like that career planning an elective. That's why you got people out there don't know what to do. Girls, they say fuck it and go in the county line. Then they sit home, watching *Donahue* and thinking, Yo if I have another baby I can make some more money. That's the way they go, getting paid, looking fly, but then they kids be home looking filthy. All because they don't teach you how to cope in this motherfuckin' society. Black kids are always going to be disinterested in school as long as school doesn't teach them what they contributed to this country. The only time you learn about anybody who looks the same as our face is in February, Black History Month, and you learn about that same motherfucker, Martin Luther King. After twelve years of that shit you know the story back and forth. Him and Harriet Tubman. They were the only two I ever learned about in school. Until rap came along you wouldn't learn about nobody else.

Tate: *Was that how you learned about Malcom X and the Black Panthers?*

Ice Cube: Yep, through rap music nothing else. Kids are starting to compare: I can learn more about my kind on a rap record than sitting here eight hours. School is a fantasy world.

Tate: What was the first rap record that inspired you to want to be a rapper?

Ice Cube: "The Message" because of how real it was. It wasn't the same old, I'm this and that. That was kind of fake, niggas just bragging. I was used to that from the basketball court. Like, Yo motherfucker I did your momma like this. Rap was the same way until "The Message" came out. Then "Roxanne Roxanne" came out and it was like boom you had all these avenues busting out for rap. I could talk about more than the kind of chain I got on, I'm so divine, and all that bullshit.

Tate: Your forte seems to be the storytelling rap.

Ice Cube: Yeah, I like to tell a story that could be true. Most of my stories have happened or could happen. Some of them I heard about, some happened to me, some I seen. I like to mix all that around and come out with an interesting story that can have a little comic relief on it so it can be entertaining. People don't realize that we're still entertainers and we're still trying to make people groove to the beat. If that wasn't the case I'd be doing poetry or something.

Tate: A lot of things you talk about, if the humor wasn't in there you'd come off very grim. You're conscious of that?

Ice Cube: I want Black people to look at themselves in my record and laugh it off but then again say goddamn. Like "Once upon a Time in the Projects." It's funny, but somebody's house is really like that. Somebody's mom selling crack out the house, black-and-white TV, kids running around, police keep coming up in there raiding all the time. That shit is sad but I put some comedy on it so it wouldn't just be a message song. You can party to it and think about it. It can hit you from all kind of angles.

Tate: What inspired you to do "You Can't Fade Me"?

Ice Cube: That was from a true experience. This girl, who I knew was a neighborhood girl if you know what the hell I'm talking about. I was like, Fuck it, I'll get with her. I came back off tour and she was like pregnant and she said, "This is yours." It was like being on trial—my mind was like, Oh no, fuck this. I was thinking all kind of shit. I'll push her down the stairs. No I'll go to jail, can't do that. Shit was going through my mind. Because I knew if my homeys found out about this shit it's over. It wasn't my baby though. It was some other motherfucker's.

Tate: *What was so terrifying to you about this?*

Ice Cube: Having a baby by this bitch, because I knew all she wanted was to dig into these pockets. That was last year, so I wrote a song about that shit. That's an experience a lot of brothers done went through.

Tate: *But a lot of them wouldn't have put it on a record in such graphic terms with such violent fantasies. A lot of people, myself included, couldn't even get past that track on the album.*

Ice Cube: Well everybody has fantasies. How many times you been in a bank and said, Damn I rob this bank I'll have all this money. Then you look up at those cameras and say, Naw I don't think so. You think that shit but you'll never carry it out. But you put this on wax and people think you're for real. People who can't get past that would be thinking the same thing but just be scared to say it. A record can't be violent, a record can't hurt you. You listen to a record, take what you can use and throw the rest back. Even on the record I say can't do that that's murder one and then I'll really get faded so I gotta think of another solution and another. It just a story.

Tate: *What do you think you would have done if it had been your baby?*

Ice Cube: Handle the shit like a man. Took care of it you know what I mean. What the fuck else can I do. Handle that shit like a man and not like a sucker. If I was a sucker, I'd be, Yo, I'm outta here.

Tate: *Do you think rap is hostile towards women?*

Ice Cube: The whole damn world is hostile towards women.

Tate: *What do you mean by that?*

Ice Cube: I mean the power of sex is more powerful than the motherfuckers in Saudi Arabia. A girl that you want to get with can make you do damn near anything. If she knows how to do her shit right, the girl can make you buy cigarettes you never wanted to buy in life. Virginia Slims and shit. The way I look at it is this. You take a young Black male and you take a young Black female. The female is watching *Dynasty* and *Lifestyles of the Rich and Famous*. The young Black male is like, Yo, I'm broke, and he sees a girl he wants to get with. She's like, I don't want you, you broke ass motherfucker. What can you do for me? What have you done for me lately, all this bullshit. So he becomes a stick-up kid, taking your shit, my shit, he's selling dope. Now he's got some status, the car and the jewelry. Now here come the girl. So what I do is I label that girl. I say, That's a bitch right there. I say, You don't want her. You don't want her. You want somebody that wants you for you, and not for what you've got. Now brothers are stepping out with a new attitude, like, You don't want me for me, later for you. Now you don't get robbed, I don't get robbed, and brothers are saying fuck the Benz, I got my hoop-dee ride. All the crime shit, dope, gangs, all that's over material shit to get women. Nothing more, nothing less. I know a lot of guys, they'd like to say fuck the bath but they don't want to step out and see the girls and be all funky. Look at all my boys out here on this video shoot, all these motherfuckers sitting out here trying to look fly, hot as a motherfucker, ready to go home. But there's too many women here for them to just get up and leave. They out there suffering, been here since eight o'clock in the morning and ain't getting paid. They came for the girls.

Tate: If you're so hostile and suspicious of women how can you find somebody who wants you for you?

Ice Cube: Can't nobody fake forever. You'll see their true colors. When I see a young lady I want to be with or wants to hang with me I'll take her out for a month and won't take her ass nowhere. I'll pick her up and say, Let's go to my house and look at TV. Long as it takes, because if the colors don't come out after two months of that shit I'll cool out.

Tate: Where did you meet Yo-Yo?

Ice Cube: Met her at a flea market. My man T-Bone said I had to meet this female who could really rap. I met her and said, "Yo, what's happening?" She acted like she was too busy to even talk. I said, "Let me hear you rap." So she rapped, I said, "You good," and she just walked on. I said, "Fuck that, we got to sign her because she got the right attitude." She writes all her own lyrics, had delivery, attitude, personality. "It's a Man's World" on my album came about because we had an argument about something sexist, like battle of the sexes type of thang. And I was like baby, "It's man's world, no matter which way you try to slay it, men run this motherfucker." She said, "Fuck that." Later on I was thinking, that's a helluva song with us arguing. So I called her up and she said, "Cube, I'm mad at you for that bullshit you were saying." I said, "Yo, hear me out." So she wrote her shit, I wrote my shit and then we sat down and came up with lines that made 'em intertwine, came out pretty dope. She got some songs on her record like "Sisterland," "Make Way for the Mother-lode," and "Put a Lid on It." Telling the girls to stop getting pregnant and giving up the boots.

Tate: What's up with "A Gangster's Fairytale"? Why did you have that kid cussin' on there like that? You didn't feel like you weren't exploiting that kid?

Ice Cube: Nope, because when he gets away from his mama he'll do that shit anyway. You can go to any elementary school and hear the same language. Because I do it on record now I'm exploiting. Come on man.

Tate: You think there should be an age restriction on hip-hop?

Ice Cube: No, because if you can turn on the cable you be exposed to the same kind of shit. If you two and Mom is asleep on the couch you *seeing* and hearing. TV is worse than I could ever be. Cartoons are violent. They got Uzis on cartoons now.

Tate: You've talked about not wanting the burden of being a role model to kids but rappers are sometimes the only heroes young Black kids have.

Ice Cube: Heroes and role models are two different things. Role models are puppets, a puppet to the community. People say, "You're a role model now you can't do what you want to do, can't do what got you to that role model status." A hero is somebody who went his own way and got justice. People say, "Man all these kids looking up at you, why you cussin' all the time?" Why do you think these kids are listening? You'll get your throat cut. They'll say, "Look at this motherfucker, now he's on some different tip."

Tate: What responsibility do you think you have to your young audience?

Ice Cube: My only responsibility is making funky records.

Tate: There's more on your records than just funky beats.

Ice Cube: Whatever I do to the records, that's on me. Whatever you get out of the records, that's on you. But my only responsibility is making hits, because I could make a record to save the world, but if it ain't a hit then it ain't gonna do nothing but sit.

Tate: Could you make a hit to save the world?

Ice Cube: Yep, but it wouldn't be my responsibility, because it's still entertainment.

Tate: You have the power to influence young minds.

Ice Cube: Do I really? To what extent? If I make a record that says, "Don't do crack," and a motherfucker is going hungry, my record is in the glove compartment. It's up to the kids. And people don't give them enough credit to make their own decisions. You have to give kids credit for having some kind of mind at some time. A rap record can't make you kill nobody. A rap record can't make you save nobody. You make that decision you get out of it what you want to get out of it. I'm just telling you like it is. The truth ain't negative or positive. It's just the truth. If it works as a scared straight tactic, or you hear it and see the light, then it's working. And even if it don't, it's still working. If you just hear that funky beat and you party to it, it's still working. I'll do anything I can to help anybody, but when it comes to music I got to do what got me in this position. I can't do nothing different.

Tate: What's your assessment of what's been happening with Luther Campbell?

Ice Cube: The whole thing is a racist situation. I think the motherfuckers don't want white kids to know about Black kids at all. I don't think they even want motherfuckers to mix. The white kids ain't going for that shit. They ain't listening to what their grandfather be saying. They're getting the real deal on the records.

Tate: Why are so many white kids checking out hip-hop now?

Ice Cube: They're sick of hearing them lies, man. They're going to school with Black kids and they're saying, Yo, we're all cool, we can all kick it. But they go home and their pops is talking about nigger this and nigger that. And the kids are like, Yo, I got Black friends in school. Fuck what you're talking about. Rap records are doing that. You go to a Public Enemy concert in '87, it was all Black kids. Now it's fifty-fifty Black and white. They don't like that shit, so they're trying to come down any way they can.

Tate: Do you think the repression of rap will only intensify, and if so how do you plan to respond to it? Censorship, your records being pulled from the shelf, people being arrested for selling your records.

Ice Cube: I'll start bringing lawsuits against the motherfuckers. I'll play the game just like they play it. They love to see a brother with a stick, they know how to deal with that. Watts riot? It's going to be a mental riot. It's some new shit brothers are starting to come up on. We'll play the motherfuckers like they play us. Like Chuck. They wouldn't let his ass in St. Louis. He said, "Fuck, I'll sue your building for discrimination." Then they were like, "Oh, no, no, we didn't say that. C'mon in, sure you're welcome." So I'll sue the motherfuckers. What else you gonna do but fight the motherfuckers the whole way? 'Cause they don't want niggas to have nothin'. So I'll go thirteen-fifteen—win thirteen, lose fifteen—because you got to be in there. But I don't let shit like that worry me, because I know I'm in a fight. Since June 16, 1969, I've been in a motherfucking fight. Why get mad now that I'm in a fight? It's either win against the motherfuckers or leave them with the same amount of scars you got and call it a day.

Tate: Do you ever think you go too far? Like the wire hanger line on "You Can't Fade Me"?

Ice Cube: Man, that's shit motherfuckers on my block talk about. Laughin' like, Your gal is pregnant man? Better get out the hanger. It's just thoughts. If I think it, why can't I say it? What's the law against saying what you think? Why I got to put my mind in prison or my tongue?

– 1990 –

Wynton Marsalis: Jazz Crusader

You might not know it, but Wynton Marsalis is one funny brother. The man has got jokes for days, even when he's being deadly serious. Hailing from New Orleans, Marsalis embodies the many virtues of the educated southern Black man. He's earthy, respectful of his elders, and sarcastically analytical of all that smacks of sham, pretense, and fakery. One of the things African Americans lost in the migration from the South to the North was our grassroots artisan tradition, the knowledge of and skill in building things by hand. Marsalis's reverence for and militant advocacy of technique and learning—as evident in his lecturing as it is in his trumpet playing—may owe as much to the presence of such craftsmen in his immediate family tree (his father, Ellis, is a renowned jazz pianist; his brothers include sax star Branford and pianist Delfeayo) as to his musical forefathers Louis Armstrong, Duke Ellington, John Coltrane. His sheer productivity in so many areas is nothing short of astounding.

In the past year Marsalis, thirty-four, has recorded his thirtieth album, *Standard Time, Vol. 4*, due out in March, and completed the writing and hosting of two distinctly different series on jazz for PBS and National Public Radio. The PBS *Marsalis on Music* series, derived from his Jazz for Young People program at New York's Lincoln Center (he is also artistic director of Jazz at Lincoln Center) is something all parents interested in their children's cultural development should own. The series for NPR invites musicians from many schools of contemporary Black music to present their work and to analyze the improvisations of artists like Charlie Parker. Participants have included those often considered—simply because they represent a differing or opposing conception of jazz—as Marsalis's personal enemies, people such as Cecil Taylor, Steve Coleman, and Marcus Miller. But Marsalis isn't out to pick fights as much as he is interested in stirring up healthy intellectual debate: Jazz musicians are often a taciturn, cultish, and enigmatic lot when it comes to sharing trade secrets.

Marsalis loves to share what he knows with as many people as will listen—and sometimes even with those who won't. His opinions on hip-hop have almost led him to duking it out in public with some well-known rappers. He's hands-down the most illuminating essayist and speaker on jazz musicology to emerge in some time. And we all know he's no joke on that horn. Nor are his talents as a bandleader, composer, and arranger anything to laugh off. All the same, Marsalis has yet to join the ranks of the jazz geniuses. No fault in that and no surprise, either: Anyone attempting monumental jazz behind what Ellington, Monk, Coltrane, and Miles laid down has their work cut out for them. What's important to consider with Marsalis is that he's even trying to rise to that challenge. Our conversation took place in my hometown of Washington, DC, where Marsalis was burning the midnight oil for his NPR project.

. . . . .

Q: How did growing up in the South impact on your development?

A: It was tremendous, 'cause you know I love the South. When I was in it, I didn't love it as much—I learned to after I left. When I was living there, I couldn't wait to leave. I left when I was seventeen, because I felt the rest of the world was going to be different. When you're in the South, you hear that it's so backward and prejudiced. But once you get out in the world you realize, whew!

Q: You got a rude awakening?

A: Very rude. [Laughs] It's like New Orleans music, man. My whole life I heard it and loved it, but I wouldn't let myself love it, because I thought it was Tomming. So when I heard it, I'd be like, Damn, I like this shit. But I had so little respect for it, I wouldn't even learn it. I'd be in parades playing and wouldn't know the songs. No respect. My daddy used to tell me, "You need to learn some tunes," and I'd be, like, "Aw, man, that's old music."

Q: *I'm curious about the funk band you and Branford were in when you were teenagers, the Creators. Apparently, from things I've read, y'all worked a lot.*

A: We were a popular band. We played proms, talent shows, lounges—we worked. We worked more than my daddy, man. We had one of those big old bands like Cameo. Took us an hour to set up our equipment. We had timbales, lead vocalist, two guitars, keyboards. We had our little dance steps and uniforms and all kinds of lights that would be blowing up. It was funny.

Q: *You sang too.*

A: Yeah, that style. A few background vocals, like [breaks into a falsetto voice] "Ooh, baa-bay." [Laughs] That was the gig, man. It was fun. We'd play whatever was popular, bruh. "Brick House," "Tear the Roof off the Sucker," "What's Going On," all of Earth, Wind & Fire's and Parliament's music. If you'd see us in rehearsal, we'd be arguing and fighting with each other for an hour over who was playing what part from the records. We were New Orleans musicians, man—just vamp and solo. Matter of fact, we had to cut back on the soloing because people started saying, "The Creators, they play jazz." Playing talent shows was the best, because when cats would lose, they'd want to fight the band. One time, some cats came up singing "Kung Fu Fighting" and they were messing up bad—then they wanted to fight *us*. We'd say, "Boy, we got so many people in this band you making a big mistake, you don't want to come up in there."

Q: *Did you always know you were going to be a musician?*

A: Not until I got to high school. That's when I started practicing and developing a certain curiosity. Man, all those years I lived with my father, he had all those jazz albums and I never was curious enough to put one on. But when I was twelve, I put on this record of Trane's, *Giant Steps*. And the only reason was because I was looking at album covers. The albums we listened to always had somebody doing something wild on the cover, like wearing some strange outfit or big glasses or wings or a wig or something. Then I looked at my albums, and cat had some vines on, and were clean, and I said, Damn, let me see what they're dealing with. So I put *Giant Steps* on, and I said, Huh, this shit don't sound bad. Every day after, I put Trane on. I didn't try to play along. This was when I was transcribing this little jazz tune Earth, Wind & Fire had on the *Open Our Eyes* album—writing it out with letters because I couldn't read music. But hearing Trane got me asking my daddy questions about "What is this?" and "Can you play along with me?"

Q: *He must have been in shock.*

A: Yeah, he was like, "What is this?" But I had been hanging around gigs since I was a little boy, and I always liked the way jazz musicians talked. All the nasty shit they were saying. You could feel that hurt in them because the people didn't like their music, but you could also hear a lot of pride. And they were smart. They'd go in the barbershop and be winning all the arguments. They'd get respect. Cats would be, like, "Hey, man, Ellis is a jazz musician, he been all over the world." My daddy was smart at all kinds of stuff. Once he coached our little league football team, and that's the only game we almost won. But they struggled, man. They had a hard time, my daddy and all of them. I remember that period very well. When the seventies started, we had a certain momentum and pride. And then that broke down. I remember that feeling in the street when Muhammad Ali won his legal battles and Marvin Gaye came on. Everybody was playing "What's Going On"—that was the anthem when cats were washing their cars or playing street football, whatever. I remember the feeling of that, man.

Q: *So what's your analysis of what happened to that feeling?*

A: Unreality. You take something unreal and you make it real. Chaos is always in the world. The question is always, How we can order it? And once them Black exploitation movies came in—and I went and saw every one of them—that was a tremendous blow. That blow has never been assessed. Everything was "bitch this" and "ho that" and "motherfucker"—that's the beginning of that shit. And the riots hurt a lot too; the downtown areas that never got rebuilt. Then there was the lack of the transferal of information from one generation to another. Toni Morrison and I went out talking one night, and she said, "You know, it seems one generation just forgot to talk." It's like a gap. All that information is still here, but what happened to the humility? What happened to the soul? Because soul don't matter about how bad your condition is. Seems like the more struggles people had, the more soulful they were. Whose people had money, man? My grandfather started out a sharecropper in Mississippi. My grandmother was a domestic worker. My father struggled. He wasn't making no money playing modern jazz in New Orleans. But no matter if we had to pick out clothes from the Sears catalog, we had respect. Respect, that's not an economic condition.

Q: *What's your definition of soul?*

A: Soul is somebody that's bringing a feeling to you regardless of your race, your sex, or your age. That feeling that everything is gonna be all right. It has a spiritual quality to it. It's a matter of having understanding and empathy when somebody wants to fight you over nothing, and you say, "Hey, man, it's all right." It's not a weak thing, though, like, "I'm just gonna go along with whatever y'all say." Because soul sometimes means you gotta pick up a sword.

Q: *Is that why you decided to hold public debate with James Lincoln Collier [author of three controversial tomes on jazz]?*

A: Collier made me mad with some of the things he wrote. Because he writes things like, "Louis Armstrong was being treated like a nigger in the real sense of the word." Well, what is the real sense of the word "nigger"? Or "Duke Ellington couldn't write long-form music." Just a bunch of assumptions. And the technical things he got wrong just shows a level of not caring about these people. Usually you can never get guys like that in a forum. But with Collier I wrote a letter in rebuttal—which Collier at first said that I didn't write because he thought I'm too illiterate to write a letter, so Stanley Crouch had to have written the letter. But when we started debating, I wasn't even proud of it, bruh, because he wasn't really prepared to debate. After twenty minutes I was ready to stop. I like to argue, man. I like to go back and forth. It's like a game. If we gonna play some ball or something, I like to have to hustle. I was looking forward to him being smoking or something, where I'd have to say, Damn, didn't think about that. But he didn't take it seriously enough to prepare for it. Now the question is, Why won't Oxford University retract and change those things that were factually wrong in those books?

Q: *In your* Sweet Swing Blues on the Road *[W. W. Norton], you wrote about a fellow approaching you and saying how he thought European concert music was better equipped than jazz to express the emotional complexities of the age, and you respond, "What jazz are you talking about?" and he says, "All of it." And you go, "Uh-huh." I could imagine a similar exchange between you and someone asking you about hip-hop.*

A: First of all, you have to have a lot of different views of a thing out in the public so people can weigh them and make their own decision. Music is music: melody, harmony, rhythm, and texture. Those elements combine to do a certain thing. Now music also interprets mythology. And there is a history of Afro-American music in this country where everything on that timeline reflects something about America. And just like you can look around our community and say, "What happened?" you can also do that same thing with our music. My whole thing is—where are the music programs? Who's teaching our kids music? We don't need to be taught? Even Louis Armstrong got music lessons in the waif's home.

Q: *Isn't there a way of looking at hip-hop as not necessarily the next state in evolution or devolution, but as something that is valid because of its innate ingenuity and resolution of certain musical problems?*

A: Well, first of all, it is valid because it exists. It's valid in reference to African American musical tradition. But once something is a part of a tradition, it has to be viewed and dissected for what it is. There's a whole tradition of talking and rhyming, Rudy Ray Moore, Slim Gaillard, ad infinitum. Some of what hip-hoppers do is creative. There's creativity in everything, man. And when you get a lot of people working on something, you're bound to come up with something.

Now one interesting thing is, a lot of times . . . [chuckling] the songs aren't really in a key. That's interesting to hear, because their relationship to sound is sonic, so they'll put all these elements together, and it's not in a key. So that's interesting. For a tune or two. But given the history of Afro-American music, for me the question becomes, how can you get everything in your art? How can you have music that will inspire boudoir activities with music that is spiritual and that has a high musical content and that's reflective of the real true grandeur of human life regardless of your economic status? How can you get some music that's terrible in terms of its depiction of tragedy and put that in three-minute form? Because we had forms that existed that led us to that point. Then suddenly—boom! It's like, okay, none of that existed, now we have this.

Q: *Yeah, but in some cases you can say that in a redemptive sense as well as a destructive sense.*

A: Well, there's always a range. You can't say all of something is bad. But if you said to me, "I want you to name fifteen hip-hop albums," you think I'd be able to do that?

Q: *You haven't been pulling too much off that shelf, huh?*

A: Whatever I think about that is coming from a limited point of reference. Now—as a musician—if you play some music for me, I can tell you what they're playing. Because I'm around kids all the time, I can tell you what they think about it. I've had this discussion about rap music ad infinitum. When I go out to eat, I got to damn near have bodyguards. Cats are, like, "You said you didn't like our music." It's become an absurd situation, where I have to say, "First, I'm not afraid of you. You're entitled to your right to speak, and I'm entitled to mine. We could talk about this all night if you want." And we can put the documents themselves on. We can read the lyrics. They're gonna speak much clearer than what I could say. If I had fifteen CDs stacked up right here, it would speak much louder than what I could say about it.

Q: You might be surprised too, B.

A: Believe me, I've checked out a lot of their music, because people bring it to me and say, "Listen to this." I mean, c'mon, I speak in high schools, man. It's like, I go in there and they say, "Oh, jazz . . ." [Laughs] You know what I'm saying? You know that group with the song "Jazz"? A Tribe Called Quest? Man, about twenty people played that one for me. Like, "Hey what you think about this? This is jazz."

For me, it's not so much a question of hip-hop as it is, what happened to Afro-American popular music once the church tradition faded out in that music? Once you let go of the blues and the instrumental tradition of improvisation, that's when a lot of things got lost. The question is not, Why don't you like hip-hop? Or do you not like the younger people? I love young people and I'm always around them. When I walk into schools and principals tell me they don't have any PTA because parents don't have any concern for their kids at all, or when I go into schools and see kids not being educated . . . you can't compete in this world like that. The world does not care about your personal situation. It's a lot of human potential being wasted. And the question becomes, How can we develop all of that human potential? Maybe the final conclusion will be hip-hop or whatever the next thing is. Hey, fine, you know. The question is, what forms promote it more?

When Afro-American music loses its sonic connection to the blues and the church and to the whole give-and-take improvisation, it loses the most important things. It's not so much that what is created is not good or creative, because if you got two million people beating on steel, forty or fifty thousand of them are gonna figure out something. So if you listen to the way all these people are combining sound and all the different ways they play with language, there's bound to be a lot of things in there that are interesting. But what're they doing with the things that are at the core and the backbone of Afro-American music? When this fad is gone, it's gonna be back to the blues—always been and always will be.

Q: *Some would say it's an extension of the blues.*

A: How would they say that? See, that's when I iced the discussion. How is it an extension of the blues as music?

Q: *Well certainly the orality of hip-hop is from the blues. Just the raw sound of the voices themselves. The tone and texture of those voices are not that far from somebody like a Howlin' Wolf.*

A: All right, I'll give them that—there's one. But what about from the standpoint of the form itself? The blues has many aspects that manifest themselves in the artifact of music. Where is the folk essence?

Q: *The properties of sound that hip-hop producers are looking for when they sample are soulful properties. They're looking for bits of soul they can build upon. Because what they're sampling is the history of Black music. And I think you could make a case for the folk essence of the blues still being in their music.*

A: What they're doing is what they do. And that's okay. Fine. I agree with you that it's part of an ongoing cycle. But after a while we got to have some music. You can go on forever riffing, but if you say, "Man, you got your instrument, why don't you come up here and play what you're talking about?" What I'm saying is not something speculative. It's what I know. But I have to have the music to show you where the form is coming from. Remember, we're not talking about re-creating the old folk blues. We're in the nineties so we're talking about the sixty–seventy-year extension of that concept. It's not that there's an element of blues in hip-hop, but how does that element reflect sixty–seventy years of musical development?

Q: *Stanley Crouch told me each successive generation was able to summarize and codify the entire contribution of the previous generation in one succinct phrase. He referenced Marvin Gaye as a sublime example of that. Hip-hop could be read as a codified reading of our history and tradition too.*

A: You can argue music forever without the music, because you're using words that are not connected to anything, because the sound is not there. If you and me start talking about rocks on Mars and I say, "Well, I've seen blue ones that look better than the green ones," what does that mean? But once you get to a piano and a record player, that discussion gets cut down by about three hours.

– 1996 –

Thornton Dial: Free, Black, and Brightening Up
the Darkness of the World

When I start making something, I gather up the pieces I want
to work with. I only want materials that have been used by
people, the works of the United States, that have did people
some good but once they got the service out of them they
throwed them away. So I pick it up and make something new
out of it. That's why we pick up these things. Negroes done
learned how to pick up old things and make them brand new.
They had to learn them things to survive, and they done got
wiser for doing, wiser by looking at the things and taking
them into the mind. You call that "smart."—THORNTON DIAL

Black folks know what they got to do to live. . . . They
want to have their own strategy for working, to use
their own energy and spirit the way it come to them
to do it—not do something because someone else make
you do it. That's freedom. . . . My art is the evidence of my
freedom.—THORNTON DIAL

If Sun Ra came out of Alabama, what else they got down there? Born
in Birmingham in 1914, Sun Ra brought science fiction and Egyptol-
ogy to bebop and swing jazz in the 1950s—musically, visually, theatri-
cally, and theoretically. The pageantry and discipline of his big bands
led to a respected career of more than forty years, during which he
provoked controversy and propelled jazz into uncharted celestial space
on a nightly basis. Ra reinvented jazz in his own futuristic Pharaonic
image with unimpeachable knowledge and reverence for the music's
past masters: Armstrong, Ellington, Henderson, Parker, Monk. But synthesizers, funk, rock, and African music all appeared in his music years
before fusion jazz and world-music became all the rage in jazz, as did
scathing political commentary and sly, absurdist humor.

We should have asked about Ra's Alabama roots a long time ago, at
least as far back as the mid-1960s, when Sun Ra and Alabama Negroes
were both bent on bringing humanist (and alienist) change to a Jim
Crow America not ready for prime time, let alone Afrocentric space-
time. As an aghast world tried to square Cold War propaganda of Amer-
ica-the-Beautiful with civil rights footage of America-the-lynch-mob,

those of us who knew Ra's visionary and pioneering work should have been more curious. If Sun Ra could come out of a Black man's hellhole like Alabama in the 1930s, what other kind of extraterrestrial brothers were they cultivating down there? Had we thought to ask, the world might have learned about Thornton Dial. Ra and Dial are both Black southerners who refused to allow the Jim Crow South's social restrictions and fictions to restrain their protean visions of art and life as fluid, spiritual, multidimensional, comical, cryptic. Dial once explained: "Art is strange-looking stuff and most people don't understand art. Most people don't understand my art, the art of the Negroes, because most people don't understand me, don't understand the Negroes at all. If everybody understand one another, wouldn't nobody make art. Art is something to open your eyes. . . . I always be looking to the future. I respect the past of life, but I don't worry too much about it because it's done passed. . . . Art is like a bright star up ahead in the darkness of the world."[1]

Thornton Dial was born in Sumter County, Alabama, on September 10, 1928. It is a year he shares with other innovators and innovations: Andy Warhol, Bo Diddley, Stanley Kubrick, Fats Domino, Karlheinz Stockhausen, and "Steamboat Willie," Disney's first Mickey Mouse movie and the first film with synchronized sound. Also on this date, the first television station began regular broadcasting in Schenectady, New York; penicillin was discovered; and the transistor was patented. Dial, an equally miraculous progeny of that era, grew up to become one of the most accomplished visual artists in human history. He also grew up to become one of the definitive practitioners of what this writer likes to dub "The Southern Black Visual Tradition." That you haven't been made aware of Dial's art before is no fault of your own, nor of his. Though Dial is over eighty years old and has been making art since he was a kid, few people besides his neighbors had seen his work before the 1980s. He is not an unknown quantity in some quarters of the art world—especially the American folk art world—but he's nowhere near as well known as Sun Ra is, even to people who don't like swing jazz, science fiction, or the very idea of spending one day in Alabama.

To those of us who loved Sun Ra, his madcap genius seemed to derive less from his Alabama upbringing than from his astral travels to Chicago, New York, Philadelphia, Egypt, or his proclaimed home planet, Saturn. This itself speaks volumes about Alabama's image in the public imagination. That image has, of course, been shaped by scenes in civil rights–era films and readings of Taylor Branch's epochal masterpiece of the movement, *Parting the Waters*. After learning about that Alabama, how could the state not seem like some medieval backwater, where the most barbaric violence imaginable against Blackfolk seems to have been damn near legal—a racialized tenth circle of Hades where, on a daily basis, bombings, shootings, lynchings, tear gas, tanks, fire hoses, and truncheons were deployed with deadly force (and by state police under the governor's orders) against unarmed men, women, and children. Deployed against folk who peaceably and stoically stood up to protest the South's denial of constitutional protections and inalienable human rights for its Black citizens.

The notion that Sun Ra's Intergalactic Myth-Science Arkestra—one of many sci-fi noms de plume Ra adopted over the years for his band of up to thirty starry-eyed virtuosos decked out turban-to-toe in a glittering rainbow of otherworldly Afronautic gear—just might have derived their flamboyant fashion sense from Ra's Alabama roots never even crossed our minds. Maybe there was a disconnect because civil rights–era television broadcast in primitive black-and-white, and the Arkestra lit up the stage in polychromatic widescreen Technicolor. Maybe it was because Ra's core northern audiences of the 1970s couldn't imagine a southern palette any richer than blue denim, red clay, and white cotton. Or maybe it was just because we didn't know about Thornton Dial back then or about others of his tradition—Archie Byron, Mary T. Smith, Purvis Young, Joe Light, Lonnie Holley, Ronald Lockett—all fellow masters of a regional art movement who were compelled, like Dial, to iconoclastically and iconographically light up one of the darkest corners of the American psyche: the twentieth-century legacy of slavery and the profound subjectivities it made these artists of African ascent unleash in their art.

In the 1960s and '70s, many of us who love and admire Dial's work today were decades away from becoming aware that Alabama was a place full of visually visionary Black American fabulists. We did not know that there were, among Sun Ra's homies, hosts of image-making mythographers who were as prismatic, ingenious, and Afrocentric with their paintbrushes, carving knives, and acetylene torches as Ra was with his pianos, synthesizers, organs, horn sections, and the Arkestra's star-hopping caravanserai of a wardrobe trunk. Nor did we know that Ra's Alabama-born painting and sculpting brethren and sistren, such as Dial, made spectacular and sardonically signifyin' works of art that likewise delineated the crossroads of earthly and extraterrestrial existence and African American politics and mysticism. And because we didn't know there was a tradition of southern Black image making just as rooted in Black consciousness, history, geography, grandeur, elegance, grace, and joy as all of the southern music we loved—blues, jazz, soul, and funk—we also didn't know that this tradition of image making was capable of producing works as aesthetically and emotionally arresting as any masterpiece by Black culture's universally recognized musical masters.

For as long as I've been Black and culturally knowledgeable, I've been of the common opinion that everything Black Americans have produced in the arts as a group sits in the shadow of our music. That when it comes to world-class accomplishment, our music leads the way and that, while there are certainly examples of Black writers, painters, sculptors, and choreographers whose work has been accorded world-class status by global scholars and arts devotees, these examples are seen as cultural exceptions and not the rule. Nowhere is this idea more acutely held than in the realm of the visual arts, where, until recently, you could count on one hand the names of Black American artists who had noteworthy, lucrative, and critically acclaimed careers within the world's gallery and museum galaxies. Because of Dial and The Southern Black Visual Tradition, we now know this idea to be, if not a lie, then an ignorant error in judgment.

Now, some of this fallacious thinking could be attributed to the opposite ways that so-called high culture and mass culture work with respect to spectatorship, audience, and connoisseurship. Black music, largely made inside the matrix of American mass culture, has always attempted to be as populist and democratic in practice and appeal as possible. (Even our most avant-garde jazz abstractionists lament the commercial forces that keep them from communicating directly with The People.) With the music's populist compulsions, there also came coded and direct challenges to racism and elitism in American life. America's visual arts establishments, on the other hand, have long been openly hostile to anything but a begrudging recognition of nonwhite Americans (and women of any type) in general. The idea that such people were capable of making statements equal to males of European descent in the American art world's Eurocentric pantheons has been anathema.

Nowhere was this hostility displayed more blatantly than in the years The Jungle, a major modernist work by the Cuban Wifredo Lam owned by the Museum of Modern Art, was hung not in the museum proper but on a wall leading to MOMA's coatroom. Critic and curator John Yau wrote about this in a landmark expose on race and curatorial practice titled "Please Wait by the Coatroom": "Its location is telling. The artist has been allowed into the museum's lobby, but like a delivery boy who has been made to wait in an inconspicuous passageway by the front door. By denying Lam the possibility of going upstairs and conversing with Paul

Cézanne, Pablo Picasso, Jackson Pollock, and Frank Stella, the museum relegates 'The Jungle' to a secondary status."[2]

Yau's essay now reads as a harbinger of the insurgent assaults on the art world in the 1990s that would force an opening in visual culture and ensure future inclusion of American artists whose ancestors were not phenotypically European males. That essay could also be seen, in light of its hard critique of art historian William Rubin, as the shot across the bow announcing that artists, critics, and curators of African, Asian, and Native American descent would soon be challenging the authority of art-world gatekeepers on cornerstone issues of artistic quality, innovation, talent, and intellect.

Unlike Black music, whose development ran parallel to the rise of the nation's entertainment industry, Black visual culture has had far fewer democratic rivers to cross. Dancing darky feet have rarely been given a chance to cast votes in the American art world. That world is proudly defensive of its elitism, and no matter how much we hear about the leveling of high and low categories since Warhol, its "deciders" still hold the keys when it comes to nurturing and encouraging sustainable careers, market-value, and scholarly recognition. All in all, these ensconced art world types tend to be a less well-rounded group than the more representative demographic who made backwoods South Carolina product James Brown a household name and a millionaire by the age of thirty-five.

If there was a Black American visual artist as ambitious, gifted, and ultimately significant as James Brown in 1956 Georgia, where Brown released his first million-selling single, "Please Please Please," we know that such a person would not have been able to launch his or her national career after being a local church performer who was a mere four years out of juvenile prison. Lacking a wide audience, much less the means to get to one, he or she could not have imagined their work being accessible to everyone within range of a radio, a television set, a juke joint, or a Victrola. Nor would they have been able to stage their work wherever there was clamor for it. Like our favorite Black southern visual avatar Thornton Dial, James Brown's visual counterpart more likely was doing whatever kind of physical labor he or she could find to make ends meet—working every kind of manual labor gig around, just like Brown's own father, Papa Joe, even after his son's superstardom in the 1960s. There is also the fact that, unlike James Brown, who had no doubt that his work was actually Music, hit records or not, Thornton Dial did not even think of his stuff as Art with even a small A.

The socioeconomic reasons for Dial's lack of opportunity within the mainstream art world will likely scream at you—race, class, education, medium, and region. Although Black music often shared the same "disadvantages," it escaped the obscurity still plaguing Black visual art for a number of critical and esthetic reasons. By the 1950s, Black music had begun to "own," as the kids say, the sound of modernity in twentieth-century life. The music also had an undeniable kinship to the "shock of the new" aspect of Western painting and sculpture since cubism. As both jazz and cubism were sparked by the distinct transcontinental conversations that had been struck up between African and European forms since slavery began, this should not seem all that strange. Nor should modernism's painters' and Black musicians' mutual attraction to a progressive zeitgeist and to improvisational techniques. Both jazz and early abstraction also profited from a discerning, discriminating, and vocal fan base with influence and of many nationalities who created a readymade market for their wares and almost instantly deemed them novel, innovative, and noteworthy.

By the 1960s, you could proclaim Sun Ra as a successor to Stravinsky, Stockhausen, and Ellington without much critical or institutional resistance. In the early twentieth century, Louis Armstrong and Picasso were both recognized as transformative creative forces to be reckoned with and to whom attention must be paid—just as Charlie Parker and Jackson Pollock were in the 1940s; Motown, Jimi Hendrix, Godard, and Warhol were in the 1960s; Stevie Wonder, Miles Davis, P-Funk, Earth, Wind & Fire, Bob Marley, Richard Serra, and Robert Smithson were in the 1970s; and Prince, Public Enemy, Robert Wilson, New York Subway spray-can art, and Jean-Michel Basquiat were in the 1980s. All the Black American musicians mentioned above are now seen as belonging to a powerful world-conquering thing called Black music, a thing which furthermore needs no defense or explanation to be understood as valid or to be politically claimed as Art in its own right. Southern Black visual culture, on the other hand, is only slowly beginning to generate a body of scholarship.

Since Dial's middling art world ascent, the idea that American Blacks have no original and sophisticated visual culture of their own has been revealed to be a shameful lie. Whether you want to label the work visionary, avant-garde or conceptual, or the southern Black visual tradition, it is easy to see from the few but important books on the subject (*The Quilts of Gee's Bend*, the two volumes of *Souls Grown Deep: African American Vernacular Art of the South*, and *Thornton Dial in the 21st Century*) that a Black visual tradition as dynamic, innovative, and profound as that of Black music has thrived unbeknownst to mainstream eyes. And many of the artworks rival (and often surpass, in my humble opinion) much that is owned, exhibited, and fawned over by major institutions as representative twentieth-century American art, in terms of visual originality, ingenuity, and intensity. Dial's work, in particular, is capable of leaping out of those books' pages with as much captivating spirituality and brio as anything I've ever heard by Armstrong, Parker, Howlin' Wolf, Miles Davis, Hendrix, Stevie Wonder, and the entire vainglorious catalogue of hip-hop music's grandmaster lyricists, MCs, turntablists, and beatmakers. The work is, in fact, the perfect visual corollary and companion to the Black soundworld mix that the world knows far better and has known about for far longer. Perhaps this too shall change as the work of Thornton Dial and his compadres—living, disabled, and dead—becomes more widespread and commonly exhibited in the nation's arts institutions. We're not taking any bets just yet, however. The major gestures toward inclusion of Dial have yet to occur and may not for another decade or so.

The respect, recognition, and place now commonly accorded Black American music is itself actually a fairly recent phenomenon, one that owes as much to the human rights rebellions of the 1960s as it does to the persistent progress of the music as a multidimensional cultural force in American society. Had the work of southern Black artists and their defenders been more in evidence when the first Black studies programs were being established on major American campuses in the 1970s, perhaps things would be different. As it stands now, though, some of Dial's best work, and that of many others in his tradition, is languishing in a warehouse in Atlanta, Georgia, leased by collector, curator, and writer Bill Arnett—primarily as a safeguard against those treasures being hauled off to the city dump. Had Arnett, Dial, and pioneer Alabama artists Lonnie Holley and Joe Minter not run afoul of a few name-players in the Atlanta, Birmingham, and New York art scenes in the 1990s, or had they not been victims of a slanted and vilifying 60 Minutes "report" by Morley Safer in 1993, then maybe the name Thornton Dial would be as well known nationally and globally as the names of other artists of African descent whose careers shot off like guided missiles in that decade: David Hammons, Cheri Samba, Lorna Simpson, Gary Simmons, Kerry Marshall, George Adiabgo, El Anatsui, Ellen Gallagher, and Kara Walker.

The exclusion of Dial, now in his eighties, from a curated palaver about other art world talents of his mien seems as nutty, on the surface, as the exclusion of the music of Stevie Wonder, Aretha Franklin, and

Jimi Hendrix from any serious conversation about postwar American music. There are some who believe the denial of Dial (and others) to his rightful place in the metropoles of the fine art world is due to malefactors high and low and to a perfidious bevy of things unseen: greed, envy, elitism, criminality, willful ignorance, and petty vendettas. Given the race and class history of this country—with much of the last two hundred years spent verifying Blackfolk's humanity to the courts, to Congress, and to various museum directors—the omission of Dial isn't all that surprising in itself. What is somewhat shocking is that Dial's exclusion has taken place over the last fifteen years, a time when many Black American artists have been awarded unprecedented amounts of fame, critical recognition, and money for their art, and in a time, as well, when Black popular culture has become a dominant, lucrative, trailblazing force in American business, intellectual life, and entertainment.

What is beyond ironic, bordering on tragic, is that the denial of Dial comes at a time when we've witnessed the election of the nation's first African American president. Thus we have the unsightly spectacle of Dial's work being treated by art world gatekeepers of all hues as if he were producing and attempting to exhibit his universal images in the segregated South of the 1930s. At the same time, there is a short list of scholars and critics who have devoted blood, brains, time, and treasure to documenting the remarkable tradition of Black American art making and who believe that this current refusal to embrace Dial is only delaying the inevitable: the reevaluation of everything we thought we knew about the canon of American visual modernism as it is expanded by and measured against the hidden-away bounty of the southern Black visual arts. The probability of this critical turnabout occurring anytime soon has less to do with the work itself and more to do with hidebound, high-faluting and exclusionary notions of who gets to be considered an Artist with a capital A in this country. Never mind that Dial's art typically tends to make space, time, and conversation stop when folk of both great and mild sophistication are in its presence.

Like most Black music of any consequence (hip-hop excepted), Dial's art originates in traditions developed by people born and raised outside of the nation's cosmopolitan centers. These are the expressive practices of folk who, like Dial, did not, by and large, possess college or, often, even high school degrees. What they did have was vision, visual ideas, and image-making acuity. They also had a complex and unique cultural ethos to draw upon: Dial is the product of a peculiarly Black and peculiarly southern racial and ethnic consciousness, a rich ore-filled cerebral cache that has remained hidden from even other Black Americans not of their group vernacular and group mentality. What paradoxically makes Dial's work so ultramodern is that it is so grounded in Black American racial consciousness and daily reality, the very same things that have always made Black music so renewable and cutting edge—resources that account for Dial's and the music's newfangled translations of African modalities through New World temperaments and American creative opportunities.

Whether plumbing the realities of America's slave-holding and Jim Crow past or wrestling with the dilemmas of our modern global world, Dial's playful examination of history, politics, and religion always appears to be the product of a highly personal symbolic language, rich in rhythm, texture, mysticism, surprise, and wit. His work is political, poetic, mentalist, formalist, folksy, fabulist, science fictional, secularist animist, and philosophical. This is also a body of art that tackles the national obsession, race, in ways that are never hackneyed or simply ironic and parodic. In fact, Dial tackles that old bugaboo race in ways that eschew cliché and elegantly transcend current conversations about representation, identity, and stereotype in Black American art by opening up more fertile and intriguing discussions about racialized cosmologies, contraptions, biomorphisms, ecologies and medicines. Dial's miraculous work operates on the premise that art should always be mystical, mysterious, and chasing immortality to be deserving of the name. His is an art that is never one-joke in delivery, though it is full of humor and deftly evokes magical practices, magical principles, and magical possessions, projecting a sense of the artist as someone casually at home in places where divination rituals and survivalism seem to have gone hand in hand.

For far too much time, Dial's work has been tethered to a critical and curatorial limbo somewhere in between high art and what's known as "folk art" and "outsider art." The difference between how those categories are received in the world often has more to do with art world agendas than with any true disparity in the cognitive and emotional powers of the work itself. Had Dial's works not derived from the hands of an unlettered Black southerner, they'd have been immediately categorized as Conceptualist projects rife with dynamic visual phenomena. Rejection of Dial's art in the metropoles then seems to derive from a fanatical presumption that Art with a capital A is not supposed to be within the intellectual skill set of southern negroes, especially those who plowed, mined, and welded for a living before turning to full-time art making once they got close to mandatory retirement age.

Dial's training as an artist, though, took place on the job, meaning any job he's ever had. He has taken all the tools and techniques he picked up as a jack-of-all-trades factory worker to reinvigorate and reenchant familiar art forms, often binding a cacophony of objects into a riotous supersymmetrical architecture of color and signifiers.

Dial once talked about his process:

> I have learned a whole lot about drawing from my work at the Pullman factory. Designs was punched out in the iron and steel works; big, beautiful pieces of steel start out with a little design. They drawed out the designs for the templates on paper, then make them on wood, then bring them to be punched into iron to go on the train car. I got to seeing how things you draw can be the design for everything.
>
> When I went to making art on plywood, I drawed it out first with a pencil, and after that I put on the other materials, stuff I find or stuff I have, like the steel, carpet and old tin, and then I paint it. . . . After while I just went to building my pieces right on to the board. I didn't need to draw them out. Cutting out tin and carpet and stuff come natural like drawing. The mind do the imagining. I got to where I could bend and twist the materials as beautiful as I could draw it out with a pencil.[3]

Dial is incapable of not converting any available scrap of cast-off industrial material or organic solid into metaphor and metacommentary. These aspects of his works alone—the vast range of transmogrified objects and transformational procedures present in them—will be delighting and confounding spectators and scholars for generations to come because they resonate and even vibrate with his crafty prestidigitator's way of drawing soulful plasticity out of whatever he touches: "I like to use the stuff that I know about, stuff that I know the feel of. There's some kind of things I always liked to make stuff with. I'm talking about tin, steel, copper, and aluminum, and also old wood, carpet, rope, old clothes, sand, rocks, wire, screen, toys, tree limbs, and roots. You could say, 'If Dial see it, he know what to do with it.'"[4]

The prodigious scope of Dial's creativity, versatility, virtuosity, and productivity, coupled with his multitude of thematic interests, renders any attempts to speak of a "quintessential" Dial all rather silly and inadequate. He is one of those rare visual talents of whom you can easily find yourself saying that you have forty favorites and you consider them all to be sui generis masterpieces, though not a one of them vaguely resembles another. Dial's titles alone clue you in to how far afield his mind frequently travels in pursuit of his muse. The titles are enigmatic yet illuminating fables unto themselves, literate indicators that draw wide and revealing circles around Dial's history, his thinking, and his vision: *Everybody's Welcome in Peckerwood City, In the Roosevelt Time: Hard Labor, Ladies at the Circus Like to Look at the Bear, Cotton Field Sky Still Over Our Head, Controlling the Ocean, Mad Cows and Cowboys, Don't Matter How Raggly the Flag, It Still Got to Tie Us Together, The Dream of the Handicapped Woman (Escaping the Jungle), Looking Good for the Price, Ground Zero: Decorating the Eye, The Last Day of Martin Luther King, Having Nothing Is Having Everything, Eve and Adam Still Looking for Christmas, Looking for the Taliban, High & Wide (Carrying the Rats to the Man), Life and Death of the Moonshine Man, Buddy Jake and the Power of the Mule, Creation of Life in the Blueberry Patch, Mercedes-Benz Comes to Alabama, Monument to the Minds of the Little Negro Steelworkers, Men on Alert (All Eyes on Iraq), Last Trip Home (Diana's Funeral).*

As an Alabaman with a global perspective, Dial is a parochial figure whose antennae are always tuned to world-historical channels, what some would call "universal" aesthetic virtues and twenty-four-hour news-cycle events. All the same, modernism can barely contain Dial as a category—no more than the Juilliard School's musical pedagogy could explain or contain a Sun Ra Arkestra—because, while he's arriving at a conclusion about what sophisticated and thoughtful art should do, he's not compelled by that canon or its self-critical intentions. Black American culture is the product of a people whose psyches were answering calls to creatively speak in ways that have more to do with that culture's interior dialogues than with exterior ones. The quality of the work on modernist terms only proves that humanity matters more than social hierarchies in the creative act.

The definition of Modern Art remains, of course, whatever the incestuous network of curators, gallerists, collectors, critics, and art historians who compose the "art world" say it is for hosts of reasons—sometimes valid, sometimes dubious, sometimes unscrupulous—sex, money, context, power, status, careerism. Dial, the self-taught, self-authorizing, self-confident Black southerner might not fit in that world at all. For contemporary Black American image makers and their devotees, Dial's art poses hard questions as well, including a consideration of how much speculative, exploratory, and courageous headroom their own visual tradition may or may not already provide outside of the museum system. We also need to claim Dial's voices, virtues, inventions, and daring as an empowering model for ourselves before Dial's accomplishments get assimilated and dissolved into the wider, consumptive art world's whiter shades of "beyond the pale" exploitation and appropriation. To quote two mavericks of Black American insurgent tradition, Charlie Parker and Huey Newton, "Now's the Time" for us to "Seize the Time" and ensure Dial's work and name become as loudly and proudly lodged in Black American psyches as the names Martin Luther King, Jay-Hova, Oprah, and Obama.

In his early eighties, Thornton Dial is now pretty much officially the long-distance runner of his tradition. He is, thankfully, still productive, prolific, masterful, and crafty. According to one scholar, he is also our American Michelangelo due to his rare and equally skillful handling of painting, sculpture, drawing, and his own hybrid variants of each that are taxonomically implacable.[5] The sheer volume of astounding work that he has produced in each medium is truly staggering. I have spent hours staring wide-eyed and wide-mouthed at hundreds of Dial's large paper drawings and spent as much time attempting to fully absorb the Atlanta warehouse full of his woolly mammoth assemblages, four-dimensional found object sculptures, obelisks, and towering widescreen canvas paintings. As they say, no experience is lost on an artist, and no material, no matter how damaged, discarded natural, or synthetic, is lost for a semiotic purpose in Dial's inventive and insightful hands.

Dial has a spacious home with sprawling acreage in Bessemer, but since his wife of fifty-odd years passed a few years ago, he prefers these days to work out of the metal fabrication shop that he and his adult sons have owned and operated for many years. On the brisk late winter day when I visited Dial Metal Patterns, there were cars and trailers up on blocks awaiting mending and renovation, and work was being completed on a ten-foot-high, fourteen-foot-wide wrought-iron gate and the kitchen for a family-size trailer home. Stacked in the back of that same airplane hangar of a room, there were also furniture, lamps, a welded statue of a duck-walking metallic Chuck Berry, as well as an elegant top-hat-doffing Bill "Bojangles" Robinson, all designed by Dial's son Richard, as expert a metal sculptor as they come.

Dial has two dedicated rooms on the premises, one for drawing and another larger studio in the very back for paintings and recombinants. At his home in Bessemer's pastoral suburbs, there are shambolic sculptural projects that rival small cranes in size. There are also on the property several fleet, white-spotted, black-tailed brown deer in a pen behind the shed, which contains several gnarly and gargantuan Dial pieces awaiting a move to a sturdier enclosure. Among those works in the shed yet to be seen anywhere else is *The Farmer's Wife*, which, like many of Dial's standing assemblages, is built up on two sides in thickets of (in this instance) dolls, manikins, repainted junk and handmade paper birds. The wife in question seems to be represented by a white manikin free-falling in truncated pieces toward heaven or hell (as it can be hard to tell sometimes with Dial whether his topography favors earth or sky—a recognition perhaps of the topsy-turvy view of life that can result from growing up needing to optically correct a hyper-racial and hyper-spatial hell on earth). Dial speaks about this piece as a tribute to the kind of women he saw working side by side as equals with farmers. This, in turn, points up Dial's adoration of the feminine and his feminist sympathies, less cryptically on view in his many erotic drawings, prolific as they are with female figures who never seem strangers to radiant sensuality, life-and-death human struggle, or animist powers of communication with fish, snakes, mules, bears, squirrels, birds, or wild men.

Ishmael Reed has identified the funkiest and most fecund aspects of Black American culture as drawing upon a venerable homemade voodoo philosophy he's dubbed "Neo-Hoodooism"—a syncretism of African and African American art making and mysticism grounded in the folklore and folkways of folk born and raised here in these continental United States. Reed sees Neo-Hoodooism as having issued from highly inventive Black Americans bent on connecting with ancestral energies, ideas, and practices from which they've been physically and psychologically separated for centuries. Reed has also identified the periodic recurrence of Africanist energies in Black America as a spontaneous and subconsciously generated collective unconscious phenomenon that he objectively, romantically, and sarcastically claims "Jes Grew." A more rationalist explanation would be that just as Blackfolk in America never stopped being Africanist music makers, they also never ceased to be Africanist image makers. The difference is they just did it in secret, in private, in disguise, using caution and discretion, under extreme pressure and in fear of violent consequences for exhibiting any thoughts, plans, or actions that might appear contrary (when not viscerally opposed) to a malevolently racist and classist social order. Some of the vertiginous mojo of Dial's art can certainly be attributed to its being incubated in an underground Black culture, a nondisclosing culture, a culture of codes and ciphers whose ways and meanings were meant to appear strange, curious, chaotic, and primitive to outsiders.

Even with full explanations and big hints from Dial himself, his work is not easy to fully comprehend, because it is not readily reductive to its aesthetic, political, or cultural implications. You don't have to know anything about American slavery or racism to be moved by the singularities of black-hole beauty in a Dial, or to even know that the artist is a Black American. His work generally appears before the eyes as a thing apart from any other art you may have seen, yet it is so rigorously and sumptuously made that resistance is futile and seduction is inevitable. Every

Dial I've ever seen instructs you that frolicsome acts of creative destruction and resurrection are going on and that invisible forces are being bound, harnessed, and manipulated like Silly Putty, that life and death, heaven and hell, chaos and supersymmetry have all been captured and enfolded in a viral and networked embrace.

In Dial's work, one can often witness what seems to be a brutally and lyrically encrypted tango going on during a bone-crushing tsunami of earth-shattering proportions. There can frequently be so much bricolage overload as to overwhelm our sensory apparatus in hallucinogenic ways, a working and reworking of material that makes you think you're gazing at a fixed object that is thrashing about in the throes of an improvisational flux and beguilingly undergoing its own fast-forward, time-elapsed evolution in real-time. So that no matter how texturally and temporally stabilized a Dial may seem on the surface, we seem to apprehend the thing as taking place in four dimensions or more, not merely three. Normal spatial cognition hardly being enough to help us make sense of what the works demand, we also know them in Time, know them as spinning celestial bodies that intend to collapse the spectator's distinctions between past, present, and future.

It is for these reasons that it does actually help to know the racial background and ethnic affinities of the artist, to know the motions of history which compelled and propelled Dial and his tradition's death-defying, risk-taking works into being by any means necessary.

So make of these facts what you will: Know that Dial worked for the Alabama-based Pullman-Standard Rail Car Manufacturing Company for thirty years and that while there, he learned to do just about every kind of factory-manufacturing job required to fabricate and assemble a rail car. His friend and fellow artist Lonnie Holley believes this is why Dial is so comfortable working in scales that rival the façades of small buildings. Dial also grew up in an Alabama that contained the ironworks firm of the Sloss family, a firm known for re-creating slave conditions in their barbaric modern-day mining and factory operations—places well documented as worksites where Black men were worked literally to death in unregulated hazardous shafts and then secretly buried in mass graves on company property. The Alabama that Dial was raised in was also infamous for some of the most violent attacks against civil rights workers by state and local police and citizens in the movement's history. This is, after all, the place where most infamously four young Black girls were blown to bits while attending Sunday school because their parents dared stand up against second-class citizenship and rampant police brutality. A place where Black ministers and their families were dynamited out of their houses on a daily basis, often as much out of habit as vicious terrorist intent. Given the level of psychopathic hatred that surrounded them, it's no wonder that Dial and his folk, purveyors of Alabama's wing of Neo-Hoodoo, kept their prophetic and provocative art safe in clandestine spaces, nor is it any surprise that they rarely provided more than a mutter and a mumble about its spirit-catching content or symbolism.

Amiri Baraka, a Dial devotee and friend for many years, once wrote in an essay about John Coltrane that one of the remarkable things about America is how much beauty exists here, in spite of how much vileness there is as well. Beauty in the extreme, the art that Thornton Dial has made and goes on making in Alabama lo these many decades is ample proof of that maddening paradox. The open acceptance of it may also be one of elite America's last chances to truly overcome a segregationist history that has denied the Constitution's promises of liberty, equality, and democracy from being self-evident in the eyes of Americans of Dial's genus and genius.

– 2010 –

Notes

Epigraphs: "Mr. Dial Is a Man Looking for Something," in *Souls Grown Deep: African American Vernacular Art of the South*, vol. 2, ed. William Arnett and William S. Arnett (Atlanta: Tinwood Books, 2001). Quoted in John Beardsley, "His Story/History: Thornton Dial in the Twentieth Century," in *Thornton Dial in the 21st Century* (Atlanta: Tinwood Books in Association with the Museum of Fine Arts, Houston, 2005), 285, 291.

1 Beardsley, "His Story/History," 291.
2 John Yau, "Please Wait by the Coatroom," in *Out There: Marginalization and Contemporary Cultures*, ed. Russell Ferguson, Martha Gever, Trinh T. Minh-ha, and Cornel West (New York: New Museum of Contemporary Art; Cambridge: MIT Press, 1990), 133.
3 Beardsley, "His Story/History," 286.
4 Beardsley, "His Story/History," 286.
5 This comment was made by Maude Southall Wahlman to William Arnett.

Kehinde Wiley

Black masculinity is already context. Already place, status, identification. Already name, rank, serial number. Already nationality and nation-state. Already a map of the world, already hotly contested territory. Already socioeconomic category. Already pedagogy, anatomy, psychoanalysis. Already in need of its own branch of physics and its own embassy. Already its opposite: Black femininity that is, and not some other form of masculinity merrily miserably merely its opposing force. Already a dream deferred sagging under its own weight and exploding. Already the death of Bigger Thomas, of Tea Cake, of Ras the Destroyer, of Brother Tod, of Milkman Dead, of Fred Hampton, of Amadou Diallo, of Sean Bell, and aye, Stringer Bell too. Already a fiction and an ethnographic narrative. Already the shortest distance between two points and the hypotenuse of a square. Already a moonshot, a roll of the dice, the luck of the draw, the pick of the litter. Last hired, first fired, only standing president to be called out by his name like so; "uppity tar baby." Rich nigra, poor nigra, White House–ensconced nigra still just a nigra. Not the boss of me, thee, dem, dose, dat. How'd that happen? Like *Pithecanthropus erectus*. Like Topsy, like Benjamin Banneker and Nat Turner too. Like Jew Grew. Like Jesse B. Semple. Like Booker T., W. E. B., Garvey, Ellington, Ellison, Elijah Muhammad too.

Duchamp frames Kehinde Wiley's actual practice better than Rembrandt. Black masculinity is a ready-made with legs and teeth, is already a context that comes with its own frame, game, and SAMO. Black masculinity is already a critical intervention at birth—a thing born performative before the gaze of Others. A thing born already in pursuit of a graduate degree in performance studies and always a reckoning and a rendering of Invisibility, the dominant theme of twentieth-century African American literature.

Black masculinity is always liminal, emergent, fugitive, subject to investigation. Already criminality itself, and already the definition of the heroic narrative, the hero's journey, the pilgrim's progress, the children's crusade, the rise of the planet of the apes, the L.A. Rebellion of 1992 aka the Rodney King riots, the OJ trial, the Million Man March. Always democracy in action, always singular and plural, elect and preterite, elite and common, Muslim and Baptist, Ethiopian and Jew, Desirable and Untouchable, Miles Davis, Dravidian, Coltrane, Lil Wayne, Toussaint Louverture, Jean-Michel Basquiat.

Black culture, declares Diego Cortez, "needs its own aristocrats too." Cortez never really explained why but this was long before hip-hop ruled the world and Black Aristo-cats were the only ones left in American life anyway. Before the most leisurely of Black masculine activities, shooting hoops, speaking in rhyming verses, posturing with swagger, had all become universal state-of-the-art markers of American male competence, elegance, dandyism, rhetorical flourish, rebel reverie reveille referencing.

Black masculinity is always many balls in the air at once. Always hit 'em high and hit 'em low. Kobe Bryant, the Italian-fluent Black Mamba of the NBA. Michael Vick, the last fox to hunt hounds on American soil, pay the price, then jaunt from the life of the endangered Falconer to the liberty of the protected Eagle. Does anyone in America still have to guess who Kanye West and Jay Z are coronating when they command us to "Watch the Throne"? We be claiming ourselves as benighted royals without hesitation, ambivalence, or ambiguity since the days of the Prince Hall Masonic lodge. Black masculinity means when your president is Black you need aspire to more than opulence, decadence, and luxury. You need to also assassinate all signs of disempowerment and cultural disadvantage and then further dispel any notion among your loyal opposition that they can ever meet you or beat you at eye level.

At the most base level, all of Kehinde Wiley's portraits are about the triumph of Black American masculine style over other more masculinist mythologies. All those clouds and floral patterns and noble horsemen in his work mere metaphors for urban American culture's intrinsic capacity for vertical elevation, liftoff, ecstasy, effervescence, élan, joie de vivre, savoir faire, the good life, Jordan high-tops, head fakes, tricky crossover dribbles, and thunderous slam dunks.

Hailing from Compton, California, home of Snoop, Dre, and N.W.A, Kehinde Wiley knows the name of the game is rising up over the top, and angelically flying above the rim. The virtual enthronement visible all over hip-hop's face. Black masculinity is always a game and as long as you're not playing according to the other fellas' rules you've got a decent shot at glory. Black masculinity must first be dispossessed to be redeemed. Black masculinity must first be trickster to become Trojan horse. Ralph Ellison understood this when he wrote the Trueblood section of his novel *Invisible Man*. Black masculinity is the profit to be had from the lurid racial fantasy locked up in the other fella's gaze.

Wiley posits that Black masculinity can as readily burst out from inside of the European Imaginary and defy all manner of racial binaries in the process. What contrast are we to presume of Wiley's urban American masculinities and his European painting models? The chasm between them is more existential than historical, less painterly than absurdly drawn as to confuse and conceal the painter's actual motives, which are in truth more descended from Brer Remus than Brer Verspronck—the latter, typically a painter of blonde royals, must have considered his brushstrokes' descent to the dandyish demimonde of his day a walk on the wild side. Wiley clearly required no Orphic fall to pitch his dark angel's ascension toward the light.

– 2009 –

Rammellzee: The Ikonoklast Samurai

Once upon a time in the Bronx, before hip-hop had a name, or came to be defined by the Five Elements of MCing, breakdancing, B-boying, turntabling, and the painting known as graffiti, it had Writers. These scribes wrote on the trains of New York's subway system. Mostly they wrote their names: a host of colorful noms de plume. They rendered bold abstractions of the alphabet in spray paint and magic marker, causing the letters to inflate like gaseous bubbles and explode outward with multidirectional arrows. If any figuration appeared, it would be cartoon characters and caricatures of the Writers themselves. At their most ambitious and epic, these Writings covered entire carriages from top to bottom, including the windows. Outside the culture, these mobile murals were seen as mere "graffiti." Within the culture, the act of writing on the trains was synonymous with "bombing" them. As the name implies, bombing was an aesthetic form of urban terrorism. Since bombing involved defacing and vandalizing city property, it was also considered a crime by the authorities, so much so that those powers eventually put barbed wire, attack dogs, and undercover cops in the train yards to foil raids on the carriages during Gotham's graveyard shift. It took the city a decade of aggressive policing, and a new line of Writing-proof trains made in Japan, to drive Writers away from the system forever.

In its heyday (roughly 1970–85), Writing seemed a permanent fixture and irrepressible feature of life in the city. At times the Writers functioned collectively, like a Renaissance guild, routinely exchanging ideas, techniques, energy, and adrenalin for their consuming mission to "bomb all lines." Their efforts paved the way not only for hip-hop as an art form but also for the scale of commodification and self-promotion that defines today's hip-hop.

The originator of Writing is generally thought to be a Greek immigrant who made a name for himself around 1970 by plastering the walls of the metropolis with the tag "Taki 183." Inspired by his example, a fame-hungry generation of alienated, disenfranchised youths in the Bronx, Brooklyn, and Harlem began throwing their tags up on city walls. One day, some genius of ghetto self-promotion got the bright idea that if you really wanted to have your name seen around the city, why not throw it on the side of a parked train car? By 1976 this idea was taken to its zenith by hundreds of graf crews who took up the challenge of trying to bomb as many as sixteen cars in one night. While Gotham slept, Writing crews, sometimes in pairs or groups of up to thirty strong, executed their work in the yards and underground tunnels. If your fellow Writers considered your bombing beautiful, you had made a "burner." Those who couldn't produce burners were considered "toys."

There is another theory of Writing's origins which says it all began with the medieval monks of the fourteenth and fifteenth centuries, who produced illuminated manuscripts in the script we now call Gothic. In this version, the monks were prevented by the Catholic Church because their letters had become so ornate that the Pope and his bishops could no longer read them. This set of beliefs emanates from a gentleman and hip-hop icon known to the world as Rammellzee.

To understand Rammellzee, especially for the uninitiated, it's best to begin with basic facts. Ramm was born in 1960 in Far Rockaway, Queens. He began writing on the trains in the midseventies, influenced by legendary Writers like Phase One and Dondi, who became something of a mentor. In 1980 he stopped writing on trains and, like many of his peers, began showing his paintings and sculptures in international galleries and museums. Around this time he began developing the notion that Writing was actually an act of war, a military assault he code-named "Gothic Futurism" and "Ikonoklast Panzerism."

Fans of hip-hop, and of the film *Wild Style*, first became aware of Rammellzee not as a theorist or a Writer but as an MC. In the film he freestyle duets with his partner Shockdell in the nasal bark he calls "Gangsta Duck." This performance is thought to have served as the template for the vocal styles of both the Beastie Boys and Cypress Hill.

In 1983, Tartown Records, under the aegis of producer Jean-Michel Basquiat, released a twelve-inch called "Beat Bop" by Rammellzee versus K-Rob, a one-off that immediately entered the canon of hip-hop masterpieces. The song went on to become the unofficial theme song for the documentary *Style Wars*, the definitive statement about Writing culture that still stands as the most revelatory film about hip-hop ever made. Strangely enough, Ramm does not appear in the original, though in the two-disc DVD version he is discussed in detail by Dondi in an outtake and given his own exhibition space in one of the extra features. Ramm also appears in Jim Jarmusch's feature debut *Stranger Than Paradise*. In the original script for Julian Schnabel's *Basquiat*, there is a re-creation of his rather infamous interrogation of Jean-Michel, brought on because he and other writers felt Basquiat had been unduly crowned king of graffiti painting by the art world despite having never sprayed a burner up on the trains.

The moody music that plays behind the two MCs on "Beat Bop" is a sighing, whinnying ambient shuffle full of funk and suspense that creeps through your head like a slow-moving ghost train. While K-Rob's lyrics detail urban corruption and misery in a subdued variation on Grandmaster Flash's "The Message," Ramm's oblique streaks of surreal verbiage suggest William S. Burroughs doing cut-ups on acid. In the eighties Ramm recorded sporadically with Bill Laswell and Death Comet Crew. The latter joint presaged the dark cinematic settings RZA crafted for the Wu-Tang Clan by a decade. On *Bi-Conicals of the Rammellzee*, released this month on German label Gomma, Ramm reunites with K-Rob and Shockdell. The beats on *Bi-Conicals*, created by several different producers including Death Comet Crew and Munk, sound a bit too 1982 retro/electro/"Planet Rock" for my taste, but it's wonderful to hear Ramm return to recording. This is not to say the *Bi-Conicals* are not without zany lyric charms: for example, when Ramm preaches the gospel of Gothic Futurism or duels with Shockdell over living space on "Pay the Rent." Potentially more satisfying is a Japan-only CD, reportedly more dubwise in approach and mimicking the massive reverb envelope utilized on "Beat Bop." Currently, however, there is no Western distribution for this, and label details could not be secured at press time.

For as long as I've known Ramm—going on two decades now—he has lived in a two thousand-square-foot space in Tribeca, Lower Manhattan. The narrow, ramshackle building, abutting a loading dock, has three floors. Fittingly, Ramm lives on the top: the mad monk in the attic. The crib's only window faces south. On 11 September 2001 he had a clear, elevated view of the Twin Towers' collapse from a distance of no more than twenty blocks.

Still tall and rangy, though with the inevitable middle age spread that forty-four years can put on a brother, Ramm remains a man of mystery and profound contradiction. Yet he is not without appetites, a human history, and a superhuman ego to complement his prodigious gift of gab. He loves his Olde English 800 as much as the next gangsta rapper. "Not because it gets me drunk," he professes in his heartiest Viking voice, "but because it's beer!" Like his brethren among postmodern African American apostles George Clinton, Sun Ra, and RZA, you can take his playful philosophies as seriously as you want. He cracks himself up constantly. Ask him how he came to believe the Pope is the enemy of the letter and he'll guffaw, "I don't know!" and mean it. He'll admit to being as mystified as anyone by the stuff that spontaneously exits his mouth. He never writes anything down and though he speaks of having derived his terminology from "dictionaries," the only publications visible in his domicile are magazines with articles about him and a pornographic calendar I had to move aside before taking a seat on his couch. What you'll mostly find in his home is twenty-five years' worth of paintings (on canvas and carpet), sculptures (most prominently a four-foot-high gold-painted replica of an Egyptian ankh symbol), costumes, and toys. A profusion of spray-painted and glued mask artifacts made out of junk and skateboards salvaged from the scrap heap hang from the walls and the ceiling, taking up about two-thirds of the room (he claims there is even more work in his mother's garage in Queens). A newer series features the letters of the alphabet rendered as three-dimensional wildstyle transformer weapons on wheels. You can feel the sweat and the anal, outsider art obsessiveness that went into constructing all these pieces. They are in the vein of African power sculptures, assemblages with hidden powers and meanings waiting to be activated by their builders and makers.

Ramm grew up in Far Rockaway, Queens, in a working-class neighborhood close to JFK Airport. He describes his family as mostly made up of "cops and military police," with himself and a cousin (who did time in NYC's most infamous prison, the Tombs) as the criminal element. His initiation into Writing's master level came via the legendary Dondi.

"I came down from Queens to the Bronx," he reminisces, "because that's where the culture was coming from. All the guys who also rode the A Train—Phase Two, Peanut Two, Jester—all these guys influenced me in this manner of Writing. I used to cut out from school and meet other people who were toys. We were using flash lighters with erasers and store market ink. It would leak all over your pockets, but you could hit a train. 'Course, when you got home you got your ass beat because your pants were all fucked up. One day a guy heard me talking about writing on the train and he said, 'I know Dondi.' I hit the window right behind him to prove I was a Writer. I went to Dondi's house and he didn't want to let me in until this guy said, 'No, he's great.' I had a great time with Dondi for about four or five years. Dondi saw something developing—he couldn't see how the idea of an arrow turning into a missile could have come from someone from Far Rockaway. [He thought] it should have [come from] somebody [dead up] in the culture, from the hierarchy. I was far away. I shouldn't have those thoughts in my mind.

If I'd been born in Brooklyn," he adds, "I wouldn't have come up with my style of Ikonoklast Panzerism. I would have been too close to too many masters.

"I was part of United Graffiti Artists along with everybody else," Ramm continues. "I was known as Stimulation Assassination: Tagmaster Killer. I owned the entire 1, 2, 3, 4, 5 lines. The letter music notes and weather notes that were done down there reached a point where you didn't need to kill a person. The piece itself became a weapon: the letter itself. So fame was the most interesting to take out. How do you know George Washington? You know him through a name. You shoot the letter on the train at the other name and it takes out that name. So therefore homeboy has no identity. Why should I kill him? He'll just be dead anyway because nobody will know who he is. He'll just be a walking zombie.

"Don't let him be dead," he asserts. "Because that's what they want to do to you. They sell your art, they sell your music and exploit it and then all you have left is exploitation. So why don't you at least have your own name? Give that to them and what do you have after that?"

Ramm believes that when Writing moved from the trains it gained the world's attention for fifteen minutes but lost its soul. Not so much because the Writers got pimped and disposed of by the galleries but because, except for himself and the painters A-1, B-1, and C-1, the original Writing culture discontinued the path of armoring the letter and furthering the war they had started on the trains against a biologically diseased alphabet. As he told the online grafzine @149st, "We failed what could have been 'our culture.' Writing for fame or name is a poor excuse to be a monk and is the reason why this culture is a subculture. I went [to an auction] in 2000. Everyone who was anyone in this 'subculture' had works for sale. No one sold except for a few. I felt that the 'culture' died right there. There was too much mannerism, not enough 'burner'! Our futurism! We should have stuck to our principles, left by the monks. We should have only stuck to doing 'the letter' and joined together to fight the light dwellers, but we will always be 'Kings from the Dark Continent.' It's hard to become a real live painting in B-boy style but I managed, and we all could have managed."

If you are fortunate enough to see Ramm perform, you will see him dressed in full body armor—mechanized costumes whose details and personae express his philosophy in visual form. In his heavy metal B-boy samurai gear, Ramm freestyles and cavorts, at times with a vocoder attachment which makes self-evident the connection between his Gangsta Duck delivery and George Clinton's Sir Nose D'Void of Funk persona.

Looking at these creatures arrayed in his apartment, I ask for a formal introduction to each one as Ramm walks down the line.

"These are gods called the Ramm Ell Zee," he intones. "Each one of them has a part to play in the mythology called Gothic Futurism. Some of them are from different time periods. The Purple People Eater over there is China, the Cosmic Bookie. We all gamble one way or the other. He places his bets with the Horrors, and the Horrors gamble galaxies. The Wielder is dealing with Chronologics. He spins around and deals with Ovulization. He has to deal with the bet called 'Womb versus Man.' What he does is calculate all movement in the universe, or as I call them, the transverses. Ovulization, or the cosmic flush, is the same thing as when a wombman has her period. Times burns out as a cosmic flush called 'men o pause.' This is a trick made by the clergy: Man versus Womb Man.

"There's Wind, she's a mother of natures. The one with the white beard and the pitchfork is a loan shark. He takes bets and hands them to the Horrors. There you have Destiny and Destiny, the double-headed wombed man. What they do is separate themselves like Adam and Eve.

"That brings us into the style of Gothic Futurism and the first two people, and their attitude towards an apple or orange. Anything round is silly because since space has no curvature and there's no down or up, the only thing that could actually represent that is a steeple. I believe the first spaceship is a steeple." Cosmology or mere child's play? You be the judge. Ramm don't care 'cause Ramm don't stop. I'll only say that every time I suspect he is putting me on, the scientific theory checks out.

For many, our first encounter with Ramm's militant and contentious body of thought came via the May 1983 issue of *Artforum*, a special edition about the future in which he was quoted at length by writer Edit Deak. Many of us weren't ready for this articulation of hip-hop's message. No matter how much we loved Writing, rapping, turntabling, and breaking, and despite our ardor for the sight of a ten-carriage-long series of burners unfurling from the tunnels during morning rush hour, Ramm had us scratching our heads in confusion and wonderment. He dropped knowledge that wasn't easy for the average bear to assimilate. In that issue of *Artforum* he not only revealed his philosophy of Writing's military function, but suggested he'd done the math, come up with a unified field theory of space-time, electromagnetism, biochemistry, and mysticism.

"The monks started what we do," he told Deak. "We extend off their science. The bishops in 1582 stopped their knowledge because they couldn't read the monks' tax papers. They were getting too fancy so the bishops said, 'I can't read this to tax the people.' If you look in the dictionary you'll see that the bishops stopped the monks because their power was becoming too strong with the letter. Those damn monks contradicted what the kings wanted. They wrote it the way they wanted to write it, in their style. The calendar monks sent a letter to the one place God cannot go: Hell. The light we had draws from a knowledge that was dim down there, so the knowledge was very faint but yet it was real, and with its energy passing through our bodies, we received it."

Composer and painter Danny Hamilton believes Writing stopped being interesting once it stopped being about vandalism. To hear Ramm tell it, the essence of writing on the trains was all about taking something back—not Krylon spray cans from local art supply and hardware stores, but the alphabet itself, whose true symbolic nature was mathematical, not phonetic. Ramm believes our native tongue was imposed on the letter by our biologically diseased species, especially the Roman Catholic Church. As Einstein did with his equation $E = mc^2$, Ramm employs the letter as a stand-in for universal electromagnetic forces. Surrounding the Earth, the charged particles we know as the ionosphere determine the structure of every living thing, from the weather to DNA. Before the Writers on the trains were stopped, just like the monks before them, they were subconsciously armoring the letter against exploitation and misdirection—hence the repeated imagery of arrows and missiles. Emblazoned with these symbols, the trains became moving combat vehicles akin to the German tanks of World War Two: Ikonoklast Panzerism.

Rammellzee believes that information is encoded within the mathematical structure of the alphabet that will allow human beings to leave the planet ("this mold," as he calls it), freed from the demands of both the church and the human reproductive system. As long as science, religion, and biochemistry are bound together, he believes human beings will be unfit for interstellar travel. Like Sun Ra and George Clinton before him (whom he acknowledges as conceptual forebears along with Gene Simmons of KISS, AC/DC, and the Hell's Angels), Ramm believes mankind's true home is among the stars. If that means we must all exchange flesh for robot parts to get there, he's cool with that.

In 1985 he told me, "Rammellzee is a military function formation. . . . I am ramming the knowledge to an elevation and I am understanding the knowledge behind the Zee. Since we are dealing with Roman letters, we have to go back to the day when the Romans were using the ram to break down doors. Our situation today is to break down a door of knowledge hidden behind society. We're going to work our way around it instead of breaking it straight up. Whereas before you'd be trying to break through and you would be on the bottom of the pile. We're talking about where graffiti originated, where hard-core war went down, with markers against markers and letters against letters. You think war is always shooting and beating everybody up, but no, we had the letters fight for us.

"All my art and all my teachings are about Gothic Futurism," he continued, "and the knowledge of how a letter aerodynamically changes into a tank. I tell people, phonetic value does not apply to any letter's structure because the sound is made by the bone structure of the human species, which has nothing to do with the integer structure quality. The letter is an integer. Chinese letters are carbonetic, but ours are siliconic. Arabic symbols are disease—cultural chemical symbols. They cannot be armored. They cannot be made Ikonoklast. They cannot be made into a vehicle in motion. Silicon-based symbols can be moved forward and have no phonetic value. What they're saying in Arabic equals the structure of the symbol. What we're saying does not equal structure, but the difference in values between silicon and carbon."

Hip-hop evolved in a war zone within a society in love with its own firepower. The culture of Writing reflects the context and the pent-up aggression of its alienated, disenfranchised urban soldiers. "Our symbols could be armored because this culture has military power," he says now. "Our generation's poverty and despondency made us turn a letter into a missile. Whereas the Japanese were more spiritual, they were 'peace peace peace' after they had a bomb dropped on their ass. The first act of terrorism was America dropping the bomb on Hiroshima.

"Furthermore," he persists, "the letter appeared from the first dimension. The first dimension has total power over everything because it is total electromagnetic energy. It is an integer by itself. No one controls the alpha-beta. If you drop the [last] 'a,' it becomes alphabet. That's what they did, but is it total control or is that foolish control? Bigotry and the rest of that bullshit."

On Rammellzee's website, you can download a formal paper expanding on these thoughts titled "Iconic Treatise on Gothic Futurism." In a document strictly for the hard-core enthusiast with some basic gleaning of theoretical physics, Ramm lays out in great detail the knowledge and power he believes reside within the twenty-six structures of the alpha-beta, from A to Z. Although Ramm never calls a spade a spade or the white man the devil, at times you can feel his Afrocentricity seeping through his quantum intellect.

"There's a point where people will steal the idea of the ratio envelope, the number and the letter, combine it together and say since we own this, we own you," he says. "Numbers were stolen from India, brought up to the Arabic countries and they sabotaged it then. Zero was stolen from the Mayan Indians. We have this government that doesn't want you to remember alphabeta, they want you to remember the alphabet. We're not going to speak their bullshit anymore. We want our own sound for the letter now. We want you to take the letter, put it in the computer and find the sound that emanates from that integer which is called the aura of the letter. Do that and you get ultrasonics. Ultrasonic sound wars is what they're going to have soon. I'll probably be the first one to do it. I just finished building a tank that shoots ultrasonic sound—it's called a Weather Note. It's a metropostasizer. It controls the atmosphere. It also acts like a sundial, points out the cloud projections, then shoots the cloud. Disintegration of clouds comes from radioactivity. Microwave that shit and it puts out a sound burst that's too thick for the atmosphere. Depending on whether or not it's an iodine cloud, you reverse the polarity of that shit. Ultrasonics, instead of going at high frequency, goes at a high hum. And it gets trapped by heat and auto-emissions. It's similar to making a tornado."

Before dismissing Ramm's verbal confections as the quasi-fascist fantasies of a robot fetishist, take note of a project of the U.S. Department of Defense known as High Frequency Active Auroral Research Program (HAARP), based in Alaska. Its main installation consists of 360 seventy-two-foot antennae spread over four acres and fueled by a rich reservoir of natural gas. HAARP's antenna towers are designed to beam radiowave radiation into the ionosphere, creating a charged particle build-up that can be directed toward specific targets on Earth. The disruptive electromagnetic pulse created by atomic explosions can now be accomplished with the music of the heavens. It is to the world of sound what nuclear bomb technology is to the atom. At least twelve military/corporate patents have derived from HAARP research to date. U.S. Patent #4686 605, held by HAARP scientist Bernard Eastlund, describes "Method and Apparatus for altering a region in the earth's atmosphere, Ionosphere and/or Magnetosphere." HAARP technology has diverse weaponry uses—surveillance imaging, deep-sea submarine communications, guided missile communications interference, and, most alarmingly, human behavior. According to geophysicist and U.S. military advisor Gordon J. F. MacDonald, "Accurately timed artificially excited electronic strokes could lead to a pattern of oscillations that produce relatively high power levels over certain regions of the Earth. In this way one could develop a system that would seriously impair the brain performance of very large populations in selected regions over an extended period." By MacDonald's reckoning, "the key to geophysical warfare is the identification of environmental instabilities to which the addition of a small amount of energy would release vastly greater amounts of energy." The U.S. Air Force, which oversees HAARP, says, "[Electromagnetic] systems would be used to produce mild to severe physiological disruption or perceptual distortion or disorientation. In addition, the ability of individuals to function could be degraded to the point where they would be combat-ineffective. Another advantage of these systems is that they can provide coverage over large areas with a single system. They are silent and countermeasures may be difficult to develop. . . . One last area where electromagnetic radiation may prove of some value is in enhancing abilities of individuals for anomalous phenomena."[1] Suddenly Ramm's symbolic sound-war machines don't seem so far-fetched. If the government is out to play us with HAARP, Ramm's ideas beg that we at least prepare certain conceptual countermeasures. For all his anti-Christian warp and woof, gravel and guff, he ultimately reveals himself to be a utopian.

"We're advanced in terms of science and technology," he says, "but the attitude of the population is still Gothic. We still do not know what we're doing. We still do not know how to leave this planet the right way. We'll bring religion out into space and it'll be stopped. Because in the 1400s the word 'religion' was restriction on a legion. Gothic is the architecture of the letter that was lost back in the fourteenth century. You can have four alternatives to human nature—genocide, plain old socialism like bees and ants have, love and dictatorship, which is what we have now, or you can have a lot of high powered mega-structured knowledge where everything becomes not a socialistic bee-type state but a militant state with megastructures. That's the way it should be—mass thinking, mass brain power as one."

– 2010 –

Note

1 Quotes from Nick Begich and Jeane Manning, "The Military's Pandora's Box," http://www.haarp.net.

Richard Pryor: Pryor Lives

Unrepentant and reflective, the most profound and influential comedian of the late twentieth century laughed in the face of divorces, drug addiction, and disease. Like all great minds, Pryor helps us appreciate how noble and absurd a creature man is. And he's still mad funny. True confession time: When my editors first offered me the Richard Pryor assignment, I didn't exactly leap out of my seat to claim it. Neither my sense of the tragic nor the comic is so bloodless as to relish reporting how the once hyperactive Pryor copes with the ravages of multiple sclerosis. (MS is a degenerative disease that affects the central nervous system, causing uncontrollable muscle tremors and paralysis in some patients.)

Richard Pryor is, of course, the most profound and influential comedian of the twentieth century. Combine the pathos of Charlie Chaplin with the raunch of Redd Foxx, the critical insight of Dick Gregory and Lenny Bruce, and the wide-eyed wonder of Bill Cosby, and you might create a stand-up mutanoid, but not a Richard Pryor. As hilarious as these funny men are, Pryor made comedy more than raw; he made it ass-out, naked, and confessional. He brought the blues to American comedy— that laughing-to-keep-from-crying aspect of Black life that often pushes us beyond decorum to deconstruction, or more plainly, tellin' it like it muhfukn is.

You literally have to go to Shakespeare, James Joyce, or James Baldwin to find readings of human folly as incisive as Pryor's. Yet Pryor has it one up on those masters of the word: He didn't need exclamation points—his body movements were his function.

Pryor has left us some wonderful films of his stand-up talents (1979's *Richard Pryor—Live in Concert* is the funniest of the four) and of his dramatic acting abilities, most notably in *Lady Sings the Blues*, *The Mack*, and *Blue Collar*. But to his fans, there always seemed to be two Richard Pryors: the hero of his stand-up romps, and the chump of his Hollywood choices. Sometimes the twain did meet, like in Michael Schultz's *Which Way Is Up?* or his four movies with Gene Wilder, but not often enough.

As Pryor's art, celebrity, and wealth increased in the seventies and eighties, so did his personal chaos: divorces, drug habits, diseases, and self-doubt. When he burned himself up in a drug-induced haze in 1980, the episode seemed more like a skit than a coke fiend's cul-de-sac.

These incidents and more are now chronicled in his autobiography, *Pryor Convictions: And Other Life Sentences* (Pantheon), written with Todd Gold. Alongside them are ribald tales about Miles Davis, Pam Grier, and Billy Dee Williams; tough remembrance of growing up poor in his grandmother's whorehouse in Peoria, Illinois; and reflections about his struggle to find his own comedic style. Further documenting Pryor's work are the six Loose Cannon Records reissues of Pryor's LAFF Records comedy albums; the full catalog of twelve will soon be available.

Up until I walked into his Encino mansion and looked into his eyes, I didn't know how things were going to go. For once, I did not prepare questions. I figured I'd sit down, roll the tapes, and let the love flow. With me was Peter Harris, a fellow Howard University alum, a Pryor fanatic, poet, journalist, and family man who rolled up on me in Los Angeles the day before the interview. What neither of us counted on was the presence of Jennifer Lee, Pryor's ex-wife, now his best friend/manager/cheerleader, who complicated and enriched the session. In Pryor's bio, Lee comes off as confused, maternal, and much abused. In person, she is a centered and mature woman whose bond with Pryor seems more motherly than wifely at this point, but no less passionate and protective. (And he needs that. Lee estimates that Pryor's been bilked out of some fifty million dollars by lawyers and hangers-on.)

Before I began the interview proper, I caught this exchange between Lee and Pryor:

"Would you prefer that I leave?" Jennifer asked. "Would that make it better?"

"No," Pryor replied. "It would probably make it worse."

. . . . .

Greg Tate: When you started working on the book, did you know you were going to be as open and honest as you were with your cowriter?

Richard Pryor: No.

GT: Did you think you'd be more evasive?

RP: Yes, lots of times. It was a hard thing to do this book. 'Cause it's the truth. And the truth was something I avoided at all costs.

Jennifer Lee: Not really. I mean, look at your work . . .

RP: Oh, fuck that. That's work. That's for money, you know what I mean?

GT: You've said that when you went to Africa, you didn't see any niggers, and so that word got excised from your vocabulary. How come "bitch" didn't follow?

RP: I thought a lot about that at the time. Because if I see one, I have to see the other. You're more right than wrong. My grandmother used to say that to the pimps and stuff who used the word "bitch": "Excuse me, son, did your mother teach you how to say that?"

GT: *What did your grandmother think about the women that worked for her?*

RP: Good. She was an okay boss. I didn't see it for what it was. I was a kid. I saw the house different than what it was.

JL: But how was Mama, Richard? Because I remember when she beat me over the leg with a stick like she was back in the whorehouse.

RP: Listen, we're talking about Mama now. She's gone. Leave her alone. Ain't nothing we can do.

JL: But how did she treat those women?

RP: I imagine she treated 'em like shit.

GT: *Did you think the way you felt about women was affected by how she treated them, or what you saw growing up in a whorehouse?*

RP: I think what I saw affected me. But see, they were beautiful to me, in my mind's eye. They were like fucking fabulous. I didn't see them for what they were or nothing. I said, God, this is fucking great. But I was a kid. I really was a kid once. I really was. It's been a mystery to me how that affected me all my life, and I'm fifty-four. I don't care.

JL: He picked women who wanted to try and fix him. I sure as heck tried to fix him.

RP: Did you?

JL: Yeah, I did. It was terror, living in that scene.

RP: Wasn't an ax murder?

JL: A train wreck, maybe.

GT: *An earlier version of the book has one passage that struck me as being a revelation for you. You write about women behaving like lunatics when you got ready to leave. It's like you drove them mad. You talk about how in relationships, violence can work like a hex, like a spell.*

JL: Brilliant point.

RP: I'm glad you like it.

GT: *When did you realize that?*

RP: Probably when I wrote it. You know, it's amazing. I'm embarrassed to say this, but I used to be a violent man, except I'd only fight women.

I'd never fight with a man. Now listen to me: This movie company that they gave me, Indigo [Columbia Pictures gave Pryor his own production company as part of a forty-million-dollar deal], I hired Jim Brown to run it and realized I made a mistake. And I said to myself, If I don't knock this motherfucker out, or at least make the attempt, then I never gonna hit nobody, ever again. And that's the truth. I said, You know, I'm so bad. I bulldoze people all over, but I ain't bulldozed this motherfucker, so there ain't shit to my stuff.

GT: *What was the moment like when you did finally tell Jim Brown that he was fired?*

RP: He fucked around and turned down Prince's *Purple Rain*. That movie would have been great for us, but Jim thought it didn't have enough Black people among the production assistants or whatever. I said, "So?" "No, see, you got to have Black people. This is a Black thing." I said, "What we gonna do, Jim?" I felt like I was mad. I was insane. I told Jim Brown over lunch that I didn't want this company, and Jim cried. Jim Brown said I was either going to die right there or live with a broken face. I didn't care because I was tired of his shit.

JL: You lost the art. You guys lost the big picture. Plus it was two male egos in there too, right? Don't you think so?

RP: I don't think so. It's just that I have the ego, and if you come with your shit, ain't nothing for me to do but hit you in the head with a hammer.

GT: *You set the stage for Spike Lee and John Singleton and the Hughes brothers. Before Indigo, who was ever thinking a Black man could be in control of his career in Hollywood? There were other milestones in your career too, like getting paid four million dollars for* Superman III.

RP: But the movie, man. It wasn't my fault. They did give me the four million, so I did what the director said. But I didn't get to do shit in it.

GT: *You've talked about what a lot of us were thinking back in the day— that you were never as in command of your talent in a Hollywood film as you were doing stand-up. You had so much room onstage. It was your world.*

RP: It was. For a minute.

JL: You still rule, Richard.

RP: Shut up.

JL: I just want to see you work again.

GT: *You did do a tour a while back. You say it made you realize that you got more courage than stamina because of the MS.*

JL: He's had too many martinis too. You want me to leave yet?

RP: No.

GT: *Did you feel drugs gave you more energy to work night after night, or was cocaine just part of your lifestyle?*

RP: Hey, listen, doing cocaine was for me like being a smart kid. I knew it was wrong. But shit, cocaine made me feel like I had something so many people liked. And since I had it, I could say, "Hey, want some?" and not even look at the roll [of bills]. I could say, "Here, have some more." I didn't understand how insane that was then. My friend Burt was the first person I saw smoke it and he said, "I saw God. God is here talking to me." He sat in that chair, and I looked back at Burt, and I said, I'm gonna try some of this shit because he's fucking gone.

GT: *When did you realize you were addicted?*

RP: I was talking to Redd Foxx. I said, "Why do I want, Redd? I get so much and still I want more. Why?" He said, "'Cause you a junkie." That went past me like, choo! I'd never been called a junkie before, but it was true. And I always thought, cocaine doesn't hook nobody. I was under the impression that the Lady don't be bad to you, 'cause she's a Lady.

JL: He's still addicted to cigarettes.

RP: She doesn't like my addictions.

JL: I hate the cigarettes because I think you could really help your disease if you stopped smoking. That's all.

RP: That's what you say.

GT: *What is MS like for you on a day-to-day basis?*

RP: It's not pleasant, but I look at it like this. I've seen people a lot worse with MS. I've seen people fucked up, man, and it scared me. I saw 150 people with MS when I'd never seen anybody else with it.

JL: Richard's actually walking again with a walker.

RP: The other night when I was in the walker, I couldn't wait until I could get to the table and sit down. Because that's a frightening thing when you're walking and you feel your legs going, "Hey, wanna give me a break?" And there was another fifty feet and everybody wanted to show me the food. They said, "Hey, Rich, food's over here." And I didn't want to see no food and shit.

JL: Maybe MS is a way of keeping you alive.

RP: Maybe, 'cause I'm alive. But where's the money? And the pussy?

GT: *You talk about being addicted to laughter too. How do you deal with not being able to access your talent?*

RP: It makes me angry. I say very angry and maybe that's pushing it, but I'm angry because I can't do shit. I can't jump up and do the things I want to do. I have to learn something else. I don't know what, but I'm learning it.

GT: *Do you still think of yourself as being an artist, an entertainer? Is that still in your definition of Richard Pryor now? Or is that gone?*

RP: No, it's not gone, but it's fa-a-ar away. Like it's through this veil and I can't see it. I know where it is but I can't reach it.

Peter Harris: For the cats who were coming up when you were doing the work, it wasn't just comedy to us. It was like hearing your grandfather talk, or your big brother. Do you have a sense of the type of impact you had on people when you were at your peak? Or even now?

RP: I like hearing what you're saying. If you were around here before, and I had listened, I would have felt different about myself.

GT: *How much of an inspiration were people like Miles Davis to you?*

RP: Miles . . . I met Miles at a bar on Eighty-Sixth Street in New York. A guy said, "Miles, I'd like you to meet a nice young man." Miles said, "What the fuck you know?"

GT: *Did he ever talk to you about your work?*

RP: Yeah. He said, "You a funny motherfucker." I told him once, I said, "Miles, I got a script about Charlie Parker." Miles said, "Charlie Parker was greedy." I said, "What you mean, Miles?" Miles said, "He was really gonna rape everything. He fucked everything, and he played every-thing." It was too much. With Miles, all I ended up doing was saying, "Please stop, Miles. Stop." Because he just be talking. But I picked up on it, because I said this is real shit here. Bless his heart. But there is another side to being honest, you got to remember, because it's a very dangerous blade. It swipes and cuts off thousands of heads.

GT: *What's your relationship with your children? Do you have more time for them now?*

RP: Hmmm, hmmm, hmm. It's like that. I didn't know that it was going to be forever, but they are. That's something I'm understanding now. To have kids, you got to have 'em forever. I admire their mothers. I really do. Their mothers call me up to ask for things, and I know what they're going through because I had them for a little bit.

JL: Well, in some cases, having kids was a career choice, right?

RP: No, it was never a career choice for people. You didn't do it.

JL: No, thank God, I didn't do it.

RP: No, but you got two vicious dogs.

GT: *Has there ever been a time when you didn't help someone, and you should have?*

RP: Please don't make me think of those things. Was there ever a time I could've helped and didn't? Well, I didn't go to 'Nam, that's the only thing I could think of. I wish I was in Vietnam. I don't know why. I really don't, but I just feel like I belonged there at the time. I should have been there.

JL: No, you shouldn't have. You were doing more important things. Why should you be over there killing people and killing yourself?

GT: *So you think that maybe you're experiencing guilt for the young men that came up in your hometown and died in Vietnam?*

RP: [Softly] Umm-hmm.

GT: *As hard as you worked, did you ever feel like, "Why me? Why was I the one to become successful?"*

RP: Oh God, yes. I beat myself up a lot about that. And then I met Ethel [his term for women].

PH: What kind of therapy do you have to do?

RP: The therapists massage my legs, and I walk on the walker. I hate that fucking walker, I hate it. She says that I'm doing great. And I say to her, "But I'm on this fucking walker."

JL: If you're physically diminished, that doesn't diminish who you are . . .

RP: Okay, then sit on my face . . .

JL: Oh, stop it, Richard. Oh God.

RP: See, I can't make you do that, so that's diminishment.

GT: *Does poverty scare you more than death?*

RP: No. I know about poverty. I know it very well. Very well. I just think, poor people, they're not nice. I mean, they don't mean to hurt you, but they're not nice. And I don't want to be around them if I can help it. Poverty will make people come in your house and say, "Motherfucker, you in a wheelchair, what the fuck are you talking about? You had fifty million dollars, and what did you do with it? Fuck—lemme have a dollar."

GT: *How did success separate you from the people in the street, from the very thing that had made you successful?*

RP: I never understood that having a dollar made me different or separate like you say. I never understood that the way, maybe, other people do. But them's the breaks, hey? Makes me sad . . . not remembering what I was going to say. I was going to say something. It was standing right here, and then I picked up this cigarette and it just said, "Fuck you."

GT: *Folks say success doesn't change you, but changes the people around you. Is that what happened?*

RP: Yep. My Uncle Dickie.

JL: Yeah, he used to cry, "Oh, Richard, I just need $50,000 to get that damn truck out the garage."

PH: Damn, what a paint job. Better have some sparkles.

JL: No, he'd come back the next day with rhinestone glasses with his initials and a truckful o' pot and a new pink polyester suit and ten women on each arm. Dickie was terribly lovable to Richard, and he knew it.

RP: He was what he was and I always thought, "If my father were alive, he wouldn't do this to me."

JL: No, Buck would have kicked some ass.

RP: Yes, I know so. But also, the other side of that is kicking ass was a bad habit with Buck. His leg would start kicking, and he didn't know how to control it. He'd say, "Down, leg! 'Cause your ass could go too."

PH: We got to say, man, we're trying to get you to understand that you can take *That Nigger's Crazy*, put it on at a gathering of Black folks in 1995, and you could still stop a party. With the wino and the junkie, and the cat hollering at Dracula—that's breakthrough stuff. I know you can't stand up on stage, but what you think about in terms of storytelling now?

RP: I don't know what I—that I think of anything. I think I'm tired. That's okay, but I'm tired.

PH: What about a Mudbone movie? The way films are done, you could do the whole Mudbone character sitting.

JL: Some people are interested in purchasing the rights and writing with Richard. I think Richard is Mudbone now.

GT: *Is it important to you that your work is remembered? That you have a legacy?*

RP: Yes, very much so. And you gentlemen have impressed upon me that I'm alive. I feel like that Frankenstein movie. "It's alive!" [We are interrupted by the sound of a helicopter overhead.] I have dreams about a helicopter crashing in my backyard. In the dream, I run out and help the people. Then the helicopter blows up. Only I don't know if the helicopter blew up while I was out there, or after I left. So that's a thought I have all the time. What am I going to do when this helicopter crashes for real in the yard? I don't know if I'll go out and try to help the people, or if I'll stand in the doorway and go, "It's gonna blow!"

PH: Have you figured out any mysteries you didn't know how to answer in the early days?

RP: I'm glad I didn't go to heroin. That was a mystery.

GT: *What was the difference between that and cocaine for you?*

RP: Good question. Stalling, stalling. Cocaine. I don't want to have to think about it.

JL: Coke just kept you up for five days and made you pass out for five years.

RP: One thing about coke was, I used to go to sleep and wake up and didn't know that I'd been asleep.

JL: Yeah, absolutely. You didn't get REM with that.

GT: *You get slim.*

RP: Hey, man, the hell I saw that time when I walked in the hall and saw a man. Jennifer said it was the devil, but I thought it was me, only skinnier than me, in black shorts. He walked through a door, then he walked across me and I said, "I'm going to leave this guy alone." I went into my room, looked around and said, "I saw me, skinny, in black underwear, and in my mind it was real." Nobody believed me.

JL: I think it was you, as the devil incarnate in reverse taking you to hell . . .

RP: Oh.

JL: [Laughing to herself] I do.

GT: *In the book, you profess that God is now asking, "Hey, Rich, you ever heard that phrase 'delayed gratification'? Good. 'Cause you've done had a lot of gratification . . . Well now comes the delay."*

RP: See, the difference between me and other motherfuckers is I want all the pussy. If there's three or four billion women in the world, eventually I want to fuck 'em all. And I will.

JL: [Sighs] You've had enough, Richard, to last ten lifetimes.

RP: There can never be enough to last ten lifetimes. I'm sorry.

– 1995 –

Richard Pryor

1940–2005

Unlike Biggie, Richard Pryor really was ready to die. When I interviewed him a few years ago, he told me what bothered him the most about MS was not being able to jump around like he used to, reminding us that this most verbal of men was also as physically comedic as Chaplin. For those reasons Pryor's demise was a sweet release, a right fitting and proper breaking on through to that other side. Yet it remains a mournful event for the rest of us because, like Baldwin, Pryor—or "Richard," as we knew him in the seventies, because he was the only Richard you could possibly be talking about—always seemed less a Negro celebrity than a beloved family member, one whose death automatically becomes a nostalgic reminder that better, funkier days are behind us. Like the equally monumental departures of Rosa Parks and Luther Vandross, his exit throws into relief the incredible triteness of Black American being in this historical moment.

I have no doubt Dave Chappelle remembered that the forty million bucks Pryor got from Columbia Pictures was the beginning of the end of his ability to control the forces around him and within him. But I also know that Pryor, like every Black badass muhfuh of his generation, made his public self-destruction into a work of art and an object lesson in how Soul is a terrible thing to waste. We're smarter about money, careers, and lawyers now thanks to Pryor and Ali, who not only raised the price tag on performative Black culture but rendered unto it the currency it has today. What's been lost in the Faustian nigga bargain is that fearless, breakneck do-or-die-for-the-art-and-the-People ethic Pryor and Miles and Nina and Jimi and Marvin brought to the Culture—that quality of tortured, intrepid, and successful Black genius looking into an abyss that winked back before they laughed, then leaped into that mother, spearfishing for pearls. Lauryn Hill, D'Angelo, and Dave Chappelle are as gifted, charismatic, and sharp as any who've come before, but you get the sense they'd all rather just be crazy than be the kind of crazy about your art that has you drop a *That Nigger's Crazy, Bicentennial Nigger, Is It Something I Said?*, or a *What's Going On, Let's Get It On*, and *Here My Dear* in rapid succession.

Point being that Pryor recognized how that kind of work demanded a protection of one's nuts, one's nerve, and one's nakedness at the same time. In that regard he may have been born with a leg up on the rest of us, for Pryor was raised in a brothel where his grandmother was the madam and his mother was one of her sex workers. So though he tried hard to be one of Cosby's kids early on, he could never be comfortable in that role. When he decided it was time to get real, he took his inspiration from two other mavericks of the depths, Lenny Bruce and Malcolm X. Two of his best friends, Jim Brown and Miles Davis, were also two of his major icons, but superfreakish Black machismo was not his mask or mission. What Pryor poked and prodded us with instead was raging Black male vulnerability served on a stick, his own mostly, hung way out there to dry and never snatched back. As in the bit where he tells his lover how he's going to get some new pussy and his lover cuts back with how he'd find some new pussy right at home if he had an inch more dick.

His was the kind of comedy that often took a bullet for the home team and wrapped the humanity of the 'hood in a bow. Pryor practically invented the golden-egg ghettocentricity we lust for today, but never just for a punch line's sake—as raw as he could get you knew he was only doing it because the Black and human truths he was relating demanded every nigger shit fuck that came out his monologist mouth. Never more refined as a storytelling tool than on *That Nigger's Crazy*, the greatest Black pop album of 1974 and we now know the most prophetic. That was the year you couldn't go to any Black home in Chocolate City, from Anacostia to the Gold Coast, and not find it on infinite repeat and folk laid out convulsed with hysteria. You have to go to Chekhov or Edward P. Jones to find small lives rendered with as much epic detail and epiphanic force as Pryor unveils on that album's "Wino and Junkie," a hellacious and ruthlessly hilarious vision of life beneath the underdog that erects a totem to Black male oblivion out of the parsed lines his Boswell wino relates about his junkie Johnson: "Nigger used to be a genius, I ain't lying, booked the numbers didn't need paper or pencil. Now the nigger don't know who he is."

The apotheosis of Pryor's commitment to truth in stand-up came in his film masterpieces *Live in Concert*, *Live on Sunset Strip*, *Here and Now*, and *Live and Smokin'*, where he rose from freebase ashes and essayed on addiction, self-immolation, and killing the car his wife was trying to leave him in, and indelibly portrayed himself having a heart attack like his aorta was using him for a conga drum. Any list of Pryor's greatest hits would also include all his Carson appearances and his sweet duets with Lily Tomlin. With the films there's good, there's great, and there's atrocious, but, Denzel notwithstanding, more solid stuff to choose from than any Black actor besides Poitier when you think about it. He's a scene-stealing riot-act in our favorite blaxpolitation flick, *The Mack*; a heartbreaking wonder of empathy as Piano Man in *Lady Sings the Blues*; a slapstick marvel in *Which Way Is Up?*; a working-class hedonist in *Blue Collar*; and a fake Spanish jokebutt in *Bingo Long*. *Silver Streak* and *Stir Crazy*, his buddy movies with Gene Wilder, are as good as crossover vehicles can get. There are some in there you wish he'd never made too, like *Superman III* and most egregiously *The Toy*, with Eddie Murphy's *Harlem Nights* not far behind. But though the qualitative gap between his stand-up and his films was wide enough to drive a fleet of Humvees through, Pryor's career in total was a masterpiece of how to keep it moving. While being Black ain't easy and the pretend Blackness of most comedians might be the epitome of laziness, Pryor took on the same challenge as Miles, Sun Ra, and George Clinton. With the fluidity of bebop and the cutthroat poetics of the blues, he made Blackness articulate and conceptual in ways that respected nuance and transcended mimicry and minstrelsy. So that Pryor's greatest gift to his comedic sons and daughters—Chris Rock, the *Saturday Night Live* Eddie Murphy, Dave Chappelle, *The Boon-*

docks' Aaron McGruder, Sarah Silverman, and Wanda Sykes—lies in demonstrating that while any fool can be Black and funny, coaxing belly laughs out of Black and confrontational requires the gift of tongues and a funny bone made of pure nuts. Peace go with you Rich.

– 2005 –

Gil Scott-Heron
1949–2011

You know why Gil never had much love for that ill-conceived "Godfather of Rap" tag. If you're already your own genre, you don't need the weak currency offered by another. If you're a one-off, why would you want to bask in the reflected glory of knockoffs? If you're already Odin, being proclaimed the decrepit sire of Thor and Loki just ain't gonna rock your world.

Gil knew he wasn't bigger than hip-hop—he knew he was just better. Like Jimi was better than heavy metal, Coltrane better than bebop, Malcolm better than the Nation of Islam, Marley better than the King James Bible. Better as in deeper—emotionally, spiritually, intellectually, politically, ancestrally, hell, probably even genetically. Mama was a Harlem opera singer; papa was a Jamaican footballer (rendering rolling stone redundant); grandmama played the blues records in Kentucky. So grit shit and mother wit Gil had in abundance, and like any Aries man worth his saltiness he capped it off with flavor, finesse, and a funky gypsy attitude.

He was also better in the sense that any major brujo who can stand alone always impresses more than those who need an army in front of them to look bad, jump bad, and mostly have other people to do the killing. George Clinton once said Sly Stone's interviews were better than most cats' albums; Gil clearing his throat coughed up more gravitas than many gruff MCs' tuffest sixteen bars. Being a bona fide griot and Orisha ascendant will do that. Being a truth teller, soothsayer, word magician, and acerbic musical op-ed columnist will do that. Gil is who and what Rakim was really talking about when he rhymed, "This is a lifetime mission: vision a prison." Shouldering the task of carrying Langston Hughes, Billie Holiday, Paul Robeson, and the Black Arts Movement's legacies into the world of 1970s African American popular song will do that too. The Revolution came and went so fast on April 4, 1968, that even most Black people missed it. (Over one hundred American cities up in flames the night after King's murder—what else do you think that was? The Day after the Revolution has been everything that's shaped America's racial profile ever since, from COINTELPRO to *Soul Train*, crack to krunk, bling to Barack.)

Gil, a student of radical history and politics, knew that if you were charged with the duties of oracle, troubadour, poet, gadfly, muckraker, and grassroots shit talker, your job was to ride the times (and the *Times*) like Biggie rode beats. To provoke the state and the streets and to progress your own radical headspace. Many cats of Gil's generation became burnt-out anachronisms from trying to wage sixties battles on seventies battlegrounds; some are still at it today. Gil knew the Struggle was a work in progress—a scorecard event of win some lose some, lick your wounds, live to poetically fight another day. Keep your eyes on the prize—a more democratic union—but also on the ever-changing same. Keep it about forward movement but keep it moving too. Not so difficult if you're the type of self-medicating brother who gets lonely if he doesn't hear the yap of hellhounds on his trail.

Gil described himself best as a "Bluesologist," a phenomenological student of "the science of how things feel." Hence the vast emotional range in Gil's writings—why the existential consequences of getting high and the resultant pathos could move that stuttering vibrato to emphatic song same as the prospect of South African liberation could. We call Gil a prophet, but most prophets don't prophesy their own forty-year slow death with the precision, poignancy, and nuance he did on "Home Is Where the Hatred Is," "The Bottle," and "Angel Dust."

Gil was better than most rappers because he leaned as hard on his vulnerability as other muhfuhkuhs lean on their glocks, AK-47s and dogged-out bitches, real or rhetorically imagined. His potency as a balladeer is vastly underrated compared to the shine shown his protest vehicles. If you yearn to hear your nutsack glorified, there are reams of lyrics ready to handily fulfill your manly needs. But the dude who needs a song allaying fears that his failure at marriage will cost him his children can only turn to "Your Daddy Loves You." I don't know what Gil's relationship to his and Brenda Sykes's only daughter, Gia Scott-Heron, was in his twilight-zone years, I just know that song owns the fraught distraught father-to-daughter communiqué category in the blues canon.

Even his most topical protest songs are too packed with feeling and flippancy to become yesterday's news, though—mostly because Gil's way with a witticism keeps even his Nixon assault vehicle "H_2OGate Blues" current. Gil's genius for sound bites likewise continues to sustain his relevance.

We'd all rather believe the revolution won't be televised than hear what he really envisioned beneath the bravado—that we may be too consumed with hypercapitalist consumption to care. And damn if we don't keep almost losing Detroit, and damn if even post-Apartheid we are all still very much wondering "What's the word?" from Johannesburg. And in this moment of the Arab née African Spring we may "hate it when the blood starts flowing" but still "love to see resistance showing." "No-Knock" and "Whitey on the Moon" remain cogent masterpieces of satire, observation, and metaphor. "Winter in America" is hands-down Gil at his most grandiloquent and "literary" as a lyricist, standing with Sly's *There's a Riot Goin' On* (and the memoirs of Panthers Elaine Brown and David Hilliard) as the most bleak, blunt, and beatific EKG readings of their postrevolutionary generation's post-traumatic stress disorders. "All of the healers have been killed or betrayed . . . and ain't nobody fighting because nobody knows what to save."

In death and in repose I now see Gil, Arthur Lee of Love, and the somehow still-standing Sly Stone as a triumvirate—a wise man/wiseguy trio of ultracool ultrahip ultra-caring prognosticators of late twentieth-century America's bent toward self-destruction and renewal. Cats who'd figured it all out by puberty and were maybe too clever and intoxicated on their own Rimbaudean airs to ever give up the call of the wild. Three high-flying visionary bad boys of funk-n-roll whose early flash and promise crash-landed on various temptations and whose last decades found them caught in cycles of ruin and momentary rejuvenation, bobbing or vanishing beneath their own sea of troubles.

Just as with Arthur, James Brown, and Sly, we always hoped against hope that Gil was one of those brothers who'd go on forever beating the odds, forever proving Death wrong, showing that he was too ornery and too slippery for the Reaper's clutches. Even after all those absurd years on the dope run, and under the jail, even despite all of Gil's own best efforts to hurry along the endgame process.

Hendrix biographer David Henderson (a poet-wizard himself) once pointed out that the difference between Jimi and Bob Dylan and Keith Richards was that when Dylan and Richards were on the verge, whole hippie networks of folk got invested in their survival. But no one stood up when Jimi stumbled, left all alone, like a complete unknown, not a Rolling Stone. Gil's fall at the not-so-ripe age of sixty-two reminds me that one thing my community does worst is intervene in the flaming out of our brightest and most fragile stars, so psychically on edge are most of us ourselves. Gil's song "Home Is Where the Hatred Is" seems in retrospect not only our most anguished paean to addiction, but the writer's coldest indictment of the lip service his radical community paid to love in the Beautiful Struggle. "Home was once a vacuum / that's filled now with my silent screams / and it might not be such a bad idea if I never went home again." Mos Def reached out, gave back—magnificently so—soon as Gil got out the joint three years ago, bringing a rail-thin, spectral, dangling-in-the-wind shadow of Gil's former selves to the stage at Carnegie Hall for the last time, if not the first.

But end of the day, here we go again, just another dead Black genius we lacked the will or the mercy or the mechanisms to save from himself. End of the day, it all just make you wanna holler, quote liberally from the Book of Gaye and Scott-Heron, say, "Look how they do my life." Make you wanna holler, throw up your hands, grab your rosary beads, do everything not to watch the disheveled poet desiccating over there in the corner—the one croaking out your name as you shuffle around him hoping not to be recognized that one late eighties morn on the 157th Street IRT platform, where, even while cracked out and slumped against the wall, Gil was determined to verbally high-five you, brother to brother.

We all kept saying, "Why don't he just 'kick it quit it / kick it quit it,'" but Gil, more cunning, wounded, and defensive than any junkie born, kept pushing back harder, daring any of us to try and rationally answer his challenge to the collective's impotencies and inadequacies: "You keep saying kick it, quit it / God, but did you ever try? / To turn your sick soul inside out / So that the world, so that the world / can watch you die?" What the funk else can we say in all finality now, but, uh, "Peace go with you too, Br'er Gil."

– 2011 –

The Man in Our Mirror: Michael Jackson
1958–2009

What Black American culture, musical and otherwise, lacks for now isn't talent or ambition, but the unmistakable presence of some kind of spiritual genius: the sense that something other than or even more than human is speaking through whatever fragile mortal vessel is burdened with repping for the divine, the magical, the supernatural, the ancestors. You can still feel it when you go hear Sonny Rollins, Ornette Coleman, Aretha Franklin, or Cecil Taylor, or when you read Toni Morrison—living Orishas who carry on a tradition whose true genius lies in making forms and notions as abstract, complex, and philosophical as soul, jazz, or the blues seem so deeply and universally felt. But such transcendence is rare now, given how desperate, soul-crushing, and immobilizing modern American life has become for the poorest strata of our folk, and how dissolute, dispersed, and distanced from that resource-poor but culturally rich heavyweight strata the rest of us are becoming. And like Morrison cautioned a few years ago, where the culture is going now, not even the music may be enough to save us.

The yin and yang of it is simple: You don't get the insatiable hunger (or the Black acculturation) that made James Brown, Jimi Hendrix, and Michael Jackson run, not walk, out the 'hood without there being a 'hood—the Olympic obstacle-course incubator of much musical Black genius as we know it. As George Clinton likes to say, "Without the humps, there's no getting over." (Next stop, hip-hop, and maybe the last stop too, though who knows, maybe the next humbling god of the kulcha will be a starchitect or a superstring theorist, the Michael Jackson of D-branes, Black P-branes, and dark-energy engineering.) Black Americans are inherently and even literally "damaged goods," a people whose central struggle has been overcoming the nonperson status we got stamped and stomped into us during slavery and post-Reconstruction and resonates even now, if you happen to be Black and poor enough. (As M-1 of Dead Prez wondered out loud, "What are we going to do to get all this poverty off of us?") As a people we have become past masters of devising strategies for erasing the erasure. Dreaming up what's still the most sublime visual representation of this process is what makes Jean-Michel Basquiat's work not just ingenious but righteous and profound. His dreaming up the most self-flagellating erasure of self to stymie the erasure is what makes Michael Jackson's story so numbing, so macabre, so absurdly Stephen King.

The scariest thing about the Motown legacy, as my father likes to argue, is that you could've gone into any Black American community at the time and found raw talents equal to any of the label's polished fruit: the Temptations, Marvin Gaye, Diana Ross, Stevie Wonder, Smokey Robinson, or Holland-Dozier-Holland—all my love for the mighty D and its denizens notwithstanding. Berry Gordy just industrialized the process, same as Harvard or the CIA has always done for the brightest prospective servants of the Evil Empire. The wisdom of Berry's intervention is borne out by the fact that since Motown left Detroit, the city's production of extraordinary musical talent can be measured in droplets: the Clark Sisters, Geri Allen, Jeff Mills, Derrick May, Kenny Garrett, J Dilla. But Michael himself is our best proof that Motown didn't have a lock on the young, Black, and gifted pool, as he and his siblings were born in Gary, Indiana: a town otherwise only notable for electing our good brother Richard Hatcher to a twenty-year mayoral term and for hosting the historic 1972 National Black Political Convention, a gathering our most politically educated folk (the Black Panther Party excepted) chose to shun, denying support for Shirley Chisholm's presidential run. Unlike Motown, no one could ever accuse my Black radical tradition of blithely practicing unity for the community. Or of possessing the vision and infrastructure required to pull a cat like Michael up from the abysmal basement of America and groom him for world domination.

Motown saved Michael from Gary, Indiana: no small feat. Michael and his family remain among the few Negroes of note to escape from the now century-old city, which today has a Black American population of 84 percent. These numbers would mean nothing if we were talking about a small Caribbean nation, but tend to represent a sign of the apocalypse where urban America is concerned. The Gary of 2009 is considered the seventeenth most dangerous city in America, which may be an improvement. The real question of the hour is, How many other Black American men born in Gary in 1959 lived to see their twenty-third birthday in 1982, the year *Thriller* broke the world open louder than a cobalt bomb and remade Black American success in Michael's before-and-after image? Where Black modernity is concerned, Michael is the real missing link: the "bridge of sighs" between the Way We Were and What We've Become in what Nelson George has astutely dubbed the "Post-Soul Era"—the only race-coded "post" neologism grounded in actual history and not puffery. Michael's post-Motown life and career are a testament to all the cultural greatness Motown and the chitlin circuit wrought, but also all the acute identity crises those entities helped set in motion in the same funky breath.

From Compton to Harlem, we've witnessed grown men broke-down crying in the hood over Michael; some of my most hard-bitten, 24-7 militant Black friends, male and female alike, copped to bawling their eyes out for days after they got the news. It's not hard to understand why: For just about anybody born in Black America after 1958—and this includes kids I'm hearing about who are as young as nine years old right now—Michael came to own a good chunk of your best childhood and adolescent memories. The absolute irony of all the jokes and speculation about Michael trying to turn into a European woman is that after James Brown, his music (and his dancing) represent the epitome—one of the mightiest peaks—of what we call Black music. Fortunately for us, that suspect skin-lightening disease, bleaching away his Black-nuss via physical or psychological means, had no effect on the field-holler screams palpable in his voice, or the electromagnetism fueling his elegant and preternatural sense of rhythm, flexibility, and fluid motion. With just his vocal gifts and his body alone as vehicles, Michael came to rank as one of the great storytellers and soothsayers of the last hundred years.

Furthermore, unlike almost everyone in the Apollo Theater pantheon save George Clinton, Michael now seems as important to us as an image maker—an illusionist and a fantasist at that—as he was as a musician/entertainer. And until Hype Williams came on the music video scene in the midnineties, no one else insisted that the visuals supporting R&B and hip-hop be as memorable, eye-popping, and seductive as the music itself. Nor did anyone else spare no expense to ensure that they were. But Michael's phantasmal, shape-shifting videos, upon reflection, were also, strangely enough, his way of socially and politically engaging the worlds of other real Black folk from places like South Central L.A., Bahia, East Africa, the prison system, ancient Egypt. He did this sometimes in pursuit of mere spectacle ("Black and White"), sometimes as critical observer ("The Way You Make Me Feel"), sometimes as a cultural nationalist romantic ("Remember the Time"), even occasionally as a harsh American political commentator ("They Don't Care about Us"). Looking at those clips again, as millions of us have done over this past weekend, is to realize how prophetic Michael was in dropping mad cash to leave behind a visual record of his work that was as state of the art as his musical legacy. As if he knew that one day our musical history would be more valued for what can be seen as for what can be heard. (Having said that, my official all-time favorite Michael clip is the one of him on *Oprah* viciously beatboxing (his 808 kick sound could straight castrate even Rahzel's!) and freestyling a new jam into creation—instantaneously connecting Michael in a syncopating heartbeat to those spiritual tributaries Langston Hughes described, the ones "ancient as the world and older than the flow of human blood in human veins." Bottom line: Anyone whose racial-litmus-test challenge to Michael came with a rhythm-and-blues battle-royale event would've gotten their ass royally waxed.)

George Clinton thought one reason Michael constantly chipped away at his appearance was less about racial self-loathing than about the number one problem superstars have, which is figuring out what to do when people get sick of looking at your face. His orgies of rhino- and other plasties were no more than an attempt to stay ahead of a fickle public's fickleness. In the nineties, at least until Eminem showed up, hip-hop would seem to have proven that major Black pop success in America didn't require a whitening up, maybe much to Michael's chagrin. Critical sidebar: I've actually always wanted to believe that Michael was actually one of the most secretly angry Black race-men on the planet. I thought that if he'd been cast as the Iraqi nativist who beat the shit out of Marky Mark in Ridley and Russell's *Three Kings* while screaming, "What is the problem with Michael Jackson? Your sick fucking country makes the Black man hate his self," Wahlberg would've left the set that day looking like the Great Pumpkin. I have also come to wonder if a midlife crisis Michael was in fact capable and culpable of having staged his own pedophilic race-war revival of that bitterly angry role. Especially during those Jesus Juice–swilling sleepovers at his Neverland Plantation, again and again and again. I honestly hope to never discover that this was indeed the truth.

Whatever Michael's alienation and distance from the Black America he came from—from the streets in particular—he remained a devoted student of popular Black music, dance, and street style, giving to and taking from it in unparalleled ways. He let neither ears nor eyes nor footwork stray too far out of touch from the action, sonically, sartorially, or choreographically. But whatever he appropriated also came back transmogrified into something even more inspiring and ennobled than before. Like the best artists everywhere, he begged, borrowed, and stole from (and/or collaborated with) anybody who he thought would make his own expression more visceral, modern, and exciting, from Spielberg to Akon to, yes, okay, smartass, cosmetic surgeons. In any event, once he went solo, Michael was above all else committed to his genius being felt as powerfully as whatever else in mass culture he caught masses of people feeling at the time. I suppose there's some divine symmetry to be found in Michael checking out when Barack Obama, the new King of Pop, is just settling in: Just count me among those who feel that in Michael Jackson terms, the young orator from Hawaii is only up to about the Destiny tour.

Of course, Michael's careerism had a steep downside, tripped onto a slippery slope, when he decided that his public and private life could be merged, orchestrated, and manipulated for publicity and mass consumption as masterfully as his albums and videos. I certainly began to feel this when word got out of him sleeping in a hyperbaric chamber or trying to buy the Elephant Man's bones, and I became almost certain this was the case when he dangled his hooded baby son out a balcony window for the paparazzi, to say nothing of his alleged darker impulses. At what point, we have to wonder, did the line blur for him between Dr. Jacko and Mr. Jackson, between Peter Pan fantasies and predatory behaviors? At what point did the Man in the Mirror turn into Dorian

Gray? When did the Warholian creature Michael created to deflect access to his inner life turn on him and virally rot him from the inside?

Real Soul Men eat self-destruction, chased by catastrophic forces from birth and then set upon by the hounds of hell the moment someone pays them cash money for using the voice of God to sing about secular adult passion. If you can find a more freakish litany of figures who've suffered more freakishly disastrous demises and career denouements than the Black American Soul Man, I'll pay you cash money. Go down the line: Robert Johnson, Louis Jordan, Johnny Ace, Little Willie John, Frankie Lymon, Sam Cooke, James Carr, Otis Redding, Jimi Hendrix, Al Green, Teddy Pendergrass, Marvin Gaye, Curtis Mayfield. You name it, they've been smacked down by it: guns, planes, cars, drugs, grits, lighting rigs, shoe polish, asphyxiation by vomit, electrocution, enervation, incarceration, their own death-dealing preacher-daddy. A few, like Isaac Hayes, get to slowly rust before they grow old. A select few, like Sly, prove too slick and elusive for the tide of the River Styx, despite giddy years mocking death with self-sabotage and self-abuse.

Michael's death was probably the most shocking celebrity curtain call of our time because he'd stopped being vaguely mortal or human for us quite a while ago, had become such an implacably bizarre and abstracted tabloid creation, worlds removed from the various Michaels we'd once loved so much. The unfortunate blessing of his departure is that we can now all go back to loving him as we first found him without shame, despair, or complication. "Which Michael do you want back?" is the other real question of the hour: Over the years we've seen him variously as our Hamlet, our Superman, our Peter Pan, our Icarus, our Fred Astaire, our Marcel Marceau, our Houdini, our Charlie Chaplin, our Scarecrow, our Peter Parker and Black Spider-Man, our Ziggy Stardust and Thin White Duke, our Little Richard redux, our Alien versus Predator, our Elephant Man, our Great Gatsby, our Lon Chaney, our Ol' Blue Eyes, our Elvis, our Frankenstein, our E.T., our Mystique, our Dark Phoenix.

Celebrity-idols are never more present than when they up and disappear, never ever saying goodbye, while affirming James Brown's prophetic reasoning that "money won't change you / But time will take you out." JB also told us, "I've got money, but now I need love." And here we are. Sitting with the rise and fall and demise of Michael, and grappling with how, as dream hampton put it, "The loneliest man in the world could be one of the most beloved." Now that some of us oldheads can have our Michael Jackson back, we feel liberated to be more gentle toward his spirit, releasing him from our outright rancor for scarring up whichever pretrial, pre–chalk complexion incarnation of him first tickled our fancies. Michael not being in the world as a Kabuki ghost makes it even easier to get through all those late-career movie-budget clips where he already looks headed for the out door. Perhaps it's a blessing in disguise both for him and for us that he finally got shoved through it.

– 2009 –

Miles Davis

In the winter of 1985 Collette Valli, Craig Street, and this reporter went to hang out with Miles Davis in the midtown NYC recording studio where he was making the album *Tutu* with producers Marcus Miller and Tommy Li Puma. Miles spent a few minutes before our formal chat praising the boot maker in Italy who had hand made the very fly leather footgear he was gliding around in that day.

. . . . .

Is it still important for you to be considered an innovator?

That seems to be the case. Because, you know, you can't always come off with a new style by yourself. I just realized that myself. This record here—*Tutu*—ain't gonna sound like the regular run-of-the-mill music because we got those voices breathing and stuff. Have you heard any of it?

Reminds me of Bootsy Collins.

Well, you know Marcus Miller walks like that. He walks like he plays, funky like that. Everything he writes is on the beat. When he talks he's on the beat. Most people who have good time talk on the beat. My nephew says when I say motherfucker it's different from anybody he knows because I say it in rhythm. You know, "That motherfucker." Trumpets talk like that [taps out a rhythm on the table]. The desks want to hear things that are on the beat.

Prince wrote me a letter and sent me two cassettes. He said, "You can use this with or without the vocal and here is some other stuff I haven't finished. You can finish it." But what I'd really like him to do is go into the studio with Marcus and I. He sent me a song that goes, "Can I stay with you tonight/Can I play with you tonight." We did it in California. He sent me the master tape. I cleaned it up a little bit and sent it back. He called me up and said, "It's frightening." Prince talks like this [Miles moves his hand across his chest, palm down, a kind of flatline gesture].

Monotone.

Not monotone. He's just saving his energy. You know if you laugh and talk a lot and shit like that it burns up all your energy. Emotions really drain you before you play or something. You know, if I have to do something that I feel, I can't let it out anyplace else. So I know the feeling he talks about like this [repeats the flatline hand gesture].

We talked to Wayne Shorter and he told us how much fun you guys used to have before and after the gig, hanging out, joking. He said that's what made the music happen for him.

I didn't do all that shit. Maybe it made it happen for him. Wayne is different from anybody you will ever know. He's very talented. He can write for anything. But Black people don't get a chance to write a ballet and stuff like that. They still go for all their old masters because all of those white people who have a lot of money, they demand it. "Play Puccini." Dance Theater of Harlem, I'm going to give them some music.

Did you hear Bill Cosby's speech? The NAACP gave him an Image Award. Now I been telling Cicely [Tyson, his then wife], "What the fuck is wrong with Bill? Why he always got to cater to this or cater to that?" Well he gave the damndest speech I ever heard in my life. I sent him a telegram. I said, "If I had fifteen minutes to live after Cicely told me to wait on her, then I'd want to hear that speech you made."

He said the reason Rosa Parks did what she did was because she was tired. He said when he started with *I Spy* everybody helped him out, but when he took his new show around everybody said they couldn't believe a Black man could bring a story that everybody will listen to at eight o'clock with no curse words.

Cicely breaks up when Bill does something. Me, I don't.

You know I'm a fan of Richard's [Pryor]. But when Bill made that speech, that was powerful. More powerful than Richard's shit, that kind of style. As a friend Bill is great, but not as a comic. But that speech? It wasn't a speech, he just started talking. And he said, "*The Color Purple*'s alright, at least it's a story." Said, it's one story out of a lot of stories of our lives. I never heard no shit like that coming out of him. I knew it was bound to happen one day.

I saw Bill with Phil Donahue and Donahue was talking this shit about how he just didn't believe Bill was that talented. And I said, "Fuck him." (I can't explain anything without cursing, but Bill can.) Donahue said, "Well you had the gun in *I Spy*."

So Bill said, "That was the first Black person to have a gun but I didn't get no women."

I couldn't believe Donahue man. Motherfucker.

He don't believe Bill has that much talent?

A man that doesn't respect you, he doesn't know what you're talking about. It's like me trying to tell a white boy how to groove. I can't tell him because he don't hear it. I was telling somebody something and my nephew said, "He don't know what you're talking about. He wouldn't know if you kept on all day." That's not saying all of them are like that. All of us ain't like that. But Donahue ain't never gonna change.

But back to the music. Where did I leave off? With Prince? It's a nice little song. It has that James Brown feeling. He plays guitar and I just play in the background. He made it about ten minutes long and I'm gonna have to cut it. I said, "Prince, what's the last half?" He said, "It's an epic." I said, "What?"

But he can play. Play just as good as these jazz pianists out here. He's playing some stuff.

I'm curious about what you think of the music you made between 1972 and 1975. Haven't heard you say much about it since you've been back. That was awesome music. Way ahead of its time. On the Corner, Get Up with It, Agharta. *How do you feel about that music now?*

I can't remember it. It was good. But that was then. If somebody asked me to repeat yesterday, I'd just say, "Man I can't do that." I wouldn't care if they were going to give me a reward. The last concert tour we were on, I happened to put that on by mistake and I said, "Oh shit, did we sound like that?"

We heard some tapes from Zurich.

[Suddenly turning to Craig Street] Why you looking at me like that?

How am I looking at you? It's just a look. No different than for anybody else. You can believe that.

Okay. Zurich, it was nice, but in my head I can't make that anymore. You know how people sound when they're gonna commit suicide or something? Can't do it anymore. Rubs against everything. Wake up at night and say, "Ooh shit." What if I couldn't hear anything beyond that? You play music?

I play a little guitar.

Well then you know what you're talking about then. I heard this guy sounded like Hendrix. What was his name? Violet? [Miles means Jimi's good friend and teenage protégé, now deceased, Velvert Turner.] Met him with Buddy Miles. Sounded just like Jimi. I'm gonna knock Buddy out when I see him. I wrote that *Jack Johnson* for him and he didn't even show up. You Motherfucker. If he says he got busted, it's okay. But if he says, "Well man, I missed this and I missed that," I'm knocking him out. Step on his foot or something.

Did y'all just go in and hit with Jack Johnson *or was that real worked out?*

Why do you always think that? Don't you know you have to work out things? You don't walk in the studio and just do shit like that unless you're me. Or Prince. And Marcus. I did write the introduction, what John McLaughlin played.

What was that last thing you did for Columbia Records with an orchestra? [Miles Davis, Aura, *Columbia* C2X *45332]*

Oh yeah, that was in Copenhagen. That was one of the reasons I left Columbia Records. When you're talking to somebody and they don't know what you're talking about like [former head of Columbia's jazz department] George Butler. He said, "We're going to call it contemporary jazz." I said, "No you're not either, not as much time as we spent on it." I told the engineer to keep the master tape. I told George, "Say something, do something about the music, because it's not that run-of-the-mill music." You can't just say this is contemporary anything. Talked to him about that three weeks ago and he sounds like he's going to do justice to that last album.

The scale is made out of my name so it can't be like other music, like just chords. I mean just that new scale will make you play something different. But I hope George isn't going to say contemporary jazz because it has about ten keyboards, four drummers, and the Copenhagen Radio Orchestra and it didn't cost that much money. Columbia refused to pay for it to be switched to digital and that only cost $1,400. They wouldn't pay for it. I said, Fuck 'em. I finished it with National Endowment for the Arts money. Warner Brothers would die to get that album; Columbia, I don't know what's happening up there. I don't care who I record for but Warner's, they have access to all the arrangers. In other words it's like leaving Soho and going over to Avenue A. That's where the real art is, not Soho. I mean people from Connecticut go down there just to be hip. Everybody I know that's slick is with Warner Brothers.

And George is still trying to get Wynton Marsalis to play all that classical music. That's not his roots. They're going to turn him into a white man. I mean, matter of fact they already have almost.

Now why you say that?

Because like Bill says, you don't go up into a place just because the white man wants you to dress up in the kind of suit he wears. And you don't just say, "They know what I'm thinking," because they don't. You don't give a man that much credit just because of his color. You don't just look at a man and say, "Well you can dance," because you got some of us out there who can't do like this [claps his hands on the 2 and 4]. I hate hearin' Black people say, "They." Like, "Well you know they don't understand me." They? Who gives a fuck? You do what you feel. Don't take for granted that Leonard Bernstein knows what you're playing. He doesn't. Or say, "Well now they know I have technique." By playing their music you're wasting your time with them. It's been played before. But you know some people just don't have that gypsy in them. To be free and try to learn something and put their own thoughts on records. Something other than interpreting something that Black people don't go to see.

Wynton could do a lot better because he's a good player. He's not original or anything but he could play those Black compositions. He could just tell Wayne Shorter, "Write me a trumpet concerto." Or Joe Zawinul, or George Russell. Since he's there now like he is, he could just stretch, just reach. He'd put a wrinkle in that system. There are a lot of great composers who are Black that he could help.

Even Sting hires some jazz musicians. I hate to call 'em that. [Former Sting bassist] Darryl Jones told my nephew that Farrakhan wouldn't let them take out some Black girls because they were playing with Sting and looked like slaves up there. They got all Black, that's a Black band, right? No, it's pop. [To himself] "Miles you shouldn't say those things." [The devil in his ear] "But they're true." What I do now? Man I'm not talking to you anymore because I get to talking and people lose their jobs and stuff.

Why did you play a pimp on Miami Vice? *[as Ivory Jones, in Season 2, Episode 6, 1985, "Junk Love"]*

That's what they wanted. That's easy to do, dope and pimps, that kind of stuff. That's all they do on *Miami Vice* is street stuff. And if you ever go to get some dope or something, go to cop, that's what you run into. Pimps and dope dealers, *Miami Vice*, I know all about that stuff. Cicely said, "They got you in the right part. It was easy to do, huh, Honey?" And they helped me out a lot, Philip Michael Thomas and Don Johnson. They act that way off camera. The director says, "Miles, Miles, Miles, you say, 'You want to get these girls? You want this red-haired one, you want to touch hair. You want a man? You want a midget and the girl?'" Shit like that. But they didn't put that in there. But that's what he meant if you own a whorehouse. That's the way you talk to a john or a freak. "What you want? Two midgets or one girl or what?" But I didn't say that.

That would have made it too real.

Yeah. It wasn't nothing. I did some music for the new Alfred Hitchcock show. Did you hear that? Listen man I wrote some music for when this guy is on his way out and kisses a blind and deaf white woman. Well, the assistant director, that motherfucker man, took that out, because it was his girlfriend that the guy was kissing. I said, "Cicely—white motherfuckers!"

She said, "It aint that. It's just too powerfully strong for that scene." Because the song said they were going to fuck in a minute. The assistant director heard the song and his girlfriend was up there and she played that part, man, and I said, "Oh shit, don't let them fuck that song up." I was sick. Plus he did it without me knowing it. I had all this shit in it. Shit like Ravel. I had strings in there, and the part where he got shot, they took that out too. So I asked [bebop trombone legend and Hollywood film composer] J. J. Johnson if they ever done him like that and he said, "Man, they do it all the time." The shit you think is okay, they take it out.

You going to do any more TV?

If they write a part that I can do, I'll do it. Billy Friedkin asked me to do something he's doing called CATS, about a group inside the CIA. People ask me, "How do you do it?" Because I do it every day out here. When I get up, I start. I went into a club, man, for the first time in four years. Went to hear my good friend Gil Evans. Chuck Mangione sat in. He ain't got business doing that. He should play what he plays. Herb Alpert wouldn't do no shit like that. You know when people do shit that ain't together it embarrasses me. He can't play like that and he knows it. Man, I had to go.

Are you going to see Patti LaBelle?

Yeah. Patti is going to lose her voice the way she sings. That bitch *over-sings*. Went with Cicely to see her and Al Green do *Their Arms Too Short to Box with God* on Broadway. They're too much. Now man, y'all have to get outta here so I can get into *my* thing.

– 1985 –

She
Laughing
Mean and
Impressive
Too

Born to Dyke: I Love My Sister Laughing and Then Again When She's Looking Mean, Queer, and Impressive

Some of his best friends are Black Lesbians. Some of his best friends insist that he's a closet Black Lesbian in disguise. As in his personal manager, the Black Lesbian entrepreneur, who invites him to a girl party thrown by two Black Lesbian promoters and quickly assuages his anxiety about bumrushin' with "How could it not be cool for you to come? You're dyke of the century." As in his ex-lover the creative director who tells him, "You were my great lesbian love affair, the man who solved the mystery of what making love to a woman would be like." As in his buddy, the ex-Criplet Yale NYU law grad public defender and Black Lesbian mack of the century who often cites him as her twin. While he finds the love and embrace of these comments flattering, he also finds them bewildering since he's never fancied himself that down with the cause. Even given his self-mocking paraphrase of the *Goodfellas* line, "All my life for as long as I can remember I've wanted to be a Black Lesbian gangsta feminist."

Well, maybe not all of his life. He can trace this desire back to the tender age of nineteen when he developed a mad crush on the brilliant filmmaker and poet Michelle Parkerson. Before he could declare his love, he deflatedly learned from her coming-out poem that she was a "Shopping Bag Dyke." As queer and mysterious as all women seemed to him then, Parkerson's moment of revelation made the distaff exponentially enigmatic. As professed in his response poem "the x-girl factor" that began "Black Lesbians Unknown / These the eyed and these the unseen women in the room."

Over the years, enchantment with Black Lesbians became a pronounced feature of his persona, his circle of friends, his writing, and his music. This is why he formed Women in Love, a band that performs songs like "Just Another Flybutch in a Black Leather Jacket," written after lustily observing two sistas mack each other out on Christopher and Barrow. He claims he's not interested in what Black Lesbians do in the bed—though he'll cop to being startled by the strap-on dick concept—eschewing the mundane male gaze agape at the vision of two women doing it. In this sense and others, such as his incapacity to derive pleasure from porn or fellatio, he believes he is truly the brother from another planet.

By his reckoning he is a voyeur of Black Lesbian style, Black Lesbian cool, Black Lesbian constructions of femininity. How Black Lesbians dress, converse, and play has always seemed as magical to him as what jazz musicians do and as smoothly coded. In his mythifying eyes Black Lesbians carry themselves with more relaxed sensuality than their straight or "het" (to use the parlance) sisters. A willing tool of Black Lesbian mesmerism, he perceives their world as one where gender boundaries are collapsed and personal agency is like the universe, forever expanding. Black Lesbians seem to exist in a more fluid realm of Black humanity, having liberated themselves from repressive notions of gender and erotica.

And of aesthetics too. Not long after Parkerson came out to him, he attended a Black writers' conference at Howard University where Barbara Smith, a Black Lesbian belle-lettrist, was pilloried by a straight sister for offering a prolesbian interpretation of Sula and Nel's friendship in Toni Morrison's *Sula*. When Smith was accused of sullying a good book with her "perversion," his now lesbian-sensitized skin began to crawl. Parkerson also influenced his reading of books and films—in particular, her gift of Isaac Asimov's *The Gods Themselves*, which imagines a genderless race of extraterrestrials, and Fellini's festival of androgyny, *Satyricon*, which she took him to see. Gradually he realized that being a Black Lesbian allowed girlfriends a vantage on gender that privileged Black female eroticism and fetishized polymorphous perversity. His ease in exploring human sexual possibility in his fictional writing dates back to Parkerson opening his eyes to her world of the Other. And further explains his compulsion to place Black women protagonists at the center of several writing projects.

Out of the romance with Black Lesbians Parkerson inculcated in his late teens and early twenties have evolved friendships in his thirties that find him engaged with Black Lesbians emotionally, intellectually, artistically, and financially. (For the record, he has white lesbian colleagues and acquaintances but no white lesbian friends—in fact, there have only been three white women he's ever considered close friends.) Due to antisexist positions he's taken in various essays over the years, and the profeminist stance he's taken in certain songs, he feels he is sometimes misidentified as a feminist man. He has often wondered whether he embraces feminism (and feminists, per se) to the same degree he embraces the ruffneck Black Lesbian gals who now run his life.

As he once confided to fellow butch-hag Arthur Jafa, "I'm probably too sexist to be a real feminist man. Too much of a dog, you know?" Meaning he believed himself too compromised by his interpersonal dealings to deserve true feminist ranking—"unless you can be a feminist and a dick too. What I'm struggling to be is antioppressive toward the women who enter my cipher. I don't know if antioppressive and antisexist are the same thing."

He believes he's never harassed, stalked, or physically abused any woman in his life. He will cop however to leaving a fair share of emotional and psychological wreckage in his wake. He wonders whether the absence of sex (though not intimacy) from his Black Lesbian friendships allows those to blossom minus the melodrama usually afflicting his relations with straight women. (Though not all his women friends are ex-lovers, note that his white women friends have evaded his trauma ward due to his anxiety about interracial sex, a phobia that may require therapy.)

Like Yanks for Wim Wenders, Black Lesbians have colonized his imagination, and he loves it. If his Black Lesbian friends don't absolutely love him as a genre, he loves them as a genre. Yet this realization begs the question: Why does he feel more comfortable receiving love from his Black Lesbian friends than he does from his lovers? Why does he expect his twentysomething Black Lesbian girlfriends to be more emotionally and professionally stable than his het ones?

He might answer that since Black Lesbians demolish his categories of masculinity and femininity he sees them as human and capable before he sees them as "girls" or, worse, as sexual prey. He might also answer that since he is not a "guy's guy" the "manly" aspect of Black Lesbians stimulates the woman in him. Or that Black Lesbians appeal to the science fiction nut in him, proposing we dream a world where Black women and men can interact without tripping over who's the man and who's the bitch. Black Lesbians have also enabled him to foresee a time when Black folk will find revolutionary solidarity by celebrating rather than chastising one another's differences.

Beyond his mythifying, he's come to recognize his attraction to Black Lesbians owes something to them being women he can have raunchy sexual conversations with without swinging from Clarence Thomas's nut sack, or the justice's hairy Coke bottle as the case may be. Once he discovered that Black Lesbians could be more carnivorous sexual players than any brother this side of Wilt Chamberlain, he recognized them as his compatriots in the consumption arena. This was a terrifying thought in one respect since it suggested that what was most alluring about Black Lesbians was their doggish side. Did he love Black Lesbians for the same qualities he'd found loathsome among the locker-room cadres? Had he gravitated to Black Lesbians because they were women who could dog out other women without penis guilt? Were Black Lesbians the vicarious instruments of his repressed misogyny?

This may be too hard a read on his affection for the Black Lesbian coven. He'll say he loves his Afro-Sapphic sisters because they are so fierce and "flava-full" like he wants all his niggas to be. Still the question remains: How does his lesbophilia explain his inability to sustain relationships with sisters who ain't gay beyond a New York minute? Could his Black Lesbian affinities run so deep that he has little love for women still under the sway of Dick, even when it's his own?

Before we answer that, however, I need to say, later for him, who is me, and his literary distancing devices. That's all good, but right now I need to talk to I & I about something that happened on the way to this forum. As stated above, my manager Angel got vocalist Helga Davis and me on the bill at a girl party. I'm expecting this small and intimate affair and it turns out to be a muhfunkin' warehouse jam. So check it out: 1:30 in the morning on a Sunday night and boatloads of sisters are lined up around the block near the Jacob Javits Convention Center dropping $15 a head to party 'til thabreakadawn with about 1,500 other Black women (some of whom I discovered had flown in from Los Angeles, Atlanta, and DC). I gots to say, seeing platoons of pleasure-seeking sistas arrive on the Manhattan shore to thoroughly enjoy one another's company did mess with my head a little.

For as I stood in the hallway awaiting clearance I came to a Gadzooksean epiphany, not unlike Charlton Heston's on sighting the Statue of Liberty at the end of *Planet of the Apes*, or Einstein's when he glimpsed the speed of light. To wit: there are no more straight Black women in New York City between the ages of eighteen and twenty-five. And as unlikely and ludicrous as that might sound, it forced me to recognize that we have come to a crossroads, if not a full-blown paradigm shift where lesbian exploration is concerned in the Hood. 'Cause see, this wasn't no academic-boho-lesbian-feminist crowd, y'all. (For one thing, there were next to no white women at this gig, a statistical signifier that this was an event sparsely attended by your academic-feminist-boho Black Lesbians.) This was predominantly a working-class Black girl affair where style, complexion, and beauty standards ran the fly ghetto-goddess gamut: from ruffnecks to baby-face killers; from backward-baseball-cap-sporting hip-hop butches to plastic miniskirted video vamps; from dreads to fades to fried-dyed-crucified-laid-to-the-side Brooklyn posse girls, all my sisters, every kind of Black woman you see every day coming straight outta Bed-Stuy, Fort Greene, Jamaica Queens, and the Bronx. They wuz representin' out that piece yo. And they were all fine, bumpin' in fact, not because I say so but because they thought so, moving through the club with an ease that said, ain't we Black women bad, the joint, the haps, the dopest, hippest, happiest thing on the face of god's creation right here, right now, up in here?

We don't have to assume all these women were gay, or bi, or even testing the waters to cull that hell-of-fine sisters of all sexual persuasions just want to have fun without the Black Man being much in evidence. And while I found myself a lonely corner booth to hole up in with my het-girl and did not trip when she went off to the dance floor, I realized my anxieties about occupying womanspace were moot since the sisters did not look upon me or the four other aimless Negroes up in there with disdain. They didn't track us, gay and straight alike, as if we were interlopers or invaders; we were more like irrelevant, invisible men.

As a Jessica Rabbit–waisted cleavaged-out Latina waitress offered tequila from a spray-cannon tubed up to plastic tanks strapped across her back, one thing crossed my mind: Obviously there is a lot more acceptance of lesbian sexuality among young working-class Black women than anybody's talking about.

If one out of ten people in the population are assumed to be gay, for Black women between eighteen and twenty-five in New York that figure should probably be revised to more like nine out of ten. Like greatness, we can assume that some sisters are born Black Lesbians, some choose to have Black Lesbianism thrust upon them, and others are just making up their sexuality as they go along. Whatever sort of sex drives brought these 1,500 sisters to party that night, there was undeniable allure to a space where male members were at a minimum. While I don't subscribe to the notion that women who love women do so only in reaction to male abuse, I did feel this communion was compelled by the alienation and antipathy Black men are producing in Today's Black Woman—or, more bluntly, how tired the superwomen are of putting up with Black macho bullshit. I know girl parties have been going on as long as there have been girls, but this particular one did have the effect of making me really think about why women really love the company of women. Outside of a southern Black Baptist family reunion, I couldn't imagine a straight scene where you'd see so many happy-looking Black women.

In discussions about this phenomenon, straight Black women friends have admitted to feeling like they are now a dying breed. My ace boon dream hampton, a wannabe lesbian if there ever was one, confesses, "I'd be a lesbian if I could get over my fear of eatin' pussy. I'd be one bad bitch. I feel like I'm out of the loop. My lesbian friends say things to me like, 'You still into boys? You funny.' Like I'm being cute or corny."

"When I hang out with my gay women friends," says Miss Ards, "I say, 'Damn, they look happy. I wonder if I've made the right choice.'" Miss Ards doesn't think all Black woman bonding is in pursuit of the pleasure principle however. "I went to Abyssinian Baptist Church for a meeting of Black women and made the mistake of asking, 'How can we bring Black men's voices into this discussion?' They just dismissed me and my question." The political ramifications of Black women creating exclusive support groups in the Hood suggest that Black Lesbians aren't the only ones for whom the Black Man is not the Answer.

Now comes the hard part. With these kinds of numbers and this kind of money to be made, we are talking a demographic here, a market share. If all these Black women were out the closet, even the straight ones, in their support for Black Lesbianism, there could probably be a Black Lesbian Barney's or Bloomingdale's or WBLS even. Leading me to wonder that if this many sisters are down, then why don't they rally behind their own red black and green flag? Why is there no Black Lesbian movement for empowerment?

For answers to these questions I went to my three card-carrying Black feminist friends: Ms. Rebecca Walker, the notorious bell hooks, and my aforementioned manager, the born-to-dyke Angel Rhyan. As far as brand names go, hooks is a self-described sex radical, Walker an avowed bisexual, and Rhyan a devout homosexual. Rhyan, twenty-five, shares the working-class background of the sisters who were up in the party. Having been "in the life" since she was sixteen, it's her belief that few of the women there would "claim lesbian as the identity that they are proud of." She recounted that when Helga sang "Flybutch in a Black Leather Jacket" at the party a friend heard a sister crack, "So what's she gonna do, sing about dykes all night?" A reading at B. Dalton's for *Afrekete: An Anthology of Black Lesbian Writing* (edited by Catherine E. McKinley) confirmed this. I counted as many white women and Black men among the thirty or so folk there as Black women. Subtract the editor and the three women who read from the anthology and it would seem that the surest way to get Black Lesbians to avoid a Black Lesbian event is to raise the Black Lesbian flag.

We do need to consider the specter of homophobia (if not anti-intellectualism) when questioning why the butches didn't flock to jock the book party the way they did the girl jam. As Walker pointed out, we don't know what forms of personal resistance Black Lesbians who may seem apolitical wage in the course of their everyday lives. These women, she says, could be engaged in antipatriarchal acts that we have no aware-ness of. I agreed, but asked how could these individual acts of resistance ever coalesce into a mass movement if nobody wants to grip the Black Lesbian label. Walker countered, in that New Age peace-love-and-power way I find more naive and more revolutionary than I'll ever be, that "we have to recognize that their brand of feminism may be valid too, and as potentially transformative."

I then proposed a hypothetical scenario wherein a gay Black woman is bashed and in the fracas slaughters her attackers only to be charged with murder. Would Black Lesbians make her a cause célèbre? Rebecca found my example extreme. Angel believed some of these apolitical clubhead lesbians might support my heroine as a victim of racism or sexism but not of homophobia.

We turn now to bell hooks for an opinion on undeclared lesbianism among these young women as well as some older Black feminist icons. In her opinion, "they're just greedy"—not for ducats, but for lifestyle options. She saw this as cutting two ways: living sexually undeclared spares you homophobic assault if you're already in that high-risk Black woman category, but it also eschews the burden of heroic lesbian representation. She went on to say that she was surprised no well-known Black Lesbian intellectual had taken up Audre Lorde's mantle, since Lorde's position presented tremendous critical freedoms as well as restraints. She feels sexual conservatism is another reason otherwise fear-defying Black women warriors don't come out. As hip-hop has proven, foul language can provoke as much of a ruckus in the Black psyche as white violence. Where sex talk is concerned, we all know folks who blush and blanche at the mention of words like "dick" and "pussy" in polite discourse, but who relish putting their lips on the very genitalia those vulgar terms describe.

For years we've known that many Black women look upon "feminism" as a nasty word, too. Even though folk like Alice Walker, bell hooks, and Ntozake Shange have all made critical and inclusive interventions into the feminist discourse, we can conjecture that many Black women continue to find the discourse alienating. Though Barbara Smith says in Marlon Riggs's *Black Is . . . Black Ain't* that Black women's apprehension of the word comes from fear of incurring the wrath of Black men.

Still, what if Black Feminism thrives in silence? What if, à la jazz, the practice of Black Lesbianism in the Hood is the real Black Feminist theory? What if, to build on KRS-One's cipher, real bad girls also move in silence? Perhaps there's more of a political statement to be found in Black Lesbians quietly boosting their ranks instead of walking around with big Ls on their chests. Though Angel is proud to be a Dyke with a capital D, she envies the women she calls "postlesbians." "They are who

I want to be when I grow up," she muses. "They're comfortable in completely straight scenes. I've always thought of myself as postrace in that way. I can be the only Black person in a room full of white people and not notice. But I just can't let my Lesbian identity go in the same way."

Just so no one thinks the irony (and the outrageousness) of a man writing this essay escapes me, yes I do feel weird and conflicted. Though I generally despise white writers who apologize for being white when they write on Black subjects, I've developed some empathy for them writing this joint here. Several Black Lesbian writers have told me, I might as well go ahead and put their stuff out there since they ain't about to. They're not interested in being consumed or on display. (It seems that Black Lesbian filmmakers are more interested in publicly probing contemporary Black Lesbian life, erotica, and politics. Perhaps there's something in the power of film that encourages Black Lesbian exhibitionists. See the work of Jocelyn Taylor, Dawn Suggs, and Cheryl Dunye.)

When I presented my conundrum to bulletproof diva Lisa Jones she said, "Well I can't write about that scene because I'm too much of an outsider." And like, I'm not? To which she replied, "You're an insider by virtue of your desire to be inside of it." You think I got a snappy answer for that rape-inflected colonialist reading, you got another think coming. In considering my desire to be in on the girls' world, I'm reminded of a rhyme by Q-Tip—"The thing that men and women need to do is stick together / Progressions can't be made if we're separate forever" and of this passage from André Breton's 1944 treatise on woman and war, *Arcanum 17*: "After so many female saints and national heroines fanning the combativeness of this or that camp, when will we see a different miracle extending her arms between those who are about to grapple to say: you are brothers. Is it because the yoke is crushing womankind that she definitively abdicates before forces that are obviously opposed to her? I see only one solution. The time has come to value the ideas of Woman at the expense of those of Man. It is artists in particular who must maximize the importance of everything that stands out in the feminist world view in contrast to the masculine, to build only on women's resources, to exalt, or even better *appropriate to the point of jealousy* making it one's own" (italics added).

In ways that I am only beginning to understand, my dialogues with Black Lesbian friends, and Black feminists in general, are providing me with insights critical to my becoming a nonoppressive and non-self-destructive Black Male.

Perhaps this outing of my own Black Lesbophilia is my way of returning an embrace I see essential to Black folks surviving the twenty-first century, of shouting out to progressive brothers and sisters alike, à la James Brown (and Rodney King): Can we still take it to the bridge, y'all? Can we even locate that muthafunka?

– 1995 –

Joni Mitchell: Black and Blond

My buddy Craig Street and I used to joke that the only people we knew who liked Joni Mitchell were Black people—like ourselves and Prince and Seal and Cassandra Wilson. Younger readers may only know her music from the sample of "Big Yellow Taxi" (Reprise 1970) Janet Jackson used on last year's "Got 'Til It's Gone" (Virgin). But Mitchell—a Grammy winner and Rock and Roll Hall of Fame inductee—has been an enduring influence and inspiration on modern music for some thirty years now. Again and again, she has stretched the "folk singer" tag she received early in career beyond recognition. Listening to her tell her life's curious, circuitous tale by phone from her native Canada, I was reminded of how peculiarly "Black," one could say, and even "hip-hop" her sensibility and attitude are. Mitchell has absorbed from the culture and sometimes stepped deep up in it—like her fearless foray into jazz and Brazilian rhythms, *Don Juan's Reckless Daughter* (Asylum, 1977), or when she collaborated with the mercurial and then dying bass legend Charles Mingus for a 1979 album, *Mingus* (Asylum). But she's not a parrot, a pirate, or a parody. In point of fact she's her own damn genre. Joni Mitchell is hardcore, Sun. And like you, she couldn't stand poetry in school but has always had lyrics to go. And at age fifty-five, she just keeps going and going and going.

"At a certain point in my career, only Blacks and women understood what I was doing. The white male rock 'n' roll press really didn't get it. They'd go, 'There's no rhythm here!' When in fact there was a lot. Or they'd say that it was too 'jazzy.' That fear of jazz thing. . . . And the harmony eluded them from *Don Juan's Reckless Daughter* on. The album got reviewed in a Black magazine—accidentally, I think, because I was dressed like a brother on the cover—and they got everything about it, from the cover on. Whereas the white press said, 'What's she trying to say, that Black people have more fun?' When *Don Juan's Reckless Daughter* came out, Charles Mingus found out about it somehow. I think, for one thing, that he was intrigued that I dressed up as a brother on the cover . . . so he was curious about me. Around the same time he found out he was dying [of Lou Gehrig's disease], Charles composed six pieces of music and flattered me by calling them 'Joni One,' 'Joni Two,' 'Joni Three,' and so forth. I'd been told he was a racist, but I was intrigued, so I flew out to New York to meet him. I thought, How much of a racist can he be, he's got a red-headed Irish wife? So anyway, I went up to his room, and he was in a wheelchair with his back to me. When I came into the room, he turned around and he said, 'The strings on "Paprika Plains" from *Don Juan's Reckless Daughter* are out of tune.'

"He had a sly and mischievous quality to him that I really liked. From the beginning we hit it off. So I set about trying to parquet words to his material that would be a suitable epitaph for him. [Mingus died five months before Mitchell's *Mingus* was released.]

"In the school system I went to growing up, poetry was taught very badly. On examinations, they'd give you a piece of poetry and then ask you to paraphrase it. And then they'd say, 'No, that's wrong.' Usually it was according to some authority, not even the poet themselves. We weren't taught the poetic spirit so much as correct interpretation. But more than that, I found a lot of poetry vague. Not all of it though. I liked the things that gave me more of a direct image and a direct picture, like Carl Sandburg saying, 'The fog comes on little cat feet. It sits looking . . . on silent haunches and them moves on.' That stuck with me. Anything that was pictorial like that. I like metaphor. I've got Irish blood, and a love for metaphor seems to come along with the DNA. But a lot of the themes on the poetry they taught us seemed to have nothing to do with my life as a young person. It had a lot of Latin in it with references to Greek gods. It was poetry for people who had read other books. It didn't come right off the page and directly into your life.

"But I always wrote poetry. I wrote poetry that I never showed to any-body. Like when there was some kind of disturbing incident, like when the pheromones hit. There was a kid in our group who committed sui-cide, and I wrote about that and then put it in a drawer. It seemed to me that I could perceive something that I would call now, the poetic stance. That's the soul patting itself. As opposed to coming from an idea of what a poet should say. If you ever read the poetry in the *New Yorker*, it's really awful. You go, Hmmmph . . . so what? Or you have to dig too hard to get the message. People say, 'Isn't that profound?' and I'll think, No, you know, it doesn't say anything to me. I didn't really like Shakespeare's poetry either. I always felt that it seemed to be written on commission. He wrote these poems of seduction, basically saying, 'You're so beauti-ful, you should reproduce yourself and let me be the guy.' And I think he was gay.

"As a writer I'm more interested in what passes before my eyes than I am in second-generation realities. I think the reason I don't like the obliqueness or the vagary of what a lot of people consider to be great poetry is that I prefer the direct hit of cinema. I think a lot of my music is just frustrated filmmaking. It's an attempt to get that in music. And Black people get it. At the last Grammys, this Black woman, who was the hairdresser, came up to me and said, 'Girl, you make me see pictures in my head.' And I thought, that's one of my favorite things anybody's ever said to me. Like, All right, somebody gets it. Don't try to analyze it. Just let the picture come as if it was projected right in front of you."

– 1998 –

Azealia Banks

Fantasea
(8/10; Yellow, Mixtape; July 11, 2012)

"Welcome to the After-Future," is how the poet Mike Ladd aptly summed up the deflationary aughts of this century. A moment in history when the choices for bold, visionary expression in popular media were reduced to Team Al Qaeda or Team Abu Ghraib, Osama Bin Laden or Bush-Cheney. Fortunately, we all live in the Afro-future now—a time when a two-term Black president with an African name that isn't "Fela" looms and super-WASP wacktresses employ conversational French to chortle about their niggas in Paris.

Praise Jah, the Afro-future also seems hell-bent on expectorating a race of Black Barbarellas: Sirius Space Vixen and warp-driven Black chicks who spit, think, and morph faster than George Clinton or Eminem, and lust after haute couture and nonstop public adoration like R. Kelly pined for his jeep. Michelle Obama, Janelle Monáe, Serena Williams, and Nicki Minaj have all staked out major turf in Afro-futurism's elite Olympian Valkyrie circle. In less than a year, take-no-prisoners Azealia Banks has propelled herself within mere parsecs of membership in this superfly soul sistren-only version of *The Hunger Games*. A razor-sharp hip-hop-soul reanimator in her own right, Banks is surely no less Out There.

Even so, the Question has been lingering: Since Michelle runs Earth, Monáe romps and stomps in her own android-insurgent Futuropolis, Serena smacks Wimbledon to Compton with racket-teleportation every time, and Minaj controls the vast intellectual properties of her inner Sybil, what could this New Jill named Banks do to rocket her ship over the moon?

On her spontaneously combustive and utterly boisterous seventeen-track mixtape *Fantasea*, the coolheaded Banks supplies the hyperkinetic answer: plunge her slice of the Afro-futuristic pie like a dagger into a motor-booty affair, a place where you'll dance under extreme pressure and struggle in vain not to get wet-up or spat upon three times fast—especially when Banks catches potty-mouthed *wrek* and lets "the pussy-game speak." The water-sports division of Miss Banks's Afro-future Amusements not only features bubbly, animated purple-lipped mermaid avatars, but song titles to do Sun Ra and Detroit Techno's Drexciya proud: See "Atlantis," "Neptune," "Fantasea," "Out of Space," and "Aquababe."

Never fear: This doesn't mean Banks is any less feral, ferocious, or fun than the more landlocked inner-city rap starlet that had yawl at hello (with last year's YouTube smash "212"). Just means she's invented her own way of stepping to this pop era's most daunting gladiator-level women's event: the Lady Gaga Challenge. In essence, this your-moxie-or-your-life contest demands a grrl dress up her most surreal sci-fi visions in hypersexual trimmings—and then strangulate the opposition. The main thing a naughty cyber-glitch like Banks must do is constantly bleep and bop slack phrases. These come at meteoric tempos designed to keep fools guessing as to whether she's a drum 'n' bass infected devil-woman or Devo, or a freaky-geeky, speed-rapping succubus who graduated from Performing Arts High School and loves Sondheim. "Put your hand on your dick and take a gander at this," she commands on "Chips," before her inner Willy Wonka takes over: "My pussy good / I lift it up / I took it slow / that chocolate body / that tootsie roll / that flirty Hershey / Lord ham mercy / do it to me don't hurt me, hurt me." Reciprocity is no laughing matter in Banks's lyrical boudoir though: "I'm counting back till he lick the crack / If he acting up then he's getting slapped / If I popped the trunk and he didn't clap?? I'll pop your rump and I'll spit you back."

For all the Afro-futurism Banks has got going on *Fantasea*, Banks hasn't exactly turned into Sun Ra in a skirt as far as basic subject matter goes. (Though we love the spacey jazz noodling that closes out a couple tracks.) She still loves saltily assaulting various straw girls—"these public pool bitches ain't fit to be mermaids" and as on "Fuck Up the Fun" demonstrate the various ways her rhetorical twat knowlogy can outswim, outfemme them: "We can freak with your man this week / . . . Your pussy game weak / think I'll let my pussy-name 'Peach' / I can disappear and let my pussy game speak, huh."

Someone once asked actress Kate *Underworld* Beckinsale to name her favorite body part; she answered, "My vagina." We don't know if Banks would concur, but she certainly loves being a riot of a grrl—rudest kinda gyaal in fact. Type who takes supreme lyrical pleasure in treating sex talk like her personal Kama Sutra.

She also has a work ethic second to none—an official album allegedly called *Broke with Expensive Taste* is on its way ASAP, but *Fantasea* already makes her sounds mega-industrious. There's damn near a different dope producer on every track and all are full of that most ingeniously hybridi-nized goth-house-dubstep-drum'n'bass-dancehall zeitgeist which now defines cutting-edge-raw riddim 'n' nois. Soul-damaged types like moi appreciate that Banks's musical-theater training has bequeathed her a rich, velvety, and melodious singing voice capable of both organically hitting notes found on the piano and rocking sold-out (probably not sta-diums just yet—well, actually she just played Coachella) shows without pitch correction. Fans of femme-MC legends like Lyte, Kim, and Foxy already show Banks much luv-luv. Her unabashed blueswoman raunch and tart rum 'n' Godiva vocal timbre hot flashes them back to the nine-ties hardcore.

Not to mention her warp-factor-nine elocution—how effortlessly Banks rains snappy rhyme combinations on heads like Sugar Ray Leon-ard once bongo-drummed on furthermuckers' noggins. "Hey, feel better than exing blow / Get high from a line turn text to notes / See these nig-gas gased up like Texaco / Watch your bitch pulling Pepsico / Ever since it was a nbo / Had magic glow, young dynamo."

She also proves on "Nathan," her collab with Styles P, that even the boys' club's most frank-and-beans rappers don't intimidate her spit a whit. "Do you motherfuckers wanna gamble with your luck? . . . / I'mma roll head, crack trips / You got the nuts? I'mma call your bluff like / "I'm next, small talk."

Your reporter is also enough of an old skool race man to confess his favoritism for sweet, grown, sassy, and limber brown girls from Uptown Harlem USA who got the Bouncing Betty skills to blast to smither-eens this charge-of-the-light-bright-brigade moment in race music and American pop kulcha.

– 2012 –

Sade: Black Magic Woman

Sade's five albums have sold an estimated twenty million copies domestically and more than forty million worldwide. Born in Ibadan, Nigeria, to a British mother and Nigerian father, Sade (nee Helen Folosade Adu) left the Motherland at age four when her parents separated. She first came to pop-music prominence in 1984 with *Diamond Life* and its momentous singles "Your Love Is King," "Smooth Operator," and "Hang on to Your Love." *Diamond* was followed over the next ten years by the high-charting *Promise*, *Stronger Than Pride*, *Love Deluxe*, and a greatest-hits collection, *Best of Sade*.

In 1992, Sade, thirty-three, dropped out of public sight. On the eve of *Lovers Rock* (2000), she and her band's first album of new material in eight years, Sade generously allowed *Vibe* a peek behind her fabled Garboesque mystique and confronted a few rumormongers along the way.

. . . . .

Greg Tate: Were there times while you were away that you thought, Am I ever going to perform again, get back on the horse?

Sade: No, because, for me, being a singer isn't like a day job. Coming back was all about finding a space in my life again where I could devote myself to music. A relative of mine got really sick, and I had to get involved with that. On top of that, I had my daughter and didn't really have any desire to write at all. To do it and not have that real need just wasn't right. It might have sounded the same in the end, but the purpose behind doing your art is everything. If you don't really feel it and you're just going through the motions, the results aren't going to be satisfactory. They'll be less than your expectations of yourself.

GT: Are you nervous about coming back into the current pop climate? A lot has happened out there musically.

S: No, because people either like us or they don't. We've never tried to please people in that respect—to do the thing that's hot. Because if we did that, we wouldn't do it very well. Whether this record sells a hundred thousand or a hundred million, I've already done my best.

GT: Lovers Rock has a serious reggae and dub influence. You're also addressing racism in a more pronounced way than ever before with "Slave Song."

S: I've always loved sweet lovers' rock music [reggae love songs]. That influence has always been there. "Slave Song" is a song I've always wanted to write but I was skeptical, because it's a big issue to address in a song. I didn't want to be pretentious and I left myself the out that if it didn't work, I'd abandon it. One day we started jamming on it in a really dubby way, and I started to feel the weight of the sea and what it must have been like on the journey over to America. Then I thought about Bob Marley's "Redemption Song" and thought, Well, what is my point here? Once I knew what the purpose was, I knew if I stayed true to that it would all work out. Did you like it?

GT: Yeah. Particularly the line, "Pray to the Almighty I don't do to you what you've done to me."

S: That's what it's all about really. I've always felt Black men are under more pressure than Black women in how they're perceived generally, but I've always had that problem of Black men sometimes becoming a parody of what's expected of them in a way—because all that resentment and bitterness doesn't really get you anywhere. That song is about learning from the journey and not becoming like the persecutor. Oftentimes when people despise somebody, they become exactly like the person they despise, then ultimately they despise themselves. The song is about remembering what our predecessors had to endure in order to get us where we are. Just to keep that in mind—the real, real struggle.

GT: You pick up on those themes in "Immigrant" too.

S: That one is more personal. It relates to what my mother told me about how, when my father first came to England, they'd be shopping and she'd notice how the guy in the store didn't want to touch his hand. That affected me a lot. It's something I've always remembered from being quite young. The song is about how dignified that older generation was. It gets to me sometimes when I see an older guy walking down the street and the shabby little things he's had to endure just to get there and [how he's] been made to feel dispossessed. Those men are intelligent people with a lot of pride who weren't given the opportunity in their time— there's much more opportunity now. We just see this old guy, but that's an intelligent person who has not been able to fulfill his potential and has made the best of what he's had. The song is like a salute to them.

GT: You were born in Nigeria. Do you have strong memories of Africa from your childhood?

S: I remember things more to do with the atmosphere, the smells, the food, and my grandma. I spent my twenty-first birthday in Nigeria with my father, just the two of us. What's really strange was that I didn't feel out of place or uncomfortable even though I grew up in this sleepy little village in Essex, England. Being in Nigeria was amazing, especially meeting my grandmother, who's dead now. She was an incredibly strong woman who built her own one-story house in the village. She was also a herbalist who traveled around the country collecting plants for medicines to make special fertility soaps for the women. She wouldn't let me use the soap; she said I was too young to get pregnant—like there were these loose sperm flying through the air. Her father was a witch doctor, and everything revolved around those beliefs. She wouldn't let me touch anyone or let anyone touch me, because she was afraid of "juju." She put newspaper everywhere I sat, like I was a princess.

GT: *When did you first become conscious of race in society?*

S: I was very privileged. I grew up in a small village where Mom was the nurse. They called her the Nurse, and my brother, Banji, and I were the Nurse's Children. It wasn't until I turned eleven and went to secondary school that I had any racist incidents. I always had good friends and wasn't afraid to fight for myself, but I went home and cried after the first day at this new school, just sulked in my room. These kids said things like, "Go black home, you'll feel white in the morning." Now it sounds so infantile but it actually hurt me. Then I realized these are weak people. So I decided, Tomorrow, that guy with the spotty face and the long greasy hair, I'm going get him first. The next day, they started taunting me, and I said, "Yeah, I'm Black, but you've got dirty hair. Why don't you go wash your hair and see if you can do something about your spots?" The others got so embarrassed and fearful that I might find their weakness that they backed off. I've always found it funny that they thought they'd insult me by calling me Black. I've always been proud of who I am and where I come from. I can't feel less. I think that's what "Immigrant" is about too. You might get called a Black bastard, but it's much easier if you don't feel like one.

GT: *When did you start thinking about music as a career?*

S: I don't know that I've ever told anybody this, because it was such a weird set of coincidences. I was going to Central Saint Martins College of Art and Design [a prestigious London art school] studying fashion and making clothes. I wasn't really into that the way everybody else was. I almost envied the other students, because they were so passionate about it. Like they'd go to these designers' shops and almost fall to the floor in reverence. I liked making my things, but I didn't revere other designers. I needed to make a living, because I didn't have a benefactor, and would have liked to do painting or writing, but fashion seemed sensible. One day, a friend and I went to get some weed and we were driving along a road and saw that it was really misty. We both commented on it at the same time and decided to make wishes. My wish was that I wanted something good to happen in my life. It wasn't anything specific, just a wish for a change. After that, we went to a neighbor's house, and Clint Eastwood's film *Play Misty for Me* was on TV. Then this neighbor guy said, "Hey, Misty and Roots, the reggae group, are playing tomorrow. Do you want to go?" When we went to the concert, these guys I knew from where I grew up were there. They said, "We've got a band but we don't have a singer. Do you want to sing with us?" And I was like, "What do you mean? No way." They said, "But you're into music; you must be able to sing." In other words, You're Black. You must be able to sing. They just kept pestering me to come in until they got a proper singer and in the end I felt sorry for them and went to rehearsals trying to remember how to sing in the proper key. But after I left that group, I was known as a singer. That's why the guy who managed the group Pride [the band that eventually became Sade] thought I was a singer and asked me to audition with them. It wasn't that I had these powerful singer wishes. The other thing I found out years later is that Stuart's [Matthewman, Sade's saxophonist and guitarist] favorite standard to practice on his saxophone was "Misty."

GT: *Many women have said that becoming a mother changed their voices, tonally and emotionally. Has motherhood affected the way you approach music?*

S: The whole thing has been affected by my daughter in a strange way. I think you do grow up a bit when you've got the responsibility of someone else, although I've always been the kind of person who felt a responsibility toward my friends and other people. When I had my daughter, Ila, Stuart said he was concerned everything would change. Then he realized everything is the same except there's just a baby there who everybody loves.

GT: *What's the meaning of your daughter's name?*

S: It means "the Earth" in Sanskrit. What happened was her dad, Bobby, who's a Rasta, was coming up with these amazing names from the Old

Testament, and I was poo-poohing all of them. I had this big book with names, a history of names, that a friend had given me when my daughter was born. We were at the seventh day, and on the seventh day in Nigeria you have the naming ceremony. I felt bad that she didn't have a name, so I asked the spirit of my grandmother to help me find a name for our daughter. I opened this book and put my finger on the Hebrew name Ayla, which means "oak tree." Then I closed the book, and after about half an hour I said, "C'mon, Mama, help me again." This time I put my finger on the name Ila and said, "Wow, I'm sure this happened half an hour ago; this is the same name." So I woke Bobby up, and he said, "Yeah, that's great, everything is I-la." I thought he was speaking in tongues. I said, "Hey, man, this isn't for the moment, this is our child's name for life." But he said that in Rasta, when you say everything is I-la, it means everything is natural and lovely and beautiful. They also call the calabashes that they eat out of Ila-bashes.

GT: *Your relationship with your band has endured a remarkable amount of time for the music business. More than fifteen years. What do you attribute that to?*

S: To them having more of a desire to make the next album than I do. To be honest with you, I don't particularly like being famous—maybe this is more an English than an American thing (no, I'd be this way wherever I was), but I'm uncomfortable with it. Don't get me wrong, I'm not ungrateful. I want to give and I feel a lot of love comes back to us. But if I could send a clone out, I would. I like performing live, but to actually be out there being the star . . . no. Send in the clones.

GT: *Your career has been distinguished as much by what you do as what you don't do—no duets or collaborations or songs for films; generally no remixes. Is that all part of a plan?*

S: I've always wanted to do one thing really well as opposed to doing many things fairly well. What's good about us is what we do as a collective. I like that fact that we try our hardest to do the best we can. Also, in a way, I'm quite shy and I feel comfortable working in our own little sphere.

GT: *What do you like so much about Spain, where I've heard you spend a fair amount of time?*

S: It's more like being in Africa, like halfway between England and Africa. They're more relaxed there. They've got their approach to life and family isn't prudish or rigid.

GT: I know you were married. . . .

S: To a Spaniard!

GT: So how do you feel about the institution of marriage now?

S: Well, I was never the marrying kind. I always thought that if you love somebody and you have a bond, you don't necessarily need to announce that to the world. Marrying doesn't make you love a person more, and marrying doesn't keep you together either. My husband was the one who wanted to get married. I loved my husband as much before as after I got married. Then we got a divorce.

GT: A lot of your lyrics deal with themes of betrayal and regret, the end of the affair, that sort of thing. Do you always draw from some deep well of pain when you write?

S: Yeah, and maybe that's why I don't like to discuss personal stuff, because I've put a lot of personal stuff in my songs. It's not all me, but I'm as sensitive to other people's feelings as to my own, and it gets imprinted. I don't really dwell on stuff, but it's obviously there when I come to write. "Immigrant" is a good example. Fame and money don't stop you from being affected by the real things in life that matter. You're as affected by what hurts people and leaves marks as anybody else.

GT: An article about you reported that a British tabloid was going to write a piece claiming you were a junkie, and then your lawyer called them and said you were going to get your blood tested and then sue the hell out of them. What was all that drama about?

S: That happened a long time ago. I wasn't making myself available, so people automatically assumed there must be a reason why you don't want to be on the national lottery show. They don't understand that maybe you have things to attend to in your life that are more important. The music is important, because that's what you give. But it's like, if someone says to me, "If you do the blah-blah-blah show you'll sell a million more albums," I'll say, "I don't care." It might seem ungrateful, but I'd rather be with my daughter or go to the park with my cousin, you know what I mean? Because, in the end, that's what you're left with in your life, your relationships. The media think that's weird and they call you reclusive, but the people in my local shops don't think I'm reclusive at all. But the media started inventing all of these elaborate stories. It made me upset at the time, but I don't mind it so much now. Because I know there are people out there who are going to slag off our album and slag me off for whatever and misrepresent me and believe I'm something that I'm not, but in the end it really doesn't matter. You can't be hurt by somebody who doesn't understand you. You can't let that affect you, because otherwise you'll get bitter and twisted and want to go break legs. Even if some of them deserve it.

– 2001 –

All the Things You Could Be by Now If James Brown Was a Feminist

It's probably safe to say that James Brown was not a feminist. James Brown was, however, a liberator of Black women. How do we explain this conundrum? If y'all knew my Aunt Mother Popcorn who felt herself liberated enough by JB's 1969 single to forever claim that steatopygic matriarchal title as her own street name, I'd really need say no more. Since you don't know Aunt Popcorn, hang on, s'gonna be a bumpy ride, maybe a bit of a stretch but Lord knows that ain't never slowed us down before.

James, as we already know, was the great emancipator of Black bodies in general. There is for Black social bodies, after all, a Before and After James picture waiting to be developed. In the Before picture Negroes can be seen dancing. In the After picture Negroes can be seen doing it to death. The difference is as profound as the difference between the day Negroes heard about the Emancipation Proclamation and the day we heard about the Black Panthers brandishing their performative right to bear berets, bandoleros, and arms for self-defense on the steps of the California State Capitol. Freedom does not always come from the barrel of a gun. Happiness may not only be found in a warm pistol.

James did not invent Black popular dance but he did bring it spring it out the closet. Out the juke joint, out the bucket of blood, out the Apollo, the Palladium, the Savoy ballroom, off the blue light basement wall, up off the storefront church floor. He made folk want to act more African again in ways not seen since Congo Square. Ways that didn't deny the dirt, the dynamism, or the dignity of those who had to populate these mean American streets. He gave us a music that brought the grind of the corner and the ecstasy of a Pentecostal prayer service into everybody's living room.

It was music built to expedite and illuminate the motion of an unfree and under-pressure people on the move. A musical performance that made it respectable for Black people to own rather than disown their bodies in public spaces. In so doing, James gave those bodies a venue for public spectacle that had nothing to do with minstrelsy or the white-gloved pantomimed Copacabana dreams of Berry Gordy, or, goddess bless her, Diana Ross. The gospel of James was not a gospel in pursuit of white approval, entertainment, or legitimacy, all the bane of African American existence to this day. He'd take those things, but with emphasis on the take and even more emphasis on his own terms. Like Harriet Tubman, James believed that freedom was a road that could be traveled by the multitudes. This is what we mean by utopic democracy. This is what we mean by social justice. This what we mean by funk. I can't let this moment pass without reflecting on this morning's panel and how in his *Revolution of the Mind Live at the Apollo Volume 3* moment, James reignited the classic still-recurring schism in African American politics between assimilation and repatriation, Booker T. and W. E. B., Garvey or Du Bois, separatism or integration, King or X, the ballot or the bullet; James Brown or Black Power tyros Newton, Carmichael, and Cleaver, the latter troika being the ones who truly posed the deepest realpolitik question of the era—Were folk going to be about the pursuit of perpetual revolution or the pursuit of revolutionary reform? Or even about an opportunistic, pragmatic bootstrap Afrocentric capitalist Black nationalist fusion hybrid of the same ideologies. Next stop Palestine or next stop Parliament Funkadelic, next stop Cuba, or next stop hip-hop?

At this stage of our postslavery history we have some fair idea of what it means to be a free Black man. Even if that man is, as revolutionary activist Viola Plummer once proclaimed upon her comrades' acquittal of RICO charges, "not free—just loose."

If you ask for my historical idea of a free Black man, free, loose, dead, or alive, I've got hell-a contenders for ya, ones that don't start with J. B. or end with Jay Z. Defining a free Black woman though—if I may be so bold—in music at least, requires more imagination than defining a free Black man because to the world a dead Black man can still be sexy. A dead Black woman tho'? Hmm not so much.

Riffing on the gender difference also requires a notion of self-mastery that has more to do with Buddha than booty, more to do with high spirit than fallen flesh, more to do with the pursuit of selfish satisfactions than worldly success, more to do with owning the young libidinous moment than the veteran image award. This is what we mean by she got a right to sling the blues. This is what we mean by "Must she holler / Must she shake 'em on down?" John Coltrane's famous Cousin Mary once said Trane played the way he did because he wanted to sing like the sisters in the church but couldn't. So Trane secularized their feeling and called it his own *Love Supreme*. Jimi Hendrix didn't call his music psychedelic, he call it Sky Church. This might be what Alice Walker meant by identifying Hendrix as someone who possessed the secret of joy. This also might be what Miles Davis meant when he described the highest state of musical achievement as "a spiritual orgasm."

Betty Davis, Chaka Khan, Grace Jones, and Meshell Ndegeocello are four all-the-way-live Black giants of super secular funk who took possession of their bodies in performance like those sisters in Trane's old church took possession of their heavenly voices. All four gave us music and performance that foregrounded their bodies as instruments of transgressive pleasure-taking—*HE WAS A BIG FREAK I USED TO BEAT HIM WITH A TURQUOISE CHAIN. PULL UP TO THE BUMPER BABY DRIVE IT RIGHT IN BETWEEN. CALL IT WHAT YOU LIKE WHILE I BOOTSLAM YOUR BOYFRIEND LAST NIGHT. IF IM IN LUCK I JUST MIGHT GET PICKED UP TONIGHT. FEELING LIKE A WOMAN LOOKING LIKE A MAN. SHE ONLY WANTED ME FOR ONE THING BUT YOU COULD TEACH YOUR BOY TO DO THAT. BECAUSE IM A WOMAN IM A BACKBONE / BEAR YOUR KIDS AND BE YOUR MOTHER TOO.*

The open expression of Black female sexuality in popular music may predate Bessie Smith but its lessons do not return to the overt text of said music until the early seventies and Betty Davis's 1973 debut album, which predates Millie Jackson's equally self-emancipated *Caught Up* by a year.

The band Davis and coproducer Greg Errico assembled was a who's who of Oakland East Bay funkateers from the era. There was Errico and fellow Family Stone founding member Larry Graham, there was Neal Schon and Doug Rauch from the Santana band, Hershall Happiness and Patryce Banks from Graham Central Station, the Pointer Sisters, Tower of Power, and the legendary Sylvester. Betty took those elements and gave us funk that emulated gutbucket blues mamas like Big Mama Thornton even more overtly than J. B., Sly, and Jimi.

Before the album's release, Davis nee Betty Mabry was best known as the twenty-year-old wife and muse of Miles Davis—the woman who to jazz puritans irrevocably corrupted his music and fashion sense within the twelve-month span of their marriage. She'd had a fledgling career as a continental fashion model and R&B songwriter before she met Miles. She introduced him to friends and peers Jimi Hendrix, Sly Stone, and her own circle of buccaneer women friends who Miles was likely stewing over when he cut the album *Bitches Brew*. Betty also says it was she who strongly suggested Miles change the title from the pedestrian *Witches Brew*. We now know Miles cut an album with Betty using stalwarts from his camp—John McLaughlin and Wayne Shorter among them. This album languishes in the Columbia Records vault as Miles sat on it, in fear says Betty that it would make her a bigger star than him. We also know thanks to funk historian and reissue label mensch Oliver Wang that Betty spent the next four years after their marriage rejecting several record deals—including one with Motown—because none gave her full artistic control. We also know that upon hearing her debut's first track, "If I'm in Luck I Just Might Get Picked Up," that the NAACP called her a disgrace to the race and that several church groups demanded she be banned from Black radio.

My fellow Howard University alum Lewis Flip Barnes who arrived at our beloved Mecca of Negro Education a couple years before me had the pleasure of witnessing a full-on Betty Davis performance at the school in 1975. My man Flip is a very earthy Gemini cat from Virginia Beach and an Alpha frat brother besides. Thirty-two years after the fact his verbal re-creation of Betty's appearance in Howard's gymnasium is an urban classic that honors all aspects of his brotherly pedigree, sexist and profane.

"Man I recall the line-up was Con Funk Shun, Betty Davis, Graham Central Station, just an all-star funky line-up. Well you know how Con Funk Shun used to stank it up, right? Well Betty came on and just stanked it up even more than that. Her band came out first jamming this cold hard nasty vamp and then she, like—I won't even say she came out onstage—, it was more like she OOZED out onstage. And she just looked luscious with that big ass Afro and those hot-pants and shit. She was just wicked and she looked like she could do it all night long, funky-wise and *other*-wise. I remember her lips and her mouth just moved so sensually, so rooty-vooty nasty . . . it was everything all good funk is spozed to be. And she was just everything brothers loved in a sister back then. Because her figure was like damn, not bulging but tight, sensual. And nothing they played that night wasn't funky fast and hard. If they played a ballad that night it was a hard, funky ballad. She was so comfortable being nasty too. Not in a Millie Jackson way but Betty just gave you raw nasty funk grabbing that mic and rubbing it between her legs like, 'I'm in heat—Can you handle this animal?' And we were all—all the fellas I mean—all there at the height of our testosterone wanting to scratch and pet that animal, and soothe it. Man she was just vicious. She was delivering funk as sexuality. But I also remember that after she did her thing and Graham Central Station came on, she was sitting on the edge of the stage with her legs dangling, getting off on Graham same as we were. Like wasn't no superstar vibe, it was almost like you coulda pulled her off the stage to dance with you if you dared. It was a great night and

I remember Howard's homecoming got softer and softer after that. Like on some Al Jarreau or some shit. I mean Al is kool but you know . . . Anyhow, other thing about Betty I remember was that she didn't have a hardness about her. Like she played hard funk but she wasn't hard like a dude, like MeShell sometimes seems to me. It's kinda amazing she pulled that off too when I think about it."

Why Betty Davis's career never seemed to catch fire for all the dynamism of her performance could be attributable to many factors—not least of which is never scoring a radio hit in what was becoming a softer and softer quiet storm/disco era. Scoring hits in any era though has never seemed a problem for Chaka Khan, whose career has been defined by mass-ass acceptance from the moment she came out the box.

What connects Chaka to Brown for me is in fact that she burst into our consciousness with wildcat action-figure physicality that no sister in R&B before her had prepared us for—not Nina, not Aretha, not the Supremes. Not even Tina Turner, who might seem to set the stage for Betty and Chaka Khan, but whose lack of control over her life, sexual and otherwise, onstage and off, marked her as less liberated and even less libertine.

Like Brown, Chaka Khan has never seemed less than in full command of her career, no matter who her collaborators were over the years. It's in fact difficult to think of another woman in the history of R&B before and since whose professional life seems as self-determined and unmediated by anything resembling a man, let alone a Svengali.

What was clear about Chaka from the beginning was that she projected an aura of indomitability rooted in her whole body—voice to viscera—a body capable of charismatic artistry and potency, vocal prowess and sexual mastery, self-renewal, triumph of the will, and sexual conquest. She was a female Stagolee figure, one who always seemed more capable of exciting and satisfying herself in ecstatic public performance than any lover, or orgy of lovers ever could in private, no matter how potent the drugs.

By contrast, the career of Grace Jones is unimaginable without the run of a host of Svengalis, a plethora of men who saw her as a sleek Black canvas to objectify and project upon just about every white male fantasy in the book.

Fashion photographers, French gay bathhouse devotees, her negrophile art director husband Jean Paul Goode—a cat whose visual impact on Kara Walker has yet to be properly recognized—not to mention Island Records boss Chris Blackwell, an impresario who saw her as more

Jamaican chanteuse than Eurotrash dominatrix. Jamaican enough, in fact to be paired with the greatest reggae rhythm section in the world in Sly and Robbie for a series of albums that crushed together a hybrid of dub, funk, punk, tango, and Edith Piaf.

What connects Grace to James more than the funk though is the unabashed recognition of her own physical form as a work of art, one that in her case could be Cubistically exaggerated, deconstructed, collaged into the realm of the fantastic and the future-primitive. On that tip, it's interesting to note that when she worked with Arnold Schwarzenegger in the film *Conan the Barbarian* he was so taken aback by her ferocity he actually described her as "an animal." Even more unfortunate is that Grace turned down the runaway slave sci-fi classic *Blade Runner* to do the James Bond film *A View to a Kill*.

Back in the early nineties when Meshell Ndegeocello played bass and was the only woman in our Black rock band Women in Love, our lead singer Mikel Banks always referred to her as the dick of the band. Her bass playing has had the effect on more than a few sensitive fellas. When our veteran virtuoso bassist friend Jared Nickerson recounts her immediate effect on the New York music scene, he notes that brothers didn't hear her and say, "Oh she plays good for a girl." "Brothers," says Jared, "went home and started practicing."

Since her debut album *Plantation Lullabies* in 1994, Meshell has emerged as an iconic triple or even sextuple threat—instrumentalist, vocalist, songwriter, hip-hop lyricist, composer, producer, band leader, and a highly unlikely (and highly suspect to some conservative types) sex symbol.

Of all the figures in contemporary Black pop, she may be the only one who compares to the James Brown of legend and to Prince as innovator across several key categories: band disciplinarian, funk orchestrator, fearless social commentator, genuine human enigma, fierce defender of her own artistic integrity. Musician, mother, Muslim, lesbian, the labels attached to her seem to proliferate by year and confound reductive explanations at every turn. The inability of the music business to find a box big enough to squeeze her mammoth talent into reminds us that certain Negroes defy rationalization or ready-made analysis. In the decade or so she was on Madonna's Maverick label, Meshell was repeatedly encouraged to work with the likes of Dr. Dre and once even P. Diddy—was in fact offered an ultimatum to work with Diddy for an unlimited budget, or work with former Cassandra Wilson producer Craig Street for a nickel. She took the nickel and made the critically acclaimed cult classic

Bitter. She was also repeatedly told by her label bosses that she had no sex appeal by dint of her boyish butch profile. This charge is belied by the fact that nobody in New York draws a hotter vortex of sexy folk out to her performances than Meshell, or has a more erotic effect on her audience. There are witnesses who will back me up when I report of Meshell shows where sisters who came to the show on their boyfriends' arms left the club caught up in same-sex rapture with their formerly straight BFFs.

None of this is surprising when you learn Meshell began her career playing in DC's go-go scene with Rare Essence and Lil Bennie and the Masters. Lotta folk only know go-go, Chocolate City's homegrown boombastic Afrodelic answer to the J. B. legacy, if at all from Chuck Brown's records *Bustin' Loose* and *We Need Some Money* or E.U.'s "Da Butt" made famous by Spike Lee's *School Daze*. Lotta folk ain't got a clue as to what the hell used to go down, and I mean way lowdown-to-the-ground *down* at a real DC go-go show. Back in the day a typical go-go triple bill could mean nine nonstop hours of pure cowbell horn and conga-accented funk. I once asked Meshell why she didn't put go-go in her music. She said because go-go wasn't a style, go-go was church, a religious service. And I had to concur because the spirits go-go set loose were more interested in freeing their own libidos than following the Lord. Long before anybody down DC way had seen the inside of a reggae dancehall, a krunk strip club or a girls gone wild video, a go-go audience could be found any given Saturday obliterating whatever difference you imagined between dance as African ritual and sex as a form of African dance.

What Meshell absorbed most from those symphonic/polyrhythmic funk masters James and Chuck Brown was an almost neurological inability to play a show that ever dropped the groove, lost an iota of intensity, or betrayed their work ethic or dedication to formal precision, even during improvs.

In conclusion I'd like to offer a pair of Black Zen paradoxes: My man A.J. once said that he thought Andy Warhol was so white that he was Black. Maybe James Brown was so masculine that only the hardest-working women in showbiz are truly capable of carrying on in the name of his jockstrap.

– 2007 –

Itabari Njeri

The Last Plantation: Color, Conflict, and Identity: Reflections of a New World Black, by Itabari Njeri

Call her Ishmael. In *The Last Plantation*, Itabari Njeri plunges into the chaos of American multiculturalism. What she comes up with is brave, messy, brilliant, and caustic. A dispatch from the outer limits of the country's internecine race wars, the book reads as an enlightened take on our national obsession. It might be the most idiosyncratic interrogation of race and identity issues in American life since Ralph Ellison's *Invisible Man*. It is certainly as nuanced and picaresque about the subject as that classic, and just as Afrocentrically incorrect.

Njeri spares no one from the scythe of her wit, not even her own grandmother: "A privileged Creole princess with servants of her own in Jamaica, she was, with her bearing, education, and British colonial accent, a perfect candidate for scrubbing toilets in America." A former reporter for both the *Los Angeles Times* and the *Miami Herald*, Njeri is also the author of a memoir about her Brooklyn girlhood in a troubled middle-class family, *Every Good-Bye Ain't Gone*. Echoes of that story and storytelling technique reverberate through *Plantation*, sometimes subtly, sometimes obnoxiously, always instructively.

Though a tireless and meticulous reporter, Njeri lives to demolish the Fifth Estate's fourth wall at every opportunity. Wrapped around juicy exposés of multicultural census-box fanatics, Black-Korean scrapes over the American dream scrap heap, and the carpetbaggery of pseudomilitant poverty pimps are cervical examinations, dizzy spells, and citizenship in the Prozac nation. Never gratuitous but often disturbing, these sidebars prove as germane, by the end, as what had seemed to be her main events. Discussing race demands that the conversation turn extremely personal if you push at it, and Njeri has no problem taking it there. As an interviewer she's relentless enough to push Cornel West, the Answer Man, into admitting to a blind spot (regarding the role of psychotherapy in African American psychic healing). Her praise of the roughneck ministry of Brooklyn's Johnny Ray Youngblood comes with swipes at his sexism, homophobia, and gangsta-rap pulpit style: "We want to deal with him and make him a fucking example. . . . We intend to send a signal to the street that we are not going to take this shit."

Reporting from the race beat requires a Baldwinian narrator, one not in denial about her own niggling racial obsessions. All objectivity freaks, get prepared to kiss Njeri's ass. What the author is most obsessed with is the fate awaiting Black folks' politics (and our folk politics as well) in America's tempestuous multiethnic future. Njeri is not the first commentator to note that Black and White relations aren't going to define or dominate the face of ethnic conflict forever. She is, however, in the vanguard of those out to provide Black Americans with a wake-up call regarding the whittling away of our deck of race cards. Updating Paul Revere with her cry of "The multiethnics are coming! The multiethnics are coming!" Njeri will seem as shrill and unconvincing to many Blacks as a Spike Lee finale. Because her rhetorical scalpel owes its incisive edge to our prickly tradition of race invective, even Njeri finds it impossible to discuss race without Black American rage holding center stage. The question becomes whether "race," as we know it in America, a creation of Black/White history and Black/White mythology, actually includes anybody whose identity isn't wrapped up in our dual legacy of color-coding. Though geneticists, as Njeri points out, no longer believe race even exists as a marker of human difference, this scientific fiction forms the bedrock of American racialism and continues to dominate issues of economic and judicial iniquity. Yet what Njeri brings to the table is vital—how America's Black problem shows up as a problem for America's newer immigrants from Asia and the Middle East. The story that occupies the bulk of The Last Plantation has to do with the murder of fifteen-year-old Latasha Harlins—shot in the back of the head by a Korean woman after a dispute over a bottle of orange juice—and the bizarre tale of the community's response to it. In three years of reporting on the issue for the Los Angeles Times, Njeri covered all sides of a highly politicized trial process. She seems to have practically moved in with Harlins's dysfunctional family and uncovered details about her killer Soon Ja Du's class background that got lost at trial.

Njeri's most bizarre tale unfolds via Patricia Moore, a corrupt and ambitious street activist who once had her eyes on a state-office prize. Njeri describes Moore as "a film noir style bitch" gone berserk in a post-sixties landscape where Black Nationalist politics could be parlayed into lucrative kickback schemes. This story, worthy of Brecht, needs to be made into a dramatic vehicle about the betrayal of Black Power by real-life blaxploitation actors.

In effect, The Last Plantation tends to be mildly intriguing and somewhat alarmist about multiethnic squabbling, and more revelatory about the country's long-standing policy of Get the Nigger and that power struggle's waste products, Niggers with Pathologies. For this reason, I believe Njeri's real subject to be not multiethnic warfare but the self-hate that hate has produced. With more nods to Ralph Ellison than Gunnar Myrdal, Njeri delves into how sick and crazy Black people have become after centuries of being made bottoms in our sadomasochistic and racialized social order. The adoption of this power game by new Americans abets the conflicts that arise between African Americans and all who deem themselves superior due to being anything but Black. As in the Asian taxi driver who drops Njeri off at her posh Los Angeles address, only to rebuke her with, "You not good enough to live here." Vouchsafing her own cool, Njeri lets on that while she has her moments, she is not as crazy as the brother who lost it when told by two Hollywood hostesses that "Nigger" was the name of their jet-black feline. (The brother in question choked one matron and slashed the other. He was eventually arrested while running away from the premises like a renegade slave.)

Like many of us who write about racism, racialism, and American Blackness, Njeri has made the pen her sword and shield against the rage within and the rage without. Her command of detail is microsurgical and maniacal. She lets us know, for instance, that she uppercases Black and White not as racial adjectives but as proper nouns, considering those usages as ethnic designations rather than indicators of complexion. (This is logical, since Black certainly encompasses a wider spectrum of complexions than the LaBrea tar pits, and includes a fair number of folk who could pass for White.) Hopefully this corrective gesture will incite a riot among those copydesks and style-book fetishists who pretend that lowercasing Black is sensible and not White-power jockeying taken to the grammatical level. Foremost among Njeri's missions is to make the world realize that all New World Blacks are already multiethnic rather than monoracial as both Afrocentrists and racists would have the world believe.

Out of her life and work Njeri has developed a deep understanding of racial mythology, and has little patience for those who perpetuate and, worse, profit, from its miserable fallacies, Black, White, or otherwise. Her portrayals of Black proletarians, politicians, and street activists are sure to ruffle some feathers.

– 1997 –

Kara Walker

Can we drop the bomb on the white boy too? Can we drop the bomb on the freak crew?—TROUBLE FUNK LIVE, *STRAIGHT UP FUNK GO GO STYLE*, 1981

So we're gathered here today to talk about Kara Walker—Kara Kara Kara/Tora Tora Tora. We take our quotation about dropping the bomb on white boys and superfreaks from the book of Trouble Funk, a quite extraordinary and legendary DC go-go funk band.

Let us first say that we don't think of Kara Walker's oeuvre in terms of individual works but as an ongoing saga, a never-ending story, an unfolding nightmare, a New World African Holocaust Memorial project. Which is to say we think of her work as a conceptual whole, one that confronts a central problematic of twenty-first-century narrative and political art. Namely how can art represent the unrepresentable, speak on the unspeakable, visualize the unvisualizable? How can it frame, screen, and project those events of mass-population subjection, suffering, and victimization we've soundbitten to death with our talk of ethnic cleansing, pedophilia, exploitation, rape, fascism genocide sexism and racism/white supremacy? How can art depict or even reference such events without resorting to melodrama, sentimentality, countersupremacy? And how do you do it in ways that are seductive, sophisticated, and sublime but still terrifying enough to leave the world, as Gil Scott-Heron once said of America, perpetually in shock?

The modern visual artist who takes on this problematic has to represent not just victimhood but the organized and systemic state power, which compels these crimes against humanity. The artist must find forms adept enough to reveal the rationalization and normalization of state-sponsored terror throughout the social order—not just by military force but by law, language, and social convention. The artist must approximate and appropriate the means by which the state can disappear a people's humanity through forms high and low—legislation, media, cartoons, journalism, slang, graffiti, rumor, spin.

All this has to be done as economically, efficiently, subliminally, and swiftboatingly succinctly as the state suppression of the marginal's microhistories. Such a task places a huge burden on the painter, sculptor, or graphic novelist seeking to artfully resurrect the fate of Jews, Native

Americans, peoples of African descent, Palestinians, Iraqis, Afghanis, Pakistanis, and Persians. This work must be accomplished in the gallery in a manner akin to those swordsmen in samurai flicks whose blades slice the neck so quickly the mind scarcely has time to register that it's been decapitated.

In her translations of slavery's rationalizations, pathologies, and violence Kara Walker reminds me of the Chicago Bulls superstar Michael Jordan in his prime—dark and majestic, cunning and lyrical, relentless and dangerous.

Akin to what Art Spiegelman did more mutedly in his graphic novel about the Holocaust, *Maus*, the more blithe, brutal, and spectacular Walker has reactivated and reanimated a visual vernacular meant to musically accompany the destruction and disfiguration of African personhood in these United States.

The caricatures created to voodoo and disappear a people's oppression are also meant to substantiate the superiority of the ruling class. Simply put, you can't be a master race without having hordes of readily violated slave bodies to prove it upon again and again. The role of the state's dominant visual apparatus is to soothe their guilty conscience and their victims' raging unconscious alike, to convince both parties that the most horrible things done weren't committed against anyone who could really be considered "human." Some find Walker's hypersexual and hyperviolent slavery fantasias offensive because they resurrect and mimic not one but two offensive programs—the aristocratic illusions of insane hillbilly cotton farmers and the coonification samboification pickaninnyification and thingification of a people whose enslavement rendered the Bill of Rights a scrap of lies from the get-go.

Walker oddly draws fire for reimagining and exaggerating something beyond dispute—the routine violation of Black humanity by the beneficiaries of the antebellum slave system. She has in fact done her work so well that we should want to protest or vomit if we stare at the work too long. Walker has said in conversation that she feels driven to make work that got inside of other people's minds and "private parts" the way racism had gotten inside of hers. There might be no point to her work existing if it didn't at least disgust and repulse somebody. In this respect, her most gone-ballistic critics are actually her best audience. They honor the work's horror show intentions in ways your more detached and esthetically impressed viewers never will.

Walker's most vaunted trope—her elegant hijacking of the genteel vanity form par excellence, the cutout cameo silhouette—instantly lent force and clarity to her foremost visual desires: to make a grotesque spectacle out of antebellum slavery's sadomasochism and bestiality subtext.

Walker's critics sometimes seem to have forgotten something she apparently hasn't—that her work can never be more disgusting, awful, or cruelly creative than whatever the real thing was. What her work does do best is recognize the legally sanctioned evil that antebellum slavery required of its upstanding and proper beneficiaries and dispensed upon its plethora of victims—victims who we should note didn't all go down after taking a few with them like Nat Turner (The Real Original Gangsta), who led the most successful slave rebellion of enslaved Africans in 1831 Virginia.

The heroic narrative of New World African struggle is a powerful thing and a necessary thing and Lord knows we love it as much as the next person. Give us your tireless Frederick Douglass, your Harriet Tubman, John Coltrane, MLK, Malcolm X, Motown, Black Panther Party, BLA, Assata Shakur, Chaka Khan, Michael Jordan, give us all those homegrown real-life tales of Black mythic gods and superheroes, and we too will savor them with relish. The critical and historical problem is that for every Harriet Tubman (who herself freed and led a thousand enslaved Africans from bondage to freedom) is that there were millions more, as she observed, that she could have freed "if they'd only known they were slaves." (As a relevant sidebar please note that all knowledge we have of celebrated self-taught African American artist Bill Traylor and his work is due to Traylor finally leaving the antebellum plantation where he was born when he was well into his eighties, and well into the twentieth century, after everybody he'd ever known, family, former owners, and overseers alike, were dead and gone.)

Walker's work is clearly not about American history's Black superheroes but the many thousands they left behind in the dust gone on their way to achieving escape velocity. Her work in its own quiet way recognizes acknowledging that the heroic narratives white supremacy keeps can't pave over for all the foul, degenerate shit that happened and keeps happening to Black people, here and abroad, simply by dint of skin color. In the American instance we speak of people who were once understood as the personal property of the same ex-owner class who turned lynching into a fairground circus family picnic–type event roughly five minutes after the Civil War ended.

We would conjecture that the real problem people have with Walker's work isn't just what she puts on the walls but instead that her loyal opposition doesn't want to see a behind-the-music version of the heroic narrative, complete with all the hidden, historical, and hideously unimaginable visuals that duly explain why the heroic narrative is actually so damn heroic.

This writer knows we as a people don't want to see slavery's horrors being depicted as routine because this writer lives in Harlem. And on any given day in Harlem you can find a group of militant brothers on 125th Street displaying and selling sepia-toned historic photographs of twentieth-century southern American lynch parties—pictures of strung-up Black men and their jolly white spectators. These images are of course the same sort of sepia-toned flicks that were once commonly sent as postcards thru the U.S. mail system. Please note that the fast-moving foot traffic of Harlem always seems to be moving that much faster past these brothers' enterprising open-air exhibition of the most grotesque violation and carnage.

Let it also be noted that the heroic narrative can accommodate those street merchants of African death's curatorial project in ways it can't Walker. Not only because Walker isn't a hard-core Hebrew Israelite brother from the streets capable of withering the white gaze from fifty paces away but secondly because Walker indulges the one thing the heroic narrative cannot and will not abide—deliberately tasteless "nigger jokes," a rude sense of irony, and a perverse desire to see how much Black self-loathing, abasement, and shame you can fit into one pristine right and exact punch line. Our good friend and trenchant observer of our folkways and mores Vernon Reid likes to point out that African Americans are the only people in the world who give out (and elaborately televise) Image Awards. This a party to which we suspect Walker may not soon be invited.

All these tendencies put Walker in the bawdy, scandalous hyperviolent storytelling tradition of the blues and hip-hop where heroes are zeroes with dollar signs attached to their noms de plume and the highest praise imaginable is "Oh snap oh no she didn't say that." As when Furry Lewis sang "I'm going to get my pistol / 40 rounds of ball / I'm gonna shoot my woman just to see her fall." As when Blind Blake sang, "That woman is like a tiger got ways like a bear / gun in her pocket, a dagger in her hair. / To keep her quiet I knocked the teeth out her mouth. / That notoriety woman is known all over the south." As when Biggie Smalls rhymed, "Nigga you ain't got to explain shit / I been robbing motherfucker since the slave ships with the same nine clip." As when Ice Cube waxed, "I'm thinking to myself, 'Oh why did I bang her? / Now I'm in the closet looking for the hanger.'"

The creative literature by African American about antebellum slavery does not constitute a huge shelf, nor does the visual library. For having the will, the wiles, and the stomach to even attempt to go there places Walker in the short-list company of Toni Morrison, Suzan-Lori Parks, and Edward P. Jones, among her relative and most relevant contemporaries.

The question one keeps hearing about Walker by even some of her friends, peers, and ardent supporters is, "How long can she keep doing that stuff?" Which is also to perhaps ask, "When is Kara Walker going to stop forcing us to look at this horrible stuff?" Walker's own stock, defiant answer to that question has become that she intends to keep making her work "as long as I'm Black and a woman." This dramatic placard of an answer of course then tends to beg the question of whether her work has become schtick, redundant, so marketable that she can't afford to stop, or even a kind of outsider artist obsessive-compulsive disorder. We'd like to think that subconsciously or not something else is going on. That Walker feels compelled to recognize the productive and destructive capacity of slavery's shop of horrors via her own relentless volume of production.

Of course Walker's images of an antebellum imaginary could not be more in touch with today's screeching graphic headlines—Abu Ghraib; Don Imus's knuckleheaded comments about the Rutgers football team; the Jena Six, Genarlow Wilson, and Megan Williams incidents—nor lest we forget about the Black woman found to have been held captive for weeks, gang raped, and forced to eat her own feces in West Virginia, or the firing-squad execution of Sean Bell, or the nooses that a few years ago suddenly popped up like flies all over New York workplaces, the disgraceful ways victims of Hurricane Katrina were dehumanized, traumatized, dispersed, and became a "disappeared" population. In total, all these recent events are not only proof of how viral and virulent American racism remains but of how visually freakish and subject to dismissive, infantilizing legal, political, and media spin Black American victimhood continues to be as well. Such events also point up the degree to which Walker's obsessive not-so-old-timey image making shows little sign of being rendered anachronistic by romantic head-in-the-sand notions of "postracial" progress and enlightenment. In this respect Walker's declaration that she'll stay at her task as long as she remains Black and a woman and sees the same old–same old happening reminds me of filmmaker and theorist Arthur Jafa's description of the slave trade's "Middle Passage" as an "Auschwitz on the water"—an observation that Jafa explains with the proviso that for enslaved Africans the worst was yet to come after their death-camp boat ride.

Good artists are master tricksters, utterly effective at getting us to look at some obvious marker while they're secretly obsessed with something else entirely. This is to say that while Walker's work is easily read as commentary on the routine violation of Black women, children, and men, it's really an indictment of patriarchy as a rationalization for all manner of permissible violence. If her work has any political power at all, it is the power to seduce, to beg the question of how much esthetic pleasure can be drawn from infants with adult penises thrust in their faces or homoerotic couplings of hanging-judge masters and emasculated well-hung slaves.

Race as we know it was invented during the Enlightenment, which actually means that whiteness as we know it was invented then too. This eventually led to the invention of the Black visualizations we know from coon art but not African art, life, and culture. There is then yet another way to read Walker's work as less about Black subjection and more about that fun-loving frolicsome place the white supremacist imagination would most like to return. A rendering unto Caesar of things already Caesar's, a restaging of Caesar's repressed, inflated desires which the artist is but holding an elephantine mirror to like an avenging reverse Medusa: converting Stone Age figures into hollow men with her serpentine scissorhands and obsidian gaze.

All this in turn leads to my observation that though Walker has taken much doodoo-kaka for her works' alleged palatability to the white gaze, she has also on evidence of her scorched-earth writings and ragingly sarcastic drawings done something even more radical: found a neat way to avoid being dismissed or silenced as the proverbial Angry Black Woman—a stereotype, archetype, or both whose voice is not generally known to generate much sympathy or audience among the world's power elites in politics or the art world, Condoleezza Rice excepted. Walker may in fact be probably the angriest Black woman ever to get a MacArthur if one judges by her writings and drawings—both sets of work being more charged with personal venom and meanness toward all, friends, lovers, and enemies alike, than her more famous, more flattened, more demurely savaging wall pieces. Our suspicion is that the technical demands of work she makes by cutting mitigates, mutes, and even subdues her own repressed desire to do some real-world slicing and sawing in kind. A surgeon once told David Mamet that the most important trait a surgeon had to possess was an innate lust for cutting stuff up. Given her own suturing legerdemain with scissors and blades, Walker likely would have made a great surgeon were she not subject to the same urges that made my Tennessee-born grandmother Callie White refuse to watch the TV miniseries *Roots*. As a barber then working on a U.S. Air Force base, Grandmother Callie said she didn't watch the program because she knew her own postbellum memories would stray her strop-razor hand as it deftly slid across a general's throat.

In the final analysis, whatever one takes away from or makes of Walker's work, we should all take some solace and be thankful that while we're all just momentarily visiting her gutbucket phantasmagorias, Walker has clearly chosen to live there.

– 2007 –

Women at the Edge of Space, Time, and Art:
Ruminations on Candida Romero's *Little Girls*

In 1685 Johann Zahn built the first portable camera body. Zahn's invention collected dust for 150 years before becoming commercially applicable in the nineteenth century. The camera obscura preceded cameras as we know them by about eight centuries. Evidence can be found in Iraqi scientist Ibn al-Haytham's groundbreaking Book of Optics, *published in 1021.*

Around 1827, Joseph Nicéphore Niépce and his partner Louis Jacques Daguerre produced the first photograph that didn't vanish on contact with the sun. They deployed a sliding wooden box camera that had been constructed by the Parisian inventors Charles and Vincent Chevalier. Niépce and Daguerre's chemical process dated back to research done by Johann Heinrich Schultz in 1724—a mixture of silver and chalk that darkened once exposed to light. Daguerre refined the process in 1836, lathering a copper plate with silver and smoking it with iodine vapor, which increased the recorded image's light sensitivity.

The invention of photographic lapel processes meant images could now be preserved in-camera and not by manually tracing them before they could fade away. Room-sized cameras—with space inside for only a few people—were the norm at first; compact, handheld devices were in wide distribution by the time Niépce and Daguerre got down to business fixing images to plates in the 1820s.

> What makes you think more highly of a woman? . . . to see
> her busy with feminine occupations, with her household du-
> ties, with her children's clothes about her, or to find her writ-
> ing verses at her dressing table surrounded with pamphlets
> of every kind? The genuine mother of a family is no woman of
> the world; she is almost as much of a recluse as the nun in her
> convent.—JEAN-JACQUES ROUSSEAU

When we're dead and buried no one will step forward to account for our souls. Not even our most intimate associates. Primarily because each one of our souls is so specific to our encounters with the light of the world. So specific to this life, this skin, this interior narrative we have carved out of our gazes, tongues, and silences, from the degree of presence we bring to our reflex and bone structures.

The infancy of the camera takes us back to the time before the fall. Before Woman Child and Man fell under the dominion of Images constructed for the commercial advantage of the dream factories. We know this about the camera in the time before the fall because in its infancy the camera does not seem bent on full possession of the human soul. That moment will of course await the advent of Hollywood and the end of unmediated human identity. The rise of Hollywood will also cleave the world in two—into those deemed worthy of the camera's love and those whom it shall merely and begrudgingly tolerate.

This is to say then that in the time of the camera's infancy (and our lost innocence) the subject has yet to become aware of itself as an object, as mere prop for the photographer's self-aggrandizement. The subject of the camera's infancy does not know herself as the subaltern stock of the celebrity subject. She understands herself as someone whose persona the camera must learn to honor, cherish, obey, and surrender to.

The infancy of the camera is also, of course, our antiquity. An antiquity born within the Eden of our modernity, the Paris of the nineteenth century. A Paris infatuated with both novelty and narrative, with all things newly invented and with all things that were novel simply because they were exotic. To this Paris we owe the creation of impressionism and Orientalism, the creation of Flaubert and the flaneur.

Thanks to Monsieur Flaubert we also know something of the death in life his society (and imagination) intended for the woman entombed in an age of alpha-male adventurism—a one-sided Eden filled with curious, globetrotting Adams and sedentary, domesticated Eves, women whose designated place was to be holed up in their propriety and petticoats when the world was being rediscovered, renamed, reshaped, remapped, and remade in the image of men who believed there was no limit to their discovery or conquest of new worlds—whether in the world's colonized interior or the outer reaches of their scientific and artistic ambitions.

These seventy-five paintings/collages/assemblages/bricolages by Candida Romero straddle centuries and genres, swamps and gardens, illustration and abstraction, portraiture and ghost photography, biography and mythology. Taken in total they introduce us to a lost world and a newly discovered continent of this Afro-Gallic artist's own making. Taken in total the painter's brushstroked reconstructions evoke temporality-violating voyages made to imaginary intergalactic wildernesses and to the civilized prison houses Flaubert's Paris had ready-made for the obediently feminine. Taken in total they recombine visions of hell and visions of paradise in bold, even brazen painterly masterstrokes that crossbreed gothic romance and science fiction as ingeniously and as impetuously and as terrifyingly as Mary Shelley's *Frankenstein* did. Taken in total Romero's project suggests the cartographically rendered recollections of a lucid dreamer and a schizophrenic time traveler, as if the artist was attempting to diagram the phantasmagorical place where the expeditions of Lewis and Clark might have tripped over the writings of Hélène Cixous, Toni Morrison, and Lydia Cabrera.

In these seventy-five works (and the seventy-five source prints included nearby) Romero demands we mark the distance between the feminine ideal of then and the restlessly self-inventing and unbound woman of now. But through her excavations and recovery of ladies in waiting a century and a half old (thanks to the collection of her collaborator, poet Pierre-Jean Rémy), also comes a Promethean overgrowth of ideas, intimacies, intimations, and insights about what sort of infernos and primordial stews these women may have kept bridled, bundled, buttoned, and repressed beneath their spirit-constricting and soul-squashing bodices and undergarments. What you view here then is palette-born abstraction turned Kirilian aura imaging, canvas-based abstraction turned polychromatic ghost photography.

To see these works as "about" the wanton wildernesses and Kirlian cosmic rays we speculate Romero detected and suspected lay within the bosoms of these postcard and family-album figurines is to also question our contemporary prejudice toward Other sorts of women—all those feminine Others who don't conform to our current Western notions of freedom, expression, and fantasy—to question whether, say, our own prejudices about the modern Muslim women behind veils and burkas might not also be to mistake costumed surface for sensual depth and to confuse cultural style with erotic potentiality. The uninhibited lyricism Romero uses to contrast her expressive determinism with her lost-and-found subjects' rage to repress often evokes both psychedelia and melancholia, not to mention nirvana and nostalgia, simultaneously. The exhibition's title of *Little Girls* is of course pointed and sarcastic, since it speaks to more than the gender identity of the deceased subjects—implicated as well is our own historical relationship to the subject of subjugation and democracy.

In this respect Romero's praxis brings to mind African American maestros of female body image and history such as Lorna Simpson, Ellen Gallagher, and Kara Walker. In this respect Romero's praxis also brings to mind some of this writer's favorite Afro-diasporic music of the recent past—Miles Davis's *Dark Magus*, Bob Marley and the Wailers' *Exodus*, David Byrne and Brian Eno's *My Life in the Bush of Ghosts*, J Dilla's *Donuts*, and anything by the Wu-Tang Clan; most especially Chef Raekwon's *Only Built 4 Cuban Linx* and Ghostface Killah's *Supreme Clientele*—all albums where the composers deploy what the African American cinematic theorist Arthur Jafa has described as "dub strategies"—the re-ignition and sampling of older rhythmic and melodic vernacular forms—hard-core funk, symphonic seventies soul, Burundi drumming, Islamic muezzin songs, kung fu film soundtracks—to contribute poignant feelings of loss and pathos to more contemporaneous, calculating, and distanced pronouncements on the state of things.

Dub strategies are also understood as a relentlessly repetitious means to inculcate millennialist and revolutionary desires for what has been called "future-memories": remembrances of liberatory things not yet seen. Repetitions activated as a means then to imagine as a kind of Proustean desire engine sent into forward reversal. A "Black to the future" operation bent on aurally and visually mimicking those immense antigravitational forces astrophysicists call "Dark Energy": mysteriously alive forces from the dawn of space-time unaccountably re-creating Big Bang velocities and galactic tomorrows in a cosmos which science thought was slowing to a celestial doomsday crawl and edging toward a Big Crunch. (One can also find in the sheer volume of Romero's work here an echo of the vertigo and trance-inducing repetitions heard in those composers' works as well—a recognition by the artist that in an age of attention-spans accustomed to blinking twice before leaving a gallery there may now be a need for painters to environmentally subsume the digital-obsessive spectator.)

There is also the proposition—especially at this point in our skeptical and disenchanted postmodernity—that paintings, like all mediated practices, signify nothing more at the end of the day than what they reveal about the limits of their medium and their makers. That at this stage of history, paintings are only about the contract made between the latent artful thing and the latent talents of its artful manipulator. That paintings now are really only about paint, or at best only about the expressive limits of paint in the hands of the painter in question.

After the advent of postwar jazz, abstract expressionism, and semiotics, painting and "social meaning" underwent a divorce which no amount of interpretive gloss could ever suture back together again. So these hybrid paintings, assemblages, and collages of Romero's are seductive more for the choices and strategies visible in them than for what they attempt to say about various kinds of femininities, subaltern and radical, antiquated and progressive. Or so we might be led to proclaim and move on were it not for the stickler of a social fact that women painters, and especially those of bicultural and Afro-diasporic DNA like Romero, are still not a commonplace of the contemporary Parisian art scene. And without there being any attempt on the artist's part (or by this writer on her behalf) to claim for her a genetic exception, the racialized hierarchies of the European art world demand that we acknowledge Romero as an ethnic exception to that world's totemic status quo—and to then move on. Or then move back to a discussion of the aforementioned choices, conceits, and strategies visible in her voluminous body of exhibited works.

Even the casual observer will note that there are a large number of Romero's works that border on monochromatic and feature thick, cloudy, and unruly gray-green masses of paint and an equally large number of those which are more colorfully festive and playful in nature. Romero attributes some of this distinction to falling in love midway through the five-year creative process which yielded her seventy-five dark energy experiments (with the more rainbow-hued explorations resulting from the artist's romantic transformation in case you have to ask). Of the more verdant ones I find myself especially enamored and enraptured by *Sisters*, where the diaphanous and crystalline delicacy of the crusty green patina appears to flirt with morbidity and disease via mildewed and fungal blacks, mentholated whites, and sunset-orange spackling.

In contrast note the floral delicacy of *Sweet Heart*, where petals of pastel blues lend a dandelion's effervescence to the proceedings. The red-splattered blouses on the siblings splashed across *Little Devils* manage to suggest both murder by shotgun and the eternal renewal of grass and forests in springtime. In this painting and several others corpuscular dripping combines with the insistent cognition of text as texture. Here

Romero makes us recall Cy Twombly, another artist for whom abstraction and openhearted (when not brokenhearted) allusions to nature painting are complementary grooves for an improvisational painter. A means to explore "rhythm and hues" in a sprawling freehanded fashion, seizing every possible occasion to do what the best hip-hop MCs refer to as "busting out in a lyrical freestyle."

The casual and the copious observer alike will no doubt be surprised by Romero's placement of the material and the concrete in the boxed-in works—the honeycombs that form archipelagos in *Fillette aux Trelons*, the regal moths that weave concentric flight patterns around the profile at the center of *Golden Butterflies*, the winged and climbing formations of gold leafing which festoon the airspace around *Petit Fantome*, nods perhaps to her love for the works of Joseph Cornell, but also a way of deliberately keeping the spectator swooning in tactile lust for the solid ornaments that adorn her dreamworld altars like doorknobs and portals.

Technically accomplished and self-taught, Romero owes some of her boundless enthusiasm and perspicacity with the possibilities of canvas and paintbrush to being born and raised within the Beehive, the famous and mysterious compound of studios which her mother, painter Simone Dat, continues to help coordinate in Montparnasse (and of whom it must be said is finally now undergoing her own rediscovery by revisionist critics and scholars). Mama Romero's 1950s circle had formed partially in reaction to André Malraux's controversial declaration that abstraction had become the only acceptable road for painting. One could also read Romero's work as a subtle reaction—a kind of tripartite attempt at rejection, rebellion, and reconciliation with her parents' and teachers' counteroffensive counter-Malrauxean practices. But you'll have to ask her about that.

Romero jokingly refers to her work as "revenge" for all the portrait painters photography put out of work in the nineteenth century. This statement draws us to a technically ironic gesture found in her use of a technique favored by impoverished painters of the fifties—one that involves the use of a powdered cheese product to extend the life of the artist's oils. Though Romero, we'll safely assume, isn't nearly as impoverished as those poorer old souls, she did find herself drawn to the crusty caked grit that she found could be built up by using this peculiar and alchemical mixture of oils and denatured, granulated cow products.

For a decade in the nineties Romero worked on a series inspired by Proust, specifically the zoological passages on sexuality found in *Sodom and Gomorrah*. That engagement served her well as preparation for the five-year undertaking toward this labor-intensive exhibition, *Little Girls*.

Not least because it led to her introduction to her poetic collaborator Pierre-Jean Rémy. It was at his suggestion that Romero undertook the morphing and mutating of her current projects' photographs, all drawn from his personal and exhaustive collection.

In that sense the work presents us with a double-curatorial gaze, a selection of disinterred souls in photographic stasis, souls twice chosen to address the past and the present (and their own presence and absence) from the votive graves prepared by Romero in a shaman-artist mode of her own devising. In the final analysis, what these simpatico creators Rémy and Romero have created together is a vernacular all their own—a way of allowing words and imagery to converse, commune and even celebrate the forgotten and ignominious souls of the camera-captive dead. A mechanism capable of stirring us to reflect that in art, as in life, when the dead come to speak, you can "bet your bottom dollar" that they'll be speaking in hallucinatory volumes.

– 2010 –

Ellen Gallagher

Though she may soon become an art world superstar, painter Ellen Gallagher has no desire to become an art world superstar. That explains why you're looking at one of her pieces right now instead of some hype photograph of the woman herself.

Some folks might question the sincerity of Gallagher's reticence since her current dealer is SoHo's Mary Boone, renowned for breaking such high-profile artists as Julian Schnabel, David Salle, and Jean-Michel Basquiat. But Gallagher wasn't too crazy about the photos that came out when the Mary Boone Gallery presented her first solo exhibition in New York this past January and was adamant about not wanting her picture in *Vibe*. She'd prefer that people look at the work and not at her, which is rather refreshing in this age of shameless self-promotion. Gallagher's achievements to date suggest she'll be around for much longer than fifteen minutes, but she's clearly bent on ghosting her way through the first quarter of her fame. Chalk it up to her New England background.

The thirty-year-old artist was born in Providence, RI, to an African American father and a social-working Irish American mother. Gallagher grew up across town from the wharves of Providence, where many of her Black ancestors worked as seamen, whalers, and longshoremen. She was also exposed to the art world early, frequenting events at Rhode Island School of Design. Her own work history includes time spent on a fishing boat up Alaska way and a stint as a union carpenter in Seattle. Her decision to become an artist came about after she realized that since she was going to stay in the upper working class no matter what she did, she might as well do something she liked. ("If you're betting on poverty, why not be a starving artist?" would be the logic there, I guess.)

The painting you're looking at is called *Elephant Bones*. There's a lot of deep personal code in Gallagher's work, and a lot of deep Black code too: She's like a one-woman Wu-Tang Clan where that's concerned.

Since Gallagher's work is conceptually coming out of an abstract-minimalist-type vibration, she's not trying to make pictures where you can immediately connect the dots—even after she's elaborately pointed them out to you and even when some of those dots aren't really obscure but familiar pop imagery from coon art, cartoons, and Black sitcoms. Listen to how Sister breaks down the multiple allusions buried in *Elephant Bones*:

"Those yellow jaundiced eyes that come in from right to left form a waterfall shape that's really a trunk, and at the base they turn white, which is like this tusk. And right there I've got these two pink minstrels, and in between the minstrels there's this elephant sniffing them. As you move out of the tusks, you go into these erased blue lines, and really what I'm doing by erasing the line is making a mark that's in the shape of an elephant skull. People didn't get that—or they got it abstractly because maybe I didn't draw a good enough elephant's skeleton.

"There's also a place on the tusk where I took a needle and made a stamp of minstrel eyes and lips. So you've got these little dotted blue lips and eyes. You know, they say the first language they found was these inscriptions on bones in China. So it's like these minstrel figures have been inscribed into this elephant's skull. This comes from an idea I got watching the Discovery Channel all the time. I think it's like nature porn. My boyfriend told me that says a lot about me, because 'all that's about is power relationships, so I don't know why you're seeing sex.'

"But anyway, one thing I saw on it once that was really interesting was about these elephants. An elephant comes across the bones and skull of its mother who has been shot by these hunters, and you could see this elephant was literally mourning her. They used to think elephants had graveyards and funeral rituals, while they know now that they don't have graveyards—but they're not sure about the funeral rituals, because they stand around in a circle and pass the deceased's skull around. They say that when elephants pass over antelope bones they don't give a shit, but when they pass another elephant's bones they'll pick them up and smell them.

"So for me the painting became about recognition of the American clown and the origins of that figure in minstrelsy. Like Ronald McDonald is a minstrel, you know what I'm saying? Like Mickey Mouse is a minstrel who's become this benign American icon. I don't know if you get all that looking at it. Do you get all that looking at it?"

Actually, where Gallagher's work is concerned, I don't think you have to get it to be impressed by its craftsmanship or its playfulness. In many ways, Gallagher's painting is the visual analogue to Thelonious Monk's music: hard edged, whimsical, laconic, eccentric, historically conscious, hypnotic, and precise. She's a bit of a recluse like Monk too. Keeping her studio up in Boston allows her to avoid social distractions and maintain the work ethic. Which is not to say that notions of artistic integrity have Gallagher afraid of making loot. A story from her childhood shows me this woman ain't never been nobody's fool when it comes to getting over on your creative work:

"Do you remember those ads for UNICEF? I started to like the idea of that controlled kind of thing in my backyard. I built all these wild obstacle-course things and charged people money saying I was going to give the money to UNICEF, but of course I kept every penny. It was a big neighborhood scandal. But I didn't send away for the UNICEF kit, so I didn't want to give up any of the money. I liked the control—and the fact that people had to pay me money to come visit my little world."

– 1996 –

To Bid a Poet Black and Abstract

Modernism, as we have come to know it, reflects the tension that has existed between Progress and Nature in Western civilization since the Industrial Revolution. The conflicting desire in Western man between wanting to be a free child of nature and hoping to become a self-made god capable of subjugating the natural order. In Western visual culture this conflict has resulted in representations meant to mediate the pitched battle between rationalism and spirituality that began raging in Western consciousness with the embrace of Darwin's theory of revolution. The decentering of God and the church that followed in Darwin's wake gradually transformed the financial barons of the Industrial Age into the new, privileged arbiters of human purpose, meaning, and salvation. The subsequent questioning of classic realism which began to show up in Western painting with the impressionists exploded into full-frontal esthetic combat after World War I via the movements known as cubism, surrealism, dada, and futurism, and later, after World War II, abstract expressionism, conceptualism, performance art, and minimalism.

The formal and philosophical debts all those movements owe various iterations of Black Atlantic culture—most specifically to the geometric shocks to the Western viewer's system supplied by traditional African sculpture and those introduced by improvisational virtuosity (and emancipating spontaneity) of Black American music and social dance—are undeniable. They are also well documented though still scarcely recognized by our art history programs and canons.

Some observers detect an anxiety in American art history about the Black presence in American modernism, particularly the presence of the Black abstractionist. This apprehension is of course a microvariation on the exclusionary racist logics generally at work in American society. Those logics work overtime to socially exclude the African Other from canonical parity. The specter of the Black creative presence is overwhelming in the American abstraction project. The legendary Black abstractionist Jack Whitten has described African sculpture as "the DNA of visual perception"—suggesting that the organizing optical principles of modernist visuality find their foundational apex in African art. Whitten has also made analogies between abstract painting and the philosophy of jazz, which he defines as an art form devoted to "the expansion of freedom," literally and figuratively. Any person born into Jim Crow Alabama as Whitten was would seem a likely candidate for the freedoms offered by abstract art making but Black artists drawn to abstraction are still not at the forefront of today's critical conversations concerning the modern Black art project.

The extent to which the Black art project feels a need to make a special case for Black abstractionists has a quality of the absurd about it, if only because the history of Black American gallery artists formally working in abstraction is long and deep—stretching at least as far back as the abstract paintings Beauford Delany and Romare Bearden were making in the forties and fifties. There is also to contend with the abstraction found in the quilts of Gee's Bend and the abstract work of self-taught artists like Bessemer, Alabama's Thornton Dial, and Lonnie Holley—all pointing to underreported and underrecognized traditions of abstraction in the Black Belt South.

When we survey the sixties and seventies we recognize bona fide schools of Black abstractionists working on both coasts. We also lay claim to a broad and rich legacy of Black abstract practice grounded in historical movements, both artistic and political—a legacy stuffed to bursting with a large cast of laudable luminary imagists: Jack Whitten, Norman Lewis, Al Loving, Joe Overstreet, Tyrone Mitchell, Mel Edwards, David Hammons, Maren Hassinger, Senga Nengudi, Fred Eversley to name a prominent few.

The uptick in the visibility, viability, and marketability of Black artists in the global art world has primarily been most rewarding for those folk who deal in figuration—those whose art foregrounds representations of figures or symbols that are readable projections of familiar inventories from the Black cultural matrix. This does not diminish the significance of the figurative work (or workers) nor is it meant to eschew the qualities of abstraction and conceptual provocation in the work of artists as disparate as Kerry James Marshall, Sanford Biggers, Wangechi Mutu, Kara Walker, Ellen Gallagher, Gary Simmons, and [the late] Terry Adkins, to name another more recent prominent few. But we can hope that one upshot of all their unprecedented access and success will be a utopic leap forward. By which we mean a critical embrace for Black artists whose tribal markings and mysteries may be so abstracted and encoded as to be invisible to the nakedly ethnographic eye.

Western modernism has long fetishized artists whose projects are described as esoteric, hermetic, shamanistic, oblique, secretive even. In this respect the modernist project has been very much engaged with a reenchantment of Western art as a magical and mythical enterprise where the liminal is prized more highly than what Duchamp called "optical art." Ironically, though this desire to sacralize and ritualize Western art making stems from the impact of African art on Europeans like Picasso, few Black artists have been adopted as fellow high priests and priestesses. The Black art project can now openly claim work that represents a Blacker liminality—work that is more obsessed with becoming than representation. A Black art whose raison d'être is to surrender the spectator to the presence of things unseen—ontological artifacts that prove to be as deeply felt as the most fugitive, freed-up, expansive, energetic, and complex of Black musics.

The five young artists chosen for Mocada's *Pattern Recognition* exhibition all share a very refined sense of high esthetic seriousness—qualities necessary to create abstract forms that convey gravitas and demand the viewer seek more than mere surface decoration. Kimberly Becoat, in response to some questions I sent the artists about their philosophy and practices, gave an answer that could be considered a summary statement for her colleagues and for the field.

"Abstract work is very spiritual in nature to begin with, whether I address it consciously or not. The minute I imprint another dialect onto a surface the work resurges as its own spiritual being. We are all natural storytellers, and what is meaningful in the exchange of looking at abstract work is that everyone, while initially looking at the artist's point of view, will go into their spirit and begin to connect through their stories—which opens up more unconscious interaction surfacing to the conscious realm. Those continuums will always make the connection more complete—as it is reaching past what one sees."

– 2013 –

"The Gikuyu Mythos versus the Cullud Grrrl from Outta Space": A Wangechi Mutu Feature

I'll play it first and tell you what it is later.—MILES DAVIS

I start in the middle of a sentence and move in both directions at once.—JOHN COLTRANE

We all do do, re, mi, but you have got to find the other notes yourself.—LOUIS ARMSTRONG

In exile: An exile. A fugitive. An INS case file. A perceived African American, pending. A Maroon. A Maasai mirror image. A Maasai woman-not. A Gikuyu cosmopolite. A Nairobi composite. A Gikuyu speaker like Ngũgĩ wa Thiong'o, though one maybe not so well understood by many back home. A Gikuyu gal gone rogue. A Riot Grrrl turned back to Africa. A gender-dysphoric witch in hiding. Somebody's mama. A natural-born feminist. A cultural anomaly. But no, not a fallen Luo hero lost in the wilderness like Barack Obama's daddy.

A self-avowed artist type from the age of four. A goddess in Bed-Stuy. A shout in the street. An African princess on lockdown in the valley known as Clinton Hill. They called her everything but a child of Ngai, Mumbi, Nyasaye, and Opondo. A question mark.

The Gikuyu word for a married or mature woman is *mutumia*, which means "one who keeps quiet," but we can find no known meaning for the name "Wangechi" in that language or any other. "Wangari" is a popular woman's name in Kenya meaning "of the leopard," but that's a different thing all together. We could translate Gechi Mutu into "Geechee Woman," though that might not be cricket. The artist herself says that after years of searching she found out her name is that of a forgotten dance, one discarded with the Gikuyu's "lost generation," those who were relocated to internment camps by the British in the 1950s.

It is also a cloaked name for one of the nine daughters of the Gikuyu's ancestors, the original human pair, Gikuyu and Mumbi. But another Other thang: Mutu and her work sometimes bring to mind the Luo fable of Opondo's children—and the boy who only stopped resembling a monitor lizard when he swam in the river. And one more thing: "Is Brooklyn in the house?"

A beast. A buck-wilding beast master. A bestiary of the southern wild. "No fish and no bushmeat" did most Gikuyu eat. FYI: "An egg" is the answer to the popular Luo riddle, "What is a house without a door?" By the way: God got angry with the Luo chameleon who appeared at his door with an offering of dirty white goat fat.

Wangechi Mutu is one twisted sister. A sister who willfully, wantonly, wonderfully, gets a whole bushel of sundry things twisted. Twisted things tend to go bump in the night. Like when your spooning hand runs over your furry polysexual lover's keloid scars. Like when Barack Obama and his SEALs, Team Six, ran up on Osama bin Laden.

Unlike Barack Obama's Luo daddy, Mutu's people in Kenya are Gikuyu. Twenty-two percent of the population of Kenya Gikuyu be. They are also known as the "highlands people." The ones most aggressively colonized, penally herded even, by the British until they rose up and launched a war of terror against British labor camps and displacement. These Gikuyu were yes, the same Kenyans known later as the Mau Mau. These are the people from which our Mutu issues (though this is not why we believe her to be such a twisted sister).

Both of Mutu's great-grandfathers were Gikuyu chieftains, which, in the Disney version of her life, would make Mutu something of an African princess if the Gikuyu were monarchical. But even African princesses can get the blues. Or like the saying goes, show me an unhappy childhood, and I'll show you an artist. Or perhaps just a mutumia who refused to remain silent from the moment she decided to be an artist.

I'm not too sure where exactly I came from. Like many an artist I was born with an inner restlessness, a heightened curiosity, and an innate weirdo-ness.

At an early age I understood that I wanted to do things creatively, en-

gage with people, look at things that were seen as unconventional, travel, experiment. But my first love wasn't art, it was music. I took classes at school and learned how to read music and play the flute. I loved to sing and make up dance routines in front of my mirror. I would paint my face, dress up, create weird alternate personas for my own personal music class. I knew I was a bit of an oddball—but not so much in school, more in my family.

I was outspoken and yet pretty shy. I was melancholic—still am—sensitive, and a natural-born feminist from a very young age. When I had my last epic fight with my father, at the age of sixteen, and told him he couldn't hit me, that I was leaving home and never coming back, I set off this powerful energy that catapulted me into another world, another reality. That freed me from the noose of an umbilical connection to him that I'd grown to resent. A year later I would be boarding a plane to Wales for high school, never to live in my parents' home again.

Selector REWIND: Prior to the "big fight," my father had seen me in an operetta called The Desert Song in which I played the lead, the "Red Shadow." I was at an all-girls school, and this was the first time we had put on a play with a male lead. So, lo and behold, little gender-bendery Mutu auditioned and was picked to play the principal part in one of my first forays into a very short-lived stage life. My father hated me in this role. The night he came to see me was the big night—the Saturday evening performance. This big night was followed by the chilliest, quietest drive home. I was heartbroken because I'd become a mini-celebrity in my school and beyond, but at home I think they were embarrassed of me.

Painfully, I actualized my second birth as a self-proclaimed, fearless, freakish, uprooted, creative type. In a way I "put a spell on me" that sealed my fate as a maker of ideas and a seeker of self-emancipation through transformation and cultural immersion. It was one of the worst and best things that ever happened. It began my painful understanding of what the difference is between being an artist and a famous person, and I didn't have the emotional infrastructure to deal with my loved ones' rejection. It wasn't really a deterrent though. I was a loner and the visual arts were a perfect lab for my kind . . . and besides, there were tons of similar cold-shoulder experiences from my family that made me more and more comfortable with the idea of creating in solitude and postponing, or completely eliminating, the need for an audience's reaction. Figuring things out for myself . . . tinkering around with materials and images to fulfill my own epiphanies first and foremost was something I learned very early.

In spite of the general lack of encouragement, I was, ironically, quite *competitive. This drive surfaced through sports, through the academic rigor in my tough Catholic school, through my attempts to get some attention from my parents, through my attempts to outdo my very well-behaved, very pretty, and clever sister.*

I read and watched and listened to a lot of stimulating things growing up in Nairobi, but not often were they made by people who looked like me or who came from where I did. The combination of an adventurous, inquisitive, creative mind and a desperate need to escape, to run away, to begin again on my own terms, made me want to make things I'd have loved to see when I was a young girl. I also had a burning need to prove that girls are fierce and fearless. All these things eventually carried me very far from where I was born but closer to the life I desired to live, really hoped to be living.

The fact that Wangechi is an internationally renowned Kenyan artist born of a high-muckety-muck Gikuyu bloodline who has lived and worked in a Bed-Stuy Brooklyn brownstone for nearly a decade should be, by itself, enough to qualify her as an "Afro-futurist." If only you, or anyone else, actually knew what an Afro-futurist really is. We could hazard to say that Afro-futurism, like Afro-punk, Afro-surrealism, and neo-hoodooism, are the default Black cultural nationalist imaginaries of this historical moment. This is to say, they are all broad umbrella terms for Black née Gikuyu creatives and Black née Kenyan collectivities that privilege Black née African identity, Black née postsoul self-determination, Black weirdness, and Black SF (alternately and fluidly meaning the genres of science fiction or speculative fiction, to critical theorists of the genre).

Duke Ellington once said that the only music and musicians he was interested in were those who were "beyond category." He also told Charlie Parker and Dizzy Gillespie that the worst thing they ever did was let critics name their (Black) art "bebop," because it boxed them in. Charlie Parker himself once observed, "They teach you there's a boundary line to music. But man, there's no boundary line to art." Once upon a time bassist and composer Charles Mingus begged us to consider "All the Things You Could Be by Now if Sigmund Freud's Wife Was Your Mother." If your father and mother were the grandson and granddaughter of Gikuyu chieftains you could conceivably be Wangechi Mutu by now. Even though Mutu will tell you she doesn't know where the funk she came from. She, who answers positively to the charge of being a "cultural anomaly." "I sometimes look at my parents and wonder, 'Where in the hell did I come from?'"

The dominant ethnic groups in Kenya, Mutu's Gikuyu and Obama's daddy's Luo, could not be more different, temperamentally or territorially. The Gikuyu primarily dwell in the mountainous and sometimes chilly highlands, and the Luo are fishermen who live in the country's more tropical south, near the Great Lakes, a part of the country the British found too uncomfortable to pillage and despoil.

While the Gikuyu largely converted to Christianity under British settler rule, the rural Luo maintained their original belief system and still proudly pass it on to their descendants.

Mutu recalls her devout grandmother almost never discussing the Gikuyu's cultural past. On the other hand, she also recalls her Mau Mau–generation grandparents as being far more politically "radical" than either of her parents. She recalls that her father even came back from university studies in 1960s Michigan as something of an irate anticommunist. Kenya was never in any danger of turning Marxist, not even when Obama's daddy was briefly in Jomo Kenyatta's government. Obama's dad believed the postrevolutionary government should nationalize all the Western industries and corporations then in Kenya.

(These notions of ripping off The Man and giving back to The Motherland are ones Obama Sr. had the temerity to lay out in a white paper submitted to the State Department. This is what capsized Papa Obama's career in government and led to the downward spiral that Obama fils describes in *Dreams of My Father*.)

It is perhaps a necessary requisite of the modernist credo (and its various posts) that artists of any consequence must erase all traces of biography in their work. You therefore do not need to know that Wangechi is Kenyan and Gikuyu and not Luo to receive visual pleasure and intellectual stimulation from her work. Since most Americans, Afro or Euro, have little reason to think about Africans at all in any sort of nuanced way, Mutu's Africanness, like that of Obama pere, has largely been rendered a sidebar to the Mutu story. The world at large is generally more familiar with her as this young gifted Black beautiful successful contemporary artist with an exotic name who is Nairobi-Wales-Yale educated, Studio Museum A.I.R. program–vetted. One who makes spectacular work that spectacularly, obliquely, and conceptually alludes to many popular modern themes + phenomena + operations + apparitions: sex, death, disease, mutilation, blood sacrifices, boils, tumors, pestilence, amputation, cancer, monstrosity, sadomasochism, deformity, viral infection, biotoxins, air- and waterborne contagions, biological warfare, gun violence, mutation, nuclear winter, deforestation, pollution, genocide, genital mutilation, post-Holocaust wastes, and landscape gardening.

Mutu has made a series of videos in which she as protagonist emblematizes the horrors of the Middle Passage, Rwanda, madness, homelessness. Her installation *Exhuming Gluttony* can be seen as her riff on How the West Was Won, though there are subtle allusions to her bovine-throat-slitting Maasai homeboys in there too if you look hard enough.

We could not begin to tell you what is undeniably Kenyan or Gikuyu about Wangechi's art. Even as sophistry, this would be so much easier if her people were rural southern buck-wild Luo and not the more seminal, northerly, sedate, God-fearing, urbanized, middle-class Gikuyu.

We do know these tidbits however: All the major deities in the Luo pantheon are thought by some scholars to be goddesses. The Luo early on in their encounters with British colonizers (or the same's evangelical missionary frontmen) found Christianity to be a bore and hostile and quite incompatible with their traditional belief system, complex social structure, polygamous relationships, and gregarious natures.

Wangechi somewhat resembles Kenya's famously tall, long-necked, nomadic, cattle-blood-drinking, hand-to-hand lion-killing, gorgeously coiffed, pierced, tattooed, and adorned Maasai people. The Maasai share the Luo's Nilotic language roots, and they force their daughters to endure the torment of female circumcision and genital mutilation. Mutu of course was not raised near any Maasai but instead in Kenya's very urban, very cosmopolitan capital city, Nairobi. In her parents' time though, the ethnic distance maintained between Gikuyu and Luo people was so extreme that even in a major modern African metropolis her mother and father didn't, still don't, have any Luo friends. (Mutu says she and younger-generation Gikuyu and Luo peers do maintain friendships however.)

. . . . .

If people understood each other there'd be no need for art.—THORNTON DIAL

Thus spake eighty-year-old-plus visionary Alabama painter, sculptor, and assemblage artist Mr. Dial, who, like his Alabama homeboy Sun Ra, is a self-educated postindustrial Afro-futurist/surrealist/neo-hoodoo man. One who, like Mutu and Jean-Michel Basquiat, is also something of a cultural anomaly.

Unavoidable sidebar: A young scholar of our acquaintance, while pursuing her doctorate in art history at Stanford, told us of a colleague who confessed that the art historical academy found Basquiat a problematic figure ("defiant and undefinable," as the *New York Times* said of this year's Afro-Punk Festival), because they didn't know whether to classify him as "a Black artist, a Caribbean artist, or a European artist." We immediately thought, "Well done, my brother JMB, well done—you did your work well."

The moving finger who only left behind trace elements for them to dissect and still come up just as clueless. Defiant and undefinable. What else is any useful and insurgent notion of "Black art" supposed to be? A rogue Gikuyu by any other name is still a nomad, a traveler, a Maroon, a mermaid, a caste and ethnographic traitor, a make-believe Maasai, an imaginary Luo-alike, a full-blown Eulipion.

> There's still so much to do. Not the least of which is returning home. As much as I feel like I was dropped into my family from some alien ship—an aquatic being in the land of hills and rusty soil, my work will not mean enough to me or anyone I truly care for until I can also make it from back home. The lost lamb, the black sheep, must eventually return. My work will be most fulfilling when I connect it with my history, my people, my land. I know there's so much more I'll understand about why I feel like a "cultural anomaly" even as I am a total product of where I'm from.

– 2013 –

Come Join the Hieroglyphic Zombie Parade:
Deborah Grant

We were told it was the Information Age but it was actually revealed to be the Age of Death. An age of dead things speaking to dead things and in a neat reversal of the psychic's practice, of dead things speaking not only through the living but for them as well. Everything had been done to death and analyzed to death and what remained were the mediums of death, the icons of death, signs of death virtually everywhere, with more on the way. Life had become measured by the amount of time one spent among the already dead, the born dead, the recombinant dead half-life of the virtual. The living and the dead had made multiplatform media the new medium of exchange. The world had become more and more McLuhanesque in the bargain—a media-saturated nightmare where the mediums had become more alive, more animated, more visceral than the messengers who used them. If you listened to the African Ancients they'd have told you that the lines of communication between the living and the dead were always clogged, jammed with calls, correspondence, communiques, signs, signals, a constant ferrying of intel between this world and the next, this hex and that text. There were whole branches of Afro-diasporic faith, like Abekwa in Cuba, that were devoted to posting semaphoric/choreographic messages to the flux of attracting and repelling dark energies outsiders sometimes misapprehended as gods and that astrophysicists called "quintessence."

The Age of Death needed to be seen for what it really was—an age of crossroads and crossed signals, overlapping agendas and forced connections, obsessive sensory stimulation and synaptic saturation bombing. An endgame age where the planet was finding itself increasingly taxed by its need to create and destroy in fair measure and humanity was finding it difficult to recognize a purpose for itself that did not involve racing through the earth's remaining resources to sustain its digitized death cult. Artificially intelligent media was fast becoming the source of all sensation, the measure of all feeling.

Media defined the sacred and the sacrilegious alike, the angelic and the satanic, the apostolic and the apostasy, the agonies and the ecstasies of the time. Funny thing was that as the scope of information grew vaster the portals of entry—what some called platforms—kept getting smaller and smaller; a paranoid-schizophrenic process of miniaturization that seemed an apt metaphor for the dwindling degree of significance held by nonvirtual human experience. Thus did we go about squeezing and collapsing our capacity for life into them, flattening ourselves out in the attempt to become more two-dimensional, more wafer-thin, more molecular like the processors that kept the hungry loas of our information-afterlives well fed and fluid.

The filmmaking Wachowskis have informed us that Will Smith turned down the Neo role in *The Matrix* because he couldn't imagine people living inside machines. The question now is whether we imagine people wanting to live anywhere else?

The first prophet of this age of info-death was probably William Burroughs. Those dystopian treatises of his like *Naked Lunch* and *The Ticket That Exploded*, on the viral, consumptive, self-manufacturing, terroristic powers of information and language. Especially the cut-up books where language that had been set to type in random combinations, as if some virulent machine of language had wrested control of the novel from the writer's hands, as if language itself had become a brain-scrambling force of nature, a word-tsunami no longer capable of containment or exploitation by mere mortal ken. What Burroughs set before us was schizoid, chaotic designs of random access—an infinite horde of barbarians charging the gate of lucidity, compromising and confusing every attempt to form a coherent verbal act, written or spoken. Burroughs might be said to have his antecedents in Sterne, Mallarmé, and Jarry if not the Tower of Babel, but his own first real heir apparent was named Jean-Michel Basquiat.

Basquiat, whose own lineage finds him descended from a Haitian, a Puerto Rican, and Hanna-Barbera, and from heroin and hero worship, from cave painters and Pollock, Zip Coons and de Kooning, Melville and voodoo, griots and graffiteros, santeros and hoodoo hollering bebop ghosts, black holes and white dwarfs, Frankenstein, *Grey's Anatomy*, Miles Davis and Andy Warhol, Superfly, The Thin White Duke, Bed-Stuy, The Great White Way, the Joker, The Flash, and the Houngan.

A man of many crossroads then: a rail splitter, a boundary crosser, a lane switcher, a line jumper, a code breaker, a spell caster, a coin tosser, a card shuffler, a rhyme sayer, a Sambo eraser, a chant maker, a game player, a letter scrabbler, a verse scribbler, a vinyl scratcher, an image maker, an idolator and an iconoclast, a language manipulator, word magician, cartoonist, abstract expressionist, portrait painter, ladykiller, Madonna and whore lover, Armani suit destroyer, somebody's brother, some mother's son, some Twombly-infected enfant terrible, some unloved genius child, king of the junkie underworld, Eddie Murphy of the art world to Robert Hughes, America's Goya to me, Just Another Dead Black Genius to A.J., all of the above and then some, more or less.

Yet like Burroughs, Basquiat got fixated on verbiage as a magic system, a way of apprehending the dead by drowning them in babble and rhythm, glossolalia and repetition, ancestor worship and nonsequiturs, Old Masters and juvenilia, sexed-up cretins, and crestfallen capitalists. Now, this man down in Alabama by the name of Bill Traylor was Basquiat's grandfather. In mad spirit anyway. They both favored dead black things suspended or grounded in negative space. You can't say why really except Basquiat believed he had a mission to put Black men in his paintings because they were missing from everyone else's and Traylor because he drew everything in a way that made it seem like life and death were just two sides of the same stark, bubbly cartoon. Traylor and Basquiat seemed to recognize and render Black figures as instant messengers, portents, dark lights of the crossroads, floating markers of the constant movement and exchange between heaven and hell, paradise and inferno, upper and lower Egypt. Because we live in the age of death we understand Basquiat better now than we did when he was here in living color, can relate better to the equal value he prophetically pointed out as the difference between his nebulous, necromantic Black figures and the symbols of wealth, power, and knowledge he saw them surrounded by.

How did he know way back when that one day Jay Z's mere signature on a pair of sneakers would be worth their weight in gold, or that Jay Z would be a messenger and merchant of high-priced dead things?

We might suppose Bill Traylor came from a simpler time and place than Basquiat, but MOMA founder Alfred Barr tried to hijack Traylor's work for a pittance back in the 1940s. Traylor, born in 1854, spent seven of his nine decades on a plantation and didn't start making art until he was in his eighties. Yet he comes to the thing having already grasped the essentials—that images have to represent one thing, signify something else, and mysteriously suggest a whole 'nutha thang entirely. We know Traylor's studio was in a doorway on the street and that he slept among caskets in the back of a funeral parlor. It's easy to think he came by his magic realism naturally but artists always seem easy to figure out in reverse. Miles Davis once said Charlie Parker played the way he did because his father was a tap dancer. John Coltrane's cousin Mary thought his sound was the result of him wanting to sing like the women in their church choir. A woman who grew up with Jimi Hendrix told me all the young brothers he grew up and jammed with in Seattle played loud esoteric blues but Jimi was the one who got out and didn't wind up in prison or strung out or murdered. It's natural to want the key to the riddle. The trick is to not confuse the riddle of the Sphinx with the riddler herself.

A great rock guitarist named Ronny Drayton told me he learned to play by slowing the vinyl recordings of Hendrix, Clapton, and Beck down from 33 rpms to 16 rpms. Not to figure out the notes but to figure out the player's emotional intentions, to figure out the emotions that preceded the notes. So a man born into slavery remains on the same plantation for seventy-four years after the Civil War, sires twenty children with a wife who also leaves and then decides to go down to the crossroads at the crossroad of his life to make thick-and-thin effigies of free-spirited plants animals people and hand-cobbled objects. Deborah Grant likely doesn't have a clue to what made the monastic ex-slave Traylor tick or his emotional intentions either but as she has previously done with the iconography of Picasso and Basquiat and *Love and Rockets* comix and Freud and George W. Bush's presidential cabinet, she recognizes in his forms a language she can profligately call her own. Before the Age of Death this was called appropriation but in the Age of Death the very notion of intellectual property is antique, a relic of a hoary bygone era. The Age of Death is synonymous with the Age of the Remix.

A devout hip-hop head, Grant comes by her mixing sensibility honestly, not that authenticity matters. As Public Enemy producer Hank

Shocklee once said, back when hip-hop was reinventing the world, only one thing matters in hip-hop: "Is it dope?"

In the Age of Death the only thing that matters is whether the dead keep appearing to entertain the living.

In the world according to Deborah Grant the quick and the dead appear to make merry and myth with the symbol and the cipher, the journal and the journalist, the eternal and the temporal, the graffiti writer and the stealth warrior, the blonde Venus and the Hottentot Venus. Grant seems to think the whole world can be nailed down on a festooned cut-up and summed up in an infinitude of cross-mapped ideograms. Grant seems to think all of human consciousness can be contained in a thought bubble, The Age of Death promises not to make a liar out of her.

Björk's Second Act

Contrary to her image, Björk isn't pixyish, waifish, or fairy godmother-like. She sits across from me stylishly adorned in a flow of colorful silks and chiffons with soft sprays of greens, yellows, and blacks that look as if they've been jacked from butterfly wings. She tends to stammer when she speaks—more from trying to combine three stray thoughts into one than from any conversational anxiety. The Icelandic singer cops to sometimes turning shy during interviews, not because she's an introvert, but because she's from a place not so accustomed to celebrity. She is self-possessed, clear about her artistic convictions and very much present in this world.

After coming to public attention in the eighties as the lead singer of the Sugarcubes, she launched a solo career in 1993 that thus far has yielded three memorable albums. In fact, Björk Gudmundsdottir, thirty-four, who lives in Reykjavik, Iceland, with her fourteen-year-old son (by Sugarcube Thor Eldon), Sindri, has become a figure of occult mystery for some and cult worship for others. In this and in the pared severity of her music, she reminds me of no one so much as the Miles Davis of the seventies, whose penetrating blend of sound, silence, and electricity made him then what Björk is today—the existential soul factor in our digital sonic Zeitgeist.

Nowhere is that soul more openly on display than in her major film debut, director Lars von Trier's *Dancer in the Dark*, an extraordinary performance for which she won the best actress award at Cannes this year. In *Dancer*, Björk plays Selma, an Eastern European émigré working as a wage slave in a metal-stamping plant somewhere in the American South. The film, like von Trier's *Breaking the Waves*, is a relentless attempt to see how far you can push a woman on the brink. It also features a soundtrack by the singer and several fantasy song-and-dance numbers in which Björk performs Björk without losing her emotional grip on her character. Preparing for her next album when we spoke, Björk meditated on music, acting, and her restless creative process.

. . . . .

Greg Tate: Describe how you make music.

Björk Gudmundsdottir: Making music is a very one-on-one affair. Sometimes I feel like singing to the audience is like lying, because I don't know them. It seems to me at concerts that if you look at people's faces that the level of communication can be a little artificial. Don't get this the wrong way, but the more selfish you get, the more you're singing for everyone. I always felt that if people weren't into what I was doing that it was fine. I've always been the eccentric one. Nobody tried to change me, so I'm not going to go and say, "If you don't like my experimental electronic impossible-to-get CDs, fuck off." I think I should do what I'm doing, and if people are truly interested, they will come. I've always looked at it that way.

GT: Did you grow up in a supportive family?

BG: Yeah, it couldn't have been better. [Reykjavik is a] small village, a capital in Europe, so you've got all the technology and modern things you want and [are] still surrounded by mountains, nature. We are still where people in Europe were three hundred years ago in our relationship with nature. My family still hunts for half the food we eat.

GT: What are your fondest memories of growing up?

BG: I guess it's related to my grandparents, because my mom was a bit of a wild child and still is. She left my father when I was one. I'd spend my weekends with them. My grandmother was a painter and my grandfather would take me to see the ships, and we'd eat ice cream and porridge with raisins. And when we were really living large we would have porridge with prunes. My grandmother's a very quiet and graceful woman. I remember spending hours with her, not saying a word but still really communicating. Because my mom was a bit of a hippie, that house was always full of people. Seven or eight people lived there. I went to music school from [ages] five to fifteen, so I learned classical German stuff. And then at my grandmother's house they listened to quite a bit of jazz—Ella Fitzgerald and Louis Armstrong.

GT: *What was the first music you embraced as your own?*

BG: Hard to pick one. Let me think. I remember Ella Fitzgerald in Berlin, where she improvised quite a bit. I listened to that record a lot at my grandma's house. *Porgy and Bess* with Ella and Louis. Like all children I reacted against my mother's music, so anything to do with improvisation, guitars, psychedelics—I wanted structure. I think emotionally it's natural to be very fluid. You don't know what you're going to feel like in fifteen minutes. But that's why I like music to be the opposite, to be something that can bring out emotion because it's very beautifully structured. Otherwise, it's just a big mess.

GT: *Your character, Selma, in* Dancer in the Dark *tries to fix things through music and fantasy. The fantasy elements don't soften the tragedy of the character; they coexist. I've heard that it took about a year to persuade you to take the role.*

BG: I was just going to do the music at first. I'm, like, religious when it comes to music. I'm very loyal to it, and acting feels like an affair to me, you know? I also think I understand the ground qualities of a person who is born an actor, and I don't think I have those.

GT: *Such as?*

BG: They are so selfless—well, not selfless, because I think they've got a lot of "self," but their self is of a type that they can become this piece they're dealing with. They move differently and everything is different about them and when it's over [snaps her fingers], they snap out of it. And then you've got other types of people—like me when I was in school. When I was learning the flute, if they showed me a song I didn't like, I couldn't play it. I couldn't obey any rules and had to make up my own songs, wear my own clothes my own way, and was just very stubborn about this whole idea of identity. During the making of the film, I asked Catherine Deneuve, "How can you act?" And she said, "Oh, it's amazing when you become someone completely different. Don't you think that's exciting?" And I'm like, "No. I have no interest in it. I feel I still haven't become me. I'm still starting. I've got fifty years to open something in my head and try to get out. I've just done, like, 5 percent." Once Lars convinced me, the only way I could do the film was to sacrifice all my idiosyncrasies, and it was very painful.

GT: *You had to sacrifice all your spontaneity to become Selma?*

BG: Well, the way he did it, probably because he knew what I was like, was that it was all improvised. Lars said I couldn't learn the lines by heart, so . . . I would just know, "OK, I'm going in this room." Sometimes I would know what would be said to me, and sometimes I wouldn't. We'd just do it, and I'd react instinctively to all the situations. Quite often I'd do something he didn't expect at all. The good thing was I'd been Selma for so long that it was usually right, and it was more Selma than Björk. The music scenes were shot with a hundred cameras, and you'd just do your thing from camera to camera, which is very lucky for someone who does music because it means you don't chop it all up, you just flow. I'd say to Lars, "I don't know what's going to happen," and he would say, "That's OK." So I guess it was very spontaneous. Afterward, talking to a lot of actors since, I realized it was probably the most spontaneous film ever shot.

GT: *How did you feel before and after the first screening at Cannes?*

BG: Being a music person, I felt more like a fly on the wall. Everybody was very nice to me, and at first I was very suspicious because in Iceland we're definitely not expressive like people in New York. We're even more [reserved] than the British. But when I won the award, it felt very genuine. Those awards are very important to the French. They're a big thing. Like if England were to win the World Cup. For them, giving it to an outsider who's not only from Iceland but also isn't even a film person was a genuine gesture on their behalf. It was very intense. I slept for two days afterward.

GT: *Let's talk about motherhood and the murder Selma commits for her boy.*

BG: It's shocking because it was so personal and intimate in a way that most film violence isn't. There's no question about it: I would die for my boy. Any parent would. Once, forty paparazzi went for me and couldn't get to me, so they went for him. They were asking him questions against his will. That was one of three times in my life when I've lost control and become physically aggressive. Fortunately, or unfortunately, because there were so many cameras going, it got [broadcast] around the world.

GT: *Were you comfortable with von Trier and his crew?*

BG: In Denmark, I was in a situation similar to Selma's, where I was surrounded by people who did not understand me at all. It felt like a conspiracy, because Lars only knew what I was going through when it was us two together. When other people were in the room, he acted like nothing had happened, and when I was screaming with pain he would say, "Oh, she's just making it up." People have written quite a lot about the conflict, and the conflict was—I say this quite truthfully because I've got nothing to hide—the conflict was not between me and Lars. I gave him all of me and a lot more than he even asked, and he would be the first person to tell you that.

The conflict was between Selma and Björk, the person who made the music. People said I walked off the set, and I wish I was that adventurous person. But I only once walked off set, and that was after I was Selma all day and they had chopped up my music for the next scenes and taken some bars out and changed some things in it. There I was, still in costume with blood on my shoulders, and suddenly I had to be the composer saying, "You can't do that. Let's sit down and work this out." I'd spent everything on that music for one year, and it was being chopped to pieces by people who'd never done music in their lives. . . . So I wrote a manifesto about music things—nothing about Lars or Selma or the film. I said I have the right to mix my own songs. I will collaborate, but I have the final say. Lars and I had so much trust we never wrote anything down, but I fought battles for my songs all the way to the very last week, when they were putting footsteps and sheep on top of them.

GT: The way you use sounds and noises in your music carries over to the score, where industrial sounds become beats for tracks. I'm curious about your process.

BG: I guess it's not a choice for me. It's a way to survive. Yesterday I walked for four hours and a song came out. It's like food or sleep, a way to survive. I've even had moments when I wished I could be without it because sometimes it's not very social.

GT: Miles Davis described constantly hearing music, and having to change his style accordingly all the time, as a curse.

BG: It's hard for me to analyze myself, but I would make my life, work, and family life simple if I could just repeat what I've done—find a system and just do that. I think the noises I use are just about where I am. It's the sound of the world we live in today—like right now with all the air conditioning—so that's why the obsession with noise-music. Melodies are a lot different because they're more instinctive. I stopped using Dictaphones because I'd rather have five good melodies I remember in my head than five thousand so-so ideas on tape. You've got to trust it. Once you stop trusting, everything goes into chaos. [I was] brought up by hippies who were into astrology and numerology and sat down and worked it all out, [then] they said, "We believe in mystery." I think as the next generation I said, "No, you don't, because you mapped it all out. If you really believed in mystery, you wouldn't have to." I really believe that you've got to trust and find it exciting that you don't know what it is you're dealing with.

– 2000 –

Thelma Golden

Though she's not a rhyme sayer, Thelma Golden is a stone-cold player. A highbrow mack-diva of the first magnitude. And that's on her slow days. Now at the Studio Museum in Harlem as deputy director for exhibitions and programs (with ex–Metropolitan Museum curator Lowery Sims as director), Golden is fast becoming recognized as one of those pivotal centrist figures in African American life. The kind of iconic character (like Cornel West) we would have to invent if they hadn't invented themselves first: an art world zephyr who seems to know everyone and be everywhere at the same time, a Black postmodernist with race-woman drive and what used to be called the popular touch. For the venerable, invaluable, but formerly staid Studio Museum, she and Sims are performing not just a makeover but a resurrection. Some of the changes are cosmetic—a renovated tinted-glass facade and airy lobby that embraces rather than repels passersby—but the more significant ones are philosophical, and the philosophy bears Golden's unmistakable stamp.

Since taking an assistant curator position at the Whitney during David Ross's pluripotent tenure there in the late eighties, Golden has been climbing to doyennedom—nurturing star figures Gary Simmons, Glenn Ligon, Lorna Simpson, and Kara Walker, guiding the patronage of her friends Peter and Eileen Norton to emergent African American modernists, spearheading the Whitney's Bob Thompson retrospective, and curating the controversial 1994 *Black Male* show. Along the way Golden has also become a fixture on the *New York Times* social page, caught on camera at the sort of chichi, froufrou fund-raisers that inform the rest of us as to who's really running things in Gotham. Wining and cheesing comes with the gig—a daily multitasking marathon—and Golden handles it all with an especially deft combination of diplomacy, intellect, cheek, and dazzle. Museum administration, like university administration, requires a rare panoply of social, managerial, and scholarly skills.

You have to be as conversant with the mood swings of the avant-garde as any cutting-edge critic, as at ease in lily-white corporate suites as in grungy Williamsburg lofts, as ready to debate community activists on your museum's mission as you are to stave off the ghettoizing tendencies of that other art world. Thelma Golden in a nutshell.

Golden gives a breathless interview, answering all of your questions à la George Clinton before you ever have to ask them. When we sit down she's got good reason to be rapidly expansive: In two hours is the opening of *Freestyle*. It's her most exuberant exhibition yet, a hip and witty survey of twenty-eight emergent African American postmodernists, replete with a stylish catalog by young writers and curators of a hip-hop generational bent. Golden found her way to these artists through her usual curatorial process, more random than methodical, which privileges the recommendations and opinions of artists she respects. *Freestyle* catches Golden glimpsing who's coming around the bend in contemporary African American art for artistic and professional reasons. "*Freestyle* is me trying to begin the process of finding the next group of artists I'd be working with for the next ten years. It's nostalgia in a way, going back to the first project I did with Gary Simmons in '91, *The Garden of Hate*, trying to go back to a way of working I had with so many of those nineties artists at the beginning of their rise."

In the eighties and nineties, Golden says, "Black artists and those of us presenting them were . . . trying to make work informed by culture, race, gender, ethnicity, nations, and trying to define it in ways that were a very complex combination of content and form. On the one hand, people were trying to work away from this idea that identity-based work was work without formal quality; on the other hand, people were trying to work away from the notion that formal quality was the only thing. That generation of artists formed in the late eighties who came into their own in the nineties were the ones who very distinctly wrote the book on what I would call a postmulticultural art-making practice.

"The moment of multiculturalism was one where that was the way people formed exhibitions—a moment of discovery when people said, Let's explore; let's discover and expand. It had this real frontier quality. But then that became, thank goodness, the norm, and many Black artists moved to the forefront of our consciousness in terms of contemporary art practice in ways that didn't have to be explained through a Black History Month label. So there was no longer any need to have all those paragraphs before you got to the work on why you were showing the work and what this means and da da da pluralism we are the world hold hands kumbaya. The artists in *Freestyle* are the beneficiaries of the nineties artists' breakthroughs. But they were also formed more out of the theoretical and aesthetic arguments of the late nineties that were both a result of millennial madness and the need to look back on the whole century."

One nineties artist whose imprint Golden believes is quite legible in the show is Kara Walker, whose distinct place among the nineties artists opened a path to the future of postmodernist Black art. "There is a before-and-after-Kara quality to the show for me because Kara emerged in the late nineties, descended from the group that includes Adrian Piper, David Hammons, and Robert Colescott and later Simmons, Simpson, Ligon, and Greene. But her work created an opening for a lot of stuff happening now because of its historical quality. The other thing I find in talking to these artists—and this is where I began to feel really old—is I feel as if the great promise of the multicultural rhetoric of the eighties is true. These artists very easily cite references across very huge lines with no need for justification on any side; one artist the other day cited Robert Colescott and Sigmar Polke in the same sentence and it wasn't about one being better than the other or the need for one more than the other—like I need to cite Polke so you'll know I'm a serious artist working in the Western tradition or I need to cite Colescott so you'll know I'm down. No, it was like, PolkeColescott."

The mark of hip-hop is everywhere in *Freestyle*—formally, semiotically, referentially, from the name on. From Sanford Biggers's fat lace-blanketed Buddhas to Julie Mehretu's topographic riots to Camille Norment's sonic head-rush stripper asylum, this show unloads an obsession with reforming, reframing, and unbranding nomadic urban space. Golden, who can be charmingly, disarmingly, unhip when she chooses, has qualms about *Freestyle* being read as drawn from the boom-bip. "The one thing I was adamant about was not creating a hip-hop show. Because I am the holdout that believes there is no hip-hop corollary in visual art. I know this is where the Hilton Kramer in me comes out. One thing I thought was, What happens in a moment when popular culture is so present—and within popular culture hip-hop is ever present—when you do a show of emerging African American artists? I'm waiting to see the tag lines and headlines because I guarantee one of them is going to say, 'Hip-hop Generation.'"

A Smith graduate who took a double major in art history and African American studies, Golden found that Smith's Afro-Am people didn't bother with visual art while their art history people didn't discuss African Americans. For this reason she has had to create her own bridges between her two guiding passions. Her history with the Studio Museum dates back to college days when she interned there and a 1986 stint as an associate curator. It was during the latter that she figured out that the historical-artifact-based program of the museum was at odds with her own desire to work in an environment where the ideas and opinions of artists were valued and where installation aesthetic was a priority.

"When I worked at the Studio Museum in the eighties for a year as an assistant curator this felt like my parents' museum. When I went to the Whitney it felt exactly like what I thought or imagined working in the contemporary art world would be like. Coming back here after ten years at the Whitney was really a challenge. I have issues around the idea of a culturally specific institution. When I was at the Whitney I never wanted the title curator of Afro-American art—but what I wanted to do was only African American artists. What was beautiful about the Whitney was David Ross understood that I didn't want the title but the privilege and the power. I feel very strongly that there should be a museum for African American art and for artists of African descent that is sophisticated and intellectually formed in very profound ways. During my time at the Whitney I thought, What if there was a Black museum that was at the vanguard? What if there was a Black museum that was ahead of the curve, like Linda Bryant's Just Above Midtown was in the seventies and eighties, that was at the very beginning of things, out there and doing it and forming dialogues and arguments? It was a fantasy, because in so many other genres—film, literature, music—we're light-years ahead."

Golden cites Henry Louis Gates Jr. as someone who has done the kind of institution building she would like to incite at the Studio Museum. As Gates needed not just Harvard's deep pockets but a cadre of renowned African American scholars to make his visions of an ebony tower at Cambridge a reality, Golden can use her artists to conjure a MOMA for the hood.

"This is a moment when it could happen because the artists are already there. Even without a structure the artists have emerged as some of the most significant working in the world now, right? So half of my job is done. I don't have to legitimize and justify the artists. I'm almost in an opposite position. I need these artists to help me move this institution perhaps more than they need me to help move their careers."

Ironically, Golden is most excited about an upcoming show for the 2002 season involving African American artists who have no use for her or the Studio Museum at all. "The work that has dogged me from afar has been this hyperfigurative Black popular art that's being sold in the 125th Street mart and in upscale malls in Denver and Houston. I call it Black romantic because I believe there is something equivalent to romanticism in all the subgenres of this work—the southern nostalgia work of an idealized past, the positive Black man work, the erotica, the images of a royal African past."

Golden cites as a huge inspiration Ernie Barnes, whose paintings for TV's *Good Times* and for Marvin Gaye's *I Want You* album raised the bar for Black vernacular painters. Professional pride is also involved: Golden is uneasy knowing there's a mammoth, well-endowed Black art world out there that she is ignorant of.

"When I go around the country to present a lecture and show all my slides of all my nice freaky artists like Gary and Glenn and Lorna, someone will inevitably raise a hand and ask about "Cynthia Saint James" or whoever—and I don't even know the names. These popular Black artists rarely approach me because for the most part I don't really have anything they want. So whereas in an equivalent situation with a bunch of young Black artists who just got out of Yale's MFA program and I've felt like I was in a den of wolves, these artists have websites, syndicated cards, and wrapping paper. They don't need a Whitney show or a Studio Museum show. I've always felt like I had to come to terms with this work, like either get therapy or do a show. Some of the images make my skin crawl, like of these naked Black women with these thirty-eight DDDD breasts and forty-inch hips sitting on stools with stars and Africa coming between their legs, but when I get beyond that I am interested in the space these artists operate in because it's not kitsch or flea market art. The funny thing is this show will be the bane of my existence because I'm sure it will be the most well-attended show I've ever done in my career. But this is what I want to do here, projects that test the boundaries. Even my own."

– 2001 –

Hello
Darknuss
My Old
Meme

Top Ten Reasons Why So Few Black Women Were Down to Occupy Wall Street Plus Four More

Like the French, radical Black folk are genetically predisposed to support all signs of insurrection, insurgency, and revolutionary suicide wherever in the known universe they rear their lovely and indignant little heads. That said, some observers of the current American progressive scene have accurately noted Occupy Wall Street's paucity of participants proudly gleaming signs of African descent and dissent. Herewith a few of our idle speculations as to wherefore art thou anticapitalist Negroid rabble-rousers riled up over any of the causes now being featured at Zuccotti Park.

10. Your Basic Soap-and-Water Theory. We love the funk—metaphorically speaking. Ditto goes for colored folk's oft-stated ardor for all things "gully," "gritty," "grimy," and "dirty South." But you out your nat'chall Black mind if you think hordes of You People will be thronging any protest site that gotta be quarantined, evacuated, or sanitized before the party for rights can continue. Whether from the boojie middle rungs or the bootylicious lower depths, Black folk generally refuse to accept the bummy notion that good politics and good grooming need be mutually exclusive. And that whole open-air-food-prep-and-serving-line thing? Not so good a look in many a woogie's book. Strictly family backyard barbecue action. Bottom line: Black folk do demos, but they don't do dirt—especially all those white-gloved and odoriferous-sensitive sisters who easily account for 80 percent of OWS's sideline African Friends Group.

9. Reasons Why We Should OWS Anyway. Nomadic African women can make a lean-to look palatial in the outback. OWS could surely benefit from an Afrocentric woman's touch. OWS would become known instead as "Occupy and De-Uglify Wall Street." Imagine the difference made by scented candles, patchouli, potted plants, and colorful fabrics. Imagine her rage for spotless and sterilized surfaces set loose on Liberty Street. A rage so bordering on OCD, Pigpen himself would be too shook to leave behind one speck of unconsecrated crud. Yoga in the morning, African dance in the afternoon, prayer and meditation before bed, goddess and ancestor worship all the live-long day. That OWS shiznit would get friggin' spiritual. OWS would get closer to godliness than the Garden of Eden. No silly housecleaning ruses would ever be thrown up again.

8. Our Absence as Radical Love. Our sincere desire to see OWS stay alive has us coordinating scant, sporadic, barely visible visits to Zuccotti Park. Hence OWS doesn't come off as "a Black Thang." Because we know that once deemed so, Mike Bloomberg and Ray Kelly would feel compelled to set more upon the movement than decrepit desk sergeants with pepper spray. No longer would cops find the heart to wade alone into the crowds of wan young figures with no backup and meaty fists a-swinging. As Sterling Brown once observed, when they come after even one Stagolee, "They don't come by Ones / They don't come by Twos / They come by Tens." Trust. Thanks to our overwhelming no-show of numbers, 49,000 shots haven't been fired at OWS yet.

7. The Biggas Are Scared or Bored of Revolution Theory. Say whut? Since when? When it comes to showing radical heart, we damn sure got nothing to prove. Protest history shows our folk couldn't be turned around by deputized terrorists armed with dynamite, firebombs, C4, tanks, AK-47s, tommyguns, fixed bayonets, billy clubs, K-9 corps, truncheons, or water hoses. Stop-and-frisk has prepped most brothers to anticipate a cell block visit just for being Slewfoot While Black. We ain't never been skeered of fighting the good fight. We love a good dust-up on pay-per-view or in the street just on GP! Out there on the street, though, all we need is to feel like you got our backs like we got yours. Herein might lie the rub. People fresh to daily struggle may need to earn our trust more. Clearly we're in no hurry to make loads of new friends spanking new to police brutality.

6. The OWS Best Go Get a Late Pass Theory. The sudden realization by OWS-ers that American elites never signed the social contract and will sell the people out for a fat cat's dime—hey, no news flash over here. Black folk got wise to the game back in 1865 when we realized neither forty acres nor a mule would be forthcoming. Also, as one sharp strapping ready-for-whatever-you-got youngblood recently put it, "I ain't about to go get arrested with some muhfuhkuhs who just figured out yesterday that this shit ain't right."

5. Reasons Why We Should Reconsider Befriending Nu People Virgin to Daily NYPD Asswhuppings. Repeatedly finding oneself on the business end of a NYPD nightstick and expecting the same result is either a sign of madness or a sign of virtual Blacknuss. Either way, even your most hardened Pan-Afrikanist should now be open to giving the OWS-ers a hug of solidarity. Maybe if organized, this form of outreach could function as the larger community's first olive branch. (Air kisses and arm's length for some snooty African noses still, I know.)

4. The Prison Industrial Complex Crickets Theory. The predominant age range of OWS's paler male participants is roughly eighteen to twenty-nine. This age group among African American cats accounts for 40 percent of the country's prison population—a national crisis which predates the bailout by several decades. This disgraceful disparity could likely continue after every OWS-er has been gainfully reabsorbed into the American workforce. Although Wall Street profits from our brothers' massive enslavement by incarceration, so does Main Street. Perhaps OWS should ponder putting prison abolition on their unformulated list of demands. Until then, some Black progressives, though duly sympathetic, might not hear a roar coming from Zuccotti Park but simply *crickets*.

3. The Mom and Pops Ain't Having It and I Need My Paycheck Theory. Currently employed grown-ass Black folk will tell you they can't spare not one day off the plantation for this worthy cause. More than a few young Black folk now in college have an inbred fear of being cut off by Mom and Pop if caught on camera decrying capitalism and inviting arrest when they need to be hitting those books. Such parents might even harbor high hopes of their prodigal progeny becoming well-paid corporate shills. Coming out rad, green, and anti–Goldman Sachs in some Black families can require more heroics than coming out punk rock musician. Or even sapphic Muslim MC. One just imagines the fallout that might occur in the Herman Cain household, for example.

2. The Great Race and Class Divide / Integrated School Lunch Table Theory. It's hard to locate many instances in American radical or cultural history where goo-gobs of Black folk leaped to join predominantly non-Black movements. Or even school lunch tables. Postracial as Obama's voting bloc might have been, America remains a country more divided by race than class. Even the most progressive non-Black folk tend to only have that One Good Black Friend in their social clusterfuck. Radical politics can make for less estranged bedfellows, but OWS still has America's mucky river of racial segregation and alienation to cross. Not to mention a certain perception, right or wrong, that OWS is white privilege gone wild again. More enlightened self-interest than interrogating whiteness on the agenda.

1. Reasons Why We Could At Least Offer OWS a Spare Bag or Two of C-Town Kale or Collards. Although we used to have the dibs on kick-starting revolt, these OWS kids are onto something big and quite necessary here. The groundswell looks globally awesome from here in Harlem. How many times have you, à la Malcolm X, said, "White folk need to get their own people organized and out on the frontlines." Well alrighty then! No danger of anybody being the next Crispus Attucks here. Not unless you wanna step to the front of the line that is.

Bonus Points!
The It Ain't Called Shiv-Gank-Stomp-or-Rob Wall-Street-Theory. This rather romantic and lumpen proletarian conceit is worthy of the studio gangsta thug-life era. Especially since, as we all know, real thugs don't do demos or entertain police assault for abstract carnivalesque goals. Death Row Tupac's focus group is, as we speak, more likely to be joining that 40 percent in G-Pop after putting in work on "Black Wall Street."

The "What Would Jordan or Jay Z Do?" Theory. Sleeping when not shouting in Zuccotti Park with scruffy-haired, fair-faced young hippies is one way to register one's sudden disquiet that hypercapitalism just ain't working for ya. American Black folk, though, have had more than four hundred years to neurologically process the whole profits-before-people thing as the Game that Federal Reserve apparatchiks are most ready to die for here. From this hard-knock-won life wisdom evolved the kulcha's own 1 percenters—rappers, ballers, and George Clinton's 3 Ps: preachers, pimps, and politicians. These freebooting outliers' drive and commitment to Being on That Grind, Getting One's Hustle On, and Putting in Work also acknowledges we best gaffle three times harder (and take a hundred times more risk) than any Wall Street schmuck. Fervently lounging along said schmucks' daily footpath expecting a fair shake is simply beneath the hustler's code, Zip Coon dignity, kool trickster-genius, and ride-or-die bootstraps. The racism and disenfranchisement others see as massive obstacles, these sly devils seize upon as photo ops for personal gain. Minds like these were plotting exit schemes and expropriations before they hit the auction block. Such types haven't been preoccupied with getting a hand on Wall Street since they docked slave ships down there.

The Ism Schism Theory. Simply put, capitalism is not the "ism" whose evils tends to motivate most American Negroes to radical action, per se. Experience shows that racism can trump even greed in Amerikkka—especially in the workplace. White dudes with prison records get hired over more qualified bloods with not even jaywalking citations. You don't have to be as high up the food chain as banker-scum to benefit from white supremacy or profit sideways from the mass povertization of the Negro. Cornel West identified 9/11 as the event which affected the "Niggerization" of all Americans. ows's lack of melanin demonstrates that the N-word's first despondents have yet to experience all this widespread mutual sharing of sufferation and American Niggerdom. Possibly because all the non-Black folk we see slumming about our gentrified neighborhoods with dogs, strollers, and condos are soooo not the 99 percent.

Reasons Why We Should Be More Down Anyway. If Zionism can equal racism, then why can't capitalism equal racism, too?

– 2011 –

What Is Hip-Hop?

for dream hampton, the conversational inspiration,
and for meshell ndegeocello for being meshell ndegeocello

Buddha blessed and boo-ya blasted
These are the words that she manifested
A grim little tyke in a black pleather raincoat
She stepped to the mike and said,
"Repeat after me, there is no such thing as alternative hip-hop, there
    is no such thing as alternative hip-hop."
So Boo in the blue silk hoody pops up like,
"Hey baby you'd be a good-looking man if you worked at it but what the
    fuck you know about hip-hop?"
Now why he go and say that?
Lil Grim sez," I know hip-hop like I know your mother.
Your mother so hip-hop I seen her laying pipe in Alaska
Your mother so hip-hop she yelled ho 'fo I even axed her
Your mother so hip-hop she thinks Biz Markie's cute as shit
Your mother so hip-hop she told you, time to get off my dick
Next time you speak to your mother, send her my best."
Buddha blessed and boo ya blasted

These are the words that she manifested:

Hip-hop is inverse capitalism

Hip-hop is reverse colonialism

Hip-hop is the world the slaveholders made, sent into nigga-fied
future shock.

Hip-hop is the plunder from down under, mackin all others for pleasure

Hip-hop is the Black aesthetic byproduct of the

American dream machine, our culture of consumption, commodification, and subliminal seduction

Where George Clinton warned us about Madison Avenue urge overkill, the pimping of the pleasure principle, hip-hop embraces the
pleasures of the pimping principle

Hip-hop is the first musical movement in history where Black people
pimped themselves before the white boy did

Hip-hop pimped the funk before the white boy and heavy metal too

Hip-hop is the perverse logic of capitalism pursued by an artform

Like capitalism, hip-hop converts raw soul into store rack commodity

Like capitalism, hip-hop has no morals, no conscience, and no ecologi-
cal concern for the scavenged earth or the scavenged American
minds it will wreck in its pursuit of new markets

Unlike Sigourney Weaver's nemesis alien, hip-hop is not the other
man's rape fantasy of the Black sex machine gone berserk.

Hip-hop is James Brown's pelvis digitally grinded into
technomorphine.

Hip-hop is dope-know-logy, the only known antidote for prime-time
sensory deprivation

There is no such thing as alternative hip-hop because the only alternative to hip-hop is dead silence and we all know such silence signifies
a lack of breath

There is no such thing as good hip-hop or bad hip-hop, progressive hip-
hop or reactionary hip-hop, politically incorrect hip-hop or hip-hop
with a message.

It's either hip-hop or it ain't Shit

Hip-hop is beyond good and evil, hip-hop is beyond life and death

Hip-hop was dead but hip-hop reanimated

Hip-hop does not live on *Yo! MTV Raps*

Hip-hop currently resides beneath the noise where all the fly girlz
and boyz use hip-hop as a form of telemetry telepath and
telekinesis

Hip-hop is how you say I love you to a hip-hop junkie

Hip-hop is your password into the cult of hip-hop infomaniacs

You know hip-hop when you see it

You may not see hip-hop before it seizes you

Hip-hop is not what it is today but what it could be tomorrow

Hip-hop ain't shit but everything is hip-hoppable mad flava beatable

Hip-hop is Pumas and a hoody today but why not leather fringe and sequins tomorrow?

If hip-hop wanted to be that corny, who could argue with it but a muhfuhkuh who was faded?

What's hip-hop today could easily become passé

Arguing with hip-hop about the nature of hip-hop is like arguing with water about the nature of wetness.

Like Bunny Wailer said, some tings come to ya, some tings come at 'cha, but hip-hop flows right through ya

Hip-hop is so far gone up its own ass you can't even speak on it unless you follow the trail of hip-hop's intestines out the lower end

Hip-hop is the rattlesnake that bit off its own tail, then listened to the death rattle warning the head that it was swallowing up the body.

Hip-hop is what happened when the Black community became the

Bermuda Triangle and lost track of itself on the radar screen of Reaganomics.

Hip-hop is the blip that boom-bipped then turned up to crack, Black is back all in we're gonna exterminate our own next of kin

Pink people wanna know if other pink people like hip-hop how can it still be hip-hop?

That's like asking, if Black people like

Dirty Harry is he still Clint Eastwood?

Hip-hop is beyond Black nationalism.

Hip-hop is not hung up on counter-supremacy because it reigns supreme like all the other dope fiends

Hip-hop is half Black and half Japanese

Hip-hop is digital chips on the shoulders of African lips

Hip-hop is Black Prozac

Hip-hop is if you can't join 'em, beat 'em, if you can't beat 'em, blunt 'em

Hip-hop is Black sadomasochism

Hip-hop is where the hurting ends and the feeling begins or is that the other way around?

Hip-hop is how we rip off the band aids and pour saltpeter on the wounds

Hip-hop is Very Ralph Ellison, who once said the blues is like running a
  razor blade along an open sore.

If it wasn't for Black English and hip-hop I wouldn't have no blues at all
Hip-hop is my black cat moan
Hip-hop is my black cat scan
Hip-hop is all I need to stop
It's time for my medicine
Time to face the music again
Buddha blessed and boo-ya blasted
These are the words that she manifested.

– 1993 –

Intelligence Data: Bob Dylan

Love and Theft

"I'm not sorry for nothing I've done. I'm glad I fought, I only wish we'd
won."

Pretty wry for a spry guy, this Bob Dylan character. The codger's got
plenty kick left in him yet. "Feel like a fightin' rooster, feel better than I
ever felt, but the Pennsylvania line's in an awful mess, and the Denver
road is about to melt." Plenty parables too. There may be no second acts
in American life, but at sixty, Dylan could care less. Like Miles Davis
and his shadow, that asshole Pablo Picasso, Dylan has given us one long
act to chew on, and one long song: a peerless and exquisite display of
craft, nerve, and wit. His riddle-rhyming trail is marked by the silence,
exile, and cunning of the hermetic populist—Joyce, Pynchon, Reed,
Clinton. Occasional lapses of taste and crises of faith, periods of doubt,
self-derision, and personal revival too. Rare among American artists, he
shouldered the burden of a great and precocious gift. He crashed but
did not burn out after the sixties. Now contemporary evidence, a new
release called *Love and Theft*, suggests that the poet of his generation is
once again prophet of his age.

The current saber rattling is probably giving him more than a slight
case of déjà vu right about now. This is where he came in, way back when,
our freewheelin' troubadour, with his "Talkin' World War III Blues," his
"Hard Rain's a-Gonna Fall," his "Masters of War." Before 9.11.01, *Love
and Theft* was an abstract expressionist painting Dylan could never have
intended to carry a topical frame. Funny what a little moonlight can do:

Now poets are bringing us the news. Before that fateful Tuesday, *Love and Theft* could not have been so easily read as Dylan's contribution to the literature of the apocalypse. Now so nakedly he seems revealed, bounding out of the wilderness in high prophetic mode: "I see your lover man coming, across a barren field. He's not a gentleman at all, he's rotten to the core, he's a coward and he's steel. My captain he's decorated, he's very well schooled and he's skilled. He's not sentimental, it don't bother him at all how many of his pals he's killed." We could have gleaned as much intelligence data from the RZA, the GZA, and the Ol' Dirty BZA, but who besides your Five Percenters and wigga types were paying serious attention to a buncha crypto-alarmist niggas from Shaolin? "Get your shit together before the fuckin' Illuminati hit." Nostradamus gave advance warning, they tell me, the Book of Revelations, Rastafari. The eons-old Mayan Calendar of Cosmogenesis predicts a cataclysm will reset the world calendar to zero in 2012. The astronomical lore of the pyramids, left behind over ten thousand years ago, informs us that the earth's axis is about to reverse, flipping the planet back to the Stone Age whether we bomb the Taliban there first or not.

This may be the dawning of the age of Aquarius but some of you know we're still in the Age of Pisces—a time of severity and strife, suffering and service, a time whose ruler Neptune is the planet of mystery, illusion, and deception. Four jetliners. Nineteen allegedly surly Middle East passport–carrying muhfukuhs with knives and box cutters breeze past security when your lone Black ass can barely make it through with house keys and pocket change. Where was racial profiling when we really needed it? None but the truly twisted will find even grim solace in that observation. If there's a hell below we're all gonna go, Curtis Mayfield croons from the wings. The Jamaican family of my man Michael Richards, a brilliant sculptor whose final resting place was his studio on the ninety-second floor of Tower One, can attest to that, as can that of my man, Guyana's Patrick Adams—former proud security presence here at the *Voice* and still missing.

Dylan's impact on a couple generations of visionary Black bards has rarely been given its propers—Sam Cooke, Curtis Mayfield, Jimi Hendrix, Otis Redding, Stevie Wonder, Sly Stone, Marvin Gaye, Charles Stepney, Terry Callier, Gil Scott-Heron, Bob Marley, Tracy Chapman, Chocolate Genius would not for a second hesitate to acknowledge coming under his spell. Like Joni Mitchell, Gil Evans, and Charlie Haden, he's left deep, yeti-sized footprints in this thang we call Black music. It's a matter of record, of sublime and divine social intervention.

Like Miles, Dylan, born May 24, 1941, is a Gemini, the sign ruled by Mercury, messenger of the gods. According to Goldschneider and Elffers, those born on the day of the magnifier and clarifier also fall under the sway of Venus, but are far more skilled at communicating love than giving it. They tend to favor the dispossessed over the privileged, but must guard against sarcasm and harsh criticism of their friends and also against their own fanaticism and zealotry. "I'm gonna teach peace to the conquered, I'm gonna tame the proud." Those of Yoruba persuasion might recognize Dylan as an Elegba-Eshu vehicle, those of the Dahomean faith as Legba, devotees of the vodun syncretism as Legba-Pied Casse. Trickster gods, cosmic jokers who control the crossroads. Dylan ain't just whistling "Dixie" when he pursues archaic, fallen, and decayed American musics. There's souls in them thar hills. And a taste of our cowpoke president's newspeak as well: "George Lewes told the Englishman, the Italian, and the Jew, you can't open up your mind, boys, to every conceivable point of view. They got Charles Darwin trapped out there on Highway 5. Judge says to the High Sheriff, I want him dead or alive, either one I don't care."

The voice you hear on *Love and Theft* is not that of the cocky young rock star who wrecked folk by simply strapping on an electric guitar, nor is it the vengeful and crotchety man who dripped *Blood on the Tracks*. This Dylan is older, wiser, and grousier, but sweeter, more sanguine if still unsettled too. There's a bitter taste in his mouth, but it's not bile. He might moan but he doesn't bitch, and whether you project the immediacy and portent in his words that I do, the depth and reach of song craft remains monumental and omnivorous. *Love and Theft* presents an assured master working with a cornucopia of tuneful frames, all set out on leisurely, laconic display. There are blues forms and jazz forms here, gypsy-jazz folk forms, Tin Pan Alley and rockabilly, boxcar rounds, campfire sing-alongs and sea chanteys, cowboy songs, madrigals, and various alchemical mixtures as they're needed. His current band speaks his language, being connoisseurs of antiquity too, and are as adaptable, supple, and blissfully out of touch as any he's ever had. They understand how to support and navigate his juke-joint rhythms and cascading, sometimes colliding, cadences. Even at its most foreboding, this is good-time music. The overall impression it leaves is that of bodies in motion and bodies at rest, sometimes at breakneck speeds and sometimes arrested, of folks flying forward and folks stopped dead in their tracks, having finally looked back to see what's been gaining on them. There is an economy, transparency, and conviviality that complement the newfound humility, civility, and camaraderie of our city—a place that, achingly, feels so much smaller in scale without our twin megalopolis-marking towers of money and babble, traded in now for a massive laying-on of hands.

So many prescient, portentous lyrics beg the question: What did Dylan know and when did he know it? Some up-to-the-minute somebody at the Federal Bureau of Immigration, very few Angolans, and no Haitians at all will surely wish to inquire about the former Mr. Zimmerman's connection to Osama bin Laden: "Tweedle Dum and Tweedle Dee they're throwing knives into the street. Two big bags of dead man's bones, got their noses to the grindstone. Living in the land of Nod, trusting their fate to the hands of God." "Bye and Bye"'s breezy B-3 lounge jazz skates beneath lines I hear as fair appraisal of the conduct of our Mussolini-mad mayor and wartime consigliere, who will waltz out of office on a heroic grace note: "Bye and bye, on you I'm casting my eye. I'm painting the town, swinging my partner around. I know who I can depend on, I know who to trust. I'm watching the roads, I'm reading the dust. . . . The future for me is already a thing of the past. You were my first love and you will be my last." The national psyche, the national moment, the nightly jingoistic appeals to revive the national resolve, avenge the national honor, and spill the national blood can strangely, spookily be heard sounding their retort in this music Dylan wrote who knows how many months ago: "I'm gonna baptize you in fire, so you can sin no more. I'm gonna establish my rule through civil war, make you see just how loyal and true a man can be." Dylan's sleeping giant is more wary, weary, and diplomatic than the one who rose out of Pearl Harbor, but just as ready to applaud good old American know-how and the desire to just get the job done.

There are also intimations of the lumpy-throated suspense we're all held in now, waiting for the proverbial shoe to drop, the proverbial ax to fall, and what comes next, our collective jumpiness as it were: "Last night the wind was whispering, I was trying to make out what it was. I tell myself something's coming, but it never does." In this Dylan you can hear the banjo-strumming wagon-train ghosts of America-past riding shotgun with our after-the-innocence future shock, but because it's Dylan you also hear this place where the personal and the apocalyptic mesh. "You don't understand it, my feeling for you. You'd be honest with me if only you knew. . . . I'm here to create the new imperial empire. I'm gonna do whatever circumstances require."

"Po' Boy" is what hip-hop would be if it told the tale of all those players doomed to lives of quiet desperation—"Po' boy need the stars that shine, washing them dishes, feeding them swine." But it is in "Sugar Baby," the album's swan song, a final address to a tearful, fearful nation, that this record's kinder, gentler, crustier, creakier Dylan quietly dons his gold lamé glitter suit one last time and goes for the jugular with run-down, melancholic glee: "Every moment of existence seems like some dirty trick. Happiness can come suddenly and leave just as quick. Any minute of the day that bubble could burst. Trying to make things better for someone sometimes you just end up making it a thousand times worse. Your charms have broken many a heart and mine is surely one. You've got a way of tearing a world apart. Love see what you've done." Whether he's speaking as Dylan the martyred lover or as some kind of Jesus, the message appears abundantly clear: These may be the last days, but not even Armageddon is going to save us from growing up, and our learning curve remains steep.

– 2001 –

Hip-Hop Turns Thirty

We are now winding down the anniversary of hip-hop's thirtieth year of existence as a populist art form. Testimonials and televised tributes have been airing almost daily, thanks to Viacom and the like. As those digitized hip-hop shout-outs get packed back into their binary folders, however, some among us have been so gauche as to ask, What the heck are we celebrating exactly? A right and proper question, that one is, mate. One to which my best answer has been: Nothing less, my man, than the marriage of heaven and hell, of New World African ingenuity and that trick of the devil known as global hypercapitalism. Hooray.

Given that what we call hip-hop is now inseparable from what we call the hip-hop industry, in which the nouveau riche and the superrich employers get richer, some say there's really nothing to celebrate about hip-hop right now but the money shakers and the moneymakers—who got bank and who got more.

Hard to argue with that line of thinking since, hell, globally speaking, hip-hop is money at this point, a valued form of currency where brothers are offered stock options in exchange for letting some corporate entity stand next to their fire.

True hip-hop headz tend to get mad when you don't separate so-called hip-hop culture from the commercial rap industry, but at this stage of the game that's like trying to separate the culture of urban basketball from the NBA, the pro game from the players it puts on the floor.

Hip-hop may have begun as a folk culture, defined by its isolation from mainstream society, but being that it was formed within the America that gave us the coon show, its folksiness was born to be bled once it began entertaining the same mainstream that had once excluded its originators. And have no doubt, before hip-hop had a name it was a folk culture—literally visible in the way you see folk in Brooklyn and the South Bronx of the eighties, styling, wilding, and profiling in Jamel Shabazz's photograph book *Back in the Days*. But from the moment "Rapper's Delight" went platinum, hip-hop the folk culture became hip-hop the American entertainment-industry sideshow.

No doubt it transformed the entertainment industry, and all kinds of people's notions of entertainment, style, and politics in the process. So let's be real. If hip-hop were only some static and rigid folk tradition preserved in amber, it would never have been such a site for radical change or corporate exploitation in the first place. This being America, where as my man A.J.'s basketball coach dad likes to say, "They don't pay niggas to sit on the bench," hip-hop was never going to not go for the gold as more gold got laid out on the table for the goods that hip-hop brought to the market. Problem today is that where hip-hop was once a buyer's market in which we, the elite hip-hop audience, decided what was street legit, it has now become a seller's market, in which what does or does not get sold as hip-hop to the masses is whatever the boardroom approves.

The bitter trick is that hip-hop, which may or may not include the NBA, is the face of Black America in the world today. It also still represents Black culture and Black creative license in unique ways to the global marketplace, no matter how commodified it becomes. No doubt, there's still more creative autonomy for Black artists and audiences in hip-hop than in almost any other electronic mass-cultural medium we have. You for damn sure can't say that about radio, movies, or television. The fact that hip-hop does connect so many Black folk worldwide, whatever one might think of the product, is what makes it invaluable to anyone coming from a Pan-African state of mind. Hip-hop's ubiquity has created a common ground and a common vernacular for Black folk from eighteen to fifty worldwide. This is why mainstream hip-hop as a capitalist tool, as a market force, isn't easily discounted: The dialogue it has already set in motion between Long Beach and Cape Town is a crucial one, whether Long Beach acknowledges it or not. What do we do with that information, that communication, that transatlantic mass-Black telepathic link? From the looks of things, we ain't about to do a goddamn thing other than send more CDs and T-shirts across the water.

But the Negro art form we call hip-hop wouldn't even exist if African Americans of whatever socioeconomic caste weren't still niggers and not just the more benign, congenial "niggas." By which I mean if we weren't all understood by the people who run this purple-mountain loony bin as both subhuman and superhuman, as sexy beasts on the order of King Kong. Or as George Clinton once observed, without the humps there ain't no getting over. Meaning that only Africans could have survived slavery in America, been branded lazy bums, and decided to overcompensate by turning every sporting contest that matters into a glorified battle royal.

Like King Kong had his island, we had the Bronx in the seventies, out of which came the only significant artistic movement of the twentieth century produced by born-and-bred New Yorkers, rather than Southwestern transients or Jersey transplants. It's equally significant that hip-hop came out of New York at the time it did, because hip-hop is Black America's Ellis Island. It's our Delancey Street and our Fulton Fish Market and garment district and Hollywoodian ethnic enclave/ empowerment zone that has served as a foothold for the poorest among us to get a grip on the land of the prosperous.

Only because this convergence of ex-slaves and ch-ching finally happened in the eighties because hey, African Americans weren't allowed to function in the real economic and educational system of these United States like first-generation immigrants until the 1980s—roughly four centuries after they first got here, 'case you forgot. Hip-hoppers weren't the first generation who ever thought of just doing the damn thang entrepreneurially speaking, they were the first ones with legal remedies on the books when it came to getting a cut of the action. And the first generation for whom acquiring those legal remedies so they could just do the damn thang wasn't a priority requiring the energies of the race's best and brightest.

If we woke up tomorrow and there was no hip-hop on the radio or on television, if there was no money in hip-hop, then we could see what kind of culture it was, because my bet is that hip-hop as we know it would cease to exist, except as nostalgia. It might resurrect itself as a people's protest music if we were lucky, might actually once again reflect a disenchantment with, rather than a reinforcement of, the have and have-not status quo we cherish like breast milk here in the land of the status-fiending. But I won't be holding my breath waiting to see.

Because the moment hip-hop disappeared from the air and market-place might be the moment when we'd discover whether hip-hop truly was a cultural force or a manufacturing plant, a way of being or a way of selling porn DVDs, crunk juice, and S. Carter signature sneakers, blessed be the retired.

That might also be the moment at which poor Black communities began contesting the reality of their surroundings, their life opportunities. An interesting question arises: If enough folk from the 'hood get rich, does that suffice for all the rest who will die tryin'? And where does hip-hop wealth leave the question of race politics? And racial identity?

Picking up where Amiri Baraka and the Black Arts Movement left off, George Clinton realized that anything Black folk do could be abstracted and repackaged for capital gain. This has of late led to one mediocre comedy after another about Negroes frolicking at hair shows, funerals, family reunions, and backyard barbecues, but it has also given us Biz Markie and Outkast.

Oh, the selling power of the Black Vernacular. Ralph Ellison only hoped we'd translate it in such a way as to gain entry into the hallowed house of art. How could he know that the House of Lauren and the House of Polo would one day pray to broker that vernacular's cool marketing prow-ess into a worldwide licensing deal for bedsheets writ large with Jay Z's John Hancock? Or that the vernacular's seductive powers would drive Estée Lauder to propose a union with the House of P. Diddy? Or send Hewlett-Packard to come knocking under record exec Steve Stoute's shingle in search of a hip-hop-legit cool marketer?

Hip-hop's effervescent and novel place in the global economy is fur-ther proof of that good old Marxian axiom that under the abstracting powers of capitalism, "All that is solid melts into air" (or the ether-net, as the case might be). So that hip-hop floats through the virtual marketplace of branded icons as another consumable ghost, parasiti-cally feeding off the host of the real world's people—urbanized and institutionalized—whom it will claim till its dying day to "represent." And since those people just might need nothing more from hip-hop in their geopolitically circumscribed lives than the escapism, glamour, and voyeurism of hip-hop, why would they ever chasten hip-hop for not steadily ringing the alarm about the African American community's AIDS crisis, or for romanticizing incarceration more than attacking the prison-industrial complex, or for throwing a lyrical bone at issues of in-timacy or literacy or, heaven forbid, debt relief in Africa and the evils perpetuated by the World Bank and the IMF on the motherland?

All of which is not to say "Vote or Die" wasn't a wonderful attempt to at least bring the phantasm of Black politics into the twenty-four-hour nonstop booty, blunts, and bling frame that now has the hip-hop industry on lock. Or to devalue by any degree Russell Simmons's valiant efforts to educate, agitate, and organize around the Rockefeller drug-sentencing laws. Because at heart, hip-hop remains a radical, revolutionary enterprise for no other reason than its rendering people of African descent anything but invisible, forgettable, and dismissible in the consensual hallucination-simulacrum twilight zone of digitized mass distractions we call our lives in the matrixized, conservative-Christianized, Goebbelsized-by-Fox twenty-first century. And because, for the first time in our lives, race was nowhere to be found as a campaign issue in presidential politics and because hip-hop is the only place we can see large numbers of Black people being anything other than sitcom window dressing, it maintains the potential to break out of the box at the flip of the next lyrical genius who can articulate her people's suffering with the right doses of rhythm and noise to reach the bourgeois and still rock the boulevard.

Call me an unreconstructed Pan-African cultural nationalist, Africa-fer-the-Africans-at-home-and-abroad-type rock-and-roll nigga and I won't be mad at ya: I remember the Afrocentric dream of hip-hop's becoming an agent of social change rather than elevating a few ex–drug dealers' bank accounts. Against my better judgment, I still count myself among that faithful. To the extent that hip-hop was a part of the great Black cultural nationalist reawakening of the 1980s and early '90s, it was because there was also an antiapartheid struggle and anticrack struggle, and Minister Louis Farrakhan and Reverend Jesse Jackson were at the height of their rhetorical powers, recruitment ambitions, and media access, and a generation of Ivy League Black Public Intellectuals on both sides of the Atlantic had come to the fore to raise the philosophical stakes in African American debate, and speaking locally, there were protests organized around the police / White Citizens' Council lynchings of Bumpurs, Griffiths, Hawkins, Diallo, Dorismond, etc. etc. etc. Point being that hip-hop wasn't born in a vacuum but as part of a political dynamo that seems to have been largely dissipated by the time we arrived at the Million Man March, best described by one friend as the largest gathering in history of a people come to protest themselves, given its bizarre theme of atonement in the face of the goddamn White House.

The problem with a politics that theoretically stops thinking at the limit of civil rights reform and appeals to white guilt and Black consciousness was utterly revealed at that moment—a point underscored by the fact that the two most charged and memorable Black political events of the 1990s were the MMM and the hollow victory of the O.J. trial. Meaning, OK, a page had been turned in the book of African American economic and political life—clearly because we showed up in Washington en masse demanding absolutely nothing but atonement for our sins—and we did victory dances when a doofus ex-athlete turned Hertz spokesmodel bought his way out of lethal injection. Put another way, hip-hop sucks because modern Black populist politics sucks. Ishmael Reed has a poem that goes: "I am outside of history . . . it looks hungry . . . I am inside of history it's hungrier than I thot." The problem with progressive Black political organizing isn't hip-hop but that the No. 1 issue on the table needs to be poverty, and nobody knows how to make poverty sexy. Real poverty, that is, as opposed to studio-gangsta poverty, newly-inked-MC-with-a-story-to-sell poverty.

You could argue that we're past the days of needing a Black agenda. But only if you could argue that we're past the days of there being poor Black people and Driving While Black and structural, institutionalized poverty. And those who argue that we don't need leaders must mean Bush is their leader too, since there are no people on the face of this earth who aren't being led by some of their own to hell or high water. People who say that mean this: Who needs leadership when you've got twenty-four-hour cable and PlayStations? And perhaps they're partly right, since what people can name and claim their own leaders when they don't have their own nation-state? And maybe in a virtual America like the one we inhabit today, the only Black culture that matters is the one that can be downloaded and perhaps needs only business leaders at that. Certainly it's easier to speak of hip-hop hoop dreams than of structural racism and poverty, because for hip-hop America to not just desire wealth but demand power with a capital P would require thinking way outside the idiot box.

Consider, if you will, this "as above, so below" doomsday scenario: Twenty years from now we'll be able to tell our grandchildren and great-grandchildren how we witnessed cultural genocide: the systematic destruction of a people's folkways.

We'll tell them how fools thought they were celebrating the thirtieth anniversary of hip-hop the year Bush came back with a gang bang, when they were really presiding over a funeral. We'll tell them how once upon a time there was this marvelous art form where the Negro could finally say in public whatever was on his or her mind in rhyme and how the

Negro hip-hop artist, staring down minimum wage slavery, Iraq, or the freedom of the incarcerated chose to take his emancipated motor mouth and stuck it up a stripper's ass because it turned out there really was gold in them thar hills.

– 2004 –

Love and Crunk: Outkast

Speakerboxxx / The Love Below

Six hot jawnts into the game, the release of any Outkast album is an Event. They've given us the most scrumptious moments counter-nihilistic hip-hop has offered in recent memory. But none has loomed as more Event-ful than *Speakerboxxx / The Love Below*, because it may also be the group's last. This time the Outkast banner flies over two solo albums: the first in jewel-box order by the rowdy and irrepressible Big Boi, the second by the belovedly fly eccentric Andre 3000, latest link in a lengthy chain of supersoulful African American eccentrics stretching from Charley Patton and Jelly Roll Morton to Andre's guiding light in eclectic negritude, Prince. All folk who wielded weirdness like a scalpel, albeit one that carves order out of the cosmic slop of their free-associative funky imaginations.

Since hip-hop is now the Kmart of the American id, where our dark and unconscious shit turns into shinola, we need its democratic ideals to be messy. The Roots' Ahmir Thompson credits crack for the genius of eighties hip-hop music, and faults Bill Clinton for the generally agreed suckitude of the music's nineties genus. Fair enough, but Bill Clinton also presided over the rise of hip-hop's Dirty South oligarchies, an apt legacy for the country prez who whipped his dick out in the Oval Office. Just as Dirty Bill kept the White House close to the outhouse, southern hip-hop's progressive wing was sustaining the tradition of brain-teasing verbal panache and shock-of-the-new funk we once snootily considered the sole province of us uppity upsouth cosmopolite muh-fuhs. They also proved you could keep it thoughtful and pimpstroll-ful, goofball and gangsta, conspiracy-theoried and crunk. Being Dirty Southern means never having to say you're sorry for Master P or *The Matrix Reloaded*.

No, we ain't about to get it twisted. We know that in the rhyme-soloist MC gladiator arena New York, home of J-hova, Nas, L.L., and DMX, 50 Cent still rules the roost. But if you the kind that needs that good old

P-Funk freaknigga headcharge in your modern-day life, Outkast has been your hip-hop band for more than a minute. I'm talking about bootsylicious BASS. And Brides of Funkenstein girlchorus moments. And those Blackbyrd McKnight–style guitar fusillades tearing through "Bombs over Baghdad." And all those insouciantly inscrutable booty-snatching lyrics to go. Not to mention hip-hop's only rock star, our best-dressed clown prince of phools, Andre 3000, as much a vision to behold as a voice to be heard. Role play becomes him. Inside the new album you'll find flicks of him seminude, Dionysian centaur dude surrounded by a bevy of brown-girl space angels in an astrological space-time continuum. Worth the price of the ticket if you already think Andre's a god.

If you worship at other altars, know that Mr. 3000 talks more than he rhymes on *The Love Below* and sings profusely about Love. About Cupid and Valentine's Day and "Dracula's Wedding Day" and "Love Hater" and "Love in War" and our romantic hero's love for ladies, lap dancers, unicorns, and prototypes. There's lotsa love and nostalgia in the music too: a drunken Art Ensemble of Chicago swing thing here, an Earth, Wind & Fire torch song there, a punk rockabilly stomp, the ever Princely combo of swooping symphony and gooseneck woodblock beats, and an instrumental jungle variation on Coltrane's "My Favorite Things" up in here. One sexy, smart, stylish, tuneful, and above all silly record for starters— Andre Benjamin 3000 in a nutshell, in excelsis, in spades. Cutting to the chase: If the very thought of Andre or Gilbert and Sullivan doesn't make you smile, *The Love Below* might not be your cup of topsy-turvy ambrosia, bojangles, and laughing gas. It's a concept album and there's supposed to be a movie version next year. Yay.

In any other group *Speakerboxxx* would be the box Andre decided to start thinking outside of. But there's plenty room in Big Boi's house for the Andre Benjamins of this world as well as Ludacris, Jay Z, Big Gipp, Killer Mike, CeeLo, Lil Jon and the East Side Boyz, and Slimm Calhoun. You could hear the Big Boi disc as providing coverage for Dre the AT-Lien's space-case act of fey bravery in the unfrilly world of southern rap. But Mr. Boi more than expoobidently holds it down for all those Outkast fanatics not quite ready to join Mr. 3000 in the elysian fields of romance in psychedelic Tin Pan Alley, and proves himself no slouch with the freakness either. And Dre, still by his brother's side contrary to band-breaking-up-yo theory, produces and rhymes on the 120-bpm Eurodisco-turns-swooning-Patti LaBelle-sampling track that is *Speakerboxxx*'s first cut and graces three more before album's end.

Where Dre twists Prince remnants to his own astroboyish amorous ends, Big Boi holds up Outkast's P-Funk revival tent. "Bowtie" is very

Gloryhallastoopid, "The Rooster" could find a home on *Motor Booty Affair*, the crunkadelic Killer Mike cameo "Bust" is some *Standing on the Verge* for your shelf ass while *Trombipulation* could have used the fetching "Church." No copycatting here, though. George Clinton and company's best ideas, especially the harmonic ones, have been needing a change of venue. They've been barely touched let alone exhausted by G-funk. And never fear: Big Boi also maintains Uncle Jam and the Outkast of yesteryear's ghettocentric take on world politrix. Suckas will bounce.

– 2003 –

White Freedom: Eminem

So he's back. Presumably with another multiplatinum bitch. The kracka you love to hate. Only don't hate Eminem because he's white. Hate him because he's the only free man in commercial hip-hop. (As Lauryn is the only woman who's taken Ntozake Shange's advice and found god in herself and is loving her fiercely.) Hate him because he's the only man in hip-hop not burdened with representing the 'hood and Black sex to hip-hop's prime real estate, the vanilla suburbs. Hate him because he gets paid by the industry to be whimsical and personal. Free to be Em when such whimsical and personal Negro geniuses as Beans, Vast Aire, Jean Grae, and Prince Po got to mine the more-freelance-than-free hip-hop underground. Of course they're free too—free to never be seen on a Viacom-owned Negro entertainment station, free to never get played on hip-hop radio. But this is a price Negroes must pay when their music can't be used to score *Girls Gone Wild*.

Of course Mr. Em has his own crosses to bear, since he knows better than most how guilty he is of being white. So guilty that on *Encore* Mr. Em allots much of his time as a free man coming on humble, begging forgiveness, tripping over lines to explain himself to the Negro community for getting involved in coon bidness such as 50's beef with Ja Rule and those rediscovered ancient rhymes riddling Black girls with Mick Jagger–worthy abuse. His exercise of white freedom has also gotten him banned from Viacom-owned BET, presumably on the sensitive Negro community's behalf, for his Michael Jackson–mocking video. It has also found him scribed on the covers of hip-hop magazines as the greatest living rapper, which always makes me laugh and think of how predisposed white supremacy has made even colored journalists to crown any white man who takes a Black art form to the bank, to mo' money than

Shine ever seen, as the greatest who ever lived. Fred Astaire, Benny Goodman, Elvis, Eric Clapton, Larry Bird, take your pick. As if any of them understood the kind of casual fatalism I overheard on 116th and Adam Clayton Powell the other day, where one brother say to another, straight-faced and not a hint of irony, "He'll be out soon, he didn't get much time, he only got ten more years." All that August Wilson sheet in other words. That real Black Angst. The kind of angst that only the burdensome, belaboring crucible of white supremacy could twist into those bizarre, contorted, and comforting expressions of Black Pleasure and Irony known as bebop and hip-hop and the blues.

There's no denying that with his broken home, *Eight Mile* origins, druggy mama, and baby-mama drama, Mr. Em does the sound of white male angst as well as Iggy Pop, Woody Allen, and Bill Clinton combined, and that given how you never see another white man within ten feet of Mr. Em if he and D-12 can help it, you figure he feels he has adopted himself into the Black Guerrilla Family. You could also argue that anything that foments unity in struggle between the youth of America across color lines and late-stage capitalist hip-hop is hardly an awful thing. Especially given that being poor and white in this country is considered such a sin against god it'll make you vote for his only begotten Bush, there's little reason to doubt Mr. Em when he shares his passionate love affair with hip-hop or tells how during Public Enemy and X-Clan's heyday that love drove him to wear an African medallion and Flavor Flav clock, knowing brothers liked to snatch it from his neck. Such love of hip-hop and to such a degree that Mr. Em feels the need to share how genuinely hurt he is that a nonentity like Benzino has made him persona non grata at the *Source*, a magazine he grew up on. And to such a degree that those who found Mr. Em far funnier and more irreverent when he used his ghetto pass to hang himself, call his mama a cunt, and stab his baby-mama problem to death may well be disappointed (all the bzangin' Dre-like beats here notwithstanding) with how much quality rhyme time he gives over to apologia to the community Negro, to assaulting safe and easy Negro targets like MJ on "Just Lose It" and "Ass Like That," to the twenty-four-hour motorbootyfest known as KneeGrow Uddertainment Television. And can't nobody be mad at him for trying to rally his flock against the President's War on Iraq in "Mosh."

Yet and still, the fact that Mr. Em could get that sentiment out on music television when Dead Prez, hip-hop's most been-trigger-ready presidential assassins, never-ever will is less a testament to Mr. Em's white male freedom than it may first appear. More a testament, indeed, to the fact that the powers that be are more skeered of the Black Guerrilla Family's militant wing speaking to family about revolution through this cable-televised hip-hop medium than the angriest wigga alive. See, end of the day, Howdy Doody just don't cut it when your tired poor sleeping masses need to hear it from Malcolm X. Or god forbid from Fitty Lloyd Banks Jay Z Lil Jon Nelly Chingy Fabolous pass the smelling salts what kinda agit-prop ra ra hip-hop planet you think this is we living on?

– 2004 –

Wu-Dunit: Wu-Tang Clan

Wu-Tang Forever

Raekwon, set it off: Yo Yo What up Yo Time is running out It's for real though Let's connect Politic Ditto. Once upon a time hip-hop was something we did out of necessity and not boredom. Being down demanded urgency, like an emergency, because the shit gave you agency and currency. Like a four-alarm fire, you ignored hip-hop at your own peril. Once upon a time we thought hip-hop was the fire next time or at least the spark. Once upon a time we believed in the Easter Bunny too. Your moms got the pictures to prove it too. Just look at de chile. Sitting up there grinning at the Great White Rabbit. Hippety-hop. Grow the fok up. Hip-hop baby, your bunny been cooked.

Can you relate? It's like this you know: If not for RZA and the Wu-Tang Clan, commercial hip-hop would be irrelevant and unlistenable. Like Frank Zappa said, hard-core isn't dead. It just smells funny. For months heads been dying to know: *Wu-Tang Forever*—sophomore slump or sophomore triumph? If it's wack where does that leave us? All alone with DJ Shadow? Homey don't think so. GZA sez, "Rhymes filter through the neck before the words hit the chrome / Pro Tools editing tracks that's rough / A jam without a live MC isn't enough." RZA sez point-blank "This is true hip-hop." In the purest form. MCing! Lyrics! "This ain't no R and B. Wack nigga taking a loop thinking it's gonna be the sound of the culture."

Everything you read about hip-hop these days reads like a requiem or an obituary. How did we get here? You want to talk about your culture? Got your culture right here. Back in the day of innocence and wonder and a little will to power. Back when the song mattered more than the video hoochie. Who knew that one day hip-hop would come to this: Tupac and Biggie shot dead in the streets behind some bloodclot Bloods and Crips business? Who let the gat out the bag? Gangsta rap had to prove Bob Marley a liar: "One thing about music, when it hits, you feel no pain."

Let's blame it all on Ice Cube: two-parent-family-reared, architectural-drafting-school graduate turned gangsta rap Pandora. Updated Ralph Ellison's archetype from *Invisible Man*. The crafty, charismatic, middle-class Black boy who incites the lumpen proletariat for fun, profit, and street credibility. Brer Rabbit motherfucker. How many tar babies will choke on his mythology while he scampers away to see another West Side day? (You might want to read the early careers of Stokely Carmichael, LeRoi Jones, and Louis Farrakhan as *Invisible Man* dub versions. Then again you might not.)

The trajectory of *Straight Outta Compton* to Biggie in a casket is a straight line. We had to declare hip-hop dead after Biggie's death because we killed him; take out a moment of silence.

Now exhale.

This has been the history of hip-hop from the get-go: soon as you declare hip-hop dead, hip-hop reanimates. Michael Myers style. So let's get it straight: Death Row died, not hip-hop. And as of *Wu-Tang Forever* it's clear RZA and the Wu are on some Mitsubishi corporation-type shit. This is a thousand-year plan in motion. Afrika Bambaataa once predicted rap will be around as long as people are talking. But the Wu do more than talk. Nine young Black men in the music business who roll like a guerrilla corporate culture rather than subdivide for the dollar. How could we not be impressed? Not since George Clinton has anybody sold the same band to every major label in the book. The Wu are masters of camaraderie, Black unity, collectivity, and mad strategy. Chess Master Drunken Master Kung Fu Swordsman Five Percent Nation strategy. They're not trying to wake up one morning and find themselves victims of the industry. What sense does it make to beat the odds, survive the crack game, as most of these Staten Island project exiles have, then go out like a roach in the record business? Get your shit together 'fo' the fucking Illuminati hit. Our everlasting essence stays fired over Egypt.

Rappers aren't just the outlaw folk heroes of wigger wet dreams, but the press agents for those vertical slave ships and maximum insecurity skyscrapers, the Projects. Picture this: Dante Alighieri with a Rover, a RZA, and a pager. Or tell the brother not hip to the Wu who asks, "What are their issues, what is their message vis-à-vis that of, say, Public Enemy?": Black Male Redemption in the Projects Now. The Wu illuminate the abyss of government housing while pointing a way to the exit sign. If you never been there, they'll show you voyeurs around. If you've been there and never want to go back, they'll remind you refugees why.

If you're dodging death on the daily up in that piece, they might be your Harriet Tubman.

"Part of the lasting power of Greek drama lies in the vividness with which it presents extreme love and (still more) intense hatred within the family. Duty to the family and duty to the state may come into conflict. But no Greek tragedy is secular. Although the dramatists normally focus on the actions and sufferings of human beings, the gods are always present in the background."

Clocking in with ninety-plus minutes of gloom, doom, rumpus, and ruckus, *Wu-Tang Forever* is like the Greeks. Back in the day, Brer Plato's folk used to hold theatrical "tragedy contests." Drawn-out battles where those bold Lyricists Euripides, Sophocles, and Aeschylus strived to beat out the next man at composing tales of woe and enlightenment. Occasionally the mood would be lightened by a hypersexual "satyr play." Over the course of *WuF*'s twenty-seven cuts, the Wu borrows from this organizing principle—contrasting philosophy with metafoolishness and missionary work with sexual debasement. Method Man: "Build a devil mindstate / Blood kin can't relate / No longer brothers / We unstable / Like Cain when he slew Abel." Ol' Dirty Bastard: "Pardon me bitch as I shit on your grass / Ho! You've been shitted on / I'm not the first dog to shit on your lawn." Inspectah Deck: "Not a role model / I walk a hard road to follow / I sold bottles of sorrow / Then chose poems and novels."

Lyricists and lyrics the Wu have in overabundance, perhaps to the point of overkill, but that's probably the point—Wu comes in waves. Raekwon, Method Man, and Ol' Dirty Bastard (Wu's answer to Flavor Flav, if not Dolemite) possess the most readily identifiable voice prints among their stylists. The poetically peripatetic gully-glimmer twins Raekwon and Ghostface Killa as well as philosophical point man GZA are, line for line, the most ingenious of the Wu scribes, but Meth, the group's sex symbol, possesses a voice that's pure erotica. Coming up fast are Inspectah Deck, whose diction screams Vulcan logic, and Capadonna, whose relish for pornography rivals Larry Flynt's.

If you got Wu fever you're likely to suspend judgment as to whether *WuF* is good or evil, dope or wack. If you're too old for such mindless idolatry and want solid tracks, *WuF* got a few instant classics for your ass. In terms of continuity and quality, disc one is hit or miss, and more miss than hit for a good half, a been-there-bought-the-Wu-shirt retread. Disc two is such a tight, fluid and demolishing show of skills that other hip-hop crews will be picking shrapnel off their tongues for months. (Especially when they see the numbers—*WuF* sold 612,000 copies in its first week of release.)

It's not until track six drops on the first disc, "As High as Wu-Tang Get," that you stop feeling lethargy has set in. Suddenly there's a party going on. Ol' Dirty sets it off, GZA grinds metrics to the floor, Meth pours on the raspy charm like lava. RZA dub-theory getting you mad-lifted once again. This man gets more mileage out of two shots of bass than anybody since Lee "Scratch" Perry. (Bet you money an RZA instrumental album would go gold. Why? Because Wu cuts minus vocals equal baby-making music.)

RZA's lush and haunting string sections turn up elsewhere, and this time with an anonymous violin soloist in tow. (Word is she's Karen Briggs, on loan from Israeli New Age artist Yanni.) Not since Isaac Hayes—RZA's number one influence, we'd wager—has any Black pop artist used strings in a sexier or spookier manner. Cinematic is a term overused to describe RZA's production but it's accurate—ambience, atmosphere, mise-en-scène all matter as much to him as beats, and sometimes more so. His dramatic and profligate use of kung fu dialogue and Wu-member repartee affirms this. On most albums such material would function as cute skits. On Wu projects they play like the Zen moments in a bloody action flick.

If Public Enemy brought microsurgery to hip-hop collage, RZA brings a sculptural hand closer to the source than Cubism. Like an African carver, his Orientalist exaggerations of old-school soul song forms sounds organic rather than grafted. In this respect Tricky and RZA are similar: they both use samplers in a way that suggests they're working with flesh rather than found objects.

As Darius James said of Pam Grier and blaxploitation, the Wu-Tang are their own genre in hip-hop. They have their own sound and their own themes. Like P-Funk, Public Enemy, Ishmael Reed, and Thomas Pynchon, the Wu aren't just a band but a context, a self-referencing encyclopedic narrative. Every particle of noise invites reading as oblique commentary on the whole program. Whatever the Wu quotes, the Wu consumes and colonizes. You hip to John Woo or kung fu? Step back, son—that's now the cultural property of the Wu.

All the Wu aura in the world, however, can't salvage the lame tracks that lend *WuF*'s opening disc a less than auspicious air. Save for two gems, the aforementioned "As High as Wu-Tang Get" and "A Better Tomorrow" (what I tell you about John Woo?), I'd consign it immediately to the dustbin of hip-hoprisy. "A Better Tomorrow" is the most PC and pathos-saturated song the Wu has ever cut. Dig the chorus, a hard-core round robin that strikes the right cautionary note before slipping into sermon mode: You can't party your life away Drink your life away Smoke your life away Fuck your life away Dream your life away Scheme your life away 'Cause your seeds grow up the same way. In this tearjerker, Method Man maximizes the melancholic possibilities: Momma says take your time young man and build your own Don't wind up like your old dad Still searching for them glory days he never had. Those babies looking up to us The Million-Man March MCs get on the bus.

On the other hand, some of RZA's lines here—Y'all bitches love dances And pulling down your pants While your man is on tour you spend up his advances Your friends ain't shit All they do is drink smoke and suck dick The whole projects is trapped in sin—beg the same old tired question, and as always, I got to be the whinybutt who raises it: Why do brothers get more amped blaming poor project-incarcerated sistas for the state of Babylon than the dread Illuminati (a Wu-phemism for white supremacy)? To Black nationalism's long-standing dialectic of pimps-up-ho's-down, the Wu remains true. (Yes Nequanna, heads get confused trying to decide what's more diabolical—the 'luminati or the punanny.) It's like in *The Mack* where the pimp Goldie gets mad at the white man for selling heroin to the little brothers but got no problem with sistas hooking until they drop. As the biographies of Pablo Picasso and Miles Davis point out, you can loathe woman and still be a motherfucker in the manly modernist canon. Perhaps there's a connection between misogyny and the manly modernist muse. Perhaps we need to know where Wu-type brothers stand on the position of the woman in the revolution. Just pray your daughter doesn't bring one home for dinner, or that your son doesn't mistake their female problems for chivalry. (Per "Fuck the pussy / Give me the money and the weed.")

– 1997 –

Unlocking the Truth vs. John Cage

Last night in LOISADA Black Nerd Nirvana rained down in a most mad-random fashion. The Black Rock Coalition's Afterparty for Jeremy Xido's film *Death Metal Angola* was double booked at 107 Suffolk while a twenty-five-hour midnight gig staged by Performa 21 and performance art legend William Pope L. was happening too unbeknownst to either party.

So just dig this groovy/grimy scene: Out in the rowdy bar area Afro-punken tween wunderkind Unlocking the Truth and NY hardcore OG's Funk Face thrashed away, amps set on stun. Inside the dark and somnolent Flamboyan Theatre, Pope L. had folk of varied colors—Caleb Linzy,

Duuude—SOFTLY reading—under intense atmospheric pressure—from John Cage's Silence. The Unlocking brothers were smashing drums and thundering power chords while barely audible wisps of Cage kept being bravely droned in low monotones: "This music was not what Morton Feldman meant by Intersection Music . . . you must play it more beautifully and aggressively than anyone else. . . . Since we possess nothing everything is delightful. . . . The I Ching says those who contemplate esthetic forms must contemplate the forms of the heavens . . . the effects of these results are conducive to less separateness, less fear and more love."

Just as UTT were ending their mind boggling set of titanic instrumentals in a sick decrescendo this line by Cage floated up into the din: "And what of all those silences?" Our sweet cuz Chicava HoneyChild described this unholy collision of molten black noise and cagy white thought balloons as "magical" and so it was. Like George Clinton sez, "We are just a biological speculation sitting here vibrating and we know not what we are vibrating upon." Rarely has one's love for geek noir's many splendored forms been so organically well fed. (Kudos to Performa 21's Adrienne Edwards for soldiering on beyond the break of dawn. It's almost over my sis . . .)

– 2015 –

Screenings

Spike Lee's *Bamboozled*

Even at his most appalling, deplorable, déclassé, Spike Lee is nothing less than inspirational, phenomenal, our mediaphrenic mother of agents provocateurs, a muckraking national treasure. *Bamboozled* is hands down Spike's most complicated race-stew. True to form, it has little to say about human relations outside of that quagmire. A central paradox of Spike's films is that for all their psychological hollowness, they contain a lost 'n' found storehouse of American racial baggage, a veritable Xanadu of the attitudinizing that makes the race thing so definitive of the American id.

Problematic but bountiful, *Bamboozled* is hardly Spike's worst—that honor being reserved for the unforgettable *Girl 6*. Bad form in a Spike movie doesn't just refer to aesthetic breaches, but a feeling of "Damn, that ninja slimed me again!" (cf. the gratuitous orgy scenes in *He Got Game* and *Summer of Sam*). *Girl 6* managed the astounding feat of being prudish, prurient, and dull, and served his umpteenth revision of Irene Cara's fall from grace in *Fame*—for Spike, female sexuality is just a step away from original sin, a gateway to humiliation, degradation, and expulsion from the garden. Accusing Spike of hating women would be wrong; like many a man he has a near hysterical need to distance himself from female vulnerability—the flimsy binary veil of sexual reputation (madonna/whore) proving an especially inviting license to ill. In *Bamboozled*, Jada Pinkett Smith's Sloan must not only suffer being identified as a corporate whore by a shameless tap-dancing coon, but assume a hangdog *Scarlet Letter* expression and have no comeback. Woman you nigger of the world indeed.

If Spike's films are about one thing, it is the self-hate and defensive posturing that race hate has produced in Americans Black and white, the subrational stuff no one else in the mainstream even wants to touch. Spike's work also demonstrates that American racial identity is less a thing to be contemplated than performed—not to mention paraded, primped, politicked, and prostituted, as loudly and wrongly as possible in civic space.

Given his avowed love for musicals (seen in the soundstage artificiality of even his grittiest location shooting), *Bamboozled* appears an inevitable addition to the Spike corpus. Minstrelsy and Black vaudeville are the primal sites for both American musical theater and the visual vocabulary of racial stereotyping. Spike was destined to one day explore the link between minstrel shows and musicals—how they are constructed and romanticized in our popular culture. Though professedly a satire about contemporary Black sitcoms, *Bamboozled* is far too overreaching with its signifyin' on all comers for that declaration to hold water—no matter how many times Spike fields the asinine question of whether blacking up could come back on the UPN.

As Ted Gioia's crazed apologia for Al Jolson (and by inference Ted Danson and those tar-brushed Queens firefighters and their cop buddy caught out there two years ago) in a recent *Sunday Times* Arts & Leisure piece showed, a taste for the cork grease still whets some appetites. Enough to invoke dribble on the order of "Jolson continued to use burnt-cork makeup, perhaps not through any desire to degrade blacks, but simply to enhance the theatrical qualities of his performances." When Gioia lives in an America where some brilliant African American cantor can be forgiven for his swastika face or that uproarious Black comic surgically altered to resemble O.J. gets laughs for his endearing punch line, "Don't make me have to cut you," that'll be the day Jolson's talent is allowed to outshine his 'shine cosmetics. Historian Gioia dehistoricizes Jolson's coon mask, conveniently forgetting that the slang term for Southern segregation laws, Jim Crow, derived from the central slave figure in postbellum minstrel shows. Blackface is the slaveholder's gaze made grotesquely darkened flesh, a golem-like emblem of the deeply held desire to keep the nigra alienated and never able to satiate what Richard Wright identified as their American hunger. The NAACP protest against the Confederate flag is entertaining to the degree that it fuels cracker agitation, but hardly an emotional rallying point for most African Americans. Unfurl a white man in blackface if you want to see some bloodshed and tears.

Bamboozled covertly evades the visual offense of depicting white minstrelsy dead-on. This it achieves by having its real minstrel act occur during Michael Rapaport's high-octane performance as the Blacker-than-thou network wigger who will demean and emasculate and steal ideas from Damon Wayans's tight-assed, Harvard-trained Oreo and alleged writer-producer, Pierre Delacroix. Interestingly enough, the ham-fisted *Bamboozled* contains virtually no obvious critique of chitlin circuit television; hardly odd since Spike just made *The Original Kings of Comedy* with the cream of Black comics in television today. The real targets of this satire aren't to be found in the programmers of colored pablum but in the larger world of Black celebrity, a fact evident in the casting of the film itself. *Bamboozled* is pointedly and blatantly Spike's Revenge on Black Hollywood, hip-hop, and many other Black entertainment success stories of his generation—a Godfather-like decimation of the competitive field.

This begins with the Wayans family, whom Spike has probably never forgiven for having Tommy Davidson (*Bamboozled*'s Sleep'n Eat) skewer him in the *In Living Color* skit about Spike's Joint, where patrons are hustled to purchase "Mo' Betta Butter" and most egregiously "Malcolm Ex-Lax" and where copies of *School Daze* can't be given away. Now that was some Black TV satire for your ass. As was Spike's *Jeffersons* skit in *Crooklyn*.

Bamboozled is set in a kind of alternative universe of Black showbiz: In this one, the Roots are known as the Alabama Porch Monkeys and Mos Def isn't our Mos Def who spat at an invitation to audition for proposed slavery sit-com *The Secret Diary of Desmond Pfeiffer* but Big Blak African, a fame-hungry, pro-Black militant poseur and forty-ounce addict. Jada Pinkett Smith must mount Homey the Clown in order to mount her career ladder, and slick, sly, and wicked Paul Mooney is Homey's drunken, washed-up daddy. (There is an obvious essay to be written about the oedipal complex running through Spike's films, up-front in *Do the Right Thing, Jungle Fever, Malcolm X, Crooklyn, He Got Game*, and the unmade *The Messenger*; a less frontal exposé of his closet obsession with Black middle-class dysfunction might also be in order.)

This is a world where Savion Glover never tap-danced his way to fame and fortune in two Broadway shows, Ving Rhames and Cuba Gooding Jr. prove unable to stifle their inner coons while accepting their Token Negro Actor awards, and the overqualified Tommy Davidson must play second fiddle to a homeless tap-dance kid to work at all. The latter is unfortunately true on this side of *Bamboozled*'s wormhole. Davidson's pathos-driven performance as Sleep'n Eat is the only one where the pain doesn't seem faked (though Wayans's pain in his role is all too apparent), perhaps the saddest virtuoso-turn since the days of Bert Williams.

Bamboozled presumably satirizes the minstrel form itself, but in that aim Spike proves himself as Bamboozable as the next ringmaster. The loving, lush, lavish production values put into play for his New Millennium Minstrel Show dramatically outshimmer the drab, fluorescent mise-en-scène everywhere else in evidence. As features on video go, *Bamboozled* often makes *Hoop Dreams* seem posted up by Industrial Light and Magic if not drawn from van Gogh's palette. The New Millennium maybe didn't have to look so fly, but Spike is too much the showman to not immaculately dress his stage and his blacked-up minstrels with as much seductive surface beauty as possible, and some wickedly rhythmic digital animation thrown in for good measure. A graphic-intensive filmmaker to the core, Spike would be lying if he denied how much he loved staging those scenes. The race man in him crying "No, no, no" to Sambo's entreaties, the cineaste moaning yes, yes, yes, going cold-Molly-Bloom-up in this piece, the director's adoring eye proving, as always, a tough thing to hide behind the ramshackle bulwark of moral outrage and indignation.

Spike also reveals himself, in the flick's many brilliant supporting performances, asides, sight gags, and documentary clips, to be one of our greatest coonologists, a thinker who delights in representing the found performance poetry of unmitigated coon behavior. On that score, *Bamboozled* is frequently more fun than a barrel of frat boys.

Let me begin this graf by saying I am about to give away the ending: Now certain critics, like the two Harlem sistas who departed the Magic Johnson Theater ahead of me, have taken offense that Glover's Mantan was targeted for assassination by the Mau Maus in the riveting Dance of Death sequence, and not Rapaport's loudmouth nigger-baiting TV producer. "It's stupid," they opined. "Why kill the actor and not the guy who made the show?" The answer requires that we turn to the Norman Jewison version of Charles Fuller's *A Soldier's Story* and offer that Spike does not hail from the Howard Rollins-as-Captain Davenport/Thurgood Marshall reform perspective, nor the Denzel Washington-as-Private Melvin Peterson/Mao Tse-Tung death-to-all-running-dogs mandate, but from the Adolph Caesar-as-Sergeant Waters/Stanley Crouch school of coon-slaughter: Having found accommodations in the master's guest house to his liking, as frankly we all do, he is still not above lynching the first unrepentant jigaboo he finds cakewalking across his lawn.

For the record, Spike, like Crouch, has never really "gotten" hip-hop, the most amoral, resourceful, and cannibalistic folk music in history, which explains why his skits about forty ounces and "Timmy Hillnigger" seem flat and wildly passé viewed in the Versace and Cristal era, and less pointed than the "Tommy Field Nigger" pun I heard over three years ago, which more accurately ridicules how Tommy didn't have to advertise to the ghetto since the ghetto was gracious enough to raise him up by his bootstraps first. Lampooning Air Jordans would have more relevantly addressed the corporatized fashion enslavement of African Americans and offshore Asians, but Rage against the Machine Spike ain't.

A simpler answer to the aforementioned sistas' critique might be that *Bamboozled* is also a minstrel performance of sorts by its director and therefore shall not violate the rule of mainstream cinema that politically conscious Black men cannot be shown on screen inflicting pain on white males—especially if they're the kind of white men who greenlight film budgets. These issues aside, *Bamboozled* speaks existential volumes about the African American anxiety that neither good behavior nor bling-bling can free our minds from the ever-present fear of being "profiled," riddled by a forty-one-bullet NYPD salute, taken out for a Jasper, Texas, joyride, or suffering a Nissan loan rejection.

Those real-life scenarios declare more eloquently than Spike ever could that no Black performance, no Black male show, be it on stage or in the boardroom, can remove open-hunting-season signs and the stain of the tar brush from around Nubian necks. As that wit Vernon Reid once observed, "We're the Men in Black 24-7," AmeriKKKa's favorite-born suspects by many other names. *Bamboozled* declares symbolic war on the notion of Black performance as an escape vehicle and as emblem of Black authenticity. As the success and street cred of Eminem has overnight demolished any Blacker-than-Black pretensions left in hip-hop (if only because he's got mad flow and sounds sooo white), it's fascinating to see the Soulquarian Crew (the Roots, D'Angelo, Jill Scott, Bilal) arc Black performance back around to the sort of Pentecostal release, social commentary, and instrumental virtuosity which characterized post-Sly soul, funk, and Afrocentric fusion. Call it the new Black formalism, a bebop/P-Funk-redux privileging of communal call-and-response over telegenic posturing—though Rebecca Walker's take on D'Angelo's buck-naked "How Does It Feel" video as the auction block revisited isn't easily dismissed.

Here at the start of the twenty-first century, Zen master Louis Armstrong's arch koan "What Did I Do to Be So Black and Blue?" is no closer to being a relic of the race's American experience than Steel Pulse's (via Exodus) "How can we sing in a strange land?" *Bamboozled* argues that we will keep on singing, testifying, and coonin' for accommodations in the master's house even if it kills us. And if merely performing Blackness won't save us? I hear KRS-One in the wings whispering, "Real bad boys move in silence," Dead Prez openly declaring armed revolution to be a bigger movement than hip-hop, the Malcolm X Grassroots Movement flying their Free the Land (not Fort Greene) banner, the Witness Project archiving police-brutality survivors, the Critical Resistance posse rallying to shut down the prison-construction industry. More blood and more dread yeah, the beats and the beatdowns shall go on, la luta continua someone will likely have to translate as the struggle continues, "I have come to wound the autumnal city," now somebody give the drummer some . . .

– 2000 –

It's a Mack Thing

The joys of blaxploitation are many if problematic and exist somewhere between good ol' guilty pleasure, political incorrectness, racial chauvinism, and psychotronic cinema. Two decades later the genre's classics seem as lurid, badly acted, and bizarre now as they did back in the day. Yet they also point up the mythic distance that is both maintained around Black people and by Black people in American society. To hijack a James Baldwin refrain, to be Black and conscious in Wonderbread America is to be in a constant state of alienation. To hijack another from W. E. B. Du Bois, one is also constantly aware of one's alienness. Abysmally written films like *The Mack* depend on the alienness and freakishness of seeing Black glamour portrayed onscreen. Blaxploitation movies, sheerly by exaggerating and centering Black visual difference, capture this existential condition spectacularly if unconsciously. The way they do this has little to do with art or politics and everything to do with the clothes, chile, and who's decked out in them. Worn on the stars' svelte African frames like casual wear, those outlandish, superheroic costumes point up how Black skin tones and body language can rhythmically transform the wackest of gear into some ol' mad haute couture shit. (In *Foxy Brown*, Pam Grier sports some yellow lapels wider than her big-head Afro and still looks fly.)

In blaxploitation, the stars had to perform the function of set design, play the role, and be the mise-en-scène just like the great Hollywood stars. Transcendence is found in the ineffable power of Black faces, figures, and fashions in motion. We're talking ballet here, we're talking African dance, we're talking *Soul Train* with close-ups. The Romanesque noses of Pam Grier and *The Mack*'s one-trick pony Max Julien are worthy of whole essays by themselves. What might Fellini have done with such schnozzes?

As amateurish as much else about those films may seem, clearly somebody in the casting department recognized that Grier, Julien, and *Shaft*'s Richard Roundtree had classic movie star faces. The kind of faces that fill up the screen with glamour, sensuality, and the illusion of a rich and mysterious inner life. Blaxploitation's creation of Black movie stars is interesting considering the difficulty today's young Black filmmakers have in developing bankable stars. Perhaps the director-driven nature of today's projects doesn't allow actors to flex and eclipse the auteur behind the lens. Whatever one thinks of Tarantino, and I think highly of him, he has no problem letting his actors run away with the picture. If brother QT has learned anything from blaxploitation it's how to deploy over-the-top performances, personas, and presences as a narrative device. So that the driving force of *Pulp Fiction* isn't what happens next but what are those crazy muhfuhkuhs Sam Jackson, Bruce Willis, and John Travolta going to do next. I await the day when a young Black filmmaker eschews morality-play naturalism for the mayhem for mayhem's sake one finds in early N.W.A. Black nationalism's Black is beautiful campaign was a necessary Black supremacist corrective to Hollywood's white supremacist beauty standard. Blaxploitation producers picked up on this reversal, subverting and perverting it for their own nasty ends. While white people are almost always villainous in blaxploitation, the crime they seem most guilty of is being white, not to mention corny, ugly, and neurotic. Less than a handful of Black films since blaxploitation have attempted to foreground beauty as the ultimate narrative hook: Julie Dash's *Daughters of the Dust* and Isaac Julien's *Looking for Langston* being the most notable of them.

The Mack is the most existential of blaxploitation classics, the most inert action movie ever made. Its star, Max Julien, who could have passed for Huey Newton in a dark alley, always looks like he's in a coke-induced trance. Even in scenes with Richard Pryor, Julien appears so deep in his own purple haze that you'd think he was reciting his lines to virtual rather than real actors. His character, the novice pimp Goldie, drifts to the top of the macking game without much resistance from the established players. We rarely see him do more than talk shit, brood, and look fly in a dazzling assortment of colorful, foppish gear. I'm extremely partial to his high-collared cloaks and skin-tight paisley jumpsuits.

There are few plot gears in *The Mack*. Even the requisite revenge killings—of one of the white cops who killed Goldie's mama and his lone Caucasian hooker—carry little emotional weight, possibly because we don't see the cops commit either murder. But the problem with having a pimp for a hero is that no one cares about his moral outrage. When Goldie tells a dope-dealing mafioso scumbag that he's like "a disease," you want to holler something at the screen like, "Who you think you are nigga? Penicillin?"

What makes *The Mack* memorable is how enthralled the filmmakers were with the bacchanal aspects of the players' game. There are scenes of pimp pageantry that serve no purpose other than to document the player lifestyle: There's the players' picnic, the players' ball where Goldie is crowned Mack of the Year, and then there's the players' pool championship where Goldie's number-one competitor, Pretty Tony (Dick

Anthony Williams), loses one of his prize hos to Goldie ("You know the rules of the game, Pretty Tony. Your bitch just chose me").

Blaxploitation films are considered transgressive for their consistent indulgence in mutilation and sadism and *The Mack* does not disappoint with the killing of Pretty Tony. Mistakenly assumed by Goldie to have rubbed out his mama, Pretty Tony is ordered by Goldie's bud, Richard Pryor, to stick himself with his own knife-tipped cane. This before they stick dynamite in his mouth and blow him to smithereens. *The Mack*'s most philosophical moment occurs right before Goldie blows away the most racist of the bad white cops, who, rather than beg for his life, desperately tries to get Goldie to realize that they're cut from the same cloth. It's mercy pleas like that which make blaxploitation read as Black science fiction, Black cinema from another planet.

– 1995 –

Sex and Negrocity: John Singleton's *Baby Boy*

Black people can be found #!@$ing in John Singleton's *Baby Boy*. Rawdog, pardon our French. Your usual euphemisms need not apply. Not your having sex making love makem whoopee or knocking boots nor your beast with two backs gettin' it on gettin' busy gettin' down doing the do the deed the nasty the wild thing. No. Just dead all that. Negroes are #!@$ing in this movie. Rawdog. Simulating that real deal with a license to ill deal sex. That sweaty, steamy, comical, contortionist, desperate, anxious, African stuff. #!@$ing isn't all people do in *Baby Boy*, a film also fixated on life, death, familial dysfunction, repair, and redemption, not to mention one twenty-year-old man's fear of cutting the umbilical cord though he has children by two working women. All the ribaldry does figure into that equation, though, primarily as a harbinger of death, rebirth, and raison d'être. Truth to tell, the bedroom scenes aren't that graphic—there's more male nudity than distaff and that of the spear more anal than frontal. Yet Singleton's shtupping bits are grounded in live-wire, fully fleshed characters who show up demanding you feel them very deeply—and get your chuckle on with them too. Coital hilarity abounds, as when Ving Rhames's Melvin (ex-Crip and two-strikes ex-con turned landscape gardener) informs A.J. Johnson's hausfrau Juanita, "Girl you're going to give me a cavity," during one contest requiring hydraulic lifting and carrying. The director attributes the vigor of Rhames and Johnson's bouts to some ice-breaking improvs. "Soon as A.J. came in for the first day of rehearsals, Ving picked her up, put her on his shoulders, and acted like he was eating her out, like, Hey, what's up? Then he was smacking her ass and she was like, "I don't feel that. I said, Yeah this is what it's about. I wanted this movie to be almost as soulful as a Marvin Gaye record, and man, these actors bared their souls for me."

That must have been a good day for the randy Singleton, who was strictly forbidden by producer Scott Rudin from giving Shaft (the artist formerly known as the Blackprivatedicksexmachinetoallthechicks) some booty in last summer's remake—perhaps the most unsexy blaxploitation flick in history. "There's talk of a sequel, but Sam and I want it in our contracts that there will be some sex. You can look at *Baby Boy* and see all the sex that was frustrated on *Shaft*. I put it down in this one, boy. The reason I think they were so restrictive about sex in *Shaft* is because they don't—and even some Black filmmakers don't—see us in terms of our sensuality and roundedness as a people. The lovemaking in *Baby Boy* is celebratory. Melvin and Juanita have been through so much shit that they're almost having a teenage romance."

As regards the star-making tumbles turned in by Tyrese (who knew?) Gibson as Jody and Taraji P. Henson as Yvette, Singleton reports that his R&B hunk was unable to perform until his costar got to jukin' at his pride. "We cleared the set and made it real intimate, but the only person who had a problem with the sex scenes was Tyrese. He was doing it like he was shy and I was like, 'Naw, man, you got to hit that like a thug. You got to come with it.' He said, 'Man you got me out here naked,' and I said, 'Fuck that, this is what the girls want to see.' Then Taraji was like, 'You're fucking up my scene. You better come over here and fuck this shit.'" There's irony in Henson gaming on Gibson to get her way, since the film hinges on Jody's manipulative use of his sexual charms for self-aggrandizement and selfish gain. The social reality bursting through every frame is that of relations between African Americans being now defined by who provided sperm and who provided ovum. Who your babymother, who your babyfather, so to speak.

Singleton, father to five children with four different sisters, isn't gazing at the issues from afar. "I observe human behavior like other people watch the Discovery Channel, and I see those guys come into the mall, beating their chests and fucking with these teenage girls' minds, telling them, I want you to have my baby. The story came out of that and out of my own dysfunctions, me purging my own demons. Jody's not me—I've been on my own since I was seventeen—but I thought, What if I still lived with my mother and what if I never knew my father? There are parts of Jody in me. I've been selfish like that.

"The film was also inspired by seeing all the different dysfunctions in the Black community. Like how you're not a man unless you're a killer and who're you talking about killing? Your brother. Jail has become a rite of passage now. Like the Masai kill a lion or an Indian kill a bear, our rite of passage is you're going to jail."

The script was originally written for Tupac Shakur, paradigmatic figurehead of a generation with a death wish. Singleton's feelings about him are complex, critical, loving, angry. "There's a huge mural of Tupac in Jody's room because Pac's journey could be Jody's journey. Tupac was a baby boy. He didn't know whether he wanted to be a thug or a revolutionary. He had all this brilliance but not enough time or purpose and no mentoring at all. By the time somebody was ready to mentor him he wasn't ready to accept it. That's that whole thing of this generation thinking they know everything and they don't know shit." Best known for his debut *Boyz n the Hood*, Singleton, like his inspiration Spike Lee, has pursued an idiosyncratic and independent course in the mainstream. Though he set off the 'hood genre, he hasn't really gone back until now, given *Higher Learning*'s campus setting, *Poetic Justice*'s road bonhomie, *Rosewood*'s historical grasp, and *Shaft*'s eye on summer popcorn. He openly credits Spike's Brooklynphilia with forcing him to reveal his own regional accent. "Spike had an off-kilter vision. Even if it was within the Black community, it was so Brooklynized. When *Do the Right Thing* came along I was miffed. I said I got to do my own motherfucking movie. Spike was so strong on Brooklyn, I thought, What's so special about me? I've got to come with L.A. I think the generation that came after us is more Hollywoodized, with a few exceptions like Ted Witcher and George Tillman. There's a segment of this generation of Black filmmakers that are just like the white boys. They're just doing the same thing and we are not the same thing. I'm trying to make movies where half the people may like them and half may hate them, same as you find with hip-hop music. It's young, audacious, and brash, but you're either going to dance to it or you're not."

According to Singleton, some from Black journalism's upper class have not left previews of *Baby Boy* dancing in the aisles. The phrase "walking around with a pole stuck up their asses" might be a more accurate description of their posture. Some have even proclaimed a sudden unfamiliarity with the Black folk on screen. Singleton's not feeling them either. "People like that are just *boojie* and they can kiss my ass if they think they can tell me what kind of movie I'm supposed to be making. Get real. This is very much an ethnographic film of this time, just like

Boyz was. There are no cops, no white people, it's all insular, and doesn't point the finger at anyone else. It stays in the community, all right there. The acting is so on-point you don't see the wheels turning and you feel like you're really in the ghetto watching some people fight and fuck. That kind of realism is unsettling to some people."

Undaunted by the haters and the denialists, Singleton plans to keep on going against the assimilationist grain. "Everything we do now has to be like *The Best Man* or *Soul Food* because they were successful, but I need to continue making films I'm passionate about. South Central is like Queens—it's multiethnic, a dozen stories could come out of there. Nobody wants to go there now because they're too highbrow. I'm trying to make gutbucket, soulful movies that really hit your thing."

– 2001 –

Lincoln in Whiteface: Jeffrey Wright and Don Cheadle in Suzan-Lori Parks's *Topdog/Underdog*

In the current constellation of African American actors, Jeffrey Wright and Don Cheadle are our dark stars, orbitally unpredictable, supernaturally backlit, aglow. Gliding between the Scylla of Sambo for Hire and the Charybdis of Dignified Token in the Window, they turn in performances light-years in nuance and demeanor from some of their more clamorous cousins. Now sharing a stage at the Public Theater in Suzan-Lori Parks's *Topdog/Underdog*, the two are igniting the joint with volatile, virtuosic energy. Theirs is a balanced duet brimming over with wit, panache, funk, and what Ntozake Shange once identified as "the relaxed virility of our champions." In *Topdog/Underdog*, directed by George C. Wolfe, Wright and Cheadle enact the sibling sparring matches of Lincoln and Booth, two blood brothers who share a shoddy, single-room apartment and a world of pain, shame, and illicit gain via stolen goods and three-card monte.

. . . . .

Both of you have musical backgrounds—guitar and drums for Jeffrey, sax and piano for Don. How much do you reference music in your craft?

Wright: More and more I see plays as music and math. Particularly with this play, because it becomes a linguistic event if it's done right. A carnival ride on language. So much of it is musical equations—I find myself playing a lot of musical phrases to give it something beyond naturalism.

Jeffrey, in this production you play the older, craftier Lincoln character, but you played the Booth part in last year's workshop. Did Booth offer you the same opportunities for those kinds of flights?

Wright: I think so, but Lincoln is more of a performer within the performance, so I can find variation within it. Simply because he wears masks. He takes them off, he puts them back on.

A friend remarked on the lack of competition that was evident onstage— which is kind of ironic, given what the piece is about. Is there a space in this kind of work for one actor to try to outflex the other?

Cheadle: Any type of grandstanding would really subvert the play. One of its strengths is when one of the characters gives in to the other character, and then takes over. Dangling out there and getting so invested in needing the other character that, when you don't get what you need, you're on the precipice looking over the edge.

Wright: I'm competing every night. And that play is kicking my ass. It's really like you're in competition with the play.

Like Wynton Marsalis talking about how every night he goes out to do battle with the blues.

Wright: That's right. It's doing battle with the thing that doesn't exist. It's about trying to whittle away all the bullshit.

A big attraction for the audience is the opportunity to see two virtuosos onstage at the same time. How long did it take you guys to create a comfort zone with one another?

Cheadle: When I heard Jeff was going to be the other actor, I was excited because I'm a big fan of his work. I was also excited about being onstage again in a situation that was really small. Two actors, the writer, and a director. But the play is very difficult, so comfort is not a word that comes into it.

Wright: It's about building an uncomfort zone.

Someone once asked Olivier about what quality was most important for an actor to have, and he said physical strength. When you guys come back for your bows, it seems there's a whole lot of exhalation going on.

Wright: Pretty much the whole piece, when it's done right, feels like you take a breath when you begin and let it out at the end.

Topdog/Underdog *is so tightly wound around those characters that it never slips over into being some didactic commentary about fratricide in the Black community. But playing it, are there didactic notes you guys may be trying to hit?*

Cheadle: I'm not. I'm so busy trying to concentrate on making sure we're keeping the pressure on from moment to moment.

Wright: I do like the whiteface Lincoln wears. I like the inflection of this subsistence mask that is seemingly necessary and at the same time suffocating. I like this struggle to maintain a societal relationship that requires an amputation or a façade. That a relationship with your brother is predicated on the suffocation of yourself.

This piece is a meditation on hustling, but then again, it could be read as a meditation on acting.

Wright: On performance. Suzan-Lori Parks frequently has characters in her plays who are performers.

In your careers as Black actors, you've been able to sidestep the burden of savage nobility and the burden of only playing the stereotype or clown. They say that there are no small parts, only small actors. Is that as true for Black actors as for anybody else?

Cheadle: Oh, there's definitely some small parts. I've been fortunate to work with people I've liked and respected. But things are changing for me now that I've got a family and a school-age daughter. If I'm going to make this my livelihood, I don't want to be away for months at a time, and I don't want to pull her out of school for months at a time. It's going to be interesting to see how it pares down. To see if I have to go back to school and learn how to computer program so that I don't have to make this my livelihood in a way that would pimp it.

Jeffrey, you've taken a slower pace when it comes to movies, and you're about to become a daddy, too.

Wright: I've found film work to be, with maybe two exceptions, unfulfilling as a craft, because I don't edit my performance. The director does—it's a director's medium. But it's difficult to find directors whose voice I respect and who share a perspective on the work and the world. With film I often have to put on a mask to reveal a mask, much like Lincoln does. I find that very difficult sometimes—to put on a lie to reveal a veiled truth. I didn't go into acting to make money. I went into it to get some shit off my chest.

Talk about working with George Wolfe.

Cheadle: This is a first time for me. He's pulled my coat on a couple of things. I just think he's so smart and really odd in a very good way—in the way he thinks and the way events shake down for him in the basement of this piece, not just up high. He's been very generous and available. It's not like, "This is my artistic process. Do what I say and shut up." He's been available to harvest the shit out of these characters.

Wright: There's a line in *Angels in America*—I think it was Roy Cohn's character, but, you know, the villain often speaks the truth. He says, "No one in this world makes it unless someone older and wiser takes an interest in them." George is like that person for me.

I don't think you've let him down yet.

– 2001 –

The Black Power Mixtape

The difference between the Black Power movement and the civil rights movement is one of geography as much as ideology, of regional radicalized realpolitik versus a more conceptualist and performative approach to the problem.

Black Power emerged in Northern and Western America as ineluctably as desegregation had found traction in the American South. Civil rights transformed the way racial discrimination could be fought forevermore in all U.S. courts but Black Power changed the way Black Americans perceived themselves. It turned every negative about being Black into a positive and potentially revolutionary act. Civil rights was concerned with racial equality; Black Power was focused on racial identity and visibility. These philosophical tensions between Black activists, race thinkers who desired full citizenship, versus those who wanted to confront white supremacy wherever it reared its ugly head. One produced a Martin Luther King, the other a Malcolm X. The Black America we have today is a hybrid of King's pursuit of legal remedies to racism and Malcolm's rage to amplify the voice of Black American consciousness. Without King there'd be even fewer Black students and professors at Harvard, Princeton, and Yale; without Malcolm there would be no Africana Studies programs at any of those esteemed institutions. No King and no Black American executives on Wall Street, without Malcolm no millionaire rappers or multibillion-dollar global hip-hop industry built on their loud, proud viva le Black difference self-articulations. Civil rights expanded the literal physical space Blacks could occupy in lily-white America; Black Power extended the range of our metaphysical assault on the American racial imaginary. Civil rights gave Don Cornelius the legal right to produce and own his nationally syndicated TV show but Black Power ensured that show would be called *Soul Train*.

The Black Power Mixtape 1967–1975 is an exotic document of this turbulent, extremely violent and transitional moment in American race history. Exotic because it is the culmination of the near decade an intrepid Swedish TV news team spent interviewing prominent Black American radicals of the day—Stokely Carmichael, Huey Newton, Bobby Seale, Eldridge Cleaver, Elaine Brown, and Angela Davis. All were dramatic, eloquent, charismatic figures of their time who, except for the still-active Davis, are hardly household names to the average Black American under forty of today.

Like Jimi Hendrix or Bob Dylan they all still seem incredibly well prepared to intellectually set the world aflame at twenty-five and dominate the media but far less prepared than the Viet Cong or Fidel Castro to withhold the withering brute attacks on them and theirs directed by the U.S. government, especially the FBI's fascistic overlord J. Edgar Hoover.

Time has not diminished their critiques of American power or racism or their undeniable star power—any one of them and their radical histories could easily sustain a documentary or narrative feature film of its own. The *Mixtape* captures most of them relative moments before they would be tried, convicted, or exiled by Hoover's stated and maniacally implemented obsession with preventing the "rise of another Black prophet" after King.

The footage of Carmichael and Davis is the most poignant and illuminating. Though the film doesn't say so, it was Carmichael who brought the phrase 'Black Power' into vogue, famously goading King to give it airtime near the end of the two-week-long march to Selma, Alabama. The film tacitly demands those in the audience who don't know these figures go spend a little Google time with them afterward. On film the jocular Carmichael proves so at ease in his own skin that he could have given Sidney Poitier leading-man competition in the period and challenged Bob Marley as a composer and performer of lyrical protest ballads.

Carmichael invites himself to take over an interview the filmmakers had wrangled with his mother in the Chicago projects he was raised in. He then patiently extracts from her the pained admission that his

Trinidadian immigrant father, a skilled carpenter, was a lifelong victim of employment discrimination. As noted in progressive hip-hop MC Talib Kweli's voice-over analysis, Carmichael emerges here as a regular guy who also happened to be an incendiary and mesmerizing speaker— one still so provocative that Kweli recalls being accosted by FBI and TSA agents at an airport after 9/11 for merely listening to a forty-year-old Carmichael speech. Some may take Kweli's intimation of wiretaps as conspiratorial and apocryphal but no one familiar with Hoover's paranoia and surveillance of Black progressives will probably be among them. (The biggest laugh in the film comes from FBI director J. Edgar Hoover's statement that the most dangerous threat to the internal security of the United States was the Black Panther Party's free breakfast program. Hoover, however, was not joking.) The progress of the film is also a tacit record of the Panthers' offscreen dismantling by Nixon and Hoover's COINTELPRO conspiracy against Black leadership. The Panthers' demise by exile, imprisonment, and judicial malfeasance is presented at a glance here, but all the political capital the Panthers had was certainly expended by the campaigns to free Huey Newton, Bobby Seale, and Angela Davis. Her prison interview here offers the most astute and moving rationale for extreme Black retaliation to American racial extremists. When asked to justify the advocacy of Black violence, Davis speaks from childhood experience of her Birmingham, Alabama, community being routinely bombed by Klansmen at the behest of notorious county sheriff Bull Connor. That furthermucker, Davis recalls, deployed local radio to promote and direct such violence on a weekly basis. The extreme close- up of Davis's angry watering eyes when she speaks of four classmates' body parts being discovered after the infamous 1963 Birmingham church bombing provides all the justification for retribution any rational person should need.

Davis also emerges as the figure from that time still alive, active, and of significance to her community. Hip-hop MC and folksinger John Forte, who came to midnineties prominence with the Fugees, spent eight years in federal prison on drug trafficking charges. He recalls how Davis's contemporary broadside advocating the abolition of the American prison system was something he often shared with fellow prisoners. The Swedes' interest in Black America begins to wane in 1975 with the Vietnam War. From there the team's gloomy focus briefly turned to the devastation high-grade heroin was wreaking on Harlem. Their last interview is with a cherubic woman barely out of her teens who seemed to have barely overcome a former life of addiction and prostitution. It captures the bleak promise hanging by threads among the ruins of the movement. International media wouldn't return to reporting on Black America with much vigor until hip-hop and the crack epidemic created a new generation of fiery Black progressives—ones whose commentary made urban America's misery index newsworthy enough to warrant the world stage again.

– 2015 –

Race, Sex, Politricks, and Belles Lettres

Clarence Major

There is such a thing as an exemplary literary life. Clarence Major, groundbreaking novelist, poet, professor, and peripatetic, has already lived it to workmanlike excess. Among his more than twenty books are nine novels, nine volumes of poetry, two fiction anthologies, and a dictionary of African American slang. His novels, particularly *All-Night Visitors*, *No*, *Reflex and Bone Structure*, *Emergency Exit*, and *My Amputations*, have made him the premier purveyor of experimental writing in the African American novelists' camp, mostly because he plays fast and loose with the verities of the trade—memory, identity, lush language, acidic wit, conversational non sequiturs—like ain't nobody's biz if he do. Thulani Davis, Jessica Hagedorn, and Ntozake Shange would all cop to taking cops; Ishmael Reed just might be his only long-running peer.

A painter as well as a National Book Award–nominated poet, Major brings his plasticity and pictorial sensitivity into his narratives. In *Reflex*, where sex, revolution, and pop culture converse and convulse in a surreal postseventies haze, he makes grand, sometimes grotesque imagistic leaps, fracturing the identity of his characters. In *No*, Major adroitly collapses sexual awakening and cosmological consciousness in the psyche of a young boy growing up in the Crayola-tinged South. In *My Amputations*, he turns the paranoid spy thriller on its head.

His new book, *Necessary Distance: Essays and Criticism* (Coffee House Press), is a collection of essays, criticism, and lectures, less mind-bending than his fiction, but valuable for the insights it provides into his working-class Chicago upbringing and his love affair with the worlds of ideas and painting. The anecdotes drawn from his stumbling, naive steps toward literary community and comprehension are acutely moving. The reviews portion of the collection offers appreciations of writers as diverse as Donald Barthelme, Claude McKay, Carlos Fuentes, Joyce Carol Oates, and John O'Hara. Criticism is not among Major's strongest suits, but his travel writing on trips to Paris and Yugoslavia gives him ample room to put his astute novelist's powers of observation to winsome use.

When I spoke with Major by phone he sounded as warm and encouraging as he had a quarter century ago when I attended his creative writing class at Howard University. Now a professor of English at the University of California at Davis, Major offers that African American fiction has a strong experimental bent which precedes him by several decades.

"You can go back to people like Charles Chesnutt and Jean Toomer and find things that are formally adventurous," he bantered from his house on a quiet Sunday. "LeRoi Jones—not Amiri Baraka—was doing groundbreaking things with his first novel. There are also the plays of Adrienne Kennedy to consider. Even Ellison, if you think about the moment when *Invisible Man* appeared, that really is a very experimental novel and I think he thought of it that way. Paule Marshall's first collection of short stories in the fifties was very experimental too. Actually, the word I'd prefer to use would be 'innovative' rather than 'experimental.' Experimental somehow sounds like it's unfinished."

Self-interrogation is the uber-theme of the African American novel, just as self-invention is in its white American counterpart. Major's prose and poetry—particularly *My Amputation* and *Surfaces and Masks*—revel in the expansion of self possible for Black Americans once they leave the country. In "A Paris Fantasy Transformed," one of the new collection's deft, detailed autobiographical essays, Major writes, "Paradoxically, Paris gave me my national identity, although I hadn't gone looking for that part of myself."

He explained, "I first came across that thought in Jimmy Baldwin long before I went to Paris, but I didn't know what it meant on a gut level until I was there and saw how I was received and perceived by the French."

In the essay, Major notes that though there was undeniably racism in Paris it was not directed at him but Algerians. "As soon as the French discovered I was not an African or Arab from one of their former colonies, I was treated well. This was an ironic and ambiguous position to be in. All my life, in my own country, I had seen Americans treat Africans and Arabs—people they had no historical ties to—with the same kind of dubious respect. The point is, in Paris—as pathetic as it sounds—I felt American for the first time."

Like their author, Major's characters often take the road less traveled into the Black subconscious. Major's tendency to subject Black figures to surrealist treatment was not always by design.

"In my own writing the emphasis on self-consciousness was a gradual thing that I learned by writing my first novels. The notion that identity is a fluid thing is, I think, the great American theme. It started in the nineteenth century with people like Melville. You can even see that in American writers who may not seem so conscious of it, like Hemingway. Toni Morrison looked at that very closely in *Playing in the Dark*."

Carnal knowledge spills from every other page of Major's early work, which still reads as bolder and more unblinking than anything of recent vintage by African Americans. Major's recombinations of metaphysics and sex were interpreted as bearing a strong Henry Miller influence when they were first published. He doesn't contradict this view, but advises we recognize which Miller was influential on him. "I didn't read his erotic novels until much later because they weren't available when I was coming up. The books by Miller that I read were the nonfiction ones like *The Cosmological Eye, Colossus of Maroussi,* and *The Air-Conditioned Nightmare.* Miller was a writer who was not a part of the establishment and really talked about America as it was without, as Bob Dylan would say, pussyfooting around. He was an outsider taking a hard look at America without being mean-spirited."

Because he's a writer whose work seems to have found as much of an embrace outside of the African American community of readers as within, Major seemed a good person to ask whether writing by African Americans was still perceived as Black first and writing second.

"That whole focus on sociology and pathology I thought was finished. That was certainly something Jimmy Baldwin was trying to put to rest in the fifties with his essay 'Everybody's Protest Novel.' There are all kinds of books that show that the African American experience is not monolithic—the schlocky romance stuff and the detective novels are not all bad. What has gone on in the last twenty years is far more astonishing, rich, and diverse than anything that happened in the Harlem Renaissance. I'm not knocking it, but it doesn't compare at all in terms of subject matter, voice, and style." To underscore this, we need only refer to the range reflected by such luminaries as Thulani Davis, Danzy Senna, Colson Whitehead, Walter Mosley, Octavia Butler, Gayl Jones, Jeffery Renard Allen, Samuel Delany, Suzan-Lori Parks, August Wilson, Edwidge Danticat, Omar Tyree, and E. Lynn Harris.

Reflex and Bone Structure is my favorite among Major's novels for its adroit blend of hard-boiled sentences and schizophrenic, artsy-militant characters who are like me and my peeps. "I was living in New York when I wrote that book and I consider it to have a New York nervous system," Major said of its genesis. "I would get up every morning and try to write these little episodes, and things that were going on out the window or the radio all fed into the nervous system of that novel. But I want you to know that I never reread any of my novels and I'm leery of looking back on something I was doing then and imposing on it something that isn't true. I'm not quite sure I'm telling you the truth, I just want you to know."

Never expect a straight answer from a dealer in metafiction. Don't sleep on this Major dude either, no matter how much you may have to spend online to acquire the out-of-print *No, Emergency Exit*, and *My Amputations*.

– 2001 –

The Atlantic Sound:
Caryl Phillips's *The Atlantic Sound*

Everybody, or at least everybody Black and conscious, talks about the Middle Passage, but nobody ever does anything about it. In *The Atlantic Sound*, noted Black British novelist Caryl Phillips endeavors to prove himself an exception to the rule. Conceived as a series of inquisitive travelogues—revisiting the primary ports of the notorious triangular trade between Liverpool, Africa, and the New World—the book begins with Phillips traveling between Guadeloupe and Britain on a cargo freighter, as his parents did forty years before, and ends with his journey to Israel to visit the two-thousand-strong community of African American Hebrew Israelites. Between those landmarks Phillips provides an impressively researched bevy of bittersweet tales about the places and people haunted to this day by the moral and psychological consequences of the European trade in Africans.

To his credit, Phillips is an astute and engaging narrator who uncovers some startling new wrinkles in the record of African bondage. Notably, he resurrects the saga of a Reverend Phillip Quaque, a Christianized West African who served as chaplain at Cape Gold Castle, the slave-trading fortress through which literally millions of his brothers and sisters were sent off to New World bondage. Who knew?

When Phillips goes to Charleston, South Carolina, he dredges up the voluminous story of one Judge Waring, a man who suffered extreme contempt from his Caucasian fellows for daring to love Negroes more than whites and for writing legal briefs damning American apartheid and, worse, the Southern social contract. This chapter is a fascinating rendering of the intimacy and intrigue that characterized Black-white relations in the South then, machinations of a kind more familiar to readers of romance fiction than to viewers of *Eyes on the Prize*. His novelist's instinct to unveil the savagery behind social graces, a tenet of his fiction, has never been more right on. Unfortunately, he never resolves his research, anecdotes, and vignettes into any kind of summary thoughts—in fact he seems rather evasive on what all the dislocation, relocation, and alienation mean to him. You don't need a thesis to go on a journey, but you should be gracious enough to offer the reader a summation when your subject is as large as the existential legacy of slavery.

Though never explicitly stated, Phillips's driving obsession is exile and how it bedevils cultural nationalists of African descent and their sympathizers. But Phillips—a well-educated and successful first-generation Black British intellectual—never gives a sense of where he falls on the matter of Black folks' assimilation blues within English society. There is a kind of bloodless and disembodied quality to his reportage, a sense that he's on the outside looking in on other people's refugee camps, never investigating his own.

The people Phillips conjures up via his diasporic mouthpieces are not so much in exile as in limbo, adrift between Africa, Europe, and the New World. Phillips's guide in Liverpool, for instance, is Steve, a young Jew-baiting nationalist who sees slave profits all over his native city where Phillips sees only architectural magnificence. But because Steve is Phillips's only contact in Liverpool, you leave this section feeling as if you've just wandered out of a ghost town, having heard nothing from the old families who loathe postwar latecomers like Phillips's parents, or some sense of whatever angst Phillips's parents may carry as Caribbean émigrés.

These absences beg for a chapter on what tribe Phillips belongs to—no matter whether it's academics or a favorite aunt whom the author feels comfortable to let it all hang out with. Without such self-examination, Phillips's dispatches seem issued from a kind of literary Flying Dutchman—albeit an observant and sardonic one, as he proves in this bit of uproarious cultural reportage from a Pan-Africanist festival.

> Suddenly to the chaotic sound of drums, whistles, cowbells and the random firing of rifles, the "royal procession" arrives. They are led by the "warriors," who appear to be badly dressed unemployed youth and old men. After the "warriors" come the more formally dressed and dignified "elders." Suddenly every white person in the audience seems to own a video camera. The more bold among them are jumping and dancing.

In the Ghana section there is, crucially, the story of Phillips's driver, Mansour, an ambitious, resourceful young man who wound up prey to England's immigration system before being deported. Phillips guides us down the grueling and labyrinthine paths by which Mansour escapes Africa by his wits. When Mansour asks Phillips for $5,000 so he can leave Ghana to pursue a work-study plan in the U.S., Phillips snidely upbraids Mansour for presenting himself as a "'third world' victim." But a victim of his third world status Mansour certainly is, because no British or U.S.-born Black citizen with Mansour's grit, perseverance, and intelligence would be subject to draconian deportation laws for daring to work and study at the same time.

Phillips's concluding section about the Hebrew Israelites seems hasty by comparison, reading more like snapshots than detailed portraits. He also seems incapable of fathoming the African Americanness they've held on to in their conversion to Judaism. What's so strange about Black Jewish girls twirling batons in the land of Jesus's birth? Or their mothers and fathers listening to soul and jazz? If history has shown us anything, it's how relentless Black Americans can be in funkatizing whatever they come in contact with. Phillips seems to have confused the Hebrew Israelites' desire to escape from white America with his sense that they want to run out of their African American skins. In critiquing their Americanness he fails to recognize that nothing could be more American than lighting out for the frontier and starting your own apocalyptic religion.

Phillips should know how consistent such a move is with the improvisatory nature of Black American identity. In what appears a syncretism as profound as any of Duke Ellington's, the Hebrew Israelites have developed a religious community that sees no contradiction in sustaining Black American cultural practices as orthodox holy-land Jews. You can only wish there was as much judgment-free detail on them as the author provides on Judge Waring or the slave fort chaplain, and that his revised Middle Passage accounts came without an ax to grind about quixotic American Africanists.

– 2000 –

Apocalypse Now: Patricia Hill Collins's
Black Sexual Politics; Thomas Shevory's
Notorious H.I.V.; Jacob Levenson's
The Secret Epidemic

R. Kelly, Kobe, the Jacksons—the pop figments of Black sexuality are everywhere these days. The Janet Jackson episode proved that where Black libidinous activity is concerned, a part stands in for the whole— one raw titty can produce a panic about the thing itself. Apocalypse now: live Black yoni in your living room. Easier to tabloidize than to theorize about, Black sexuality awaits its Foucault—with good reason. Any writer whose project is American racial and sexual politics has a lot of historicizing on their hands: a legal history to unpack, from slave ownership and slave rape to lynching to the trials of Anita Hill and O.J. Simpson, and the irony that much of what's perceived as Black sexuality is a corporate media construct. There's the communion of Black sexuality and subjectivity—the "Monster Speaks" aspect of the thing, the voice of our sexual selves as displayed in the scant films and literature we can find that are unmediated by the corporate gaze. There are statistics (pregnancy, abortion, AIDS in Africa) and the charged politics thereof, with welfare, housing, and public medical policy demanding inclusion. There is Black homosexuality and Black homophobia, and then there is class: working-class strippers, prostitutes, and those upper-middle-class Black Atlantans who convene weekly sex parties in their posh homes. Then comes the problem of making sense of it all. Three recent titles take up the challenge from widely differing vantages. A mash-up of this trio, with recent books by Tricia Rose and Jill Nelson, could produce a Black-sex dream text.

Patricia Hill Collins's *Black Sexual Politics* is one of the most steaming mad books on sexuality since the days of Andrea Dworkin—a brief but dense attempt at totalizing racial and sexual politics in American life. For riled-up ambition alone it constitutes a breakthrough. Her chapter titles are provocatively au courant ("Booty Call: Sex, Violence, and Images of Black Masculinity"). Collins is boldest when putting forth the notion that racism and heterosexism are intertwined forms of oppression. She lambastes notions of Black community that squeeze out non-church- or non-nationalist-approved difference: "a narrow Black identity politics that demands an unquestioned loyalty to one version of Blackness consistently privileges some versions of Blackness and disadvantages others. Such politics routinely derogate and exclude African Americans who are the wrong sexual orientation; who love significant others that are the wrong color." A jeremiad against reactionary gender and race politics, BSP doesn't have time to identify their practitioners in a nuanced fashion.

Thomas Shevory's *Notorious H.I.V.* is more coherent and incisive, focusing on Nushawn Williams, drug dealer and alleged one-man AIDS epidemic. His story began in upstate New York and went national after he was found to have had sex with thirteen women while knowing he'd been diagnosed as HIV-positive. Shevory notes that in initial reporting the number became inflated to as high as three hundred and Williams's area of infection spread, via journalistic fiction, to at least eight states. The majority of those women were white, some even upper-middle class. In the press, the case became a microcosm of American racial mythology, where Williams was labeled a monster who traded drugs for sex with his white slaves and knowingly transmitted HIV to his victims. Much of Shevory's book is concerned with language, law, and knowledge—how Williams's case was misrepresented and spurred a call for the criminalization of HIV-positive folks who don't share that info with their partners. (Legal trickery got Williams convicted not for viral transmission or drug dealing but statutory rape.)

Shevory interviewed Williams several times in prison, and *Notorious* provides a complicated portrait of an erratic, impulsive, and fairly typical teenage drug hustler. Shevory's Foucauldian interests in the case have less to do with Williams per se than how race provided the state a means to begin criminalizing the behavior of those who carry the disease.

Jacob Levenson's *The Secret Epidemic* is the most disappointing of these books, if only because it doesn't come alive on the page as the rallying cry it intends to be. Though he has moving accounts from a variety of African Americans—some victims, some activists—the organization of the material diffuses the cumulative emotional impact. If Collins is too sweeping and full frontal in her approach, and Shevory purposefully narrow, Levenson never seems to enter the story as an on-the-ground investigator to provide the immediacy and intimacy this tragedy demands. There is a fair amount of information culled from studies by Black medical researchers and Black AIDS activists, dating back to the late eighties. But without revealing AIDS's current status as a "Black" disease, *Epidemic* lacks a dramatic sense of the present—not least because it only touches on how the poorest of African American communities in the South are confronting AIDS devastation. Levenson unveils the link between crack use, poverty, and the epidemic, but never produces the kind of relationships with African Americans that would give his book the currency his subject requires. The *Random Family* of the African American AIDS crisis has yet to be written.

– 2004 –

Blood and Bridges

Human rights movements are different from the rest. Unlike revolutions, which come together in order to overturn empires, or labor unions, which exist to boost wage increases from capitalists' pockets, human rights movements tend to coagulate over the egregious spilling of human blood, preferably that of an Innocent. They are vampiric in that way, feeding off the sainted veins of martyrs, sacrificial lambs, and causes célèbres. For this reason human rights activists often come off as ambulance chasers, morgue cruisers, demagogic ghouls prowling the autopsy room in search of an appropriate victim-myth whose body tag they can snatch, raise up high, and fly like a righteous banner.

Unlike vampires, these activists aren't seeking eternal life but temporary means of moral persuasion against the State. Human rights movements also, ironically enough, require monsters, devils, archenemies who would as soon shoot the people as look at them. Enter Bull Connor, enter Pik Botha, enter Rudolph Giuliani, though we all know it's actually been exit Rudolph Giuliani from any future hopes in politics ever since Diallo's mother fainted at the death scene. Her and her husband's regal bearing and regalia revealed that the deceased was not the "immigrant peddler" of the *Daily News*'s incessant description, but a product of centuries-deep familial roots. Surveying the joyous multitudes at last Thursday's March against Police Brutality, photographer Jules Allen opined that this grand movement-building event probably wouldn't have ever happened if Giuliani had "just said 'I'm sorry,' or 'It was an accident,' something. But to just leave it at 'Fuck you'? Was that crazy or what?"

In spite of City Hall's imperious grand wizard, last Thursday's march across the Brooklyn Bridge Cadman Plaza to Federal Plaza felt more like a victory dance than a protest rally—a voodoo-against-racism frolic so full of good cheer you'd think the order of the day was heigh-ho, the king was already dead, Viva la revolución, Rome is once again free, and all known fascists are now on the run.

Human rights rallies aren't by necessity humorless, but as soon as this reporter came out of the High Street subway station, he knew that this rally had jokes for your ass. First in the form of the young Hispanic cop who told the bewildered gentleman out just before me scouring the empty streets for signs of activity that he'd hardly seen anyone that day. This said as, not so far off in the distance, the bridge was visibly swarming with bodies. Once I got to the rally at the plaza proper (where it became clear that the march was backed up all the way from Manhattan into the streets of Brooklyn) and caught sight of a costumed Grim Reaper accessorized as a policeman, a sickle-, badge-, and billy-club-laden avatar of doom on loan from the extras crew of *Maniac Cop 3*, I got wind that comedy would be fueling this day of the dead as much as rage.

Don't get me wrong: folk were soberly chanting down Babylon as required, dropping all the familiar science—No Justice No Peace The People United Can Never Be Defeated—but they were also giddily returning cheers and power salutes from supporters and well wishers in vehicles crossing the bridge headed into Brooklyn on the roadway to the appropriate left of the march.

The first thing my mate asked when I got home that night was, "Were there enough white people there?"—meaning enough to make the media and the police not dismiss the gathering as another yawn-provoking, overtime-paying display of Angry Negro Syndrome. But yes there were, dear, so you had Black Panthers walking arm in arm with Gray Panthers and Pink Panthers, and hosts of representatives voicing other diverse concerns as well. There was so much interracial, interfaith, cross-gender coalition and alliance building going down on that bridge you had to wonder whether you were on the Brooklyn Bridge or the Golden Gate, coming straight out of Crooklyn or straight out of Berkeley.

Say what? Coalition politics were supposedly as dead or withering on the vine in New York as industrial labor elsewhere in globalized America, but this Diallo thing was not only providing Black and Hispanic leadership a reason to powwow but for your Socialist Workers and your Revolutionary Communist Party people and your well-represented Local 371 Social Service Employees members to commune with the sister passing out flyers promoting her call-in show about healing the rift between Africans and African Americans. There was even love for the fringe character who came up asking for money to feed the homeless but whose literature spoke of wanting to police homeless folks' dating practices and make AIDS testing mandatory for them.

The temper of the day was best declared, though, by the variety of vendors on the make, the brother offering not-for-free chew sticks at the foot of the bridge, the whistle man whose neck was his vending table, the Giuliani-as-Dracula button hawker, the cat passing out flyers to this year's run of the Universal Soul Circus, and perhaps most of all by my man with the "FUCK Giuliani" T-shirts who claimed to have sold two hundred or so at $8 a pop, six to an NYPD officer who gave him his car keys and asked that the vendor clandestinely load them into his vehicle. "FUCK Giuliani" is cool, but some marchers thought more clever would be mo' betta and threw up signs of "Arrest Giuliani" and "Impound Giuliani." From the book of Funkadelic came Rude-Off Fool-i-ani; from the book of *Saturday Night Live*, according to my man Marc Ribot, we got Giuliani and Milosevic, Separated at Birth.

As much as human rights movements need their Diallos and their Draculas they also need their archangels, and without question the handling of the Diallo case on the streets and in the media has been our right Reverend Al Sharpton's finest hour, his statesmanship graduation ceremony, and for all those who must recall and cannot forgive his baby-curl days as a boy preacher, James Brown fan-club booster, police snitch, FBI informant, televangelist for Tawana Brawley, December 12 movement coalition splitter, all must also remember as I pointed out in these pages some years ago that Sharpton is not a man but a messenger, in the tradition of the Yoruba trickster deity Esu-Elegba, who like Sharpton is fabled to swim in waters murky, dirty, and crystalline, an agent of chaos who must be feted and fed before any momentous journey is undertaken or any road can be safely traveled.

Hence the gaiety that prevailed on the Yellow Brick Bridge last Thursday as the masses blithely waltzed into the Emerald City to the mellifluous strains of the People United Can Never Be Defeated, a slogan for once more fact than fable. Certainly it seemed that way from the sheepish, hangdog looks on the faces of the NYPD foot soldiers and mounted police (and one imagines the helicopter pilots and boat patrols as well). You got the impression they were loitering at the rally rather than policing the darn thing, some finding their only moment of levity when a brother began shouting "Live here! Work here!" at them in reference to the residency requirements the movement is pressing for. Not in a million years, said the guffaws. Speaking of call and response, however, I must also report that the event's most bloodcurdling moment occurred when a movement exhorter got us going on a cry of "Amadou! What did he do?" Then he got us counting shots: "1! 2! 3! 4! 5! 6! 7! 8! 9! 10! 11! 12! 13! 14! 15! 16! 17! 18! 19! 20! 21! 22! 23! 24! 25! 26! 27! 28! 29! 30! 31! 32! 33! 34! 35! 36! 37! 38! 39! 40! 41!"

In this digital age where only perfectly structured sets of zeros and ones are supposed to get anyone excited, the bullet count was a reminder of what humanity loses when a brown body mysteriously morphs into a carnival game or a pinball target behind the alphanumeric eyes of four type-A porcine specimens. Four pigs to be precise, more detached and hardwired than Schwarzenegger's Terminator, capable of using a dead man's feet for target practice, secure in the long-standing American belief that a Black man has no rights a white man should feel compelled to respect, safe in the conviction that no white policeman has ever been convicted for killing a Black man in this country and that as Ice Cube once observed, the mission is to serve, protect, and break a nigger's neck.

One new slogan I heard thrown into the mix that day was also directed at cops: If We're Not Safe, You're Not Safe. Thankfully the festive atmosphere was counterbalanced by a little madman theory just to keep things in dialectical perspective, as seen to by the Parliament Funkadelic refugees handing out flyers promoting the formation of a People's Mi-litia and quoting Gandhi to the effect that violence becomes necessary whenever there is no possibility of punishing the wicked. Call it a cau-tionary device—a way of saying to the powers that be that if a Simi Valley jury shows up for these four elite white cops, last Thursday's party-down Rainbow Warriors just might start acting a tad more belligerent. Rodney King 2 in Gotham City? After last Thursday? Are they crazy?

– 1999 –

Nigger-'Tude

"Nigger" is no ordinary noun. No other single epithet in the English language could justify a memoir and career profile as juicy as "nigger," a word whose manifest destiny exercises a hold over the world as var-ied and virulent as Hollywood's. No other appellation in the American idiom has led such a rich, vibrant life; no other sobriquet has acquired such a juju-fied life force nor been the cause of so much continuing pain, pleasure, and acrimony. Not to mention ongoing controversies in our courts of law and public opinion. No other word has proven itself so em-blematic of the host culture's worst and best features, meaning white su-premacy and Black resiliency. "Nigger" has been everywhere, seen every-thing, known and influenced players high and low, insinuated itself into all things American, moved freely from the bedroom to the boardroom, the outhouse to the courthouse, the locker room to the stateroom, from our killing fields to our fields of higher learning.

Randall Kennedy, an African American Harvard law professor and former clerk for Thurgood Marshall, recently published *Nigger: The Strange Career of a Troublesome Word* (Pantheon). Trouble has already come for Kennedy in the form of strong condemnations from Houston Baker, Patricia Williams, and Julianne Malveaux, three leading Black intellec-tuals. In a nutshell, Kennedy is arguing for the fluidity of the word in American life, noting that the "protean n-word" shifts in meaning and affect depending on who's using it, how, in what context, and to whom. To buttress the point, he draws Richard Pryor, Quentin Tarantino, Ice Cube, and various of the nation's appellate courts into the fray. Much of what he cites from court records is perversely funny, making the book read like one long, drawn-out nigger joke. People like Baker, Williams, and Malveaux who would deny "nigger" any leniency in the market-place of ideas, Kennedy tags "Eradicationists." He himself, though, finds so much salacious joy in this project as to risk being labeled a nigger-fetishist. Kennedy often walks the fine line between being both an adjudicator of nigger-'tude and a nigger apologist.

Oddly he doesn't touch upon the word's place in the British Raj in India or during the high period of African colonization, nor spend much time on its tactical use by U.S. slaveholders in lobotomizing the African part of the African American brain. Tacitly we get that "nigger" now instantaneously refers to us American Blacks. The author might have spelled out how this ahistorical, ontological, etymological, and epistemological twist came about. I suspect he didn't because that would have required spending more time discussing white power rather than his beloved nigger. (More on that later.)

Instead, Kennedy, an American-law scholar and author of the acclaimed *Race, Crime and the Law*, treats us to the tortuous reasoning and outcome of numerous legal cases where debates over the use of the word "nigger" held lives and judgment fees in the balance. Some are less tragic than darkly comic—like the college basketball coach who asked his realnigga players for permission to rally the team by using "nigger" as they used it, as a supermasculine signifier separating the pussies from the truly hard motherfuckers. This gambit, Kennedy rightly argues, cost Coach his job, though the writer is sympathetic to Coach's Rodney-can't-we-all-just-love-niggers-King naïveté. No friend of the academic hate-speech code on campuses, Kennedy is less understanding toward the "hypersensitive" Black student who led a successful campaign to get a white professor fired for referencing "nigger" in a discussion of hateful speech.

Some of the less ambiguous, and less offensive to the Black upper-middle class, cases involve lawsuits against white employers and supervisors who deployed the term with extreme prejudice. Some of these cases were lost or never even got to trial because their judges found no great harm in bosses' heatedly spraying "nigger" around their shops at Black underlings. One judge went so far as to claim "nigger" had simply become a "convention of the workplace" and therefore couldn't possibly qualify as inflammatory or discriminatory. Be a cracker beat-down convention at most workplaces I know of thanks to Title VII of the Civil Rights Act, whose limits Kennedy reports with stinging jurisprudence. Black folk who've traded in the hot knuckle sandwich for the steamed legal brief get rebuffed a lot.

Questions of nigger-context and who has license-to-nigger clearly delight Kennedy, who finally betrays his own fetish for the N-word's

lumpen, transgressive powers when he speaks of certain Black entertainers as exhibiting a "bracing independence" when using the word, as
if only their relationship to it mattered. He also praises them for their
daring to "eschew boring conventions including the one that maintains,
despite massive evidence to the contrary, that nigger can mean only one
thing." Some would describe this "bracing independence" as the new
minstrelsy, since postgangsta, just being Black and wrong isn't as energizing or emancipatory as it used to be. It also doesn't seem anyone is
arguing against nigger's multiple meanings—just that it still means the
same thing to those in power and remains one of their weapons against
the Black and powerless who tend not to be Harvard ensconced.

As stated above, "Eradicationists" is how Kennedy identifies those
African Americans uncomfortable enough with the word to demand
Mark Twain's removal from high school English classes. But though he
is quick to admonish those like Spike Lee and Ice Cube, who emotively
claim the word and off-limit it to whites, Kennedy never comes out and
says how much of the word's power comes from its position as a marker
of white power—especially in working-class situations that find one-
paycheck-from-poverty Black employees in the thrall of abusive white
supervisors. As with most things in life, power separates the men from
the boys more than context per se.

Kennedy points out the word has wantonly attached itself to the for-
tunes and infamy of Richard Pryor and Quentin Tarantino's careers. Only
in the endnotes does he enter into evidence Pryor's heart-wrenching decision to stop using "nigger" after returning from a visit to Africa nor
does he address Tarantino's specious if not disingenuous claim that he
used the word because he thought it had too much power. Since white
power is the only power "nigger" could have, the world is still waiting
for proof of Tarantino's contribution to white disempowerment. And
for the first Black filmmaker who will be lionized for his witty way with
Jew baiting.

To Kennedy's credit, he does point out that there are white suprema-
cists who eschew "nigger" yet do far more harm to Black social advancement with their power than those who use it all the time. He argues
that though "nigger" was documented as a conversational favorite of
Harry Truman and Lyndon Johnson, both did good things for the Negro,
though he fails to specify exactly what. (Integrating the armed services
and signing the Civil Rights Act of 1964 were both cool, propitious moves,
dude, but let's help the historically challenged out here, all right?)

Kennedy is too hopeful about nigger's demise as an insult as it becomes more of a trope in the hands of African American musical and

comedic entertainers. That African Americans have a genius for subverting, perverting, and commodifying English is beyond argument. You can go to Addis Ababa, Ethiopia, now and hear locals dream of coming to America to live the "Thug Life." "Nigger" is further proof that African American speech possesses the secret of juju, what some Afrocentrists identify as wordsoundpower, a force akin to that which novelist Frank Herbert ascribed to his character Muad'Dib in *Dune* who understood his name as a "killing word." A central, philosophical question that should be on the table of every Black forum going today is, What are the limits of Black symbolic, legal, and moral victories over white power in America? Another way to ask the question might be, Whatever happened to Black Power? Or Foucauldian *Power*, for that matter?

Kennedy aptly and professorially demonstrates the limits of the law when it comes to using a white supervisor's flagrant nigger-usage as Proof of Racism but never takes on the power surging through, around, under, and beyond that nigger-talking offender.

– 2002 –

Triple Threat: Jerry Gafio Watts's *Amiri Baraka*; Hazel Rowley's *Richard Wright*; David Macey's *Frantz Fanon*

Black rage and its malcontents. Black alienation and its discontents. For centuries these subjects have provided the bailiwick and special baggage claim for writers of African descent everywhere, offering a launching pad for their racial reflexes and remedies, their race-fired synapses and neuroses. In the long war of words that has sought to define the power struggle between European and African descendants over consciousness and culture, Richard Wright, Frantz Fanon, and Amiri Baraka rank as protean, Promethean figures—shape-shifters packing gifts of tongues and fire.

All three arguably caught the attention of the world community by forwarding and lyricizing the notion that retributive, revolutionary violence against white people could be a form of liberation within itself. (Though Fanon posed it in terms of "natives" and "settlers," the French hardly missed the inflection.) Devising a form of Black literary terrorism seems at the heart of their best publicized works, *Native Son*, *The Wretched of the Earth*, and *Dutchman*. To the extent that their writings suggest that Black people can be more than just the victims of racist violence, can in fact perpetrate it, they easily got under the skin of white audiences. A production of *Dutchman* in Hartford last year demonstrated the play's continued ability to unsettle liberal whites. Fanon's famous line about the "cleansing" qualities of antiracist violence has an eerie and ironic genocidal resonance today; the blood trail that leads from the murder trial of Wright's Bigger Thomas to O.J. Simpson seems abundantly apparent. All three writers were more complex and learned characters than their desire to bring the pain to white folks may suggest—what we know of their lives provides a sense that immense stores of vulnerability stoked their rages and their exiles.

A peculiar coincidence of publishing has delivered big, booming, thoughtful, and provocative biographies of this troika to our desks. Read together they provide a bounty for students of Black-white conflict, Black-white writing, and Black-white political adventurism, folly, and failure. The resonances and critical differences between their lives are remarkable, none more so than that all were men of the pen who lived lives (ongoing, thankfully, in Baraka's case) that read like the stuff of novels. This trio ranks as preeminent among Black male writers in their quest to always psychologize the politics of Black liberation and the Black radical subject—their toughest explorations of Black pathology and suffering manage to be both compassionate and critically unsparing.

Each was also a vaunted Negro First, to use *Ebony* magazine vernacular. Wright was the first African American novelist to conquer the world stage, the first prominent Black intellectual to vehemently and unquietly defect from the Communist Party, the first to exile himself to Paris, the first to tackle the subject of postcolonial Africa on the ground, the first to write a book of militant haikus, and probably the last to write an entire book on Spain and bullfighting. The life of Fanon, the only world-renowned Black psychiatric theorist, is so sui generis as to defy comparison with anyone. A decorated Martinique-born veteran of World War II, he studied a very progressive form of clinical psychiatry in France but opted for a mental hospital post in Algeria, arriving just in time for the anticolonial war launched by Front de Libération Nationale guerrillas against France in 1954. Fanon, who would go on to become an FLN propagandist, practically invented third world and postcolonial studies. Papa Baraka's mercurial transformations—from fellow traveler of the beats to the Original Don Dada of the Black Arts Movement to pro-Black Marxist-Leninist-Stalinist-Maoist to the only unrepentant, unbowed, unrehabilitated sixties radical figure still around—have made for a nonpareil life in literature and politics.

A friend recently said about the oratorical style of the young poet Saul Williams that "he has the kind of voice that makes white people sit up and listen." Wright, Fanon, and Baraka were all masterful and sophisticated writers who harpooned white readers with incendiary, race-baiting texts meant to prick and alarm their guilt-driven fears of Black-on-white violence.

The biographies form a testament to the impact each had on intellectual life in their time: Wright knew Gertrude Stein, André Gide, Nelson Algren, Simone de Beauvoir; Fanon had ties with Patrice Lumumba, Sékou Touré, Beauvoir, and Jean-Paul Sartre. (For hours he harangued Sartre, who wrote the introduction for *The Wretched of the Earth*, and when Beauvoir begged Fanon to let the old man hit the sack at 2 a.m., Fanon kept him up until eight in the morning, later complaining to a friend how he detested people who "spare themselves.") Baraka's close ties to William Burroughs, Allen Ginsberg, Thelonious Monk, John Coltrane, and painters Larry Rivers and Bob Thompson have been well documented.

If you accept the construction of Wright, Ralph Ellison, and James Baldwin as postwar African American writing's Big Three, Baraka easily reads as that alliance's prodigal son, a powerful synthesizer of Wright's feel for the lower depths, Ellison's faith in the redemptive and resuscitative powers of folklore and jazz, and Baldwin's gift for lyrical moral debate. Baraka never had Baldwin's faith in America, Ellison's faith in literature, or Wright's faith in his gift as a form of weaponry. His writing and life have frequently seemed driven more by passions than convictions, more by iron will than any grand sense of purpose, more by a desire to sustain his own cult of personality than to build effective organizations. The job of dissecting the artist formerly known as LeRoi Jones has been taken up by one Jerry Watts, a noted African American professor of American studies and political science at Trinity College in Connecticut. Though Watts's book copiously disinters the well-trod ground of Baraka's literary salvos, its biting analysis of the man's political campaigns breaks new ground in the public burning of Baraka, who himself burned many bridges on the way to the demagogic forum.

In conversation the film theorist Clyde Taylor has fondly and sarcastically remembered the sixties as a time when "brothers were freelancing their imaginations." None more so than Baraka, who appears to have almost magically walked out of the pages of his own volatile early essays, plays, fiction, and poems to become a major player in sixties radical activity. Along the way he would become known for turning on former comrades like a rabid dog. Watts seems to have largely embarked on this project in order to convict Baraka on charges of contrived militancy, hypocrisy, destructive self-indulgence, infantilism, and tactical naïveté at every political turn. Free-jazz pioneer Sunny Murray recently and sardonically recalled Baraka weeping profusely over the death of JFK, calling further into question the man's get-whitey posturing of the sixties. Concomitantly, Watts expends great energy toward making Baraka's political quick changes seem dishonest, cheap, and opportunistic while begrudgingly acknowledging the integrity of his lifelong stance as a counternormative radical intellectual.

Begging to differ with Baraka's self-serving comparisons to his idol Malcolm X, Watts reminds us that Malcolm rebuked a Black anti-Semite at one of his lectures with an impolite and unbrotha'-ly "Sit down and shut up." Ultimately Watts believes Baraka's politics were more often motivated by a militant variation on bohemian individualism than anything else. Recounting a race relations panel held in the East Village in 1964 where Baraka and musician Archie Shepp acidly dismissed the deaths of the murdered white Freedom Riders Goodman and Schwerner, Watts accuses the two of deflecting—basically inferring they were too punkass to put their own bodies on the line.

Watts believes the one constant in Baraka's politics is the choosing of "the power of rhetoric and spectacle" over substantive discourse. In Watts's view, all Baraka's ideological mood swings and games of political chairs have been juvenile shows of individualism run amok and have disrupted or destroyed every organization he was ever a part of. For this reason, the author's summary arguments are brutal:

> Baraka owes many black Americans a debt he cannot pay. Because of his public actions many political opportunities were either lost or distorted beyond viability. Yes he was committed to black freedom. And yes he was seemingly inexhaustible in his commitment to the struggle. But yes he advanced a political line that was socially retarded even for the times. The viciousness of his sexism, the obscenity of his anti-semitism and the ridiculousness of his pipe dream to usher black Americans into African feudalism demand a day in public court. Baraka and Karenga [sixties Baraka crony] came far closer to advocating an atavistic black neo-fascism. . . . It is not enough to say that Baraka meant well.

Baraka is certainly a worthy, weighty subject for an American studies and political science professor, and an easy target as well. The failures and vices of sixties Black radicalism implicate far too many for Baraka to have to shoulder so much blame alone. His isolated position in contemporary Black America, self-willed or not, seems harsh enough a judgment without hysterical demands for "a day in public court." That moment in Black American rebellion still deserves its own Best and Brightest if not its own *War and Peace* to settle all the scores.

Watts also seems quite upset at Baraka for not providing him with a viable answer as to how one can function as a credible Black artist-scholar-intellectual superstar and a credible grassroots activist. Admonishing Frank Lentricchia for his comment that "struggles for hegemony are sometimes fought out in colleges and universities, fought undramatically yard for yard and sometimes over minor texts of Balzac. No heroes, no epic acts," Watts then engages in a convoluted defense and condemnation of Black public intellectuals. He asks with thinly veiled angst, "Are there circumstances in which the radical literary intellectual should put down her pen and leave her desk?" Yet the crux of Lentricchia's argument, his fragmentary "no heroes, no epic acts" line, actually leads us away from the charismatic cowboy model of Black activism that decimated Baraka's generation of struggle martyrs. Where it takes us is back toward the dull and unsexy grunt work of authentic organizing, every bit as nerdy, text-ridden, and bureaucratized as any academic department, give or take a protest rally or two.

Watts fails to acknowledge the revolution Baraka's generation of radical intellectuals did win in academe—the one evident in the booming business of African American studies, which might have helped Watts get a job after graduating from Harvard. Nor does he acknowledge that while the countersupremacist Blackness-for-Blackness's-sake ethos of Baraka's project had its crude, malformed moments, it also provided the necessary background radiation from which, for better or worse, the writings of Toni Morrison, Stanley Crouch, and August Wilson would emerge, as well as the ghetto fantasias of the blaxploitation flix, Richard Pryor, George Clinton, gangsta rap, and the lucrative Afrocentric New Age spiritualism of our Iyanla Vanzant types. Contemporary commodified progressive Black culture, in all its separate but Afrocentric bliss, would be unimaginable without Baraka.

Richard Wright's biographer, Hazel Rowley, best known for a bio on writer Christina Stead, makes superb use of the small battalion of papers his wife, Ellen, bequeathed to Yale. Of the three works under discussion, it is the most traditional and gossipy. Unlike many major postwar Black cultural figures, Wright left a paper trail that included voluminous notebooks, diaries, and even love letters. He frequently even turns up as a topic in the letters Beauvoir was writing to her lover (and Wright's old friend) Nelson Algren in the fifties. Wright's rites of passage—from Mississippi sharecropper's son to Chicago Communist Party youth leader to the internationally celebrated writer of *Uncle Tom's Children*, *Native Son*, and *Black Boy*—are lavishly and lovingly recounted by Rowley.

After those initial successes, however, Wright, in Rowley's telling, became a struggling middle-aged American writer out to keep his family fed in their city and country houses in postwar Paris. His residence there relieved him of the daily indignities 1950s America threw at a prominent Negro intellectual with a white wife. The initial rush of Paris life seems to have thwarted his productivity by introducing him to existentialism and the French attitude toward less than discreet extramarital affairs. The hyperproductive first act of Wright's early adult life becomes, by the second act, a bourgeois domestic drama with Wright desperately trying to sustain a soured marriage and his properties with dwindling royalties. A quixotic third act, perhaps brought on by middle-age crisis, made a thirty-nine-year-old Wright abandon his family for a year to attempt a film version of *Native Son* in Argentina in which he played teenage Bigger. Not long after this sojourn, Wright went to Africa for the first time, donned safari gear and cameras, and was perplexed over how anyone could tell he was a tourist. In Ghana he met and bemused Kwame Nkrumah before marching into the interior and returning with a disgust for life in the African bush that reads like something out of Conrad.

No friend of the U.S. Communist Party (though his reasons for leaving had to do with being denounced as decadent for deeming Gertrude Stein a fit model for working-class literature and disdaining Harry Haywood), Wright will unknowingly be used as an anti-Red critic by CIA operatives who publish his essays in their French magazines. He will also become the target of other African American émigrés jealous of his status, most prominently James Baldwin, whose oedipal relationship to Wright found its nadir in Baldwin's essay "Everybody's Protest Novel," which singled out *Native Son* as an egregious example of the genre. While Baldwin assailed Wright's art, two now-forgotten émigré African American journalists attempted to put Wright in jeopardy with the CIA—which, Rowley intimates, may have had a hand in his death, as it certainly did Fanon's.

Fanon's and Wright's paths crossed at the publication Présence Africaine's historic Second Congress of Black Writers and Artists, held in Rome in 1959—appropriately enough, since Fanon routinely and naively referenced Wright's and Chester Himes's work when discussing the American race scene. Under David Macey's indefatigable pen, Fanon—

whose dual wartime experience probably helped him suffer less fuzzy romanticism about Africa or revolution than Wright and Baraka—emerges as one of the most complex personalities of this or any other century. Macey, one of whose previous books was *The Lives of Michel Foucault*, is well up to the task. Telling Fanon's life story requires a polymath engagement of French and Arabic linguistics, African and Afro-Caribbean literature and politics, French psychoanalytic theory and history, and nothing less than a thorough narrating of the intricacies of the French-Algerian war from inside both military camps.

Wright and Baraka come across in print as complicated men capable of great complexity as writers. Fanon is a different sort of animal entirely: a knotty and recombinant mixture of Hamlet, Freud, Che, and Dr. Jekyll all rolled into one. He was complex in his choice of profession and projects within it, in his loyalties and defections, complex even in his critical and therapeutic lapses. Macey notes that Fanon's passing familiarity with Freud and Marx did not get in the way of his spot-on analyses of alienation among the colonized brown people and the unique forms socialism was taking in fifties Africa. Fanon's story demands numbing detail, and Macey's book is a two-in-one deal: everything you ever wanted to know about the man coupled with everything you never knew about the French-Algerian war.

Fanon's identification with the Algerian struggle was of such a fierce degree that he intimated in his writings that he had willed himself into being an Algerian. In the name of the cause he will twice disrupt historic gatherings of African intellectuals with remarks so pointed and caustic about the rest of Africa's betrayal of Algeria that a commemorative text of the second event, published twenty years after the fact, completely erased his presence.

Fanon's medical integrity allowed him to treat both the victims of French police torture and the cops themselves. One incident almost begs for the auteur treatment. A police patient of Fanon's left the examining room and wandered onto the grounds, where he fainted upon seeing one of his victims. The former victim, seeing his torturer, ran away and hid, certain he was about to be tortured again until Fanon coaxed him out, convincing the poor soul his illness caused such hallucinations.

Fanon the humanist is less well known than the Fanon who advocated the "cleansing" effects of anticolonial violence. Though *The Wretched of the Earth* was published as Fanon lay on his deathbed, it would go on to become a standard issue of serious revolutionaries and revolutionaries manqués in the sixties, inspiring Eldridge Cleaver's hyperbolic boast that "every brother on a rooftop" could quote Fanon. Macey takes to task those who would claim Fanon glorified violence, noting that if he had substituted "armed struggle" for "violence," his work would have seemed less inflammatory to liberal sensibilities. But his intended readers probably saw themselves being cleansed. Like Baraka, Fanon was not above writing with intent to cause white intellectuals to shudder. The confiscation of every available copy of *The Wretched of the Earth* in Paris on the day of his death indicates the degree to which he terrorized the powers that be.

The lives and writings of Wright, Fanon, and Baraka have easily generated enough heat, light, and space to keep an army of academic squirrels critically jockeying for decades. As far removed as we all seemed before 9.11.01 from the passions, dialogues, and barricades that defined their times, these biographies can make one long for the days when the most brilliant minds of African descent threw caution and careerism to the winds in pursuit of answers and actions appropriate to reversing a global wave of racial retardation and despair.

– 2002 –

Bottom Feeders: Natsuo Kirino's *Out*

Natsuo Kirino's *Out* is truly a universal tale, meaning a truly multiculturally applicable novel, meaning one that will be understood anywhere in the world where there are loan sharks, illegal casinos, and middle-aged working-class women toiling like galley slaves on the night shift in grueling dead-end assembly-line jobs. In this case the gig is packing prefab food into lunch boxes from midnight to 6 a.m. only to return home to abusive, cheating husbands who blithely relate how they've gambled away the family savings before punching wifey in the gut, or docile deadbeats who run off with all her pay, or dour, self-absorbed types disinterested in everything about the little woman—her mind, pussy, problems—save her penchant for putting dinner on the table like clockwork. This doesn't begin to describe the all-around appeal of various children (and in one case an infantile mother-in-law) who are either young and needy, 'ho-ing and greedy, or expert in the use of silence as a passive-aggressive weapon. None more so than the son who, in the first words his mother has heard from him in years, nearly sells her out to the police, then cries out, "Thanks for nothing, bitch," when she informs him she might be leaving the family.

True to that maxim, "Don't let a woman tell it because she'll tell it all," *Out* may be the most ghetto Japanese novel you ever read. It contains all the necessary genre ingredients and then some: a murder, a corpse-dismembering enterprise, a disintegrating team of coconspirators, a yakuza sociopath, a yakuza extortionist. The vive la différence in this case is that the murderer is the perfect housewife, her accessories to murder are her girls from the assembly line, and both yakuza cats, the sociopath and the loan shark, secretly fall in love with the assembly-line gang's hardtack, worldly ringleader, Musake, whom glass-ceiling misogyny drove from corporate life to bento-box wage slavery.

The scarily omniscient Kirino knows not only everybody's business but everybody's mind—her way with interior monologue is pungent and prismatic, shuffling between characters' ill-ass reveries on the same insane incident. There is a lot here about Japanese sexism, of the ageist and pedophilic kind, and the psychology of Japanese female self-loathing and existential despair. Like Walter Mosley she exploits the beat-down potential of the hard-boiled novel to depict life on society's bottom in ways that subtly read as one part social protest, one part sadomasochistic entertainment. Perhaps the most pointedly Japanese aspect of Kirino's writing is the way she eroticizes, even romanticizes, sexual violence, up to and including two homicidal rapes. As much as the Japanese are supposed to be enamored of all things American, after reading Kirino you can easily believe Western feminism never became the rage.

– 2003 –

Scaling the Heights: Maryse Condé's *Windward Heights* (Translated by Richard Philcox)

Maryse Condé does for Emily Brontë and *Wuthering Heights* what Bernie Worrell did for Bach: She funkatizes the mother. This is one mean little book, mean in spirit and mean in design. It's mad comical too, but in a cruel-to-the-bone, sadistic kind of way, the kind of book where tortured souls die horribly only to discover there's no peace in the hereafter either.

Condé was born in Guadeloupe but has lived and taught extensively in Africa, Europe, and the United States; presently she teaches in the francophone literature program at Columbia. Going afield for source material is nothing new for the author. In her best-selling *Segu* and *Children of Segu* series she reimagined an eigtheenth-century Mali torn between Islam and animism; in *I, Tituba: Black Witch of Salem* she got into the head of the only recorded Black woman to be accused in the Salem witch trials; *The Last of the African Kings* moves comfortably between Martinique and South Carolina. In all these works Condé essays on a Black humanity that is neither superheroic nor pathological, just neurotic and scraping by like folk everywhere. To her Brontë experiment she brings her usual admixture of race consciousness, literary gamesmanship, and meticulous research. By the time you put the book down you'll know the Caribbean caste system inside out.

Condé's Heathcliff is named Razye, after the Creole name for the heath-covered cliffs of Guadeloupe. As in the original, the orphaned protagonist was discovered roaming the wilds by his benefactors. Razye grows up the child of a poor family whose youngest daughter, Cathy, is the love of his life. Beaten by his stepfather for his attraction to her, he leaves to fight against José Martí's followers in Cuba. When he returns he finds that his tragic mulatto obsession, Cathy, has married a weak, liberal white man for wealth and security. Razye, denied his soul mate once again by class and race prejudice, embarks on a revenge plot against Cathy's white husband, Aymeric de Linsseuil, meant to cause suffering across three generations. Razye's ferocity creates an atmosphere of instability, anxiety, distraction, and self-destruction. There is much catching of the vapors in the book—several major characters waste away in bed from various contagions or after giving birth—and a lot of sins of the father deluging daughters and sons.

Surprisingly enough, Condé's retelling of Brontë, while hyperbolic, reads as neither literary parody nor political satire; her interest, as with Brontë, is the way social conventions inform and deform character. The Condé edition is likewise a fictive testing of romantic passion's earthly boundaries. Where she goes beyond Brontë is in illuminating the racial subtext of revulsion at Heathcliff's darkness dimly discussed in the original (in Brontë he's described as a "dark-skinned gypsy" who covets the light hair and blue eyes of his antagonist as much as his wealth) and having it fuel Razye's Grand Guignol of obsessive vengeance, rape, domestic abuse, and incest.

As should be expected, a monsoon of melodrama floods these pages: Joining the Socialist Party formed by an emergent Black Creole gentry, Razye uses his warlord position as a pretense to pillage and burn Aymeric's estate and drive him into poverty. Upon realizing that his beloved Cathy is beyond reach, Razye seduces Aymeric's sister Irmine into a wretched life of unwanted childbearing and neglect. Razye later adopts Justin-Marie, who is Cathy's nephew and spitting image, but the boy defects to the Aymeric camp where he hysterically rapes an Indian servant's daughter while in his tubercular death throes at age sixteen.

Where Brontë used Heathcliff's tenant and housekeeper to narrate *Wuthering Heights*, Condé allows a multiplicity of minor characters to narrate including various maids, workers, fishermen, and witch doctors, all of whom cross the path of the two accursed bloodlines. It's through these characters that Condé is able to go full press about her real business, detailing the sordid pecking order mulattos and Blacks evolved in a postemancipated Caribbean. Her descriptions of Black self-hatred are evenly matched by passages about mulatto scrambling, desperation, and impotence.

Though the Razye/Cathy story sets the book in motion, Condé's best writing is reserved for characters who shuffle in from the sidelines only to shuffle out of the picture once their particular island tragedy has been lined out. Chief among them being the woebegotten Sanjita, mother of Justin-Marie's rape victim Etiennise, whose monologue prophetically recalls Sanjita's own father's proud story about his mother being raped by a wise man—sort of a polished-turd version of a less-than-immaculate conception. Though Razye's rages in the world of angry Black revolutionaries are passingly related, Condé gives closer scrutiny to the women barely holding shit together through grinding seasons of poverty, disease, and war:

> That year Guadeloupe suffered a terrible calamity. Typhoid fever landed off the boats with the oxen from Puerto Rico, those colossal animals driven to the slaughterhouse, whose quarters, blackened by flies, can be seen hanging by the feet in the meat booths of the market. In three months the typhoid fever laid out 3,265 people. Five hundred survived with nothing but skin on their bones; the rest went to fill the places reserved for them in the cemeteries. . . . In the churches unending novenas were said, and the priests from their pulpits begged the blacks and the mulattos to repent. Why were they persecuting the white Creoles? Why did they steal their cattle and set fire to their cane-fields? For this reason the Good Lord was no longer good, and his wrath was burning the island.

Windward Heights is a confident and incisive Caribbeanization of a European master text by a master novelist of African descent, but it ultimately resonates more as a book about the social character of the island than as a novel driven by character revelations; the author's guiding hand

and didactic streak is perhaps a bit too evident for that. In the book's final chapters, the conceit of Razye's relentless revenge devolves into a fatalistic gimmick; the author seems compelled to tie up loose ends and finish raising the misery index in ways that seem more dutiful than engaging and complex.

Condé has said the book partially grew out of a debate with Patrick Chamoiseau, author of *Texaco* and *Solibo Magnificent*, over whether the francophone Caribbean novel would best find its voice, as Chamoiseau believes, in poetic and Creolized deconstructions of French or, by Condé's reasoning, culturally specific narrative techniques such as polyphony. For the reader, this argument would seem to turn on whether you derived more pleasure from a Joycean or a Proustian approach to syntax, storyline, and the writing of human consciousness. Narrative unfortunately becomes a straitjacket for Condé in *Windward Heights*, constraining reader and writer to drag themselves to a windy and piffling denouement. While Condé's previous books have displayed considerable powers of invention and insight, devotion to Brontë's formal limitations seems ultimately to have hemmed her in at the end.

– 1999 –

Fear of a Mongrel Planet: Zadie Smith's
White Teeth

We don't usually look to Black women's lit for jokes, bioethics, or those narrative schools known as the picaresque, the postmodern, or the encyclopedic. It's not like these absences arise from a lack of mordant wit or from an inability to unspool a shambolic story about the meaning of existence (think of Scheherazade, think J, think of Gayl Jones and Lauryn Hill). Actually, it's only because we've been waiting for Zadie Smith, now twenty-four, who has composed as gut-busting and auspicious a debut novel as Pynchon's *V.* that is two guffaws ahead of the zeitgeist and saturated with all manner of postcolonial subjectivities—Jamaican, Bengali, Arabic, Italian, neo-Nazi eugenicist. Deconstructing race for the twenty-first century is Smith's bailiwick, her coal-mine canary, Rosetta Stone, and tolling bell. Beware it tolls not for thee.

Big, multigenerational, and very British in the way of scathing social satire, *White Teeth* is partially about what it feels like to be an assimilated brown-skinned Bengali subject of the queen, and partially about the pervasive fear of a mongrel planet. As befits a book here to inform

Ishmael Reed, David Foster Wallace, William Gibson, Paul Gilroy, and Gayatri Spivak that There's a New Sheriff in Town, *White Teeth* wears its brains and brainy bons mots on its sleeve: "But it makes an immigrant laugh to hear the fears of the nationalist, scared of infection, penetration, miscegenation, when this is small fry, peanuts, compared to what the immigrant fears—dissolution, disappearance."

The novel is full of lovely dagger-turning sentences like those. Imagine Charlie Parker with a typewriter, Coltrane with a laptop. Cheeky like ain't nobody's business if she do, Smith spares few in her all-out assault on the nuclear family, racial purity, paternalism, bad hair, eugenics, any hint of hypocrisy committed in the name of Allah, and the frightful brotherhood of impotent, disenfranchised men.

Playing the role of perpetual patriarchal asswipe in this black comedy of postcolonial manners is Samad Iqbal—Bengali Muslim immigrant; undistinguished war veteran; disgruntled one-handed headwaiter; husband to the wise, feisty Alsana; father to twin sons, roughneck Millat and effete Magid; and best friend of Archie Jones. Archie, head of the book's second significant household, is husband to Jamaican lapsed Jehovah's Witness and denture-wearing bombshell Clara, and father to Irie. The child, who belies her feel-good name with excruciating struggles with book learning, buck teeth, bad hair, worse weave jobs, big bones, and a broken heart, is the book's most heartwarming character. Rounding out the portrait of put-upon patriarchy is Marcus Chalfen, scion of a long-running intellectual aristocracy, husband to Joyce, hippie botanist and a designer of genetic monstrosities.

These portrayals would register as so much clever juvenilia were *White Teeth* not so insightfully character driven, exquisitely plotted, and secretly fueled by that rage Baldwin identified as a constant companion of the Black and conscious—never mind Black and female—mind. Every so often Smith peels back the sarcastic surface to reveal a character's demiurge, as with butcher Mo—why it's not too good to turn the other cheek in a white man's country too long: "general fascists, specific neo-Nazis, the local snooker team, the darts team, the football team, and huge posses of mouthy, white-skirted secretaries in deadly heels. These various people had various objections to him: He was a Paki. . . . They were all white. And this simple fact had done more to politicize Mo over the years than all the party broadcasts, rallies, and petitions the world could offer."

Reviewers keep praising *White Teeth* for not being your typical autobiographical first novel. *White Teeth* is atypically diverse as first novels go, but so is Willesden, the North London neighborhood where Smith grew up.

The social journeys one can imagine a savagely observant overachiever and self-described stoner might take growing up there, especially one from a Jamaican-British union as Smith is, seem consistent with *White Teeth*. I'm betting the cultural complexities she wrings out of waiting tables at an Indian restaurant and the mathematical theorems of the Jehovah's Witnesses are likely as familiar to her as discussing the intricacies of pathogenic mutagens.

White Teeth is virtuosic and prodigious beyond belief in its command of epic and epoch-raiding Pynchonesque novelistic technique. That said, one can only wish for Smith's work to grow as emotionally resonant as her symphonic command of the form. For as wicked and chocked with memorable incidents as *White Teeth* is, it doesn't leave gaping wounds. It can hurt your sides from laughing, but it doesn't haunt you.

In attempting to cauterize the invisibility blues of colored British folk with vicious sarcasm, Smith takes a nail-paring authorial voice so above the fray that her characters' internal wranglings don't seem fraught with much mortal consequence. In a lesser talent this failure wouldn't matter, but Smith is extravagantly gifted enough to be held accountable for how movingly she renders the complexity of human vulnerability.

Ralph Ellison's great critique of Richard Wright—that Wright couldn't imagine a Black person as evolved as himself living in his fictions—may be applicable to Smith, though it's much too early to tell. *White Teeth* is a grand and masterful performance and a phenomenally fast read, but it wears a tongue-in-cheek mask, walks on comedic crutches, and keeps the author's own cards so close to her chest they read like embroidery and not the stuff deferred dreams are made of. The novel also seems, for all its heft and multiple cultural perspectives, remarkably slight, if not evasive, on the matter of how people of African and Afro-Caribbean descent interact with one another on British soil. You could say that's another book and you'd be right. But as someone who knows hella-alienated negroes in the U.K. and something of their crabby barrels, I'm just puzzled—why do I get the feeling she'd rather write about any mess but that one? Though on the other hand, who can fault Smith, who's avoided the Black Public Intellectual soapbox so far, for keeping a few secrets and subject positions to herself? If nothing else, that reticence points to her knowing how the world conspires to set agendas and steal young, gifted, and successful Black artists from their work desks. Incredibly enough, Smith just might be even smarter than her smackdown writing declares her to be.

– 2000 –

Adventures in the Skin Trade: Lisa Teasley's
Glow in the Dark

The threat of violence never strays far from desire in Lisa Teasley's stories of interpersonal horrors. Under her pen the apprehension and dread which accompany human sexual need are rendered as malicious blood kin, murderous kissing cousins. Her characters are an exotic blend of the neurotic and the noirish—tense, hungry, dangerous folk of diverse ethnicities who crave understanding and stimulation but would be better off left alone. "Don't Stand So Close to Me" could be considered the theme song, if not the battle cry, of *Glow in the Dark*.

In "Baker," Marty, a hapless white guy who exposes himself to his Black lover's daughter, welcomes a cocked gun at his head. In "Meeting for Breakfast" a woman suspects an erratic male friend of killing someone she had dreamed about strangling, then discovers he may have been lying about the person being dead. In another tale a beautiful woman uses a horse-riding incident to break off with her hypochondriac fiancé when she suspects he is terminally ill.

What saves these setups from potboiler-dom is Teasley's wickedly laconic prose. She gets to her clinchers obliquely through edgy, emotive dialogue that borders on Too Much Information. Her observations focus on the tactile as much as the psychological.

> Mrs. Gaines had the fishbowl in the bedroom now, and she didn't know why but after staring at the fish swimming around there on her dresser with its flaming fins . . . she started touching herself, and just a bit embarrassed she turned to see if her husband's picture was face down, and then feeling a bit daring she picked up the picture so that it faced her and then she . . . touched herself all over, abandoning more and more of her stipulations and confinements of the mind. This felt quite good as long as it lasted. But then it was over, and she got up and went into the bathroom to throw up.

Teasley not only wants us to get under her characters' imaginary skins, she wants us to get physical with them too, learn the heft and weight and burden and loathings of their bodies. In "Wanting Girlfriend with the Pink Hair," Emerald has an imaginary dialogue with her beautiful gay brother, Cy: "My legs are too short really. They are much too short. Why couldn't I have gotten your legs? Cy. Or only your lips, even. I'd take your spider lashes, and be happy really. . . . You're all Mom, really, gorgeous Mom with the symmetrical everything and here I am lopsided with these crazy knock knees."

Though Teasley's stories take place in New York, California, and Paris, there is something vaguely West Coast about her spatial and racial sensibilities—her presentation of so many mobile, spontaneous, restless, couch-aversive, thirtysomething types who seem only tangentially attached to land, tribe, or profession. (The exceptions are her incidental Mexican characters, who occupy the circumscribed oppressed-lower-class ethnic camps other African American writers reserve for their own poor folk in literature.) Teasley's people give off an air of being wanderers, stragglers, and slackers. Day trips and road trips figure prominently. Unrequited sex and lust send several protagonists into a frenzy of head games, hidden designs, fateful betrayals, rages, and at least one suicide.

As cultural critic Rick Powell once intimated about the romantic combatants in Jean Toomer's *Cane*, Teasley's women seem to have more erotic energy than they know what to do with while her men seem a bit sapped (making them more loopy and likely to lash out). Teasley, pun irresistibly intended, loves to tease out the explosive backlash and karmic retribution sure to follow whenever someone vents their repressed feelings. In the world Teasley's creations inhabit, knowledge that someone got the fever for the flava can be a bitter if not fearsome thing. The lesbian adventure embarked upon by a road-tripping older and younger woman dumped by the same man in "Nepenthe" comes as no surprise, but the horny buildup is as brittle, anxious, and suspenseful as a Hitchcock scene. The incestuous undercurrent of the brother-sister relationship in "Pink Hair" startles less than the admission that their Black mother always referred to their long-lost papa as "your father the trick."

Like the Meshell Ndegeocello of *Bitter*, Teasley privileges the excavation and display of pent-up feeling, eschewing conventional morality about fidelity to respect the destructive power of envy, jealousy, alienation, and, most of all, unavoidable intimacy. The circumscribed closeness that comes with taking on friends, lovers, and family is the same feeling that could drive some folk to hurt, abandon, maim, or kill. Without embracing cynicism or denying the risks, Teasley lights up the plunge into the abyss that can result from knowing people far too well.

– 2002 –

Generations Hexed: Jeffery Renard Allen's
Rails under My Back

This pungent, wrenching first novel defies easy categories. At the risk of excessive alliteration, this reader finds in Jeffery Renard Allen's masterful text invocations of the three D's: Samuel Delany (especially his postapocalyptic gang warfare novel *Dhalgren*), Don DeLillo, and Donald Goines. As Delany did in *Dhalgren*, Allen gives you the inner city as protagonist; as with DeLillo's *Underworld*, the writer conjures a cosmology from a familial microcosm. Like Goines he treats ghetto folklore as a stray cousin of magic realism.

As dark, spooky, and ghetto-operatic as any Wu-Tang production, the book is also enthralled with the marvelously mundane texture of working-class folk (the way Charles Burnett was in the film *Killer of Sheep*). Like that film, *Rails* transgresses the taboo terrain of Black storytellers—the African American father. Reading Allen makes one realize how few memorable patriarchs turn up in the literature; as rectification he presents exploded views of several in all their intestinal glory.

The families in question are joined in marriage by the unions of two brothers, John and Lucifer, to two sisters, Sheila and Gracie. The narration probes their tales with microscopic tools, rendering precise and chromatic images of their parents, children, war and work histories, and inner demons. Chief among these is John and Gracie's son Jesus, whose devilish, thug-nigga ways are intimated to have started in his mother's combustive and corrosive womb. Adept with parallel narratives, Allen counterbalances Jesus with Lucifer and Sheila's kids—bookish, dreamy, musical Hatch and flygirl Porsha.

In blunt sociological terms, the novel is about the center that couldn't hold the African American working class together when can-do agrarian Southern roots supercollided with vampiric Northern project-housing and welfare culture. Though the families live outside the killing fields of the Red Hook and Stonewall projects in the book's postindustrial Midwestern city, the forbidden aura of those places seduces the children to find what they need to satisfy respective lusts for worldly knowledge (Hatch), sensual love (Porsha), power (Jesus). Though *Rails* is also ostensibly about why modern African American men can't stay put ("We martyr to motion"), Allen hardly gives short shrift to the women his urban Odysseans leave pining behind. In his portrayals of the mothers Sheila and Gracie, and Sheila's daughter, Porsha, Allen pumps out such thorough excavations of body and soul as to suggest that authorial empathy can be the gateway to full-throttle telepathy: "The danger increased with her increasing belly. Hundreds of threads streamed out from her navel. [Gracie] was so weak it took her half an hour to reach the bottom of the circular staircase. . . . The black willing blood of the baby bubbled inside her. Her umbilical cord popped electric life, a telephone that transmitted the infant's threats: I'm gon fuck you up."

In depicting Porsha's ardor for the project-masculinity of her lover, Deathrow, Allen mines the hip-hop-laden paradox of good girls charmed by roughhouses:

> He wasn't stuck on sex. He knew the value of a hug and would hold her all night sometimes, her head on the boulder of his shoulder.
>
> Equally drawing were his wild dangerous moments. Once . . . he just up and grabbed a waitress at Davy's Garden. Some homely white girl who was working another table. Grabbed her by the arm and pulled her face next to his as if he had a secret to tell. He put his tongue in her mouth. He let her go. She cleaned her lipstick from his mouth with a cloth napkin. She tore up the check. He sat back in his chair, belly poked out with satisfaction.
>
> Did you have to do that?
>
> He looked Porsha full in the face. Clean draws can't hide a nasty booty.

As much as there is to admire in Allen's rhapsodic language and characterization skills, his symphonic mastery of novelistic form is equally awe inspiring (not to mention his intimate familiarity with the whole damn human comedy—his broad panoply of minor characters all have epic stories to tell; he pries into their secrets and petty volatile marital rages like a domestic combat veteran). Allen's handling of time and memory is circular, bearing forth an understanding of them as elastic and transdimensional. True to the feeling one often has in Black families and communities that every era of our history has been clamorously stuffed and tacked onto our sense of the now, Allen demands we recognize that all of the African American yesterday remains evocatively embodied in somebody living today. He treats temporality as randomly as one of Vonnegut's Tralfamadorians, as if past, present, and future were simply stations to be channel zapped at will.

A cruel conceit of the book is that when wanderlusting Black men leave, the world swallows them whole, and that while they may be missed, they are nonessential personnel. Though Jesus murders a major character well before the denouement, Allen, driving the point home, shocks by providing no account of bereavement or mourning for this stalwart pillar of the family. (Colder still, he only references it as a TV report about a random street shooting seen by blissfully ignorant family members.)

Rails is a book that reveals its intentions to the reader in teasingly slow, detailed, and luxuriant fashion, saving its secret heart—a rumination upon the spiritual fates of sons Hatch and Jesus, cursed with their forebears' frontiersman-like lust for self-invention—until almost the very end. Echoes of Ellison's *Invisible Man* appropriately appear in identity-forming epiphanies that spring for Hatch from a riot scene and for Jesus from an underground lair. The book is pervaded by a sense that we are reading about a tribe ancient, dusty, long dead, one whose myths and mother tongue have proven more enduring and sustainable than their civilization, whose remnants seem to be shredding as they speak. It's this quality of fiction digesting culture that makes *Rails* the kind of Black storytelling that could only be done in a novel, where the collective unconscious can be atomized and examined without any compromise of complexity, integrity, or richness. Allen has given us a great gift, a bleak, staggering, and elliptical monument to the African American family in this millennial moment. Talk about it.

– 2000 –

Going Underground: Gayl Jones's *Mosquito*

Gayl Jones is the Black writer we all want to be when we grow up, or at least when we hit the half-century mark: dark, devious, scientific, folkloric, mass-culture savvy, book smart (enough so that her erudite throwaway essays about horse grooming, Masai medicine women, French wines, never appear to be for showing off), and wise about people too (enough so that she can make a Nazi chemist character seem as human as an African American anthropologist). When Jones published *Corregidora* and *Eva's Man* while in her twenties, she arrived at the head of the class of late twentieth-century American novelists who happen to be Black, female, and brilliant. Even with the twenty-year hiatus separating *Eva's Man* and 1998's *The Healing*, she's still a top ranker.

The publication of *The Healing* was unfortunately overshadowed by the personal tragedy that ensued not long after its appearance on the shelves: her husband's dramatic suicide after a standoff with police and the author's own subsequent psychiatric detention. A similar fate awaits

Mosquito, a six-hundred-plus-page ramble that's kinda about an African American woman truck driver in Texas and her involvement with the Sanctuary movement, dubbed by Jones "the new Underground Railroad" for its work in supporting Latin American border crossings.

In both *Mosquito* and *The Healing* Jones emerges as a modern-day Zora Neale Hurston—a writer who organically projects country gal and cosmopolite. Her stance is that of both staunch race woman and steely-eyed cultural anthropologist—she knows and loves African American culture to the degree that she won't simplify, apologize for, or demystify it.

In *The Healing*, her heroine Harlan—traveling evangelist, rock-star manager, and wife to an anthropologist, among other things—unapologetically answers "beautician" when another academic wife inquires about her profession at a dinner, allowing Jones to quietly address the airs, presumption, and bad manners of so-called sophisticated folk. *Mosquito* mines this vein of social observation in a far less pithy way. Synopsizing the book is a fool's task: When a pregnant Mexican woman steals aboard Mosquito's truck, she helps the Mexican escape, an act that brings her to the attention of the Sanctuary movement as well as to the attention of sensitive activist Ray.

Except the book is less about the bonding of Mosquito, Ray, and Mexican stowaway Maria than it is about the philosophy and opinions of Mosquito and her bartending, aspiring-novelist Chicana friend Delgadina. Some of the arcane subjects include Mosquito's cactus-handled teacup, shrubbery and architecture, marine-animal camouflage, and most prominently multiculturalism, a notion Jones clearly finds quite ripe for savaging. "Delgadina say them whites that's all for multiracialism just want to use the multirace as a buffer, you know. 'Cause somebody told them that in the next millennium the white people be the minority, so they wants as many people as they can to identify with them, rather than the other colored peoples. So now they's modifying they racial purity myth, 'cause it's in they best interest." There are also choice riffs on the difference between French and German writing; white girls who pass for Mexican; Mexican bartenders who want to turn actresses because they think they look like Susan Sarandon, Sean Young, Kim Basinger; and current U.S. immigration law.

Inside every serious Black novelist there's a Racial Authority screaming to be repressed. In *Mosquito*, Jones, who till now had kept the beast at bay, ups the ante by speaking on behalf of our Latin American brothers and sisters too and doing it at a length that might kindly be called self-indulgent, if not incredibly demanding of even her most sympathetic readers' time, tolerance, and intelligence. One thing some of us used to love about Jones, whom literary scholar Imani Wilson called the Only Real Black Woman Writer ("because everybody hates her") is that she is not now nor has she ever been a Black Public Intellectual. She was instead a reclusive and enigmatic sister from Kentucky who wrote books that explored scar tissue from the inside and told exquisitely excruciating stories in terse, evocative, plainspoken language and hardly ever seems to have had her picture taken.

Now that Jones has become a story more gripping than any she's ever written, *Mosquito* can't help but seem a desperate attempt to keep pace with her reality. There will be a great temptation to read *Mosquito* as the writing of a crazy woman because of Jones's recent events, and because it is long-winded, disassociative, plotless, cutesy, full of hairsplitting deconstructive debates. But *Mosquito* also confirms that when it comes to dovetailing ivory-tower literacy with a working-class worldview, Jones is a peerless synthesist who loves to signify, as when the title character gets roped into a Hollywood cocktail party by her friend Monkey Bread, gofer for a blond movie star who always gets cast to play "ethnic types":

> We's sitting at the table with them, and they's treating us like we's human. Well, they's kinda treating me like I'm Monkey Bread's pet.
> Didn't I see you in that new Robert Townsend movie? one of them asks.
> I'm nibbling on some caviar and drinking a can of Budweiser. Monkey Bread say the star ordered that Budweiser especially for me. The others got champagne. The room they's having the cocktail party in is one of them modern rooms. . . . All the furniture is arranged in geometric patterns on the rug, so that the room outside the rug is free for the cocktail people to roam around in, like they's in the margins. . . .
> Naw, I says. I owns a little restaurant in Cuba. . . .
> And before I can tell him it's Cuba, New Mexico, he's thinking I mean that other Cuba.

When white boys write books as cunning and convoluted as this one we call them postmodern, experimental, exemplars of the literature of exhaustion; when B-boys drop prose this polemical we call them conscious rappers; when musicians of African descent take this much space to tangentially riff, we declare them avant-garde. There is a possibility that Jones is satirizing that sort of prolix, polyglot white-boy book in *Mosquito* as well as paying homage to such freestyle masters as Chuck D, KRS-One, Cecil Taylor, and the Art Ensemble of Chicago. It is also worth considering as one attempts to plow through this wordy book that at this stage in world history, if you are a Black woman writer who the state put on lockdown mere seconds after you'd broken a twenty-year silence, your next move had best be a long, unbroken howl, full of glossolalia and fury.

To her credit *Mosquito* is also an extended millennial meditation on border crossing of many kinds—geographic, racial, genetic, literary—from the hidebound perspective of an independent African American woman truck driver whose egalitarian if critical roaming among other cultures and Cultured Others reveals her as the ultimate universalist. Which might be the point of this very digressive book (albeit with the saving metafictional grace of the writer knowing she's breaking all sorts of conventional narrative contracts). *Mosquito* is Gayl Jones unbound, but certainly not untethered nor without her still prodigious storehouses of language, craft, and storytelling prowess. All those who believe in keeping the faith ought to say a little prayer for Gayl.

– 1999 –

Judgment Day: Toni Morrison's *Love* and Edward P. Jones's *The Known World*

Toni Morrison doesn't just write novels, she writes judgments, and we all stand naked before her—niggas and krackas alike. Mostly these judgments concern the violence our racialized culture has done to our collective humanity, and particularly the damage done to Black women's sense of propriety, if not their good old-fashioned common sense. In these judgments, two kinds of Black women receive contempt: those who'll do anything in the street, and those who'll allow anything behind closed doors. But there's a third Black female archetype here: practical, intimidating, indispensable—that is, a witch. She knows the value of sacrifice and getting things done. Her life is one of purpose, service, sorrow, and defeat because her job is to keep chaos at bay, and in the world of American Negroes, that's one thankless task.

Morrison's new novel, *Love*, is devoted to the declamations of four women raised better prepared for life in the open rather than behind closed doors. *Love* is a judgment about how wild women are made, about the impropriety violation may produce. You may have read that it's about a charismatic Black beachside resort owner, Bill Cosey, and his four women, but Cosey's full story will have to await telling by someone for whom the women are not fascinating grist for Morrison's judgmental mill.

Of the four, Heed and Christine could be called his women; Heed because he bought her from her father and married her when she was eleven, Christine because she is his granddaughter, the only child of his only child. What binds Heed and Christine isn't their love of Cosey but their hatred of him, which becomes a hatred of one another; in the world of proper American Negroes, there's nothing more forbidden than for a Black woman to express a bad opinion of a successful Black man. Morrison has been tagged a Black man hater, but with the exception of still wondering why in God's name the Pauls in *Beloved* had to fuck cows, I've never thought that. Being herself the kind of purposeful, binding-force Black woman who can get the job done, Morrison expects no more from Black men than she does anyone else; her judgments tend not to be prejudiced unless the case involves the kind of Black woman who'll do anything in the street.

Call this character She Who Is Without Proper Womanly Boundaries. Call her Sula, call her Beloved. In *Love* her name is Junior. From the opening lines you know Judgment and Propriety are on the warpath; from the parsed and clipped sentences, you know Morrison has a few issues with this current generation of wild women.

> The women's legs are spread wide open, so I hum. . . . Back in the seventies when women began to straddle chairs and dance crotch out on television, when all the magazines started featuring behinds and inner thighs as though that's all there is to a woman, well, I shut up altogether. Before women agreed to spread in public, there used to be secrets.

Morrison unexpectedly puts her powers of chiseled description to work on sadomasochistic sex. Giving herself a grand opportunity with the proverbially "fast and loose" Junior, *Love*'s hot-young-thing bête noire, Morrison goes for blood.

In *The Known World*, Edward P. Jones miraculously does things with African American bondage that his predecessors haven't. The dilemma in portraying American slavery is conveying the power (Ovidian and Orwellian, fantastic and fascistic) required to transform human beings into legal property, as well as the humanity of propertied beings. It's a slippery slope. Too much Negro sentimentality and white savagery can lead to manipulative, shallow ruin; too much detachment, and you may as well be writing history rather than literature. The writers before Jones all recognized the need for a distancing device: Morrison got all

Gothic, with violations and ghosts and Pyrrhic victories; Ishmael Reed worked the vein of sardonic irony and historical satire; Octavia E. Butler used the conceit of time travel to literalize the distance; Djuna Barnes Africanized and universalized man's inhumanity to man. Jones seems to ring variations on the same, but he goes deeper, re-creating the mundane surrealism of antebellum slavery.

Using the knowledge that there were African Americans who owned other African Americans during slavery, Jones has found a distancing device capable of seductively rendering the banality of slavery's evil. Arguably the most evil thing about slavery was its legal reduction of Black people to non-Being and then into pack mules, household appliances, and patriarchal conveniences. *The Known World* identifies the invisible price tags hung on individual slaves, as well as the law that normalizes their sale from white man to white man and renders the exchange so mundane that even a Frenchman jailed on murder charges can negotiate a price for two slaves from behind bars. Jones peppers this novel with plenty of similar anecdotes, letting us come to our own emotional conclusions about the daily experience of what being property means, with hardly a whiff of editorializing.

Jones also describes how Hartford-based insurance companies profited from slavery. Where he truly works miracles is in depicting the complexity of those designated slaves by the law—the folly and the absurdity of their every aching feeling rendered all the more tragic by their capricious, circumscribed lives.

– 2003 –

Black Modernity and Laughter, or How It Came to Be That N*g*as Got Jokes

The Negro has got jokes. N*g*as got jokes too. If anyone but a Negro or a N*g*a had written those words they would be considered outright offensive. Since one did they can described as outrageously cheeky, reliably colloquial, and obviously vernacular. Given the topic at hand these are all acceptable rhetorical strategies and conceits for brother-man to open up a comical essay with.

We've been asked to write about Black humor in the context of modernity, but writing about humor is never quite all it's cracked up to be. For one thing it derives from a Greek word that is meant to identify the very stuff, the vital juices as it were, which gives folk the capacity to laugh. Now, we think laughter is great, medicine for the soul and all that, and, as a Negro, I can testify that N*g*as not only got jokes but know how to laugh at them. Problem with writing about laughter though is that any fool or group of fools can be found who will laugh at just about anything. That said we could then switch-up our nomenclature and claim to be writing about Black Comedy but there again we run into semantic confusion, not just because Black Comedy could lead some folk to be confused about whether we want to be in discussion about the firm of Foxx, Pryor, Cosby, Rock, and Chappelle or that of Beckett, Barthelme, Vonnegut, and Pynchon, but because writing about comedy is generally a more dismal and joyless proposition than dancing about architecture, for writer and reader alike. Essayists gifted with a far more adroit light touch than I have taken up the task and failed miserably. Zadie Smith, one of the few drop-dead funny writers of contemporary literature, recently wrote the most melancholic if not, indeed, the dreariest piece of her career around the topic of British comedy for the *New Yorker*. If Sister Zadie couldn't make the subject vaguely entertaining, I'm not so foolhardy as to even brave the attempt. Because, you see, the number one problem with writing about comedy is that it requires you not only to translate the comedic genius of a Richard Pryor or a Dave Chappelle to the page but to then provide some very bloodless and academic reasons why the work is genius and hilarious at the same time—never a good look from where we sit. For one thing comedy is all about timing; for another thing great comedians not only say funny things but they say things funny. The Pryors, Rocks, and Chappelles of this world are people who just look inherently funny from the moment they appear to open their mouths. You kind of want to start laughing with them and at them before a single word has been uttered. In other words great comedians tend to also be great clowns—they have funny faces, funny minds, funny bodies, funny tongues, and, of course, funny bones. So the question must arise, if we are not going to talk about Black Humor or Black Comedy, what are we going to talk about to honor the spirit of the lavish invitation to essay upon Negro Laughter which the Tate Liverpool has bestowed upon this particular Negro? (One who himself tends to be rather fond of professional funny n*g*as with jokes.) To wit: We, dear friends are going to discuss Wit; Negro Wit to be specific.

Now the beauty of essaying on Wit as opposed to comedy is that you can actually measure Wit by an almost scientific standard and you're not under the same burden of comedic translation. No one has to love your wit; they just have to be convinced you're not a twit or a wit by half. This, you see, is because examples of Wit don't have to labor under the necessity of proving to be as funny on the page as they were on the stage. Wit can be visual or it can be verbal but all I have to prove with Wit is that my examples are clever, occasionally poignant or profound, well-aimed and slightly barbed. Wit doesn't have to have a target but when Wit comes lancing, its intended victims need not be appropriate or even opprobrious so much as they have to be punctured with accuracy, aplomb, verve, and a small taste of venom.

Fortunately for this writer the best examples of Negro Wit in Black Modernity can be readily found in the lyrics of many hip-hop songs. One thinks, for instance, of the two-woman stand-up hip-hop team Salt-N-Pepa who once made a song called "Never Trust a Big Butt and a Smile" while being women in full possession of both attributes in such abundance that many a man we know would have risked romantic betrayal for the privilege. One also thinks of the late great lyricist Biggie Smalls, who made a small art form out of describing acts of pure thuggery in the most shameless but witty terms possible. My own number one favorite example from Big's mugger's oeuvre would have to be "I been robbing motherfuckers since the slave ships"—primarily because that lyric violates every politically correct ancestor-worshipping bone in my pro-Black Pan-Afrikanist socialist body and dares me not to love the prickly sensation. In this genre of malice toward all and offense for everyone there are also the witticisms of Ice Cube to consider, a guy whose idea of fun was first laid bare in the song "Fuck tha Police" when he was in the band with the wittiest name in the history of hip-hop, N.W.A, short for Niggas with Attitude (as if those without attitude would be arrogant enough to assume success in American pop culture would readily follow from calling themselves the N word!). Biggie and Ice Cube are hip-hop's premiere representatives of that branch of wit we tend to describe as mordant, the sort of wits who charm and delight us while laughing at (and perpetrating) the faces of death.

Some rappers are too serious minded to deal in the sort of deadly low comedy favored by Big and Cube but the best of them don't lack for gut-socking punchlines either. One thinks of Public Enemy's Chuck D, who ingeniously injected several lines of sly and witty wordplay into a rather melodramatic song about a prison riot—most notably: "My plan said I had to get out and break North / just like Oliver's neck I had to get off." (You may need to Wiki "The North Star" and "Oliver North" to apprehend just how witty that line is if you were born after 1982 and have yet to take a course in African American history with strong emphasis on the Underground Railroad.) Now some fellow scholars of hip-hop verse find even more clever the militant nonchalance of the song's opening line: "I got a letter from the government the other day / I opened and read it / It said they were 'Suckers.' / They wanted me for their Army or Whatever / Picture me giving a damn I said 'Never.'" We, on the other hand, find ourselves more partial to the grace under pressure and dry wit Chuck displays in his follow-up line: "I wasn't with it but just that very minute it occurred to me / The Suckers had Authority."

Hip-hop is also where one is most likely in Black Modernity to find examples of that style of wit known as Absurdist. The lyricist known as MF Doom is perhaps our most uncanny contemporary purveyor of that style. Not least because he walks around onstage and off wearing a metal mask obviously modeled after that of the Marvel Comics villain Dr. Doom—but sometimes also sends younger, thinner, and even whiter-looking acolytes onstage to lip sync his songs—a gambit which has brought no shortage of ire and consternation from paying fans who demand the "real" Doom be brought before them and of course seem not to get the joke. (That being Doom's pointed send-up of current rap's rather dull devotion to theatrical naturalism or "realness" as we say here in the surreal 'hood of Harlem.) Doom, it should be noted, also deploys not just his own gruff speaking voice to tell his tall tales but also does neat impersonations of mousy cartoon characters, cornball office plebes, mentally challenged persons, superheroic talk show hosts. Doom's sort of absurdism piles on so many silly in-jokes and obscure references that you may at first easily feel fanboy brilliant for catching them until you realize the joke's on you. Being able to footnote Doom's roll call of cultural waste products we've come to realize is, though mad fun, no sign of intelligent life:

How they gave his own show to Tad Ghostal
Any given second he could go mad postal
Stay wavin that power band space cannon
And have the nerve to jump in the face, of Race Bannon
Punked out; luckily he deaded it
And guess who's the schmuck who's credited with editing it?
Your man Moltar, the cop out
Ain't have no other career choice, he dropped out
Since when the Way-Outs included Zorak
Way back he used to rub his thorax in Borax
      ("Space Ho's," from *The Mouse and the Mask* by DangerDoom)

The history of Wit in Black Modernity didn't begin with hip-hop of course. Where one finds the first evidence that African Americans were going to confront personal tragedy with a comic twist was found in that uber-body of Black literature known as the Slave Narratives. There one finds letters like the following written by our long-deceased brother Jourdon Anderson, a self-liberated person of African descent. It was composed and sent to his former concentration camp warden, one Colonel P. H. Anderson of Big Spring, Tennessee, on August 22, 1865.

Anderson's letter was apparently written in response to one from the colonel asking if Jourdon and his family would consider returning to their former confinement facility. The record shows no evidence of the colonel's written response.

Sir:

I got your letter and was glad to find you had not forgotten Jourdon, and that you wanted me to come back and live with you again, promising to do better for me than anybody else can. I have often felt uneasy about you. I thought the Yankees would have hung you long before this for harboring Rebs they found at your house. I suppose they never heard about your going to Col. Martin's to kill the Union soldier that was left by his company in their stable. Although you shot at me twice before I left you, I did not want to hear of your being hurt, and am glad you are still living. It would do me good to go back to the dear old home again and see Miss Mary and Miss Martha and Allen, Esther, Green, and Lee. Give my love to them all, and tell them I hope we will meet in the better world, if not in this. I would have gone back to see you all when I was working in the Nashville hospital, but one of the neighbors told me Henry intended to shoot me if he ever got a chance.

I want to know particularly what the good chance is you propose to give me. I am doing tolerably well here; I get $25 a month, with victuals and clothing; have a comfortable home for Mandy (the folks here call her Mrs. Anderson), and the children, Milly, Jane and Grundy, go to school and are learning well; the teacher says Grundy has a head for a preacher. They go to Sunday-School, and Mandy and me attend church regularly. We are kindly treated; sometimes we overhear others saying, "The colored people were slaves" down in Tennessee. The children feel hurt when they hear such remarks, but I tell them it was no disgrace in Tennessee to belong to Col. Anderson. Many darkies would have been proud, as I used to was, to call you master. Now, if you will write and say what wages you will give me, I will be better able to decide whether it would be to my advantage to move back again.

Mandy says she would be afraid to go back without some proof that you are sincerely disposed to treat us justly and kindly—and we have concluded to test your sincerity by asking you to send us our wages for the time we served you. This will make us forget and forgive old scores, and rely on your justice and friendship in the future. I served you faithfully for thirty-two years and Mandy twenty years. At $25 a month for me, and $2 a week for Mandy, our earnings would amount to $11,680. Add to this the interest for the time our wages has been kept back and deduct what you paid for our clothing and three doctor's visits to me, and pulling a tooth for Mandy, and the balance will show what we are in justice entitled to. Please send the money by Adams Express, in care of V. Winters, esq, Dayton, Ohio. . . .

We trust the good Maker has opened your eyes to the wrongs which you and your fathers have done to me and my fathers, in making us toil for you for generations without recompense. Here I draw my wages every Saturday night, but in Tennessee there was never any pay day for the Negroes any more than for the horses and cows. . . .

P.S.—Say howdy to George Carter, and thank him for taking the pistol from you when you were shooting at me.

From your old servant,
Jourdon Anderson

The American Negro it turns out has long had jokes, has long had in fact quite a modern comedic sense, and has for just as long been nurturing a lancing, mordant, absurdist, and extremely dry sense of sarcastic wit at the world, even while being considered under the U.S. Constitution as fit to be tied up as the legal property of the likes of Colonel P. H. Anderson. One also finds evidence of this dark sarcasm in the letters written by some of the African American soldiers who served in Lincoln's army during the Civil War. One of these, by one Corporal James Henry Gooding, had the temerity to not even spare the Great (if very very reluctant) Liberator from Gooding's mock-self-deprecating wit and playfulness when he wrote Lincoln and informed him of wage inequities and other Union Army policy offenses against the race:

Your Excellency . . . Today, the Anglo Saxon Mother, Wife, or Sister, are not alone, in tears for departed Sons, Husbands, and Brothers. The patient Trusting Descendants of Africs Clime, have dyed the ground with blood, in defense of the Union, and Democracy. Men too your Excellency, who know in a measure, the cruelties of the Iron heel of oppression, which in years gone by, the very Power, their blood is now being spilled to maintain, ever ground them to the dust. But when the war trumpet sounded o'er the land, when men knew not the Friend from the Traitor, the Black man laid his life at the Altar of the Nation, and he was refused. When the arms of the Union were beaten, in the first year of the War, and the Executive called more food for its ravaging maw, again the black man begged, the privilege of aiding his Country in her need, to be again refused. And now, he is in the War: and how has he conducted himself? Let their dusky forms, rise up, out the mires of James Island, and give the answer. Let the rich mould around Wagners parapets be upturned, and there will be found an Eloquent answer. Obedient and patient, and Solid as a wall are they. All we lack, is a paler hue, and a better acquaintance with the Alphabet. (September 28, 1863)

Hmmm, methinks if Gooding had any better acquaintance with the Alphabet he'd stand accused of committing Unnatural Acts with English typefaces, but we digress. The Black comedic sense that has descended to us moderns from nineteenth-century Black folk like Anderson and Gooding (both further proof of my long-standing belief that today's Negroes are just bold knockoffs of 1800s brethren and sistren with access to better technology) has evolved in ways that make clear a desire to distinguish itself from that of Aristotle's *Poetics* and the Greeks, in general, who seemed to have thought of Homer's *Odyssey* as a comedy (a story with a happy ending) and the Oedipus legend as a tragedy (a story with a sad ending). Black culture as we understand it would have to beg differently since no Black person we'd call friend would relish the prospect of returning home after fifteen years of fighting gods, monsters, and rocks only to then be informed he'd have to kill 108 fools who'd spent years scheming to get in his wife's undergarments. We fail to see any part of a happy ending there. By the same token, since the alleged tragedy of Oedipus produced the most indispensable word in the Black comedic lexicon, we must again claim bewilderment before the Greek court. Yes, we mean That One: "Motherfucker" or, more precisely, Muthafucka, which is by turns the most lyrical, epic, comic, poetic, and dramatic epithet Black modernity has ever known. It may in fact be the most versatile and musical word in the English language when used by the most well-versed modern Black speakers considering that given appropriate context and inflection, it can express love, rage, hysterics, hilarity, pathos, pain, the slings and arrows of outrageous fortune as well as the most laconic means known for icily lampooning an utter fool. (Now we speak of producing the barely audible and more-felt-than-heard spoken-under-one's-breath usage known best as You Stupidass Muthafucka.)

Hip-hop of course has built upon this linguistic tradition of tonal delivery and creative insult and combined it with equally virtuosic forms of braggadocio. Through such hybridity hip-hop has come to exponentially expand the rhetorical vocabulary of modern American English now used throughout the globalized world.

It has also globally popularized that branch of Black comedic thought known as "the dozens," more commonly known as Yo Mama jokes. As in "Yo mama so fat that she went floating in the ocean and Spain claimed her for the New World." As in "Yo mama so poor she went to McDonald's and put a milkshake on layaway." As in "Yo mama so poor she can't afford to pay attention." As in "Yo mama so poor your family ate cereal with a fork to save milk." As in "Yo mama so stupid it took her two hours to watch 60 *Minutes*" and "Yo mama so stupid she put lipstick on her head just to make up her mind," and so forth. Because the bon mot dozens are generally spontaneously invented and tossed about in rapid-fire street-corner contests, it's easy to see how the practice evolved into those Olympic battles of Wit we in hip-hop know as the Freestyle Contest, where one must not only wittily volley insults at one another but nimbly do so on the beat. In the most exacting of these rituals one is not even allowed to use any obscene or profane language, really putting a contestant's gifts for creative insult to an ultimate test.

When one moves to the arena of the professional Black comedian, the Mount Olympus of comedic Black modernity, however, that realm where the deities of African funnymen and women dwell, the Pryors, Rocks, Sykes, Mableys, Chappelles, and Katt Willamses, you find virtuosos of bebop fluency who combine all the strands of the form into a seamless, eloquent, flowing body of verbal, physical, narrative, role-playing, Yo Mama–reeling, president-offending, crack addict–impersonating, more-absurdist-and-philosophical-than-Samuel-Beckett stream of funk-da-fied hand-jive and hambonin' delivery. That said, we can think of no greater homage to the depths and shallows of Black comedic form and tradition than a retelling of a routine created by one of the idiom's true masters, the late Richard Pryor, for a monologue by his elderly Southern gent character, Mudbone. In it two Negroes reputed to have the largest penises in the world go out in the world to measure up, see who indeed has the biggest dick.

They were trying to find a place where they could have they contest, see? And they wasn't no freaks—didn't want everybody looking—

so they walking around, looking for a secret place. So they walking across the Golden Gate Bridge and Niggas seen that water and made 'em want to piss, see? One say, "Man I got to take a leak." So he pulled his thing out, took a piss, other Nigga pulled his thing out, took a piss. One Nigga said, "Goddamn! This water's cold." Other Nigga say, "Yeah, and it's deep too."

(Fully apprehending the assonances and resonances deployed in this conclusion may require investigating the double-entendre meanings of "cold" and "deep" in standard African American slanguage unless that should seem too terribly academic an enterprise given the unabashed, bawdy, ribald buffoonery and chicanery of the preceding narrative.)

– 2010 –

Kalahari Hopscotch, or Notes toward a Twenty-Volume Afrocentric Futurist Manifesto

Two

All conversation about Black Futurism inevitably propels us forward-ever-backward-neveryon. All Black Futurism conjures thoughts of a Blacker and brighter African past and a bleaker yet more bodacious African today and mañana. The yin and the yang of our kulchural language and interplanetary funkmanship.

Ten

So three questions that have been on my mind a lot recently are, Why so much revived interest in African-centric Futurism? Why now? and Why is there suddenly so much curiosity about Black Futurist-knowlgy in Germany of all places? Why is it that every time this writer gets invited to speak in Germany it's to *sprechen* to the Deutsch on imaginary Black tomorrows? After a while you find yourself asking, Why are progressive German intellectuals so curious about what American Negroes have to share about the future? Do they really think we Pre-Cog like that? Think *Minority Report* is for reals? Imagine we gonna step off the podium, get down in the dirt, do some freestyle Ifa divination for 'em with pfennigs instead of cowrie shells, or whut-whut on the luv-luv? Or did Sun Ra's Omni Science Myth Arkestra really turn GermanVolk out like that back in those early 1970s Berlin concerts?

We have several thoughts on this matter, and we'll share them a bit later. We do first feel a need to acknowledge ourselves as an entity with a long history in this emergent field of Black Futurism. Our thoughts about the Germans' fascination with blackfolk need first to address the importation of "futurism"—an early twentieth-century pro-fascist and militarist European art movement—by writer Mark Dery into the Afro.

By adding the prefix "Afro," Dery rendered the artsy Euro-Wehrmacht into something warm and pop-fuzzy. In Germany, the German interest in African cosmology and Black American conceptualism in music—Sun Ra, P-Funk—is long-standing, but I&I speculates that there's a psychological seduction (and mischievous delight) in our critical embrace of verboten concepts like futurism, ethnocentrism, nationalism, Armageddon, countersupremacy, et al. Notions that all decent modern Germans are inhibited from freely, frivolously, or fruitfully claiming in any progressive sense due to the burden of Nazi history.

Eleven

As a Black American male of a certain age and background I believe myself generationally predisposed to be a Black Futurist from birth. The now-defunct Soviet Socialist Republic sent their Sputnik rocket up ten days before I was born in 1957, thus initiating the race for space between East and West during the atomically anxious Cold War years. The first reading I did as a child was science fiction; the first movies I loved were horror and sci-fi; and like almost nearly every Black American male I know born post–World War II, I was a voracious reader of Marvel Comics and the neurotic and visionary creations of Stan Lee, Jack Kirby, and Steve Ditko—Fantastic Four, X-Men, Spider Man, the Hulk, Dr. Strange, and the Black Panther. Marvel's Panther, T'Chaka, presciently appeared in the comics several months before Huey Newton and Bobby Seale launched their famed party for self-defense in 1966 Oakland (and almost simultaneously with the Lowndes County, Alabama, self-defense organization founded by author/activist Robert "Negroes with Guns" Williams).

Simultaneous with those readings of America's graphic literature of the fantastic, Black Americans were out in the nation's streets rioting, rebelling, and rhetorically advocating the creation of a radically and racially transformed America. We saw Martin Luther King envision a future America where the relentless power of organized love would legalize economic and social justice for his people. We heard Malcolm X describe an American nightmare whose resolution would come by either the ballot or the bullet or the briefcase or the shotgun, to use Brother Omar Little of *The Wire*'s later opposition.

What made the science fiction of Marvel Comics more resonant with my generation of young Black Americans was that all its superheroes were tormented supercreatures full of rage, self-loathing, and anxiety about the state of the world, their own human frailties, and the freakish powers they'd been given to combat evil and engage the chaotic fluidity of modern identity.

For the Black Futurists who came of age in the 1960s and '70s, the vision was always more apocalyptic than utopic and because of what was going on in our popular culture—which at the time also included our radical-politics kulcha—the Panthers; the Black Arts Movement; Parliament Funkadelic—the future seemed to be already moving in an Afrocentric direction—one where post–civil rights middle-class Black America was already living and thriving—at least in the concert arena and on the dance floor. Even as the post-King riot corridors multitudes of us lived in were visibly beset by spirit-strangling poverty, environmental ruin, and walking-dead dope fiends.

For those of a progressive bent, Black music—electronic freedom jazz especially—Black feminist literature, and dub wise reggae became beacons of infinite, transdimensional creative possibility, options and outlets which superseded the demise of the Black Power movement. Alice Walker, Toni Morrison, Toni Cade Bambara, Gayl Jones, and Ntozake Shange were Black woman creatives we believed to be on a par with Sun Ra, Miles Davis, and Bob Marley.

Those of us who studied under Haile Gerima at Howard University in the late 1970s also got exposed to third world cinema, C. L. R. James, Frantz Fanon, and Amílcar Cabral. All expanded our sense that Blacknuss was a place with wide vistas and utter disregard for intraethnic boundaries, and an infinitely-receding horizon line.

The history of Afro-futurism and Black science fiction as genre is rooted in the coterminous forward-moving and recuperative histories of Pan-Afrikanism and Black cultural nationalism in the 1960s and '70s.

Seven

The defining trope of Black American literature is invisibility—not just the invisibility produced by the white social gaze during and after slavery but the invisibilities, voids, silences, repressed desires, and apprehensions produced by gazing too deeply within the Black American Self for too damn long. It is for this reason that our literary tradition has always been more prophetic, phantasmagorical, and surrealist than social realist or superrealist. This recognition also helps explicate why the Black American canon reads like a litany of ghost stories about various manner of fantastically radicalized ephemera: *The Confessions of Nat Turner* as told to Thomas Gray, *The Mystery*, *The North Star*, *The Autobiography of a Slave*, *The Bondwoman's Narrative*, *Blake; or, The Huts of America*, "We Wear the Mask," *Sports of the Gods*, *The Souls of Black Folk*, *Autobiography of an Ex-Colored Man*, *The Conjure Man Dies*, *Their Eyes Were Watching God*, *Mules and Men*, *Tell My Horse*, *Native Son*, *The Long Dream*, *Invisible Man*, *If He Hollers Let Him Go*, *Go Tell It on the Mountain*, *Giovanni's Room*, *The Fire Next Time*, *The System of Dante's Hell*, *The Dutchman*, *Blues People*, *The Autobiography of Malcolm X*, *Soul on Ice*, *Revolutionary Suicide*, *Blood in My Eye*, *Blind Man with a Pistol*, *If They Come in the Morning*, *The Quality of Mercy*, *Black Magic Poetry*, *Shadow and Act*, *Dunford Travels Everywhere*, *The Catacombs*, *Scarecrow*, *Sister X and the Victims of Foul Play*, *Groove, Bang and Jive Around*, *The Wig*, *The Bluest Eye*, *The Color Purple*, *For Colored Girls Who Have Considered Suicide / When the Rainbow Is Enuf*, *Beneath the Underdog*, *Bloods*, *In Search of Our Mothers' Gardens*, *Sassafras, Cypress and Indigo*, *Daughters of the Dust*, *Rhinestone Sharecropping*, *Beloved*, *Corregidora*, *Mumbo Jumbo*, "I Am a Cowboy in the Boat of Ra," *Axis: Bold as Love*, *Electric Ladyland*, *Band of Gypsys*, *Last Days and Time*, *Rainbow Bridge*, *Nova*, *Dhalgren*, "It's after the End of the World / Don't You Know That Yet?," *Maggot Brain*, *Mothership Connection*, *The Clones of Dr. Funkenstein*, *Stars in My Pockets Like Grains of Sand*, *All-Night Visitors*, *Things That I Do in the Dark*, *Reflex and Bone Structure*, *Scarifications*, *I, Tituba, Black Witch of Salem*, *Devil in a Blue Dress*, *Wild Seed*, *Parable of the Sower*, *The Healing*, *Negrophobia*, *The White Boy Shuffle*, *The Brief Wondrous Life of Oscar Wao*, *Joe Turner's Come and Gone*, *Who Fears Death*, *Through the Valley of the Nest of Spiders*, *The Broken Kingdoms*.

These titles do not suggest the literature of an oppressed people but the literature of a shamanistic and mystical people. The literature of a hoodoo voodoo and a "What the Fuck Are You People?" A mythophrenic people whose writing refuses to distinguish between excoriating the living, conjuring up the dead, or projecting starry-eyed thoughts about Armageddon. A literary canon seemingly composed by a race of angelic aliens already fallen to Earth and breeding like rabbits.

Thirteen

Black Futurism is a temporally troubled matrix that thrives on opposites and oppositions, flowing lines and nonlinearity, conflict resolution and asymmetrical warfare. It prefers the mad dash on shifting sands while in pursuit of higher ground and safe havens. Such are the creative benefits bestowed on Black Futurism by the implosive depths of Black trauma, Black liminality, and the sharp edges of Black transcendentalism.

Black Futurism is, simply put, how human truths crushed to Earth rose to engage in symbolic warfare in the twentieth and twenty-first centuries of this Common Era. How a mutating nation of nobodies turned into more than the punch line of a brilliantly ironic Bert Williams song. By seeing institutional exclusion, hyperinvisibility, and massive social erasure not as impediments but as incitements, Black Futurist avatars are inspired to repurpose oppression and re-create the world anew every Goddamn day. Racism understood as a series of epic-making and epochal opportunities.

Sixteen
As Morpheus illumined about the Matrix, Black Futurism is everywhere around us.

One
The question should never be "What is Black Futurism?" The question, instead, should be, "What is not?"

Twelve
Having ceded the racial ground war to Enlightenment-era imperialism somewhere back in the seventeenth century, Black Futurism determined that the fiery realms of the symbolic, the mythic, the rhetorical, the spiritual, the wickedly stylish, sonic, and polyrhythmic would become our kulcha's bailiwick, raison d'être, and culturally triumphalist battleground.

Nine
Race not space looms as the final frontier. Black people didn't need to wait for late twentieth-century genomic science to figure out that race as we know it was a convenient social contraction of Black eternal being.

Six
No overseer or plantation owner is a hero to his valet.

No man who needs slavery to feed his empire can much impress his coerced labor force with claims to dominance, supremacy, and master race status. The degree to which notions of white supremacy took hold of the slaver's delusions about himself make him a worthily psychopathic opponent but hardly an invincible or unassailable one. Central to the master-slave paradigm is the delusional belief that fellow homosapiens were no more observant of human foibles than horses or garden tools simply because of dark pigmentation and proof of purchase.

Who but a lunatic would make laws that forbid his shovels, rakes, plow, and hoes from running away? Or demand that those human farm implements present identification when traveling between plantation stations? Or cut off the hooves of recaptured fugitive horses to frighten any neighing stablemates who might also catch drapetomania and dream of going AWOL?

Four

The early foot soldiers of the Black Futurist army made captives in antebellum America knew that Black consciousness alone was enough to disrupt the slaver's impossible task of subhumanizing our folk. "I think, read, and write, therefore I am not a slave, just imprisoned" became quickly grasped as the primary operation by which the owners' fragile devaluing of Black humanity could eventually become undone.

Five

Fred Moten's crucial intervention into Marxist economics and labor theory becomes of paramount interest here. Moten demands Marxists reconsider the riot of ruptures that must occur when commodities can speak. Not as a speculative fictional "What if?" but as an incontrovertible and undeniable biological fact. When the monster speaks, all bets are off for the slave systems' social engineers. This is why the incendiary *David Walker's Appeal*, published in 1830, was banned—less as an incitement than as a dangerous idea. The thought crimes in Walker's jeremiad of a word-juju readily explain why:

> If you commence, make sure [you] work—do not trifle, for they will not trifle with you—they want us for their slaves, and think nothing of murdering us in order to subject us to that wretched condition— therefore, if there is an attempt made by us, kill or be killed. Now, I ask you, had you not rather be killed than to be a slave to a tyrant, who takes the life of your mother, wife, and dear little children? Look upon your mother, wife and children, and answer God Almighty; and believe this, that it is no more harm for you to kill a man, who is trying to kill you, than it is for you to take a drink of water when thirsty; in fact, the man who will stand still and let another murder him, is worse than an infidel, and, if he has common sense, ought not to be pitied.

From the moment commodified Africans realized their very thoughts could violate the delusions of white exceptionalism, the physics of the owners' universe began to disintegrate. Next came the realization that they could organize revolts, incite rebellions and Haitian revolutions, act out Nat Turner's countergenocide plan, or engage in thirty-five-year-long Seminole Maroon wars against the U.S. government. From those days forward, the game of white supremacy was lost by the American continent's self-appointed master race.

Fourteen

All that we call Black art and Black music and Black history and Black culture and the Black experience in America is actually an alternative reality built upon the impoverished ruins of the white supremacist imaginary that summoned it into Being (and into being so perpetually badass). That most badass Black American film director Melvin Van Peebles will now address the benefits of living in a racist country. "We always talk about the downside of racism but there's an upside to racism as well: When people think you're stupid, you can do anything you want to."

Seventeen

Black Futurists believe all of Africa's tomorrows belong to our weltanschauung and all of Western end-time as well. Black Futurists believe as Sun Ra instructed: "It's already after the end of the world—don't you know that yet?" Black Futurists second that emotion with what Public Enemy's Professor Griff said: "Armageddon has been in effect—go get a late pass."

Sun Ra envisioned no difference between a Paradise Lost for African people and a transdimensional intergalactic African utopia. Both were dream worlds where Black people wouldn't be lynched by hordes of white nuclear families seeking a little roasted-darky-meat entertainment while out on picnic.

Twenty-One

In the mid-1970s when George Clinton toured Parliament Funkadelic *Mothership Connection* starship to arenas like Washington, DC's 18,000-seat Capital Center, there were very few white people to be counted among those 18,000. This was a time when the population of the nation's capital was 70 percent African American and Dr. Funkenstein could righteously and rightfully declare "God Bless Chocolate City and its vanilla suburbs." If one was raised as this reporter was in a Black Futurist utopia like 1970s DC aka "CC" aka "Chocolate City," you understood Black kulcha as a thing in total—a unified field theory best described as such during the period's critical race referendum. Within this alternate-reality construct everything that had ever been conceived by a Black imagination for local and global consumption was grist for our critical and performative mill.

The song lyric that best describes the Black Futurist program is another George Clinton verse, "We have come to reclaim the Pyramids / Partying on the mothership."

What Clinton locates for us in one scrap of scrappy verse is that Black Futurism is just another name for African epistemology and whut Emma Goldman said: "If I can't dance then I don't want to be part of your revolution."

Nineteen

The greatest dancing rebel in American history was James Brown—an alchemist who transformed funk from an adjective to an action word and a meme for a transcendent body in motion. George Clinton however was the Dude who harnessed that force and converted funk into a 'hood-massive post–Black Power semiotic movement.

"Here's our chance to dance our way out of our constrictions," Clinton sez in another song, while in a third he postulates that "with the rhythm it takes to dance to what we have to live through you can dance underwater and not get wet."

Twenty

In the wake of American housing's post-prime-lending apocalypse we cite the phenomenon of underwater mortgages—contracts between home consumers and banks that force the consumer to cover the loan-shark bank's loss on a loan for a now worthless property. Statistics show that Black and Hispanic homeowners were the disproportionate victims of these loan-extortion policies and thus more viciously subject to mass foreclosure and home-ownership loss.

Any Black Futurist project that did not ask how dancing underwater while not getting wet was working out for those made homeless by the Bush administration's subprime loan policies would be irresponsible and useless to our struggle for urban social justice. Not to mention pointless, politically speaking, and too precious for words.

Twenty-Three

Black Futurism should be observant about race and power relations in this historical moment. This Black Presidential moment that Vernon Reid declares isn't "postracial" but "most racial." Black Futurism implies a dissatisfaction with the Black American status quo that must be mediated by aggressive magic and supported by George Clinton's market-savvy colloquialism, "rhythm and business." (A necessary footnote here would be Black Futurist free jazz icon Cecil Taylor's response to the question of what white people would never understand about Black culture. "The magic of rhythm" was Taylor's typically pointed yet mysterious reply—albeit less inscrutable now in the rhythm-crazy post-hip-hop posthouse post-Afro-beat frenzied young America of today.)

Twenty-Five

This emergent field that we call Black Futurism must be considered a set of narrative operations that unfolds in four or five dimensions simultaneously. There are the many documented artifacts and avatars of Black Futurism we know from music, film, and literature—the canon as it were. There is also a need to recognize Black Futurist claims on a historical timeline—from the carbon-dated birth of proto-human life and society in southern Africa's Kalahari Desert during the tool-making kinship-forming fire-creating time of early humanity.

Black Futurism recognizes the origins of human language, consciousness, art, music, and spirituality among our oldest chromosome-dated human ancestors, the Khoisan people of the Kalahari—especially since their elegant and stylish cave paintings depict dreamtime encounters with elongated transhuman hybrids.

Black Futurism also appreciates the speculation on what has been described as a "natural" nuclear reactor in Gabon over two million years ago. We also note that the Godfather of Soul James Brown's favorite place to visit in Africa was Gabon. Coincidence or natural attraction? Synchronicity or elective affinity?

The history of Black Futurism is not shy about reclaiming the pyramids nor the great wall in Zimbabwe nor any of the Nilotic valley cultures that produced the Cushite Empire, the Nubian kingdoms, and Pharaonic Egypt. Nor can it avoid the cosmology source material known as voodoo in Benin-Dahomeyan Orisha worship within the Yoruba-speaking cultures of West Africa. (Of poignant note here is the astronomically correct interstellar references found in the divination and belief system of Mali's Dogon. There is also to be considered the supposition that Benjamin Banneker, one of America's first great polymaths—mathematician, clockmaker, astronomer, and architect—was the progeny of a Dogon-born father and an Irish mother. And our freedom struggle's original celestial navigator, Harriet Tubman. These connections are also not lost on Black Futurism. Nor is the centrality of Benin-Dahomean vodun belief systems to the strategic successes of the first successful revolution led by Blacks in Western history on the island of Haiti/San Domingo in 1801.)

Fifteen

Given the appearance on the antebellum scene of Moses Dickson and the Knights of Liberty (a Black Masonic secret society over which Dickson presided and which is said to have freed 70,000 enslaved Africans and conspired to organize 50,000 free Black men to march into Atlanta to crush the citadel of slavery by force) the banning of *Walker's Appeal* can be deemed both logical and ineffective. Of course Nat Turner needed neither Masonic freemen nor Walker's fiery diction to become inspired to war against slave owners.

Black Futurism couldn't help but be moved by the fact that Turner's inspiration for radical insurgency was driven by visions of dark and light angels warring over cornfields and dripping esoteric writing in blood on the leaves and stalks.

Black Futurists also claim a precedent for their field in the esoteric newspaper names chosen by those famed Black American abolitionist-editors-in-chief, Martin Delany and Frederick Douglass: the *Mystery* and the *North Star*. We must also applaud Delany for composing what was surely the first Black science fiction novel in America—*Blake: or, The Huts of America*, about a fugitive superspy who travels around the Southern United States and Cuba fomenting antislavery rebellions.

Black Futurism later finds its first real-life superspy in the person of the woman known as "Black Moses," Harriet Tubman—she who will personally rescue over a thousand American-born Africans from American chattel slavery and lead them to the promised land.

During the Civil War, Tubman leads the legendary 1863 attack on the Combahee River plantation in South Carolina that will liberate seven hundred of her people. Tubman gathers intelligence that serves to sweep the Union Army into a battle replete with modern and archaic weaponry: Swords, guns, sea mines, bombs, bullets, and ship sinkings converge in a scene spectacularly worthy of any James Bond climax. Before Tubman leaves this mortal plane she offers us these wise, cautionary lines about the colonized Black imagination: "I have freed a thousand slaves. I could have freed a thousand more if they'd only known they were slaves." She also bequeathed the Black Futurist tradition an aphorism that also presages Martin Luther King by nearly a century: "Every great dream begins with a dreamer. Always remember, you have within you the strength, the patience, and the passion to reach for the stars to change the world." (Her sister in struggle Sojourner Truth provided an astronomical echo when she prophesied, "*I am not going to die, I'm going home like a shooting star.*")

"In dreams begins responsibility" would seem to have been the battle cry of Black Futurism long before Delmore Schwartz uttered the phrase. What we have from the beginning of the genre is a recognition that reality would have to be repurposed to accommodate a nation of very active dreamers. Starry-eyed and Bible-Black dreamers at that.

Black Futurism and Black American radical activism have tended to ride the same rails down to the same crossroads and have always profited from their fruitful encounters there.

What distinguishes the Black American radical tradition from any other is the degree to which it is addressed to changing not reality but the perceptual apparatus and hallucinations of a white supremacist nation. Black Black Futurist and the Black Radical tradition have always been at war with a phantom army—even when they didn't appear under cover of night as a cowardly pack of murderous ghosts on horseback in white sheets and hoods.

At what point did it occur to Black America that we were in a fight for our lives against creatures whose most romantic and lionized reflections of themselves were not as human beings but as monstrosities, demons, devils, colonizers, slavers, Injun killers, and slave catchers?

Eight

The nightmare of American racialism and the brutal history of same blossomed a child more radiant than the shit from which it arose. It begat a nation of beautiful dreamers, radical futurists, romantic warriors. The imagineers who conjured this mode of critical inquiry, spiritual espionage, and cultural mythography into being believed they had world enough and time. They also knew they had invisibility, God, W. E. B. Du Bois, double consciousness, and the devil's music on their side. Double consciousness—the darker side of an already black moon—meant that there was always going to be a hidden shadow dimension to the African in America.

The ideation of double consciousness by Du Bois is the most significant American intervention into the history of modern psychiatric thought. Du Bois's articulation establishes Black subjectivity as a fundamental consideration for all subsequent discussions of race in America. In one rhetorical stroke Du Bois invents the Black American subject as a profoundly alienated and widely distributed American psychological type. One whose numbers were already legion when he wrote— something on the order of eight million nominal citizens. Nominal because these numbers denote people who would have to wait another sixty years before their government would be forced to legally recognize them as deserving of equal protection under the law.

At the end of the Civil War there were a staggering 3.5 million Black Americans who could then be identified as "former slaves," and another 500,000 were designated as "free." These numbers are equivalent to the contemporary populations of both the State of Palestine and Puerto Rico or, roughly, the entire current populations of Los Angeles and Chicago.

So suddenly there were four million doubled and deeply troubled Black consciousnesses ready to exercise their capacity for dreaming and reaping meaning from the land. Their social status made them native-born aliens who jes' grew to cultural fruition in a world of difference, otherness, strangeness, self-sufficiency, and interdependency. It was a moment of human awakening that can only be compared with that moment in evolution when the species first recognized itself as a species apart because of the complex questions it asked of the world outside of its head. The very same questions asked by the fugitive-slave replicant Roy Batty in *Blade Runner*: "Who am I? Where did I come from? Where am I going? How long have I got?"

The end of slavery created the addition of four million more Black Futurists because what other country could they claim for their own but "the country of the future"?

One
Gil Scott-Heron: "Gotta move on / Gotta see tomorrow / Gotta move on / Gotta get ahead / Can't look back there's nothing there but sorrow / Gotta move on, gotta get ahead / What you call nostalgia / Really ain't what I'm after / What you call reminiscing / Ain't what my Life's been missing."

Sources

1. The Black Male Show

"Amiri Baraka": "Amiri Amour: Baraka in Memoriam," *Ebony*, January 14, 2014.

"Wayne Shorter": *B. Culture* (JAM Gallery), 1985.

"Jimi Hendrix": "Inside Hendrix: Beyond the Burning Guitar," *American Legacy*, Summer 2010.

"John Coltrane": "Coltrane at 80—a Talent Supreme," *SFGate*, September 22, 2006.

"Gone Fishing": "Gone Fishing: Remembrances of Lester Bowie," *Village Voice*, December 7, 1999.

"The Black Artists' Group": "Black Artists Group," *Wire*, no. 329 (July 2011).

"Butch Morris": "Jazz Explorer," *Vibe*, August 1997.

"Charles Edward Anderson Berry and the History of Our Future": "Roll Over Beethoven: The Life and Music of Chuck Berry," keynote lecture, Case Western Reserve University, October 25, 2014, https://rockhall.com/event /keynote-lecture-by-greg-tate/.

"Lonnie Holley": "Lonnie Holley," *Wire*, March 2013.

"Marion Brown (1931–2010) and Djinji Brown": "Black-Owned: Jazz Musician Marion Brown and Son Djinji," *Vibe*, November 1994.

"Dark Angels of Dust": "Dark Angels of Dust: David Hammons and the Art of Streetwise Transcendentalism," in *Art in the Streets*, edited by Jeffrey Deitch, Roger Gastman, and Aaron Rose (New York: Skira Rizzoli, 2011).

"Bill T. Jones": "Start Black-Owned: Combative Moves," *Vibe*, March 1995.

"Gary Simmons": "Start Black-Owned: Conceptual Bomber," *Vibe*, February 1995.

"The Persistence of Vision": "The Persistence of Vision: Storyboard P," *Wire*, April 2013.

"Ice Cube": "Manchild at Large: One-on-One with Ice Cube, Hip-Hop's Most Wanted," *Village Voice*, September 11, 1990.

"Wynton Marsalis": "Wynton Marsalis," in *The Vibe Q: Raw and Uncut*, edited by Rob Kenner and Rakia Clark (New York: Vibe Street Lit, 2007).

"Thornton Dial": "Thornton Dial: Free, Black, and Brightening Up the Darkness of the World," in *Hard Truths: The Art of Thornton Dial*, edited by Joanne Cubbs and Eugene Metcalf (Munich: Prestel, 2010).

"Kehinde Wiley": London: National Portrait Gallery, 2009.

"Rammellzee": "Rammelzee—the Ikonoklast Samurai," *Wire*, April 2004.

"Richard Pryor: Pryor Lives": "The Vibe Q: Richard Pryor," *Vibe*, August 1995.

"Richard Pryor": "Richard Pryor, 1940–2005," *Village Voice*, December 6, 2005.

"Gil Scott-Heron": "Gil Scott-Heron, R.I.P.," *Village Voice*, May 31, 2011.

"The Man in Our Mirror": "Michael Jackson: The Man in Our Mirror," *Village Voice*, July 1, 2009.

"Miles Davis": *B. Culture* (JAM Gallery), 1985.

2. She Laughing Mean and Impressive Too

"Born to Dyke": "Born to Dyke: I Love My Sister Laughing and Then Again When She's Looking Mean, Queer, and Impressive . . . ," *Village Voice*, June 13, 1995.

"Joni Mitchell": "Black and Blonde; Domepiece: Joni Mitchell," *Vibe*, December 1998, 96.

"Azealia Banks": "Azealia Banks, 'Fantasea' (Self-Released Mixtape)," *Spin* July 16, 2012.

"Sade": "Sade: Black Magic Woman," *Vibe*, January 2001, 104.

"All the Things You Could Be by Now If James Brown Was a Feminist": "All the Things You Could Be by Now If James Brown Was a Feminist," lecture, Princeton University, 2007.

"Itabari Njeri": "Saving Race," *Village Voice*, June 3, 1997.

"Kara Walker": "Strategies of Representation," lecture, Whitney Museum, 2007, http://projects.ecfs.org/Fieldston272/Readings/Walker.pdf.

"Women at the Edge of Space, Time, and Art": Preface to *Candida Romero: Little Girls*, text by Pierre-Jean Rémy (Montreuil, France: Éditions Gourcuff Gradenigo, 2010).

"Ellen Gallagher": "Ghosting Her Way to Fame," *Vibe*, April 1996, 40.

"To Bid a Poet Black and Abstract": "Pattern Recognition," New York: Museum of the Contemporary African Diaspora, 2013.

"The Gikuyu Mythos versus the Cullud Grrrl from Outta Space": "The Gikuyu Mythos vs. the Cullud Grrrl from Outta Space," in *Wangechi Mutu: A Fantastic Journey* (Durham, NC: Duke University Press, 2013).

"Come Join the Hieroglyphic Zombie Parade": "Come Join the Hieroglyphic Zombie Parade: Deborah Grant," unpublished manuscript.

"Björk's Second Act": "Bjork's Second Act," *PAPER*, October 1, 2000.

"Thelma Golden": "The Golden Age," *Village Voice*, May 15, 2001.

3. Hello Darknuss My Old Meme

"Top Ten Reasons Why So Few Black Women Were Down to Occupy Wall Street Plus Four More": "Top 10 Reasons Why So Few Black Folk Appear Down to Occupy Wall Street," *Village Voice*, October 19, 2011.

"What Is Hip-Hop?": "What Is HipHop," *Vibe*, October 1993, 104.

"Intelligence Data": "Intelligence Data," *Village Voice*, September 25, 2001.

"Hip-Hop Turns Thirty": "Hiphop Turns 30," *Village Voice*, December 28, 2004.

"Love and Crunk": "Love and Crunk," *Village Voice*, September 30, 2003.

"White Freedom": "White Freedom," *Village Voice*, November 9, 2004.

"Wu-Dunit": "Wu-Dunit," *Village Voice*, June 24, 1997.

"Unlocking the Truth vs. John Cage": "Unlocking the Truth vs. John Cage," unpublished manuscript, 2015.

4. Screenings

"Spike Lee's *Bamboozled*": "The King of Coonology," *Village Voice*, October 31, 2000.

"It's a Mack Thing": "It's a Mack Thing," *Village Voice*, August 1, 1995.

"Sex and Negrocity": Sex and Negrocity," *Village Voice*, June 26, 2001.

"Lincoln in Whiteface": "Lincoln in Whiteface," *Village Voice*, July 24, 2001.

"*The Black Power Mixtape*": "Fight for Rights, Will to Power: *The Black Power Mixtape 1967–1975*," British Film Institute, April 1, 2015.

5. Race, Sex, Politricks, and Belles Lettres

"Clarence Major": "Major's League," *Village Voice* Literary Supplement, May 2001.

"The Atlantic Sound": "Land of the Lost," *Village Voice*, October 17, 2000.

"Apocalypse Now": "Apocalypse Now," *Village Voice*, May 4, 2004.

"Blood and Bridges": "Blood and Bridges," *Village Voice*, April 20, 1999.

"Nigger-'Tude": "Nigger-'tude," *Village Voice*, January 29, 2002.

"Triple Threat": "Triple Threat," *Village Voice*, October 16, 2002.

"Bottom Feeders": "Bottom Feeders," *Village Voice*, September 16, 2003.

"Scaling the Heights": "Scaling the Heights," *Village Voice*, September 21, 1999.

"Fear of a Mongrel Planet": "Fear of a Mongrel Planet," *Village Voice*, May 9, 2000.

"Adventures in the Skin Trade": "Adventures in the Skin Trade," *Village Voice*, March 26, 2002.

"Generations Hexed": "A Tale of Two Families: Generations Hexed," *Village Voice*, February 8, 2000.

"Going Underground": "Gayl Jones's Literary Sanctuary: Going Underground," *Village Voice*, February 16, 1999.

"Judgment Day": "Judgment Day," *Village Voice*, November 26, 2003.

"Black Modernity and Laughter, or How It Came to Be That N*g*as Got Jokes": "Never Trust a Big Butt and a Smile," *Tate Etc.*, January 1, 2010.

"Kalahari Hopscotch, or Notes toward a Twenty-Volume Afrocentric Futurist Manifesto": "Kalahari Hopscotch," in *AfroFictional In[ter]ventions: Revisting the BIGSAS Festival of African(-Diasporic) Literatures 2011–2013*, edited by Susan Arndt and Nadja Ofuatey-Alazard (Münster: Edition Assemblage, 2014).

Index